BARRON'S

GED

WRITING WORKBOOK

by Katherine S. Hogan

BARRON'S

AKNOWLEDGMENTS
To my family, especially Joe

All inquiries should be addressed to:
Barron's Educational Series, Inc.
250 Wireless Boulevard
Hauppauge, New York 11788
http://www.barronseduc.com

International Standard Book No. 0-7641-0238-9

Library of Congress Catalog No. 97-34264

Library of Congress Cataloging-in-Publication Data

Hogan, Katherine S.
  GED writing workbook / Katherine S. Hogan.
    p.   cm.
  Includes index.
  ISBN 0-7641-0238-9
  1. English language—Composition and exercises—
Examinations, questions, etc.   2. General educational
development tests—Study guides.   I. Title.
LB1631.H557 1998
808' .042'076—DC21   97-34264
                              CIP

PRINTED IN THE UNITED STATES OF AMERICA

9 8 7 6 5 4 3 2 1

CONTENTS

TIPS FOR THE STUDENT

The GED Test

WHAT IS THE GED TEST, AND WHY SHOULD I TAKE IT?

The GED, the Tests of General Educational Development, is a key that opens doors. The GED examines the same material that students learn in high school. It has five exams that cover writing skills, literature and the arts, social studies, sciences, and mathematics. Some states require an additional test on the U.S. Constitution or state government. The GED test, which is offered by the American Council of Education, is designed for adults who do not have a high school degree. A GED certificate is viewed by employers, colleges, and technical schools as comparable to a high school diploma.

The GED certificate creates opportunities. Students who earn GED certificates have the chance to pursue various careers and educational options. Many employers, technical schools, and vocational programs require a high school diploma or the equivalent. Likewise, colleges and universities will only enroll students who have a high school diploma or the equivalent.

The GED is offered in English, Spanish, French, and Braille. It is also available on audio-cassette and in large print.

WHERE AND WHEN CAN I TAKE THE TEST?

The GED test is offered throughout the year at many different sites in the United States, Canada, and some territories. To find the location nearest you, call the GED Hot Line at 1-800-MY-GED (1-800-626-9433). The GED Hot Line, which is available 24 hours a day, also will give information about adult education centers in your area.

WHAT SCORES DO I NEED TO PASS THE TEST?

Passing scores vary from one place to another. To get the most recent information for your area, contact your local GED testing center or call 1-800-MY-GED (1-800-626-9433).

Each section of the GED test is scored separately. The scores are then calculated to get a total score and an average score. Most areas require a minimum score on each test and a minimum average score for all five tests. Texas, for example, requires a minimum score of 40 and a minimum average score of 45. This means that GED students in Texas must earn at least 40 points on each test and an average score of 45 on all five tests.

Students who want to improve their scores may retake some or all of the tests. However, the rules for retaking tests vary from one area to another. Before retaking a test, contact your local adult education center and check the GED testing regulations for your area.

Test Preparation

WHAT WILL BE ON THE TESTS?

The GED tests material that is taught in high school. Note the test descriptions in the box.

TIMETABLE OF THE GED TESTS
TOTAL: 7 HOURS, 35 MINUTES

Test	Topics	Length of Test (Minutes)	Number of Questions	Description
Writing Skills, Part I	Sentence Structure Usage Mechanics	75	55	Sentence Structure (35%) Usage (35%) Mechanics (spelling, punctuation, capitalization (30%)
Writing Skills, Part II	Essay	45	1	Essay on a given topic
Social Studies	Geography U.S. History Economics Political Science Behavioral Science	85	64	History (25%) Economics (20%) Geography (15%) Political Science (20%) Behavioral Sciences (20%)
Science	Biology Earth Science Physics Chemistry	95	66	Biology (50%) Earth Science Chemistry } 50% Physics
Literature and the Arts	Popular Literature Classical Literature Commentary	65	45	Popular Literature (50%) Classical Literature (25%) Commentary About Literature and the Arts (25%)
Mathematics	Arithmetic Algebra Geometry	90	56	Arithmetic (50%) Algebra (30%) Geometry (20%)

Note: Format and timing are subject to change

WHAT IS ON THE WRITING SKILLS TEST?

WRITING SKILLS TEST, PART I

The GED Writing Skills Test has a multiple-choice section and an essay. Part I, the multiple-choice section, tests sentence structure, punctuation, capitalization, spelling, and usage. In Part I, there are several passages, which are followed by questions. Each question focuses on one or two sentences from the preceding passage. For Part I of the Writing Skills Test, you will have 75 minutes to answer 55 questions.

The test questions for Part I are divided into three categories: sentence structure, mechanics, and usage.

	WRITING SKILLS TEST, PART I: CONTENT	
Content	**Percentage**	**Description**
Sentence Structure	35	These questions focus on writing complete sentences that are punctuated correctly. You may need to rewrite sentences, combine sentences, or correct sentences.
Mechanics	30	These questions focus on correct punctuation, capitalization, and spelling. You will need to find errors and correct them.
Usage	35	These questions focus on using the right word for a particular job. They may ask you to choose the correct pronoun, verb, or verb tense.

There are three different types of questions for Part I. Note the descriptions in the following box.

Type	Percentage	Description
WRITING SKILLS, PART I: TYPES OF QUESTIONS		
Sentence Correction	50	These questions will focus on one sentence from the passage. The sentence may have one error, or it may be correct. You will need to find the error—if there is one—and correct the sentence. The sentence may require replacing a word, correcting punctuation, or moving a phrase.
Sentence Revision	35	These questions will have one or two sentences with underlined sections. You will need to decide the best way to write the underlined section. You may choose the original version, or you may change the wording or punctuation.
Rewriting or Combining Sentences	15	These questions will focus on one or two sentences. You will need to write new, correct sentences that have the same meaning as the original sentences. For some items, you will be required to rewrite one sentence using a different word order. Other questions will ask you to combine two sentences into one clear, correct sentence.

WRITING SKILLS TEST, PART II

Part II of the Writing Skills Test is an essay. You will be given a topic, and you will be asked to write a composition of about 200 words. The completed essay, which should have five paragraphs, will be scored based on content, organization, clarity, and use of standard English. For Part II, you will have 45 minutes to write one essay.

Sample Essay Topic

The television has become standard in most American homes. The television has improved our lives in many ways, but it has also had negative effects.

Write an essay of about 200 words that describes the effects that the television has had on modern life. You may describe the good effects, the bad effects, or both.

Although each unit in this book will help your writing skills, Units 5 and 6 will focus specifically on the essay in Part II.

HOW CAN I PREPARE FOR THE WRITING SKILLS TEST?

Start with this book, which will help you study effectively. After you take the Pretest, work through the whole book and focus on areas that are challenging for you. Make sure that you complete the exercises carefully and practice writing essays. When you feel confident about the material, complete the Posttest and review sections as needed.

In addition to completing this book, you may want to enroll in a test preparation class. GED study programs are offered at adult education centers, libraries, community colleges, and religious institutions. These preparation classes provide individualized instruction in a relaxed setting. To find a GED program in your area, contact your local library or call 1-800-MY-GED (1-800-626-9433).

STUDY SKILLS

The following skills can make a big difference:

- GET ORGANIZED. Set up a schedule so that you can study regularly, either every day or a few days a week. Use a separate notebook or folder for each subject, and keep all of your materials in one place.
- FIND A GOOD PLACE TO STUDY. You will need a quiet, comfortable place with no distractions. If you do not have space in your home, try your local library or an open classroom at a nearby school.
- READ AND WRITE OFTEN. Like other skills, reading and writing improve with practice. Read newspapers, magazines, and books. Write shopping lists, notes, letters, and journals. Read and write things that are part of your everyday life or items that simply interest you. As your skills improve, focus on materials that are more challenging.
- IMMEDIATELY USE WHAT YOU HAVE LEARNED. For example, after you learn to spell words correctly, write them in a letter. Likewise, once you have mastered pronouns, say them correctly to family or friends. Make correct grammar a natural part of your daily life.
- KEEP TRACK OF YOUR PROGRESS. Make a list of the topics that are hard for you, and spend extra time in these areas. Once you have mastered a difficult topic, check it off of your list and reward yourself.

Test-Taking Strategies

THE DAY BEFORE THE TEST

- VISIT THE TEST CENTER. Make sure that you know which route to take, how long you will need to get there, where to park, and which door to enter.
- ORGANIZE YOURSELF. Gather everything that you will need for the test including: your admissions ticket (if necessary), identification, two or more ballpoint pens, three or more sharpened No. 2 pencils, erasers, a watch, and food.
- RELAX! Eat a good meal and get to bed early. If you prepared well for the test, your work is done. Cramming now will not help you.

TEST DAY

- EAT WELL AND DRESS COMFORTABLY. A good meal will give you energy and help you think. On the other hand, uncomfortable clothing will be distracting.
- PACK FOOD. If you will be testing all day, bring a lunch. Otherwise, a snack may be enough.
- ARRIVE EARLY. Be at the test center twenty minutes before the test is scheduled to begin. Find the room where you will take the test, the nearest bathroom, and a water fountain (if necessary).

STRATEGIES FOR THE WRITING SKILLS TEST

- READ THE DIRECTIONS CAREFULLY. If the directions are unclear, ask the test administrator for help. (Remember, it may be inappropriate for the test administrator to answer some questions.)
- BE AWARE OF THE TIME LIMIT. Part I is 75 minutes long, and Part II is 45 minutes long. Write down the finish time for the test and check your progress.
- READ THE PASSAGE FIRST. If you notice obvious errors while reading the passage, circle them. Then answer the questions. Refer to the sentence in the passage before you choose an answer—especially if the question focuses on verb tense.
- ANSWER EVERY QUESTION. If you are not sure of the answer, cross out answers that you know are wrong and make an educated guess. (Students who repeatedly read answers that they know are incorrect often get confused.)
- CHOOSE THE BEST ANSWER. Read every option and cross out answers that you know are wrong.
- BUDGET YOUR TIME. Do not spend too much time on any one question. If a question is particularly hard for you, go back to it later. (If you skip a question, carefully check the numbers on your answer sheet to make sure that answers are correctly marked.)
- FILL IN YOUR ANSWER SHEET CLEARLY AND CAREFULLY. Mark only one answer for each item and erase mistakes completely. When you are done, make sure that you have answered every question on the answer sheet. (Double-check items that you skipped.)
- RELAX! If you have prepared for this test, you should feel confident.

How to Use this Book

Regardless of your writing skills, this book can help you. All students should complete the Pretest and the Pretest Skills Chart before starting the units. After you have identified the skills that are hard for you, work through the book. Depending on your skill level, you may choose to focus on specific sections or complete the whole book.

Note the following useful features:

- The Pretest and Pretest Skills Chart will help you identify your strengths and weaknesses.
- Chapter previews will highlight the information that you need to learn.
- Each chapter is divided into sections that are easy to master.
- The symbol ∞ will help you locate summaries for each section.
- Exercises will help you test yourself on each section and chapter.
- Study hints will help you with spelling lists and words that are easily confused.
- A step-by-step guide to essay writing will walk you through the writing process.
- The clear, complete answer key will help you learn from your mistakes.
- After you have completed the book, the Posttest and Posttest Skills Chart will help you decide whether or not you are ready to take the actual GED test.
- A glossary and an index will help you locate information quickly.

After you have finished the units, take the Posttest and complete the Posttest Skills Chart. The Posttest will help you decide if you need more review.

Good luck!

Writing Skills, Part I

Directions

1. This test has paragraphs with numbered sentences. The sentences may have errors, or they may be correct as written. First read the paragraphs. Then answer the related questions. Choose the best answer for each question. The best answer should be consistent with the point of view and verb tense that is used throughout the passage.

2. Answer every question. If you are not sure of the answer, make a logical guess.

3. Allow yourself 75 minutes to answer the 55 questions. When time is up, underline the last item that you completed. Then finish the test. This will help you monitor your time for the actual GED test.

4. Write your answers to the questions on the answer grid. For each question, mark the number that matches the answer you chose.

5. After you have finished the test, check your answers and complete the Pretest Skills Chart to see which sections are difficult for you.

Example:

Sentence 1: **Parents need to give their children a lot of atention.**

What correction should be made to this sentence?

(1) replace *Parents* with *Parents'*

(2) change *their* to *there*

(3) replace *need* with *needed*

(4) change *atention* to *attention*

(5) no correction necessary

1. ① ② ③ ● ⑤

In this sentence, *attention* is spelled incorrectly.

ANSWER GRID

1. ① ② ③ ④ ⑤
2. ① ② ③ ④ ⑤
3. ① ② ③ ④ ⑤
4. ① ② ③ ④ ⑤
5. ① ② ③ ④ ⑤
6. ① ② ③ ④ ⑤
7. ① ② ③ ④ ⑤
8. ① ② ③ ④ ⑤
9. ① ② ③ ④ ⑤
10. ① ② ③ ④ ⑤
11. ① ② ③ ④ ⑤
12. ① ② ③ ④ ⑤
13. ① ② ③ ④ ⑤
14. ① ② ③ ④ ⑤
15. ① ② ③ ④ ⑤
16. ① ② ③ ④ ⑤
17. ① ② ③ ④ ⑤
18. ① ② ③ ④ ⑤
19. ① ② ③ ④ ⑤

20. ① ② ③ ④ ⑤
21. ① ② ③ ④ ⑤
22. ① ② ③ ④ ⑤
23. ① ② ③ ④ ⑤
24. ① ② ③ ④ ⑤
25. ① ② ③ ④ ⑤
26. ① ② ③ ④ ⑤
27. ① ② ③ ④ ⑤
28. ① ② ③ ④ ⑤
29. ① ② ③ ④ ⑤
30. ① ② ③ ④ ⑤
31. ① ② ③ ④ ⑤
32. ① ② ③ ④ ⑤
33. ① ② ③ ④ ⑤
34. ① ② ③ ④ ⑤
35. ① ② ③ ④ ⑤
36. ① ② ③ ④ ⑤
37. ① ② ③ ④ ⑤
38. ① ② ③ ④ ⑤

39. ① ② ③ ④ ⑤
40. ① ② ③ ④ ⑤
41. ① ② ③ ④ ⑤
42. ① ② ③ ④ ⑤
43. ① ② ③ ④ ⑤
44. ① ② ③ ④ ⑤
45. ① ② ③ ④ ⑤
46. ① ② ③ ④ ⑤
47. ① ② ③ ④ ⑤
48. ① ② ③ ④ ⑤
49. ① ② ③ ④ ⑤
50. ① ② ③ ④ ⑤
51. ① ② ③ ④ ⑤
52. ① ② ③ ④ ⑤
53. ① ② ③ ④ ⑤
54. ① ② ③ ④ ⑤
55. ① ② ③ ④ ⑤

Questions 1 through 7 refer to the following paragraph.

(1) Carbon monoxide, CO, is a colorless odorless gas that can be deadly. (2) In the United States, carbon monoxide was the chief cause of poisoning deaths. (3) Every year about 250 people are fatally poisoned by carbon monoxide. (4) Carbon monoxide is caused by the incomplete combustion of fuel. (5) The main sources of carbon monoxide are motor vehicles heaters ovens and fireplaces. (6) There are symptoms for carbon monoxide poisoning, but it varies greatly. (7) As a result, many people are unaware of there exposure to the gas. (8) Carbon monoxide detectors, that are available in most hardware stores, can warn people if the dangerous gas is present in their home or business.

1. Sentence 1: **Carbon monoxide, CO, is a colorless odorless gas that can be deadly.**

   What correction should be made to this sentence?

   (1) remove the comma after *CO*
   (2) replace *that* with *which*
   (3) change *colorless* to *colerless*
   (4) insert a comma after *colorless*
   (5) no correction necessary

2. Sentence 2: **In the United States, carbon monoxide was the chief cause of poisoning deaths.**

   What correction should be made to this sentence?

   (1) change *poisoning* to *poisening*
   (2) replace *was* with *is*
   (3) remove the comma after *States*
   (4) change *United States* to *united states*
   (5) no correction necessary

3. Sentences 3 and 4: **Every year about 250 people are fatally poisoned by carbon monoxide. Carbon monoxide is caused by the incomplete combustion of fuel.**

   The most effective combination of sentences 3 and 4 would include which of the following words?

   (1) which
   (2) because it
   (3) when they
   (4) who
   (5) although

4. Sentence 5: **The main sources of carbon monoxide are <u>motor vehicles heaters ovens and fireplaces.</u>**

   What is the best way to write the underlined portion of the sentence? If you think that the original is best, choose option (1).

   (1) motor vehicles heaters ovens and fireplaces.
   (2) motor vehicles; heaters; ovens; and fireplaces.
   (3) motor vehicles, heaters, ovens, and fireplaces.
   (4) motor vehicles: heaters: ovens: and fireplaces.
   (5) motor vehicles', heaters', ovens', and fireplaces'.

5. Sentence 6: **There are symptoms for carbon monoxide poisoning, but <u>it varies</u> greatly.**

   What is the best way to write the underlined portion of the sentence? If you think that the original is best, choose option (1).

   (1) it varies
   (2) they vary
   (3) it will vary
   (4) they varied
   (5) it did vary

6. Sentence 7: **As a result, many people are unaware of there exposure to the gas.**

   What correction should be made to this sentence?

   (1) remove the comma after *result*
   (2) move *of there exposure* after *result*
   (3) replace *are* with *is*
   (4) change *there* to *their*
   (5) no correction necessary

7. Sentence 8: **Carbon monoxide detectors, that are available in most hardware stores, can warn people if the dangerous gas is present in their home or business.**

What is the best way to write the underlined portion of the sentence? If you think that the original is best, choose option (1).

(1) detectors, that
(2) detectors which
(3) detectors, which
(4) detectors that
(5) detectors; that

<u>Questions 8 through 16</u> refer to the following paragraphs.

(1) The United States has long been known as a nation of immigrants. (2) War, poverty, famine, and persecution have driven people away from their homelands and to America the land of opportunity. (3) From 1880 to 1920, over 23 million immigrants came to the United States. (4) These immigrants were mostly from southern and eastern Europe.
(5) Since that time American immigration has changed in many ways. (6) Today, most emigrants come to the United States from Asia and Latin America. (7) In addition, various laws have restricted whom may enter the country legally. (8) Nonetheless, 15 million new immigrants are expected to enter the United States in the 1990s. (9) Millions more are expected to illegally cross the borders and settle permanently. (10) Although some people debate the pros and cons of immigration for America's future, the United States remains the land of opportunity for people from around the world.

8. Sentence 1: **The United States has long been known as a nation of immigrants.**

What correction should be made to this sentence?

(1) change *United States* to *united states*
(2) insert a comma after *nation*

(3) change *immigrants* to *immigrents*
(4) change *United States* to *United States'*
(5) no correction necessary

9. Sentence 2: **War, poverty, famine, and persecution have driven people away from their homelands and to America the land of opportunity.**

What correction should be made to this sentence?

(1) insert a comma after *America*
(2) change *their* to *they're*
(3) remove the comma after *famine*
(4) change *America* to *america*
(5) no correction necessary

10. Sentences 3 and 4: **From 1880 to 1920, over 23 million immigrants came to the United States. These immigrants were mostly from southern and eastern Europe.**

The most effective combination of sentences 3 and 4 would include which of the following words?

(1) who were
(2) because they
(3) which was
(4) that were
(5) since they

11. Sentence 5: **Since that time American immigration has changed in many ways.**

What correction should be made to this sentence?

(1) replace *has changed* with *will change*
(2) move *in many ways* after *time*
(3) insert a comma after *time*
(4) change *American* to *american*
(5) no correction necessary

12. Sentence 6: **Today, most emigrants come to the United States from Asia and Latin America.**

What correction should be made to this sentence?

(1) change *Asia and Latin America* to *asia and latin america*
(2) change *emigrants* to *immigrants*

(3) insert a comma after *and*
(4) change *come* to *came*
(5) no correction necessary

13. Sentence 7: **In addition, various laws have restricted whom may enter the country legally.**

    What correction should be made to this sentence?

    (1) remove the comma after *addition*
    (2) change *have* to *has*
    (3) change *country* to *contry*
    (4) replace *whom* with *who*
    (5) no correction necessary

14. Sentence 8: **Nonetheless, 15 million new immigrants are expected to enter the United States in the 1990s.**

    What correction should be made to this sentence?

    (1) remove the comma after *Nonetheless*
    (2) change *million* to *Million*
    (3) replace *are* with *is*
    (4) insert a comma after *United States*
    (5) no correction necessary

15. Sentence 9: **Millions more are expected to illegally cross the borders and settle permanently.**

    What correction should be made to this sentence?

    (1) insert a comma after *borders*
    (2) replace *are* with *is*
    (3) change *permanently* to *permenently*
    (4) move *illegally* after *borders*
    (5) no correction necessary

16. Sentence 10: **Although some people debate the pros and cons of immigration for America's future, the United States remains the land of opportunity for people from around the world.**

    If you rewrote this sentence beginning with:

    Some people debate the pros and cons of immigration

the next words should be

(1) for America's future; however, the United States
(2) for America's future. But the United States
(3) for America's future; therefore, the United States
(4) for America's future. Because the United States
(5) for America's future, and the United States

Questions 17 through 28 refer to the following paragraphs.

(1) Better health care is something that millions of Americans need. (2) In 1993, Americans' spent more than $900 billion on health care. (3) Yet, people often did not recieve the medical treatment that they needed. (4) Many people are covered by Medicaid which insures low-income Americans, or Medicare, which insures older Americans. (5) Others are covered by private insurance companies, who generally work through employers. (6) The remaining individuals, over 25 million Americans, have no insurance at all. (7) Generally, these people either pay for they're medical expenses out-of-pocket or do without treatment.

(8) Some political leaders and private citizens want a National insurance plan, which would insure every American citizen. (9) Under this system, the federal goverment would use tax dollars to pay for all medical expenses. (10) Although the plan for every citizen would guarantee health coverage, it would also have drawbacks. (11) Critics of the plan argues that many Americans would not have the quality health care that they currently enjoy. (12) Americans believe that health care is a problem for our country but few can agree on a possible solution.

17. Sentence 1: **Better health care is something that millions of Americans need.**

    If you rewrote this sentence beginning with

Millions of Americans need

the next word would be

(1) something
(2) better
(3) health
(4) is
(5) care

18. Sentence 2: **In 1993, Americans' spent more than $900 billion on health care.**

    What correction should be made to this sentence?

    (1) remove the comma after *1993*
    (2) replace *than* with *then*
    (3) change *Americans'* to *Americans*
    (4) move *on health care* after *1993*
    (5) no correction necessary

19. Sentence 3: **Yet, people often did not recieve the medical treatment that they needed.**

    What correction should be made to this sentence?

    (1) remove the comma after *yet*
    (2) change *recieve* to *receive*
    (3) insert a comma after *treatment*
    (4) change *they* to *it*
    (5) no correction necessary

20. Sentence 4: **Many people are covered by Medicaid which insures low-income Americans, or Medicare, which insures older Americans.**

    What correction should be made to this sentence?

    (1) replace *are* with *is*
    (2) insert a comma after *low-income*
    (3) change *Medicare* to *medicare*
    (4) insert a comma after *Medicaid*
    (5) no correction necessary

21. Sentence 5: **Others are covered by private insurance companies, who generally work through employers.**

    What correction should be made to this sentence?

    (1) replace *who* with *which*
    (2) change *companies* to *Companies*

(3) change *Others* to *Others'*
(4) remove the comma after *companies*
(5) no correction necessary

22. Sentence 6: **The remaining individuals, over 25 million Americans, have no insurance at all.**

    What correction should be made to this sentence?

    (1) remove the comma after *individuals*
    (2) change *Americans* to *americans*
    (3) replace *have* with *has*
    (4) remove the comma after *Americans*
    (5) no correction necessary

23. Sentence 7: **Generally, these people either pay for they're medical expenses out-of-pocket or do without treatment.**

    What correction should be made to this sentence?

    (1) remove the comma after *generally*
    (2) replace *or* with *nor*
    (3) change *they're* to *their*
    (4) change *expenses* to *expences*
    (5) no correction necessary

24. Sentence 8: **Some political leaders and private citizens want a National insurance plan, which would insure every American citizen.**

    What correction should be made to this sentence?

    (1) insert a comma after *leaders*
    (2) change *National* to *national*
    (3) remove the comma after *plan*
    (4) change *citizen* to citisen
    (5) no correction necessary

25. Sentence 9: **Under this system, the federal goverment would use tax dollars to pay for all medical expenses.**

    What correction should be made to this sentence?

    (1) change *goverment* to *government*
    (2) remove the comma after *system*

(3) move *to pay* after *system*

(4) replace *would use* with *used*

(5) no correction necessary

26. Sentence 10: **Although the plan for every citizen would guarantee health coverage, it would also have drawbacks.**

What correction should be made to this sentence?

(1) remove the comma after *coverage*

(2) move *for every citizen* after *coverage*

(3) replace *it* with *they*

(4) change *would* to *wood*

(5) no correction necessary

27. Sentence 11: **Critics of the plan argues that many Americans would not have the quality health care that they currently enjoy.**

What correction should be made to this sentence?

(1) insert a comma after *care*

(2) change *Americans* to *americans*

(3) change *Critics* to *Critic's*

(4) replace *argues* with *argue*

(5) no correction necessary

28. Sentence 12: **Americans believe that health care is a problem for our country but few can agree on a possible solution.**

What correction should be made to this sentence?

(1) change *believe* to *beleive*

(2) replace *is* with *was*

(3) insert a comma after *country*

(4) change *possible* to *posible*

(5) no correction necessary

Questions 29 through 35 refer to the following paragraphs.

(1) When the Constitution of the United States was ratified, leaders from several states insisted that we should guarantee certain rights. (2) As a result, when the first Congress met in spring, 1789, it drafted amendments that would protect people's rights. (3) On December 15, 1791 ten amendments, the Bill of Rights, formally became part of the Constitution. (4) These amendments pledge to safeguard freedom of expression, protect persons who are accused of crimes, and the power of the national government will be limited.

(5) Over the years, the Bill of Rights has been challenged by various controversial issues from abortion to gun control. (6) The different sides of the debates insist that the Constitution support their position. (7) In the end, the U.S. supreme court decides how the Bill of Rights applies to each situation.

29. Sentence 1: **When the Constitution of the United States was ratified, leaders from several states insisted that we should guarantee certain rights.**

What correction should be made to this sentence?

(1) remove the comma after *ratified*

(2) replace *we* with *it*

(3) change *Constitution* to *constitution*

(4) change *several* to *sevral*

(5) no correction necessary

30. Sentence 2: **As a result, when the first Congress met in spring, 1789, it drafted amendments that would protect people's rights.**

What correction should be made to this sentence?

(1) remove the comma after *1789*

(2) change *people's* to *peoples*

(3) remove the comma after *spring*

(4) change *Congress* to *congress*

(5) no correction necessary

31. Sentence 3: **On December 15, 1791 ten amendments, the Bill of Rights, formally became part of the Constitution.**

What correction should be made to this sentence?

(1) insert a comma after *1791*

(2) change *Bill of Rights* to *bill of rights*

(3) replace *became* with *becomes*

(4) remove the comma after *Rights*

(5) no correction necessary

32. Sentence 4: **These amendments pledge to safeguard freedom of expression, protect persons who are accused of crimes, and the power of the national government will be limited.**

    What is the best way to write the underlined portion of this sentence? If you think that the original is best, choose option (1).

    (1) safeguard freedom of expression, protect persons who are accused of crimes, and the power of the national government will be limited.
    (2) safeguard freedom of expression, protect persons who are accused of crimes, and limit the power of the national government.
    (3) safeguard freedom of expression. Protect persons who are accused of crimes, and the power of the national government will be limited.
    (4) safeguard freedom of expression; protect persons who are accused of crimes; and the power of the national government will be limited.
    (5) safeguard freedom of expression: protect persons who are accused of crimes: and limit the power of the national government.

33. Sentence 5: **Over the years, the Bill of Rights has been challenged by various controversial issues from abortion to gun control.**

    If you rewrote sentence 5 beginning with

    Over the years, various controversial issues

    the next word would be

    (1) Bill
    (2) to
    (3) have
    (4) from
    (5) gun

34. Sentence 6: **The different sides of the debates insist that the Constitution support their position.**

    What correction should be made to this sentence?

    (1) change *support* to *supports*
    (2) replace *their* with *there*
    (3) change *different* to *difrent*
    (4) change *Constitution* to *constitution*
    (5) no correction necessary

35. Sentence 7: **In the end, the U.S. supreme court decides how the Bill of Rights applies to each situation.**

    What correction should be made to this sentence?

    (1) remove the comma after *end*
    (2) replace *applies* with *applied*
    (3) change *supreme court* to *Supreme Court*
    (4) change *Bill of Rights* to *Bill of Rights'*
    (5) no correction necessary

Questions 36 through 46 refer to the following paragraphs.

(1) The foods we eat provide nutrients that help our bodies grow and stay healthy. (2) Carbohydrates, proteins, and lipids for example give our bodies energy. (3) Vitamins, that are used in small amounts, help our bodies perform necessary chemical reactions. (4) Likewise, minerals, such as calcium and iron, is used to perform chemical reactions and to maintain specific body parts, particularly teeth and bones.

(5) The digestive system breaks food down so that our bodies can absorb the nutrients that it needs. (6) As soon as food enters the mouth, digestion begins. (7) In the mouth, teeth break the food into smaller pieces saliva makes the food easier to swallow. (8) When food is swallowed, it moves into the Esophagus, a long, muscular tube that connects the mouth to the stomach. (9) In the stomach, it is combined with chemicals that break the pieces down even more. (10) The stomach pushes the partially digested food into the small intestine. (11) The

small intestine absorbs important nutrients though the villi. (12) Material that can not be digested then moves to the large intestine, which prepared the waste that will leave the body.

36. Sentence 1: **The foods we eat provide nutrients that help our bodies grow and stay healthy.**

What correction should be made to this sentence?

(1) insert a comma after *grow*
(2) replace *help* with *helps*
(3) change *bodies* to *body's*
(4) replace *that* with *which*
(5) no correction necessary

37. Sentence 2: **Carbohydrates, proteins, and <u>lipids for example give</u> our bodies energy.**

What is the best way to write the underlined portion of this sentence? If you think that the original is best, choose option (1).

(1) lipids for example give
(2) lipids, for example, give
(3) Lipids for example give
(4) lipids; for example, give
(5) lipids for example gave

38. Sentence 3: **Vitamins, that are used in small amounts, help our bodies perform necessary chemical reactions.**

What correction should be made to this sentence?

(1) change *amounts* to *amonts*
(2) remove the comma after *amounts*
(3) change *bodies* to *body's*
(4) replace *that* with *which*
(5) no correction necessary

39. Sentence 4: **Likewise, minerals, such as calcium and iron, is used to perform chemical reactions and to maintain specific body parts, particularly teeth and bones.**

What correction should be made to this sentence?

(1) replace *Likewise* with *however*
(2) replace *is* with *are*

(3) change *perform* to *preform*
(4) insert a comma after *teeth*
(5) no correction necessary

40. Sentence 5: **The digestive system breaks food down so that our bodies can absorb the nutrients that it needs.**

What correction should be made to this sentence?

(1) replace *it needs* with *they need*
(2) change *breaks* with *broke*
(3) change *digestive system* to *Digestive System*
(4) replace *nutrients* with *nutrients'*
(5) no correction necessary

41. Sentence 6: **As soon as food enters the <u>mouth, digestion</u> begins.**

What is the best way to write the underlined portion of the sentence? If you think that the original is best, choose option (1).

(1) mouth, digestion
(2) mouth: digestion
(3) mouth. Digestion
(4) mouth; digestion
(5) mouth, but digestion

42. Sentence 7: **In the mouth, teeth break the food into smaller <u>pieces saliva</u> makes the food easier to swallow.**

What is the best way to write the underlined portion of the sentence? If you think that the original is best, choose option (1).

(1) pieces, saliva
(2) pieces: saliva
(3) pieces; saliva
(4) pieces; therefore, saliva
(5) pieces because saliva

43. Sentence 8: **When food is swallowed, it moves into the Esophagus, a long, muscular tube that connects the mouth to the stomach.**

What correction should be made to this sentence?

(1) remove the comma after *swallowed*
(2) change *moves* to *moved*
(3) replace *connects* with *connect*
(4) change *Esophagus* to *esophagus*
(5) no correction necessary

44. Sentence 9: **In the stomach, it is combined with chemicals that break the pieces down even more.**

What correction should be made to this sentence?

(1) remove the comma after *stomach*
(2) replace *it* with *the food*
(3) replace *that* with *which*
(4) replace *is* with *are*
(5) no correction necessary

45. Sentences 10 and 11: **The stomach pushes the partially digested food into the small intestine. The small intestine absorbs important nutrients through the villi.**

The most effective combination of sentences 10 and 11 would include which of the following word groups?

(1) intestine; therefore,
(2) intestine, because
(3) intestine who
(4) intestine, yet
(5) intestine, which

46. Sentence 12: **Material that can not be digested then moves to the large <u>intestine, which prepared</u> the waste that will leave the body.**

What is the best way to write the underlined portion of the sentence? If you think that the original is best, choose option (1).

(1) intestine, which prepared
(2) intestine, that prepared
(3) intestine, which prepares
(4) intestine; that prepares
(5) intestine, which did prepare

Questions 47 through 55 refer to the following paragraph.

(1) Henry Ford, a mechanic from Michigan dramatically changed the automobile industry in America. (2) His company created cars that the average citi-zen could afford through mass produc-tion. (3) He designed the Model T Ford with an engine that could be repaired easily, and he did sell over 11,000 Model Ts in one year. (4) By 1925, his company produces over 9,000 cars a day—almost one car every 10 seconds. (5) Fords laborers, who worked on fast-paced assembly lines, earned more than most laborers in the early 1900s. (6) The high-er wages helped Ford reduce absen-teeism and his employees were enabled to purchase cars. (7) Henry Ford profited from his well-run company he supposed-ly made over $25,000 a day throughout the 1920s. (8) As a result, he became a billionaire and an American folk hero. (9) Nonetheless, other companies, such as general motors, became more compet-itive over time, and Henry Ford had to share the automobile market.

47. Sentence 1: **Henry Ford, a mechanic from Michigan dramati-cally changed the automobile industry in America.**

What correction should be made to this sentence?

(1) insert a comma after *Michigan*
(2) change *Ford* to *ford*
(3) remove the comma after *Ford*
(4) change *Michigan* to *michigan*
(5) no correction necessary

48. Sentence 2: **His company created cars that the average citizen could afford through mass produc-tion.**

What correction should be made to this sentence?

(1) insert a comma after *cars*
(2) change *his* to *his'*
(3) move *through mass production* before *his*
(4) change *citizen* to *citisen*
(5) no correction necessary

49. Sentence 3: **He designed the Model T Ford with an engine that could be repaired easily, and he did sell over 11,000 Model Ts in one year.**

What correction should be made to this sentence?

(1) replace *that* with *which*
(2) remove the comma after *easily*
(3) replace *did sell* with *sold*
(4) change *11,000* to *11000*
(5) no correction necessary

50. Sentence 4: **By 1925, his company produces over 9,000 cars a day— almost one car every 10 seconds.**

    What correction should be made to this sentence?

    (1) change *9,000* to *9.000*
    (2) remove the comma after *1925*
    (3) change *produces* to *produced*
    (4) change *every* to *evry*
    (5) no correction necessary

51. Sentence 5: **Fords laborers, who worked on fast-paced assembly lines, earned more than most laborers in the early 1900s.**

    What correction should be made to this sentence?

    (1) remove the comma after *laborers*
    (2) change *Fords* to *Ford's*
    (3) change *than* to *then*
    (4) replace *who* with *which*
    (5) no correction necessary

52. Sentence 6: **The higher wages helped Ford reduce <u>absenteeism, and his employees were enabled</u> to purchase cars.**

    What is the best way to write the underlined portion of this sentence? If you think that the original is best, choose option (1).

    (1) absenteeism, and his employees were enabled
    (2) absenteeism; and enable his employees
    (3) absenteeism. And his employees were enabled
    (4) absenteeism and enable his employees
    (5) absenteeism; and his employees were enabled

53. Sentence 7: **Henry Ford profited from his well-run <u>company he</u> supposedly made over $25,000 a day throughout the 1920s.**

    What is the best way to write the underlined portion of the sentence? If you think that the original is best, choose option (1).

    (1) company he
    (2) company, yet he
    (3) company; he
    (4) company: therefore, he
    (5) company; however, he

54. Sentence 8: **As a result, he became a billionaire and an American folk hero.**

    What correction should be made to this sentence?

    (1) change *billionaire* to *Billionaire*
    (2) remove the comma after *result*
    (3) change *became* to *will become*
    (4) insert a comma after *American*
    (5) no correction necessary

55. Sentence 9: **Nonetheless, other companies, such as general motors, became more competitive over time, and Henry Ford had to share the automobile market.**

    What correction should be made to this sentence?

    (1) remove the comma after *Nonetheless*
    (2) replace *became* with *become*
    (3) change *general motors* to *General Motors*
    (4) change *companies* to *company's*
    (5) no correction necessary

Answers to Pretest

1. **4 insert a comma after *colorless*** (See Chapter 8—End Marks and Commas: Adjectives) *Colorless* and *odorless* both describe *gas*, and they are equally important. They need to be separated by a comma. Option (1) is wrong because *CO* is an appositive that renames carbon monoxide. Option (2) is wrong because *that* is used for restrictive clauses, which do not have commas. Option (3) is wrong because *colorless* is spelled correctly.

2. **2 replace *was* with *is*** (See Chapter 13—Writing Clear Sentences: Consistent Verb Tense) The paragraph is in the present tense. This sentence should be consistent with the rest of the paragraph. Option (1) is wrong because *poisoning* is spelled correctly. Option (3) is wrong because *in the United States* is an introductory phrase, which should be set apart with a comma. Option (4) is wrong because *United States* should be capitalized.

3. **1 which** (See Chapter 13—Writing Clear Sentences: Combining Sentences) In the new sentence, *which* introduces an adjective clause that describes carbon monoxide. *Every year about 250 people are fatally poisoned by carbon monoxide, which is caused by the incomplete combustion of fuel.*

4. **3 motor vehicles, heaters, ovens, and fireplaces.** (See Chapter 8—End Marks and Commas: Independent Clauses and Items in a Series) Items in a series should be separated by commas. Options (1), (2), (4), and (5) do not punctuate the items properly. Option (5) has commas, but it also changes each item into the possessive form.

5. **2 they vary** (See Chapter 13—Writing Clear Sentences: Consistent Pronouns) The pronoun and verb in the second clause must agree with *symptoms. For carbon monoxide poi-* *soning* is a prepositional phrase that describes *symptoms*. Option (1) is wrong because *it* does not agree with *symptoms*. Option (3) is wrong because the pronoun *it* and the verb *will vary* do not agree with the rest of the sentence. Option (4) is wrong because *varied* is in the past tense, and *are* is in the present tense. Option (5) is wrong because neither the pronoun *it* nor the verb *did vary* agree.

6. **4 change *there* to *their*** (See Chapter 12—Word Choice) Whose exposure? *Their* shows possession. Option (1) is wrong because *as a result* is an introductory phrase, which should be set apart with a comma. Option (2) is wrong because *of there exposure* should be near the word it modifies, *unaware*. Option (3) is wrong because *are* agrees with *people*.

7. **3 detectors, which** (See Chapter 7—Clauses: Who, Which, and That) *Which* is used for nonrestrictive clauses, which should be set apart with commas. Options (1), (4), and (5) are wrong because *that* used for restrictive clauses, which are not set apart with punctuation. Option (2) is wrong because the clause should be set apart with comma.

8. **5 No correction necessary** Option (1) is wrong because *United States* should be capitalized. Option (2) is wrong because there is no reason to place a comma after *nation*. Option (3) is wrong because *immigrants* is spelled correctly. Option (4) is wrong because *United States* should not be possessive.

9. **1 insert a comma after America** (See Chapter 8—End Marks and Commas: Nonrestrictive Words, Phrases, and Clauses) *The land of opportunity* is an appositive that renames *America*. Nonrestrictive phrases should be set apart with commas. Option (2) is wrong

because *their* shows possession. Option (3) is wrong because the items in the series should be separated with commas. Option (4) is wrong because *America* should be capitalized.

10. **1 who were** (See Chapter 13—Writing Clear Sentences: Combining Sentences) *Who were mostly from southern and western Europe* is an adjective clause that describes *immigrants. From 1880 to 1920, over 23 million immigrants, who were mostly from southern and eastern Europe, came to the United States.*

11. **3 insert a comma after *time*** (See Chapter 8—End Marks and Commas: Opening Words, Phrases, and Clauses) *Since that time* is an introductory phrase, which should be set apart with a comma. Option (1) is wrong because *has changed* shows that the action began in the past and continues today. *Will change* is used for the future tense, which is inconsistent with the rest of the paragraph. Option (2) is wrong because *in many ways* modifies *has changed.* Modifiers should be next to the words that they describe. Option (4) is wrong because *American* should be capitalized.

12. **2 change *emigrants* to *immigrants*** (See Chapter 12—Word Choice) Emigrants exit a country, and immigrants go into a country. Option (1) is wrong because both *Asia* and *Latin America* should be capitalized. Option (3) is wrong because there is no reason to place a comma after *and.* Option (4) is wrong because *today* signals that the sentence should be in the present tense.

13. **4 replace *whom* with *who*** (See Chapter 5—Pronouns: Who and Whom) *Who may enter the country legally* is a clause, and *who* is the subject of the clause. Option (1) is wrong because *in addition* is an introductory phrase, which should be set apart with a

comma. Option (2) is wrong because *have* must agree with *laws,* which is plural. Option (3) is wrong because *country* is spelled correctly.

14. **5 no correction necessary** Option (1) is wrong because *Nonetheless* is an introductory word, which should be set apart with a comma. Option (2) is wrong because *million* should not be capitalized. Option (3) is wrong because *are* agrees with *immigrants.* Option (4) is wrong because there is no reason to place a comma after *United States.*

15. **4 move *illegally* after *borders*** (See Chapter 1—Parts of Speech: Verbs) *To cross* is an infinitive, which never should be divided. Option (1) is wrong because there is no reason to place a comma after *borders.* Option (2) is wrong because *are* agrees with *millions.* Option (3) is wrong because *permanently* is spelled correctly.

16. **1 for America's future; however, the United States** (See Chapter 13—Writing Clear Sentences: Rewriting Sentences) *Although* and *however* show a contrast between the two clauses. Options (2), (3), (4), and (5) do not show the correct relationship between the two clauses. *Some people debate the pros and cons of immigration; however, the United States remains the land of opportunity for people from around the world.*

17. **2 better** (See Chapter 13—Writing Clear Sentence: Rewriting Sentences) In the new sentence, *millions of Americans* is the subject, and *better health care* is the object of the verb. *Millions of Americans need better health care.*

18. **3 change *Americans'* to *Americans*** (See Chapter 9—More Punctuation: Apostrophes) *Americans* is the subject of the sentence, and it should not be possessive. Option (1) is wrong because *In 1993* is an introductory phrase, which should be set apart

with a comma. Option (2) is wrong because *than* is used for comparisons; *then* is used for time. Option (4) is wrong because *on health care* does not modify *1993*.

19. **2 change recieve to receive** (See Chapter 11—Spelling: Spelling Rules) Option (1) is wrong because *yet* is an introductory word, which should be set apart with a comma. Option (3) is wrong because there is no reason to place a comma after *treatment*. Option (4) is wrong because *they* refers to *people*.

20. **4 insert a comma after Medicaid** (See Chapter 8—End Marks and Commas: Nonrestrictive Words, Phrases, and Clauses) *Which insures low-income Americans* is an adjective clause that describes *Medicaid*. It is a nonrestrictive clause, which should be set apart with commas. Option (1) is wrong because *are* must agree with *people*. Option (2) is wrong because there is no reason to place a comma after *low-income*. Option (3) is wrong because *Medicare* is a proper noun.

21. **1 replace who with which** (See Chapter 7—Clauses: Who, Which, and That) Use *who* for people. Use *which* and *that* for animals and things. Option (2) is wrong because *companies* is a common noun, which should not be capitalized. Option (3) is wrong because *others* is the subject of the sentence, and it is not possessive. Option (4) is wrong because *who generally work through employers* is a nonrestrictive clause, which should be set apart with a comma.

22. **5 no correction necessary** Options (1) and (4) are wrong because *over 25 million Americans* is an appositive that renames *individuals*. The phrase, which is nonrestrictive, should be set apart with commas. Option (2) is wrong because *Americans* should be capitalized. Option (3) is wrong because *have* must agree with *individuals*.

23. **3 replace they're with their** (See Chapter 12—Word Choice: Commonly Confused Words) Whose medical expenses? Use *their* to show possession, and use *they're* as a contraction for *they are*. Option (1) is wrong because *generally* is an introductory word, which should be set apart with a comma. Option (2) is wrong because *or* is used with *either*. Option (4) is wrong because *expenses* is spelled correctly.

24. **2 change National to national** (See Chapter 10—Capitalization) *National* is an adjective that describes *insurance plan*. It should not be capitalized. Option (1) is wrong because there is no reason to place a comma after *leaders*. Option (3) is wrong because *which would insure every American citizen* is a nonrestrictive clause, which should be set apart with a comma. Option (4) is wrong because *citizen* is spelled correctly.

25. **1 change goverment to government** (See Chapter 11—Spelling: Most Common Spelling Errors) *Government* is often misspelled. Option (2) is wrong because *under this system* is an introductory phrase, which should be set apart with a comma. Option (3) is wrong because *to pay* does not modify *system*. Option (4) is wrong because this sentence is not in the past tense.

26. **2 move for every citizen after coverage** (See Chapter 13—Writing Clear Sentences: Misplaced Modifiers) *For every citizen* modifies *health coverage*, not *plan*. The original sentence implies that there is a separate plan for every citizen. Option (1) is wrong because the comma sets apart an introductory clause. Option (3) is wrong because *it* refers to *the plan*. Option (4) is wrong because *would* is spelled correctly.

27. **4 replace *argues* with *argue*** (See Chapter 4—Subject Verb Agreement: Difficult Subjects) *Argue* must agree with *critics*. Option (1) is wrong because *that they currently enjoy* is a restrictive clause. Option (2) is wrong because *Americans* should be capitalized. Option (3) is wrong because *Critics* is the subject of the sentence; it should not be possessive.

28. **3 insert a comma after *country*** (See Chapter 8—End Marks and Commas: Independent Clauses and Items in a Series) *But* is a coordinating conjunction, which joins two independent clauses. A comma should be placed before the conjunction. Option (1) is wrong because *believe* is spelled correctly. Option (2) is wrong because the sentence is in the present tense. Both verbs, *is* and *agree*, should be in the same tense. Option (4) is wrong because *possible* is spelled correctly.

29. **2 replace *we* with *it*** (See Chapter 13—Writing Clear Sentences: Consistent Pronouns) The pronoun *it* refers to the Constitution. Option (1) is wrong because the comma sets apart an introductory clause. Option (3) is wrong because the *Constitution* is the name of a specific document. When the writer refers to the particular document, the name should be capitalized. Option (4) is wrong because *several* is spelled correctly.

30. **3 remove the comma after *spring*** (See Chapter 8—End Marks and Commas: Dates, Addresses, and Long Numbers) Do not use a comma to separate a season from the year. Option (1) is wrong because the comma sets apart an introductory clause. Option (2) is wrong because *people's* shows whose rights are protected. Option (4) is wrong because *Congress* is a part of the government, and it should be capitalized.

31. **1 insert a comma after *1791*** (See Chapter 8—End Marks and Commas: Dates, Addresses, and Long Numbers) Insert a comma after a date that is used in a sentence. Option (2) is wrong because the *Bill of Rights* is a specific document. Option (3) is wrong because the sentence is in the past tense. Option (4) is wrong because *the Bill of Rights* is an appositive that renames *ten amendments*. Nonrestrictive words should be set apart with commas.

32. **2 safeguard freedom of expression, protect persons who are accused of crimes, and limit the power of the national government** (See Chapter 13—Writing Clear Sentences: Parallel Structure) Each item in the series should be in the same form. In the original sentence, the last item is inconsistent. Options (1), (3), and (4) have the same inconsistent structure. Option (5) wrongly uses colons, instead of commas, to separate the items.

33. **4 from** (See Chapter 13—Writing Clear Sentences: Rewriting Sentences and Misplaced Modifiers) *From abortion to gun control* is a modifier that describes *issues*. In the new sentence, the modifier must remain next to *issues. Over the years, various controversial issues from abortion to gun control have challenged the Bill of Rights.*

34. **1 change *support* to *supports*** (See Chapter 4—Subject Verb Agreement: General Guidelines) *Supports* must agree with *Constitution*, which is the subject of the clause. Option (2) is wrong because *their* shows possession. Option (3) is wrong because *different* is spelled correctly. Option (4) is wrong because *Constitution* should be capitalized. The Constitution refers to a specific document.

35. **3 change *supreme court* to *Supreme Court*** (See Chapter 10—Capitalization) The U.S. Supreme Court is part of the government. Option (1) is wrong because the comma sets apart an introductory phrase. Option (2) is wrong because the sentence is in the present tense. Option (4) is wrong because *Bill of Rights* should not be possessive in this sentence.

36. **5 no correction necessary** Option (1) is wrong because there is no reason to place a comma after *grow*. Option (2) is wrong because *help* agrees with *nutrients*. Option (3) is wrong because *bodies* is the plural form of *body*. There is no reason to use the possessive form. Option (4) is wrong because *that* is used for restrictive clauses, which are not set apart with commas.

37. **2 lipids, for example, give** (See Chapter 8—End Marks and Commas: Interruptions) *For example* interrupts the sentence, and it should be set apart with commas. Options (1), (3), (4), and (5) are wrong because they do not use commas to set apart *for example*.

38. **4 replace *that* with *which*** (See Chapter 7—Clauses: Who, Which, and That) Use *which* for nonrestrictive clauses, which are set apart with commas. Option (1) is wrong because *amounts* is spelled correctly. Option (2) is wrong because the comma sets apart a nonrestrictive clause. Option (3) is wrong because *bodies* is the plural form of *body*. There is no reason to use the possessive form.

39. **2 replace *is* with *are*** (See Chapter 4—Subject Verb Agreement: Difficult Subjects) *Are* agrees with *minerals*, the subject of the sentence. Option (1) is wrong because *however* signals a contrast. This sentence adds information. Option (3) is wrong because *perform* is spelled correctly. Option (4) is wrong because there is no reason to place a comma after *teeth*.

40. **1 replace *it needs* with *they need*** (See Chapter 13—Writing Clear Sentences: Consistent Pronouns) *They need* agrees with *bodies*, the subject of the clause. Option (2) is wrong because the sentence is in the present tense. Option (3) is wrong because *digestive system* is a common noun, which should not be capitalized. Option (4) is wrong because *nutrients* is the plural form of *nutrient*. There is no reason to use the possessive form.

41. **1 mouth, digestion** (See Chapter 7—Clauses: Adverb Clauses and Chapter 8—End Marks and Commas: Opening Words, Phrases, and Clauses) *As soon as food enters the mouth* is an introductory clause that works as an adverb. It should be set apart with a comma. Options (2), (3), and (4) are wrong because the punctuation is incorrect. Option (5) is wrong because *but* changes the relationship between the clauses.

42. **3 pieces; saliva** (See Chapter 9—More Punctuation: Semicolons) Both clauses are related. They show what happens in the mouth. They could be separate sentences, but that option is not offered. Option (1) is incorrect because a comma alone can not join two independent clauses. Option (2) is wrong because there is no reason to use a colon. Options (4) and (5) are wrong because they do not show the correct relationship between the two clauses.

43. **4 change *Esophagus* to *esophagus*** (See Chapter 10—Capitalization) *Esophagus* is a common noun, which should not be capitalized. Option (1) is wrong because the comma sets apart an introductory clause. Option (2) is wrong because the sentence should be in the present tense. Option (3) is wrong because *connects* must agree with *tube*.

44. **2 replace *it* with *the food*** (See Chapter 13—Writing Clear Sentences: Consistent Pronouns) *It* is too vague. The pronoun could refer to the stomach, the food, or even the esophagus. Vague pronouns should be replaced with specific nouns. Option (1) is wrong because the comma sets apart an introductory phrase. Option (3) is wrong because *that* is used for restrictive clauses, which are not set apart with commas. Option (4) is wrong because *is* agrees with *it*.

45. **5 intestine, which** (See Chapter 13—Writing Sentences: Combining Sentences) The original second sentence simply describes the small intestine. When the two sentences are combined, the second sentence becomes an adjective clause. Options (1), (2), (3), and (4) do not show the correct relationship between the two clauses. *The stomach pushes the partially digested food into the small intestine, which absorbs important nutrients through the villi.*

46. **3 intestine, which prepares** (See Chapter 3—Verb Usage: Verb Tense and Chapter 7—Clauses: Who, Which, and That) The sentence should be in the present tense because the action occurs repeatedly. In addition, *which* should be used because the clause is nonrestrictive. Options (1) and (5) are wrong because the verbs are in the past tense. Option (2) is wrong because *that* is used for restrictive clauses. Option (4) is wrong because it has a semicolon, and *that* is used for restrictive clauses.

47. **1 insert a comma after *Michigan*** (See Chapter 8—End Marks and Commas: Nonrestrictive Words, Phrases, and Clauses) *A mechanic from Michigan* is an appositive that renames Henry Ford. It should be set apart with commas. Option (2) is wrong because *Ford* is a proper name. Option (3) is wrong because the comma is necessary to set apart the appositive. Option (4) is wrong because *Michigan* is a proper noun.

48. **3 move *through mass production* before *his*** (See Chapter 13—Writing Clear Sentences: Misplaced Modifiers) *Through mass production* modifies *company*. The phrase shows how the company created cars, and it should be located near the word that it modifies. Option (1) is wrong because there is no reason to place a comma after *cars*; the phrase that follows *cars* is restrictive. Option (2) is wrong because possessive pronouns never have apostrophes. Option (4) is wrong because *citizen* is spelled correctly.

49. **3 change *did sell* to *sold*** (See Chapter 13—Writing Clear Sentences: Consistent Verb Tense) Both verbs in the sentence, *design* and *sell*, should be in the past tense. Thus, the verbs should be *designed* and *sold*. Option (1) is wrong because *that* introduces a restrictive clause. Option (2) is wrong because the comma, along with the conjunction *and*, joins two independent clauses. Option (4) is incorrect because *11,000* is punctuated correctly.

50. **3 change *produces* to *produced*** (See Chapter 13—Writing Clear Sentences: Consistent Verb Tense) *By 1925* signals that this sentence should be in the past tense. Option (1) is wrong because *9,000* is punctuated correctly. Option (2) is wrong because the comma sets apart an introductory phrase. Option (4) is wrong because *every* is spelled correctly.

51. **2 change *Fords* to *Ford's*** (See Chapter 9—More Punctuation: Apostrophes) Whose laborers? Use *'s* to show possession. Option (1) is wrong because the comma sets apart a nonrestrictive clause. Option (3) is wrong because *than* is used for comparisons. Option

(4) is wrong because *who* is used for people.

52. **4 absenteeism and enable his employees** (See Chapter 13—Writing Clear Sentences: Balanced Structure) The underlined portion shows how higher wages helped Ford. A compound verb, *reduce and enable*, balances the sentence structure. Options (1), (3), and (5) do not have balanced structure. Option (2) is punctuated incorrectly.

53. **3 company; he** (See Chapter 9—More Punctuation: Semicolons) Both independent clauses are related. The second clause provides more specific information about the first clause. Options (1) and (4) are wrong because they are punctuated incorrectly. Options (2) and (5) are wrong because they show an incorrect relationship between the two clauses. *Yet* and *however* imply a contrast.

54. **5 no correction necessary** Option (1) is wrong because *billionaire* is a common noun, which should not be capitalized. Option (2) is wrong because the comma sets apart an introductory phrase. Option (3) is wrong because the sentence should be in the past tense. Option (4) is wrong because there is no reason to place a comma after *American*. *Folk* and *American* both describe *hero*, but they are not equally important.

55. **3 change *general motors* to *General Motors*** (See Chapter 10—Capitalization) *General Motors*, the name of a company, is a proper noun. Option (1) is wrong because *Nonetheless* is an introductory word. Option (2) is wrong because the sentence should be in the past tense. Option (4) is wrong because *companies* is the plural form of *company*. There is no reason to use the possessive form.

Pretest Skills Chart

Directions:

Check your answers to the Pretest and circle the items that you got wrong. While studying for the actual GED test, focus particularly on the topics that are difficult for you.

TOPICS	QUESTION NUMBERS	PAGE REFERENCES
Parts of Speech		
Verbs	15	34–37
Verb Usage		
Verb Tense	46	61–77
Subject-Verb Agreement		78–86
General Guidelines	34	78, 79
Special Situations	27, 39	79–85
Pronouns		87–98
Possessive Case		91, 92
Who and Whom	13	92–94
Special Situations		94, 95
Pronoun Agreement	5, 40	97, 98
Clauses		107–113
Dependent Clauses		107, 108
Adjective Clauses		109–111
Who, Which, and That	21	112–113
Restrictive vs. Nonrestrictive Clauses	7, 38	113
End Marks and Commas		119–128
Commas		121
Independent Clauses and Items in a Series	4, 28	121, 122
Adjectives	1	122
Nonrestrictive Words, Phrases, and Clauses	9, 20, 47	122, 123
Opening Words, Phrases, and Clauses	11, 41	123, 124
Interruptions	37	125
Dates, Addresses, and Long Numbers	30, 31	126
More Punctuation		129–139
Semicolons	42, 53	129–131
Apostrophes	18, 51	132–135
Capitalization		
Capitalization	24, 35, 43, 54, 55	140–143
Spelling		144–155
Most Common Errors	25	145–151
Spelling Rules	19	151–154

Word Choice		
Commonly Confused Words	6, 12, 23	156–162
Writing Clear Sentences		179–199
Parallel Structure	32	180–182
Balanced Structure	52	182, 183
Consistent Verb Tense	2, 49, 50	183, 184
Misplaced Modifiers	26, 33, 48	185–187
Consistent Pronouns	29, 44	188, 189
Rewriting Sentences	16, 17	189–191
Combining Sentences	3, 10, 45	191–195

* No correction necessary for questions 8, 14, 22, 36

FUNDAMENTALS

Parts of Speech

As a writer, you are the boss, and the words are your workers. Each word in a sentence has a job to do. This chapter will help you understand how words are used in sentences so that you can use the right word for any job.

Subjects and Predicates

All sentences have a subject and a predicate. The subject is someone or something. The predicate describes the subject or shows the subject in action.

Examples:

Subject	Predicate
Charities	are important.
They	help people reach their goals.
Individuals and companies	give money to charities.

The subjects name people and things such as *charities, they, individuals,* and *companies.* The predicates describe the subject or show actions. For example, *are important* describes *charities.* The words *help people reach their goals* show the action that *they* take. Likewise, the words *give money to charities* show the action of *individuals and companies.*

PARTS OF SPEECH

Nouns name persons, places, things, or ideas: *Abraham Lincoln, child, Virginia, car, anger*

Pronouns substitute for nouns and work as nouns: *I, you, he, she, it, they, we, this, that, who, which, everybody, myself*

Verbs connect related words or show action: *is, are, talk, create*

Adjectives tell the size, shape, number, owner, or appearance of a noun or pronoun: *large, round, some, tall*

Adverbs give information about verbs, adjectives, or other adverbs: *carefully, today, soon, quickly*

Prepositions link words or groups of words: *above, behind, at, between, with, for, until*

Remember, the function of a word determines its part of speech.

EXERCISE 1: Draw a line between the subject and the predicate in each of the following sentences.

SAMPLE: Many parents / need day care for their children.

1. The girl ate a donut.

2. Some people can not afford health care.

3. Lions, tigers, elephants, and horses perform tricks at the circus.

4. Mr. Po read the poem to the class.

5. The flu strikes many people in the winter.

6. Some workers have to develop their skills.

7. Cal caught the ball, ran to second base, and tagged the runner.

8. Juan dreams of playing in the pros.

9. Parents want decent jobs, safe streets, and good schools.

10. Some people come to America to start a new life.

Answers are on page 274.

Nouns

Everything that has a name is a noun. Nouns name persons, places, things, or ideas.

Examples:

Mrs. Durkin is a great teacher.

Mrs. Durkin and *teacher* name a person.

Washington, D.C. and New York City are large cities.

Washington, D.C., New York City, and *cities* are places.

The tall tree is bending in the wind.

Tree and *wind* are things.

Most workers want success and happiness.

Workers are persons. *Success* and *happiness* are ideas.

Nouns can be found easily. Articles such as *a, an,* and *the* come before nouns. Likewise, adjectives—words that describe

the size, shape, number, owner, or appearance of nouns—often precede nouns.

> ⇨ *Note:* Certain words such as *a, an,* and *the* often come before nouns. They are called **articles.** When an article appears, a noun soon follows.

Examples:

1. The dedicated athlete won an award.
   Athlete and *award* are nouns. *The* and *an* are articles that come before *athlete* and *award.*

2. The fancy, red car sped through the intersection.
   Car and *intersection* are nouns. *Fancy* and *red* are adjectives that describe the *car. The* is an article that comes before both *car* and *intersection.*

> ⇨ *Note:* When a noun shows ownership, it works like an adjective. (Joe's cabin was destroyed. *Joe's* is an adjective describing *cabin.*)

Most nouns can be made plural by adding *-s* or *-es.*

Examples:

1. All five tests were on the same day.
   Test was made plural by adding an *-s* to form *tests.*

2. Several boxes fell to the ground.
   Box was made plural by adding *-es* to form *boxes.*

Nouns can also show ownership by adding an apostrophe (') and an *-s* or just an apostrophe. When a noun shows ownership, it works like an adjective. (See more on adjectives on pages 37, 38 and possession in Chapter 5.)

Examples:

1. Joe<u>'s</u> cabin was destroyed by the sudden flood.
2. The players<u>'</u> uniforms were muddy.

Joe was made possessive by adding *-'s*. *Players* was made possessive by adding an apostrophe ('). *Joe's* and *players'* work as adjectives.

EXERCISE 2: Underline the nouns in the following sentences.

1. The manager ran through the store.

2. The coach gave Saul a gold medal.

3. A judge ordered Chris to pay for the car.

4. The coffee destroyed Rita's notebook.

5. The fire raced through Kim's house.

6. Sean typed three letters on the new computer.

7. Lynn needs a sitter for the baby.

8. Ty wants a job with decent hours and good pay.

9. Paul's landlord did not fix the leaks in the ceiling.

10. Students want to have success in school.

Answers are on page 274.

☞ Remember these <u>facts about nouns</u>:

- Nouns name persons, places, things, or ideas.
- Most nouns can be made plural by adding *-s* or *-es*.
- Articles are soon followed by a noun.
- Nouns often follow adjectives, which are words that describe the size, shape, number, owner, or appearance of nouns.

- Nouns can show ownership by adding an apostrophe (') and an *-s* or just an apostrophe. When a noun is made possessive, it works like an adjective.

Pronouns

Generally pronouns substitute for nouns and work as nouns do in a sentence. Note the pronouns that are listed in the box.

PRONOUNS
I
everybody
he
her
herself
him
himself
it
me
myself
she
some
such
that
them
themselves
they
this
us
we
which
who
whoever
whom
whomever
you

Example:

Kathy is a doctor. <u>She</u> works with patients from all over the city. <u>They</u> come to <u>her</u> with many different health problems. <u>She</u> helps people <u>who</u> can not afford other medical services.

(*She* substitutes for Kathy. *They* substitutes for patients. *Her* substitutes for Kathy. *She* substitutes for Kathy, and *who* substitutes for people.)

Personal pronouns (*I, you, he, she, it, we, they, me, him, her, us, them*) substitute for a specific person or persons. Personal pronouns and the pronoun *who* change form in different sentences. (See more on pronouns in Chapter 5.)

EXERCISE 3: Underline the pronouns in the following sentences.

1. Leigh picked up the wallet and returned it.
2. The FBI wanted to question whomever they saw.
3. Who will volunteer to organize the bake sale?
4. After Nate cut himself, he rushed to the hospital.
5. Everybody wanted to win the prize.
6. They hurt themselves on the field.
7. I do not want this.
8. You need to fill out the forms before you see the doctor.
9. It is the only way to get her to take care of herself.
10. Which is the right way?

Answers are on page 274.

☞ Remember, pronouns substitute for nouns and work as nouns do in a sentence.

Verbs

There are two types of verbs, linking verbs and action verbs. Linking verbs connect related words (be, is, was, are), and action verbs show action (run, talk, grow).

Examples:

1. Sean and James <u>are</u> wrestlers.
   Are is a linking verb that connects *Sean and James* to *wrestlers*. *Wrestlers* renames *James* and *Sean*.
2. Suzanne <u>plays</u> the violin in the orchestra.
   Plays is an action verb. It shows *Suzanne's* action.

LINKING VERBS

Linking verbs form connections. They link the subject to words that rename or describe the subject. Think of a linking verb as an arrow (↔) that links related words.

LINKING VERBS		
Forms of *Be*	Verbs of the Senses	Unusual Linking Verbs
be	look	become
am	smell	appear
is	taste	grow
are	sound	remain
was	feel	stay
were		seem
been		
being		

Remember to test the verbs of the senses and the unusual linking verbs using a form of be or an arrow (↔).

Examples:

1. Einstein was brilliant.
   Einstein ↔ brilliant
2. The cake tastes great.
   The cake ↔ great
3. Her date seemed nervous.
   Her date ↔ nervous

Memorizing the list of linking verbs will help you find them more easily. However, the verbs that are listed do not always work as linking verbs. If you are not sure, substitute a form of *be* and an arrow (↔) for the verb. If the sentence still makes sense, the verb is a linking verb.

Examples:

1. Brianna <u>looks</u> beautiful.
   Brianna ↔ beautiful
   Brianna is beautiful makes sense. *Looks* is a linking verb.
2. She <u>felt</u> the cold weather.
   She ↔ cold weather
   She is the cold weather does not make sense. *Felt* is an action verb.
3. The cookies <u>smelled</u> great.
   The cookies ↔ great
   The cookies were great makes sense. *Smelled* is a linking verb.
4. She <u>smelled</u> the cake baking.
   She ↔ the cake baking
   She is the cake baking does not make sense. In this case *smelled* is an action verb.
5. Her grandfather <u>remained</u> sick.
   Her grandfather ↔ sick
   Her grandfather was sick makes sense. *Remained* is a linking verb.

ACTION VERBS

Action verbs simply show action. Most verbs are action verbs. The subject of the sentence either does the action or receives it.

Examples:

1. The batter <u>hit</u> the ball far.
   The subject, *the batter*, performed the action.
2. The batter <u>was hit</u> by the ball.
   The subject, *the batter*, received the action.

 Note:

Infinitive = to + verb
Always keep *to* and the verb together.
Wrong: He wanted <u>to</u> really <u>run</u>.
Right: He really wanted <u>to run</u>.

EXERCISE 4: Decide if the verbs in the following sentences are linking verbs or action verbs. Circle the correct answer.

1. That band seems awful.
   LINKING ACTION
2. Juan stayed in the hospital for days. LINKING ACTION
3. Ahmed felt the hot sun on his back. LINKING ACTION
4. My soup tastes salty.
   LINKING ACTION
5. She smells the flowers on the table. LINKING ACTION
6. Carl grew three inches last year.
   LINKING ACTION
7. Taste the cheesecake.
   LINKING ACTION
8. After the lawsuit, Ray remained angry for months.
   LINKING ACTION
9. Jill stayed in the race.
   LINKING ACTION
10. We grew tired of his empty promises. LINKING ACTION

Answers are on pages 274, 275.

HELPING VERBS

Sometimes verbs need help to show action. Helping verbs support the main verb in a sentence. The helping verb(s) and the main verb work like a team. Together they form a verb phrase. The last verb in the phrase is the main verb.

HELPING VERBS

am
are
be
been
being
can
could
did
do
does
had
has
have
is
may
might
shall
should
was
were
will
would

Example:

She <u>should have been studying</u> for the test.
HELPING VERB(S) + MAIN VERB = VERB PHRASE
should, have, been + studying = should have been studying
Some verbs can work alone or as helping verbs.

Examples:

1. Ruth and Russ <u>are</u> at the movies.
   Are is the main verb. It is a linking verb.
2. Ruth and Russ <u>are eating</u> popcorn.
   Are is a helping verb. *Eating* is the main verb. It is the last verb in the verb phrase.
3. Ruth and Russ <u>should have seen</u> a different movie.
   Should and *have* are both helping verbs. *Seen* is the main verb. It is the last verb in the verb phrase.

EXERCISE 5:   Underline the verbs and verb phrases in the following sentences. Write the main verb in the space provided.

1. Jim and Alice are at the beach.

   _____

2. The two lawyers were arguing about the case.

   _____

3. Mike and Joe could have eaten better food.

   _____

4. Khan should have thought about his future.

   _____

5. In two weeks, we will be going on a vacation.

   _____

6. Who is the best worker?

   _____

7. Pam has been working from home.

   _____

8. Keith's mom will watch the two children.

   _____

9. Jan moved to a new home.

   _____

10. The judge could have asked the jury.

   _____

Answers are on page 275

Remember these <u>facts about verbs</u>:

• There are two types of verbs, linking verbs and action verbs.

- The main verb is the last verb in the verb phrase.
- To find linking verbs, try substituting a form of *be* and an arrow (↔). Remember, this test only works for the eleven verbs listed.
- An infinitive includes *to* + verb. Always keep *to* and the verb together.

7. David broke his right elbow when he fell on the hard ground.

8. Good child care is expensive.

9. Many parents want more time with their children.

10. High-paying jobs often require a good education.

Answers are on page 275.

Adjectives

Adjectives give information. They tell the size, shape, number, owner, or appearance of nouns or pronouns. Adjectives often appear in front of the nouns they describe and after linking verbs.

To identify adjectives, you must first find the nouns in the sentence. Then ask yourself the following questions about the nouns: How many? How much? Which one? What type? Whose?

Examples:

1. John threw <u>three</u> stones into the <u>cold</u> water.
   Three tells how many stones. *Cold* tells what type of water.
2. <u>Tricia's</u> fabric was sewn into a <u>beautiful</u> quilt.
   Tricia's tells whose fabric. *Beautiful* tells what type of quilt.
3. The book is <u>large</u> and <u>red</u>.
   Large and *red* tell which book. These adjectives follow a linking verb.

EXERCISE 6: Underline the adjectives in the following sentences.

1. Rhea applied to three companies before she found her new job.

2. My small paycheck does not cover the monthly bills.

3. Kind friends helped our poor family.

4. The old, brick building was destroyed in the violent earthquake.

5. English is a hard language.

6. The best team will go to the final round.

USING ADJECTIVES TO MAKE COMPARISONS

Adjectives can compare nouns. There are three different forms of adjectives that are used for specific comparisons. Note how adjectives are used in the box.

COMPARISONS WITH ADJECTIVES

ONE PERSON OR THING = BASIC FORM tall, old, agreeable

TWO PERSONS OR THINGS = -ER OR MORE FORM taller, older, more agreeable

THREE OR MORE PERSONS OR THINGS = -EST OR MOST FORM tallest, oldest, most agreeable

Use *more* or *most* instead of the endings to help some adjectives sound better—especially adjectives with three or more syllables.

Examples:

1. Laura is a <u>fast</u> runner.
   Laura is the only person mentioned. The basic form is used.
2. However, Jennifer is fast<u>er</u> than Laura.
   Two people, Jennifer and Laura, are compared. The *-er* form is used.
3. Ellen is the fast<u>est</u> runner of the three.
   Three people are compared. The *-est* form is used.

Not all adjectives follow this pattern. For example, some adjectives change form completely; other adjectives use *more* and *most* to make comparisons.

COMPARISONS WITH ADJECTIVES		
One Person or Thing (Basic Form)	Two Persons or Things (-er Form)	Three or More Persons or Things (-est Form)
tall good bad beautiful	taller better worse more beautiful	tallest best worst most beautiful

EXERCISE 7:   Underline the correct adjective for the following sentences.

1. Susan is a (brave, bravest) girl.

2. Mark is the (better, best) player on the whole football team.

3. Our new phone needs to be (more, most) reliable than the old one.

4. I want the (more, most) careful person on staff for this job.

5. For some, Spanish is an (easier, easiest) language than French.

6. Wayne is a (more, most) talented dentist than his partner.

7. If you want to be the (better, best) salesperson in your company, you will need to work hard.

8. Chris is the (shorter, shortest) person in the sophomore class.

9. This is the (worse, worst) movie I have ever seen.

10. If you want to earn a raise, you will have to be a (better, best) waiter than Ken.

Answers are on pages 275, 276.

Remember these <u>facts about adjectives</u>:

- Adjectives give information. They tell the size, shape, number, owner, or appearance of nouns or pronouns.

- To identify an adjective, ask yourself the following questions about nouns: How many? How much? Which one? What kind? Whose?

- Adjectives often appear in front of the nouns they describe or after linking verbs.

- Adjectives are used to compare nouns.

- Adjectives usually use *-er* and *-est* endings or the words *more* and *most* to make comparisons.

Adverbs

Adverbs give information about verbs, adjectives, and other adverbs. They also can give information about whole groups of words. Adverbs often end in *-ly*, but not always. Look at a word's job in the sentence to decide if it's an adverb.

To find adverbs, ask the following questions about verbs, adjectives, or other adverbs: How? Where? When? Why? How often? How much? Some adverbs will answer more than one question.

Examples:

1. He <u>quickly</u> ran <u>home</u>.
   Quickly tells how he ran. *Home* tells where he ran.

2. <u>Yesterday</u> we <u>carefully</u> painted the sign.
   Yesterday tells when the sign was painted. *Carefully* tells how the sign was painted.

3. Bob <u>completely</u> understands the new lesson.
Completely tells how much Bob understands.
4. Mrs. Mallett is <u>very</u> happy <u>today</u>.
Very tells to what extent Mrs. Mallett is happy. *Today* tells when Mrs. Mallet is happy.

 Note: *Not* and *never* are adverbs. They answer the question *how often*. Likewise, *too* is an adverb. It answers the question *how*.

EXERCISE 8:   Underline the adverbs in the following sentences.

1. The whole crew worked very hard.
2. We often pay our bills late.
3. Today the chorus sang beautifully.
4. We never told anyone about the good news.
5. Steve is quite talented.
6. The friendly dog quickly ate his food.
7. Jay really wants a raise soon.
8. The plumber truly fixed the problem with my sink.
9. The cat ran away yesterday.
10. Edith promptly walked straight home.

Answers are on page 276.

USING ADVERBS TO MAKE COMPARISONS

Adverbs compare verbs, adjectives, and other adverbs. Adverbs also use the *-er* and *-est* endings in addition to *more* and *most*.

COMPARISONS WITH ADVERBS

ONE THING = BASIC FORM   loud, quick, beautifully

TWO THINGS = -ER FORM OR MORE louder, quicker, more beautiful

THREE OR MORE THINGS = -EST FORM OR MOST   loudest, quickest, most beautiful

If an adverb has more than one syllable or ends in *-ly*, use *more* or *most* instead of the endings.

Examples:

1. The alarm rang <u>late</u>.
Late is the basic form.

The alarm rang la<u>ter</u> today than it did yesterday.
The sentence requires the *-er* form because the alarm rang twice, today and yesterday.

Of all six days that the alarm rang, it rang la<u>test</u> on Friday.
The alarm rang six times. The sentence needs the *-est* form.

2. She <u>carefully</u> explained the information.

She explained the information <u>more</u> carefully today than yesterday.
She explained the information twice, today and yesterday. *More* is used because careful has more than one syllable.

Of all five instructors, she explained the information <u>most</u> carefully.
The information was explained five times. *Most* is used because careful has more than one syllable.

EXERCISE 9:   Underline the correct form for each of the following adverbs.

1. The hiker entered the cave (faster, fastest) this afternoon than this morning.

2. The team played (harder, hardest) today than yesterday.

3. Of all six speakers, Colin spoke (more, most) forcefully.

4. She is the (better, best) dressed woman in Hollywood.

5. Eve ran (more, most) quickly today than on Friday.

6. This shirt is the (more, most) colorful one in the store.

7. Ted yelled (louder, loudest) at his secretary than at me.

8. When Guy speaks, he rambles (worse, worst) than you do.

9. This building was destroyed (more, most) abruptly than that one.

10. Unsolicited phone calls during the day are (less, least) annoying than calls during dinner.

Answers are on page 276.

Remember these <u>facts about adverbs</u>:

- Adverbs give information about verbs, adjectives, and other adverbs.
- To find adverbs, ask the following questions about verbs, adjectives, or other adverbs: How? Where? When? Why? How often? How much?
- Adverbs often end in -*ly,* but not always. Look at a word's job in the sentence to decide if it's an adverb.
- *Not, never,* and *too* are adverbs.
- Adverbs use -*er* and -*est* endings or the words *more* and *most* to make comparisons.

Prepositions

Prepositions link words or groups of words. Many prepositions are easy to find because they are used often. If prepositions are hard for you to find, think of a preposition as an arrow (→) that points to related words. Use the following scenario to help you.

A bee can fly **about** the house, **above** the door, **across** the room, **after** the dog, **against** the window, **along** the ledge, **around** the corner, and **at** your friend. He can fly **behind** the tree, **below** the clouds, **beneath** the bushes, **between** the roses, **beyond** the fence, or **down** the hill **during** spring. **For** many hours **from** dusk to dawn, he can fly **in** the garden, **like** a butterfly, **near** the plants, **over** the farmer, and **past** the gate. He can fly **through** the window, **throughout** the house, **towards** your brother **until** noon **without** tiring.

A bee can fly
→ the house
→ the door,
→ the room
→ the dog
→ the window
→ the ledge
→ the corner
→ your friend

He can fly
→ the tree
→ the clouds
→ the bushes
→ the roses
→ the fence
→ the hill
→ spring.
→ many hours
→ dusk to dawn

he can fly
→ the garden
→ butterfly
→ the plants
→ the farmer
→ the gate

He can fly
→ the window
→ the house
→ brother
→ noon
→ tiring

An arrow (→) cannot substitute for every preposition. Nonetheless, this test may help you.

COMMON PREPOSITIONS

about	like
above	near
across	of
after	off
against	on
along	over
among	past
around	since
at	through
before	throughout
behind	till
below	to
beneath	towards
beside(s)	under
between	underneath
beyond	unlike
but	until
by	up
concerning	upon
down	with
during	within
except	without
for	as far as
from	in spite of
in	because of
into	

OBJECT OF THE PREPOSITION

Prepositions connect nouns or pronouns to other words in the sentence. The noun or pronoun is called the object of the preposition. In other words, the arrow (→) points to the object of the preposition. To find the object of the preposition, ask yourself *whom?* or *what?* after the preposition.

Examples:

1. Jamie ran <u>behind his brother</u>.
   Jamie ran *behind* whom? → *his brother*
2. He leaned <u>against the fence</u>.
   He leaned *against* what? → *the fence*

3. The police officer saved the pedestrian <u>from the speeding car</u>.
   The police officer saved the pedestrian *from* what? → *the speeding car*

Preposition	Object of the Preposition
behind	his brother
against	the fence
from	the speeding car

Usually the object follows the preposition, but in speech and informal writing the preposition may follow the object. (What is the story *about?*)

PREPOSITIONAL PHRASES

The preposition, its object, and any modifiers form a prepositional phrase. The prepositional phrase can work like an adjective, an adverb, and sometimes even a noun.

 Reminder

Preposition   a word that connects nouns or pronouns to another word in the sentence. (He ran *up* the stairs.)

Object of the Preposition   a word or groups of words that is connected to the sentence by a preposition. The object usually follows the preposition. (He ran up *the stairs.*)

Prepositional Phrase   the preposition, its object, and any modifiers. (He ran *up the stairs.)*

Examples:

1. The actor <u>with the great voice</u> has the lead role <u>in the play</u>.
   With the great voice is a prepositional phrase that describes *actor.* *In the play* is a prepositional phrase that describes *role.* Both prepositional phrases work like adjectives in the sentence.

2. The cat ran <u>up the tree</u> <u>during the storm</u>.
   Up the tree is a prepositional phrase that describes where the cat ran. *During the storm* is a prepositional phrase that tells when the cat ran. Both prepositional phrases work like adverbs.

3. <u>Over the bridge</u> is a difficult bike path.
   Over the bridge is a prepositional phrase that works as the subject of the sentence. Prepositional phrases rarely are used this way.

EXERCISE 10: Underline the prepositional phrases in the following sentences.

1. The student with the red hat is running to her class.

2. The rainbow appeared after the storm and stretched across the sky.

3. In spite of her broken arm, Jane rode the horse into town.

4. During spring break, she went to Florida with her friends.

5. Before noon, the president will tell the press something about his new staff.

6. Jong climbed up the steps and sat behind me.

7. Because of the cramp in her leg, she will only run as far as that tree.

8. The two parties differ on many issues besides crime.

9. You will find the box below the shelf in the basement.

10. Because of her hard work, Rose earned more vacation days with pay.

Answers are on pages 276, 277.

Remember these <u>facts about prepositions</u>:

- Prepositions connect nouns or pronouns to other words in the sentence.
- The preposition, its object, and any modifiers form a prepositional phrase.
- Prepositions usually come before their objects.
- To find the object of the preposition, ask yourself *whom?* or *what?* after the preposition.
- Prepositional phrases usually work as adverbs and adjectives. Sometimes a prepositional phrase works as a noun.

In this chapter you have learned:

☐ How to identify the subject and the predicate (page 31)

☐ How to use nouns (pages 32, 33)

☐ How to use verbs (pages 34–37)

☐ How to use adjectives (pages 37, 38)

☐ How to use adverbs (pages 38–40)

☐ How to use prepositions (pages 41–42)

Review sections that are difficult for you.

Chapter Review

EXERCISE 1: Identify the part of speech for the underlined word in each of the following sentences. Write your answer in the space provided.

1. The frantic student ran <u>down</u> the hall.

_____

2. The heavyweight boxer knocked <u>down</u> his opponent.

_____

3. The <u>down</u> pillows on Aunt Sue's bed are soft.

_____

4. Ellen would <u>like</u> to make jewelry for her friends.

_____

5. She acts <u>like</u> a child when she doesn't get her way.

_____

6. Peter <u>carefully</u> guided the wire through the small opening.

_____

7. Karen is <u>careful</u> with her new car.

_____

8. The coach was <u>concerned</u> about the low morale of the team.

_____

9. <u>Concerned</u> citizens went to the town meeting to discuss the future of the park.

_____

10. Juvenile crime and homelessness are real <u>concerns</u> for Americans.

_____

11. Steve's parents were excited about his <u>success</u>.

_____

12. The horse trotted <u>over</u> the bridge and into the pasture.

_____

13. The hot cup of coffee spilled <u>over</u>.

_____

14. The basket was hidden <u>behind</u> the door.

_____

15. John had to hurry because he was running <u>behind</u>.

_____

16. After Colleen lost her job, she fell <u>behind</u> in her car payments.

_____

17. <u>Mary's</u> stained glass windows are absolutely beautiful.

_____

18. When we were walking across the street, a car raced <u>by</u>.

_____

19. He must stop <u>by</u> the store on his way home from work.

_____

20. The <u>running</u> water flooded the basement.

_____

21. For the <u>past</u> five days, the weather has been terrible.

_____

22. We must study the <u>past</u> to understand current events.

_____

23. Bruce will have to work <u>past</u> noon to complete his assignment.

_____

24. After climbing six flights of stairs, Bob was <u>exhausted</u>.

_____

25. The <u>exhaust</u> from the car filled the air.

_____

Answers are on page 277.

EXERCISE 2: Identify the part of speech for each word in the following sentences. Write your answers directly above each word.

1. The dedicated athlete eventually became a professional tennis player.

2. With steady hands, Megan expertly completed the delicate surgery.

3. He studied the weather reports very carefully.

4. Cricket is a very popular sport in England.

5. Christine's new suitcase was destroyed during her flight to Chicago.

6. Jason constantly searched for a new job with better hours.

7. The retired pilot still flies his small plane regularly.

8. Without help, she carried the furniture into the house.

9. The basket of flowers filled the room with a wonderful scent.

10. Before dark, collect your toys in the yard.

Answers are on pages 277, 278.

Parts of a Sentence

In this chapter you will learn:

- [ ] How to write a complete sentence (pages 45, 46)
- [ ] How to identify objects of a verb (pages 47, 48)
- [ ] How to identify subject complements (pages 48, 49)
- [ ] How to recognize compound parts (pages 50, 51)
- [ ] How to take apart a sentence (pages 51–55)

The parts of a sentence are like the parts of a car. Alone, each part is useless. However, when the parts work together, the sentence runs well. This chapter will help you find the main parts of a sentence so that you can learn to write complete sentences and use words correctly.

Complete Sentences and Fragments

Every sentence must have a subject and a predicate. It also must give a complete thought. A group of words that does not meet these requirements is called a fragment.

Beware! Some sentences don't seem to have subjects when they actually do. These sentences are called commands because one person tells someone else what to do. The verb is stated, but the subject is not. For example, in the sentence *Beware!* you know the sentence is about you, the reader. When you see a command, the subject is *you*.

COMPLETE SENTENCES

A complete sentence must have a:

1. Subject
2. Predicate
3. Complete thought.

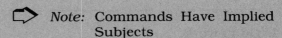 *Note:* Commands Have Implied Subjects

1. Pay attention!
2. Eat your dinner.

One person tells someone else what to do. The subject is *you*.

Examples of Fragments:

1. The big pile of leaves.
   What about the leaves?
2. Ran to the store.
   Who ran to the store?
3. Wet paint!
   What about the wet paint?

EXAMPLES OF COMPLETE SENTENCES:	
Subject	**Predicate**
1. The big pile of leaves 2. Jane and her friends 3. (You)	blew away in the wind. ran to the store. Beware of wet paint!

There are two easy ways to correct a fragment—either reword it or add words so that you have a subject and a predicate.

EXERCISE 1: **Read each group of words. If it is a complete sentence, write a *C* in the space. If it is a fragment, write an *F* in the space, and write a complete sentence using the group of words.**

1. The women with the pink shirt. ____

   _____

2. The tall man in the red hat asked me for directions. ____

   _____

3. Watch your step. ____

   _____

4. Go to work. ____

   _____

5. Great job! ____

   _____

6. I need to find a good baby sitter. ____

   _____

7. By midnight. ____

   _____

8. Wash your hands. ____

   _____

9. The man in charge of payroll. ____

   _____

10. Try to save money on your taxes. ____

    _____

Answers are on page 278.

PARTS OF THE SENTENCE

Subject does the action in the sentence. *Alice* gave Jen a gift.

Verb shows action or connects the subject to words that rename or describe the subject. Alice *gave* Jen a gift. Susan *is* a great cook.

Object of the Verb receives the action. Alice gave *Jen a gift.*(Both *Jen* and *gift* are objects of the verb.)

Subject Complement follows a linking verb and describes or renames the subject of the sentence. The cookies were *delicious.* Joe is an *engineer.*

Subjects of the Verb

In the last chapter, you learned about two types of verbs—linking verbs and action verbs. Remember, linking verbs link the subject to words that rename or describe it (be, am, is, are). Action verbs (drive, talk, run) show the subject doing something.

There are two types of action verbs. Some action verbs can be used just with a subject to make a complete sentence.

Examples:

Subject	Verb
1. The leaves	fell.
2. Time	flies.

These sentences make sense even though they only have a subject and a verb.

Some sentences need a noun after the verb to make a complete sentence.

Examples:

Subject	Verb	Noun
1. The blizzard	closed	the schools.
2. The actor	wanted	a new TV show.

If these sentences did not have a noun after the verb, the sentences would not give a complete thought. You would want to know what the blizzard closed and what the actor wanted.

EXERCISE 2: Read the next paragraph. In the space provided, write a *C* for complete sentences and an *F* for fragments.

1. This past winter was terrible. ____
2. The snow! ____ 3. Schools were closed for several days, and many people could not get to work. ____ 4. Water pipes froze. ____ 5. Some roofs collapsed. ____ 6. Bridges, too. ____
7. Luckily, no one was badly hurt. ____
8. Next winter may be even worse. ____
9. Watch out! ____

Answers are on page 278.

✍ Remember these <u>facts about complete sentences</u>:

- A complete sentence must have a subject and a predicate, and it must express a complete thought.

- In a command, the subject is *you.*
- Some action verbs can stand alone, but others need a noun to complete the sentence.

Objects of the Verb

Some action verbs need nouns to make a complete sentence. These nouns, which are called objects, receive the action in the sentence. To find the object of the verb in a sentence, say the subject, the verb, and then whom or what.

Example:

SUBJECT + VERB + WHOM OR WHAT?
1. Kyle sent a <u>gift</u> for Jean's birthday. Kyle + sent + *what?* (a gift)
2. The student body elected <u>Juan</u>. The student body + elected + *whom?* (Juan)
3. The fast, new player has been scoring <u>many goals</u> this year. The fast, new player + has been scoring + *what?* (many goals)

EXERCISE 3: Decide if the following sentences have objects. If a sentence has an object, write it in the space provided. If a sentence does not have an object, write an *X* in the space.

1. Jasmine bathed her baby last night.

   _____

2. The thunder rolled across the sky.

   _____

3. Abdul passed his math test.

   _____

4. Deena didn't win, but she tried hard.

   _____

5. Before we left, I saw the sunrise.

   _____

Answers are on page 279.

Some sentences have one more than one object.

Examples:

Subject	Verb	Object	Object
1. The coach	handed	Brian	the game ball.
2. The company	gave	the schools	free software.

The verb affects both objects in the sentence. *Brian* was handed *the game ball,* and *the schools* were given *free software.* To find the second object, say the subject, the verb, and to or for whom or what.

 Note:

Object: Subject + Verb + Whom or What

and

Object: Subject + Verb + to or for Whom or What

Examples:

SUBJECT + VERB + TO OR FOR WHOM OR WHAT?
1. The food store gave <u>the shelter</u> free meals.
   The food store + gave + *to what?* (the shelter)
2. Lynne taught <u>Kathy</u> algebra.
   Lynne + taught + *to whom* (Kathy)
3. Don bought <u>Bobby</u> a birthday cake.
   Don + bought + *for whom* (Bobby)

EXERCISE 4: Each of the following sentences has at least one object that receives action. Write the object(s) in the spaces provided.

1. Doyle offered me free tickets.

2. We mailed the check yesterday.

_____

3. The post office sent us the mail.

_____

4. The coach gave Mansi an award.

_____

5. Kim baked the cookies Friday.

_____

Answers are on page 279.

Remember these <u>facts about objects</u>:

- Not all action verbs have objects.
- To find an object in a sentence, say the subject + the verb + whom or what.
- To find a second object, say the subject + the verb + to or for whom or what.

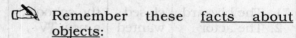

Subject Complements

Subject complements, which can be nouns or adjectives, follow linking verbs. Nouns rename the subject, and adjectives describe the subject. If you can recognize linking verbs, subject complements are easy to find. (See linking verbs on page 85.)

SUBJECT COMPLEMENTS

Noun follows a linking verb and renames the subject. Joe is an *engineer.*
Adjective follows a linking verb and describes the subject. The cookies were *delicious.*

Examples:

Subject	Linking Verb	Subject Complement
1. Many of the players	are	my friends. (noun)
2. Jill	will become	a doctor. (noun)
3. The haunted house	was	scary. (adjective)
4. The carrot cake	smelled	delicious. (adjective)

Remember, you can think of a linking verb as an arrow (→) that links related words. This may help you find subject complements.

Examples:

SUBJECT ↔ SUBJECT
            COMPLEMENT
1. Many of the players ↔ my friends. (noun)
2. Jill ↔ a doctor. (noun)
3. The haunted house ↔ scary. (adjective)
4. The carrot cake ↔ delicious. (adjective)

EXERCISE 5: Underline the subject complement in each sentence. In the space provided, write whether it is a noun or an adjective.

1. Those flowers are lilacs.

_____

2. The cars seem costly.

_____

3. The water appears deep.

_____

4. He will remain a lawyer.

_____

5. Megan will be thrilled.

_____

6. Courtney looks sad.

_____

7. The books are gifts.

_____

8. The milk smells sour.

_____

9. My ride for work is late.

_____

10. The guests are friends.

_____

Answers are on page 279.

☞ Remember these <u>facts about subject complements</u>:

• Subject complements are used with linking verbs.
• Nouns that follow linking verbs rename the subject, and adjectives that follow linking verbs describe the subject.

Compound Parts

The word compound means to combine two or more. Some sentences use conjunctions (and, but, or, nor) to combine two or more parts that are equally important. These combinations are called compound parts. Any part of a sentence can be compound.

COMMON CONJUNCTIONS

and
but
or
nor
not only...but also
both...and
either...or
neither...nor

These words combine two or more parts that are equally important.

Examples:

1. COMPOUND SUBJECT
   Exercise and a balanced diet are important for good health.

   Exercise and *a balanced diet* are both subjects. They have the same predicate.

2. COMPOUND VERB (ACTION VERBS)
   Athletes can swim, run, skate, or bike to keep in shape.

   Swim, run, skate, and *bike* are all verbs with the same subject.

3. COMPOUND VERB (ACTION VERB AND LINKING VERB)
   He not only worked hard to improve children's lives, but also was a role model for many.

   Worked is an action verb, and *was* is a linking verb.

4. COMPOUND OBJECT OF THE VERB
   Anita's mother bought her clothes and a new bike for her birthday.

   Clothes and *a new bike* form a compound object.

   Nga gave both her secretary and the custodian nice bonuses for the holidays.

   Her secretary and *the custodian* form a compound object. *A nice bonus* also is an object.

5. COMPOUND OBJECT OF THE PREPOSITION
   After the horse broke through the gate and the fence, it ran across the field.

   Gate and *fence* are objects of the preposition *through. Field* is an object of the preposition *across.*

6. COMPOUND SUBJECT COMPLEMENT
   The gentle breeze was cool but refreshing.

   Cool and *refreshing* are adjectives that describe the gentle breeze.

7. MULTIPLE COMPOUND PARTS
   Before leaving for work, Julie and Jim feed the baby, make Jack and Laura lunch, and kiss the children goodbye.

   Julie and *Jim* are subjects. *Feed, make,* and *kiss* are verbs. *Jack* and *Laura* are objects of the verb *make.*

EXERCISE 6: Underline the compound parts in each of the following sentences. In the space provided, write which parts of the sentences are compound (subject, verb, object, etc.) Some sentences have more than one compound part.

1. Neither Mike nor Joe watched golf yesterday.

   _____

2. The winner received a check and a nice plaque.

   _____

3. Both my mom and dad gave my brothers and me a lot of love.

   _____

   _____

4. Hard work and discipline help people succeed not only in school but also in life.

   _____

5. Rita and I struggled to get off welfare.

   _____

6. Either Bob or Colleen will drive you and your friend.

   _____

7. Our boss cut jobs and wages.

   _____

8. Santa brought them not only gifts, but also great memories.

   _____

   _____

9. We run, bike, and skate.

   _____

10. My mom sent Ruth and me nice gifts.

   _____

Answers are on page 279.

 Remember, compound parts are joined by conjunctions, and any part of the sentence can be compound.

How to Take Apart a Sentence

As we discussed, the parts of a sentence are like the parts of a car. You need to be able to find each part of a sentence and know how it works. These skills will help you fix writing problems so that you can write more clearly. Now that you understand each piece of a sentence, it's time to use a logical plan to take sentences apart.

STEPS TO TAKE APART A SENTENCE

1. Cross out all prepositional phrases.
2. Find the verb.
3. Find the subject.
4. If you have a linking verb, look for a subject complement.
5. If you have an action verb, look for objects of the verb.

Follow these steps to find the different parts of a sentence. You may not need to use each step every time.

Steps

Step 1: Cross out all prepositional phrases.

Step 2: Find the verb and decide if it is a linking verb or an action verb.

Step 3: Find the subject. Who or What + Verb

Step 4: If you have a linking verb, look for a subject complement. Subject + Linking Verb + Who or What?

Step 5: If you have an action verb, look for objects. Subject + Verb + Whom or What and Subject + Verb + To or For Whom or What

Hints:

Remember, prepositional phrases include the preposition, the object of the preposition, and any modifiers. Prepositional phrases cannot be a major part of the sentence, they only modify. See the list of prepositions on page 41.

If you are not sure what the verb is, look for linking verbs from the list on page 34 or for the action in the sentence. What is happening in the sentence?

Say who or what and then the verb. (Who or what ran? Who or what is?) Sometimes the subject is after the verb. *Here* and *there* are adverbs, and they cannot be subjects. If a sentence begins with *here* or *there*, the subject is after the verb.

Remember, a subject complement can be a noun or an adjective. Some sentences will not have a subject complement. Say the subject, the verb, and then who or what?

Objects of the verb receive the action in a sentence. Not all sentences have objects.

Examples:

Go over these examples without looking at the answers.

1. **Sentence:** *Many of the parents in town were upset by the coach's rude actions.*

    Step 1: Cross out prepositional phrases.

    Many ~~of the parents in town~~ were upset ~~by the coach's rude actions~~.

    Step 2: Find the verb.

    were (from the list of linking verbs)

    Step 3: Find the subject.

    Many (Who or what were? In this case, *many* is a pronoun.)

    Step 4: If you have a linking verb, find the subject complement.

    upset (Many were what? Many ↔ upset.)

2. **Sentence:** *Hoa became a surgeon after many years of medical school.*

    Step 1: Cross out prepositional phrases.

    Hoa became a surgeon ~~after many years of medical school~~.

    Step 2: Find the verb.

    became (from the list of linking verbs)

    Step 3: Find the subject.

    Hoa (Who or what became?)

    Step 4: If you have a linking verb, find the subject complement.

    a surgeon (Hoa became who or what? Hoa ↔ surgeon)

3. **Sentence:** *The huge waves crashed onto the shore, filled the beach with water, and scared many swimmers.*

Step 1: Cross out prepositional phrases.	The huge waves crashed ~~onto the shore~~, filled the beach ~~with water~~, and scared many swimmers.
Step 2: Find the verb.	crashed, filled, scared (This is a compound action verb that is joined by the conjunction *and*.)
Step 3: Find the subject.	The huge waves (Who or what crashed, filled, and scared?) *Crashed, filled,* and *scared* are action verbs.
Step 4: Skip this step when you have an action verb.	
Step 5: If you have an action verb, look for objects.	the beach (The waves filled what?) many swimmers (The waves scared whom?)

4. **Sentence:** *After the big game, John's baseball coach bought the team T-shirts with the team logo.*

Step 1: Cross out prepositional phrases.	~~After the big game~~, John's baseball coach bought the team T-shirts ~~with the team logo~~.
Step 2: Find the verb.	bought (action verb)
Step 3: Find the subject.	John's coach (Who bought?) *Bought* is an action verb.
Step 4: Skip this step when you have an action verb.	
Step 5: If you have an action verb, look for objects.	T-shirts (John's coach bought what?) the team (John's coach bought T-shirts for whom or what?)

EXERCISE 7: Write the correct part of speech for each underlined word in the space provided. Make sure that you take apart the sentence using the steps you have studied.

1. <u>Who</u> is going to the party after the show?

_____

2. Ginny bought <u>Blake</u> concert tickets for his birthday.

_____

3. Skeeter and Lynne felt <u>cold</u> at the football game.

_____

4. There are four <u>seats</u> in the front row by the dugout.

_____

5. Who called the <u>police</u>?

_____

6. I <u>drive</u> across the river and through the city on my way to work.

_____

7. Our new boss will pay <u>us</u> more money.

_____

8. The strike slowed <u>shipments</u> to the stores in our town.

_____

9. After the storm, we were <u>drenched</u>.

_____

10. The <u>man</u> in the corner with glasses wants help carrying the boxes.

_____

Answers are on pages 279, 280.

☞ Remember these <u>steps to take apart a sentence</u>.

- Cross out all prepositional phrases.
- Find the verb.
- Find the subject.
- If you have a linking verb, look for a subject complement.
- If you have an action verb, look for objects.

In this chapter you have learned:

- ☐ How to write a complete sentence (pages 45, 46)
- ☐ How to identify objects of a verb (pages 47, 48)
- ☐ How to identify subject complements (pages 48, 49)
- ☐ How to recognize compound parts (pages 50, 51)
- ☐ How to take apart a sentence (pages 51–55)

Review sections that are difficult for you.

Chapter Review

EXERCISE 1: Complete the steps for each of the following sentences. If a sentence does not have a particular part of speech, write an X in the space.

1. SENTENCE: *Laura, Jen, and Kathy skated on the pond behind their home in Connecticut.*

   1. Cross out all prepositional phrases.
   2. Find the verb. VERB _____
   3. Find the subject. SUBJECT _____
   4. If you have a linking verb, look for a subject complement.
      SUBJECT COMPLEMENT _____
   5. If you have an action verb, look for objects. OBJECT(S) _____

2. SENTENCE: *They drove the car with the sunroof to the beach on the Fourth of July.*

   1. Cross out all prepositional phrases.
   2. Find the verb. VERB _____
   3. Find the subject. SUBJECT _____
   4. If you have a linking verb, look for a subject complement.
      SUBJECT COMPLEMENT _____
   5. If you have an action verb, look for objects. OBJECT(S) _____

3. SENTENCE: *Anne gave Khoa and Marie surprise parties for their birthdays.*

   1. Cross out all prepositional phrases.
   2. Find the verb. VERB _____
   3. Find the subject. SUBJECT _____
   4. If you have a linking verb, look for a subject complement.
      SUBJECT COMPLEMENT _____
   5. If you have an action verb, look for objects. OBJECT(S) _____

4. SENTENCE: *Khan is a caring person and a great doctor.*

   1. Cross out all prepositional phrases.
   2. Find the verb. VERB _____
   3. Find the subject. SUBJECT _____
   4. If you have a linking verb, look for a subject complement.
      SUBJECT COMPLEMENT _____
   5. If you have an action verb, look for objects. OBJECT(S) _____

5. SENTENCE: *The pie in the oven smells delicious.*

   1. Cross out all prepositional phrases.
   2. Find the verb. VERB _____
   3. Find the subject. SUBJECT _____
   4. If you have a linking verb, look for a subject complement.
      SUBJECT COMPLEMENT _____
   5. If you have an action verb, look for objects. OBJECT(S) _____

6. SENTENCE: *Here are the drapes for the windows.*

   1. Cross out all prepositional phrases.
   2. Find the verb. VERB _____
   3. Find the subject. SUBJECT _____
   4. If you have a linking verb, look for a subject complement.
      SUBJECT COMPLEMENT _____
   5. If you have an action verb, look for objects. OBJECT(S) _____

7. SENTENCE: *Anh bought food, made dinner, and cleaned the house.*

   1. Cross out all prepositional phrases.
   2. Find the verb. VERB _____
   3. Find the subject. SUBJECT _____

4. If you have a linking verb, look for a subject complement.
SUBJECT COMPLEMENT _____

5. If you have an action verb, look for objects. OBJECT(S) _____

8. SENTENCE: *My dog ran across the yard, swam in the pond, and rolled in the mud.*

1. Cross out all prepositional phrases.

2. Find the verb. VERB _____

3. Find the subject. SUBJECT _____

4. If you have a linking verb, look for a subject complement.
SUBJECT COMPLEMENT _____

5. If you have an action verb, look for objects. OBJECT(S) _____

Answers are on page 280.

EXERCISE 2: In the space provided, write the words that represent each part of the sentence. If any part of the sentence is not included, put an *X* in the space. Make sure you use the steps that we just reviewed.

SAMPLE: The goat and the pig climbed under the gate and ran across the field.

SUBJECT: <u>The goat</u> and <u>the pig</u>

VERB: <u>climbed</u> and <u>ran</u>

SUBJECT COMPLEMENT _____X_____

OBJECT(S) _____X_____

1. SENTENCE: *After work, Joe gave his wife and his daughter a hug and a kiss.*

SUBJECT _____

VERB _____

SUBJECT COMPLEMENT _____

OBJECT (S) _____

2. SENTENCE: *The horse stalls and the doghouse smelled awful.*

SUBJECT _____

VERB _____

SUBJECT COMPLEMENT _____

OBJECT (S) _____

3. SENTENCE: *There are three people on the court without racquets.*

SUBJECT _____

VERB _____

SUBJECT COMPLEMENT _____

OBJECT (S) _____

4. SENTENCE: *The hard, driving rain fell throughout the night and into the day.*

SUBJECT _____

VERB _____

SUBJECT COMPLEMENT _____

OBJECT (S) _____

5. SENTENCE: *Some of my friends went to the magic show at the old movie house on 5th street.*

SUBJECT _____

VERB _____

SUBJECT COMPLEMENT _____

OBJECT (S) _____

6. SENTENCE: *After training hard for many years, Sean became an excellent athlete.*

SUBJECT _____

VERB _____

SUBJECT COMPLEMENT _____

OBJECT (S) _____

7. SENTENCE: *On our trip to Europe, we bought gifts for our friends and family.*

SUBJECT _____

VERB _____

SUBJECT COMPLEMENT _____

OBJECT (S) _____

8. SENTENCE: *Who ran to the phone and called the police?*

SUBJECT _____

VERB _____

SUBJECT COMPLEMENT _____

OBJECT (S) _____

9. SENTENCE: *Here are the photos from our trip to Greece.*

SUBJECT _____

VERB _____

SUBJECT COMPLEMENT _____

OBJECT (S) _____

10. SENTENCE: *Watch your step on the stairs!*

SUBJECT _____

VERB _____

SUBJECT COMPLEMENT _____

OBJECT (S) _____

Answers are on pages 281, 282.

USAGE

Verb Usage

In this chapter you will learn:

☐ How to form the present, past, and future tenses (pages 61, 62)

☐ How to form the perfect tenses (pages 63–65)

☐ How to form the continuing tenses (pages 65, 66)

☐ How to form the tenses for irregular verbs (pages 66–74)

☐ How to form the tenses for troublesome verbs (pages 74–76)

The subject in a sentence is like the main character in a film. Subjects make things happen. The verb, on the other hand, is the action; it shows what the subject is doing. This chapter will teach you about different verbs. You will learn about verb tenses, irregular verbs, and verbs that are troublesome.

Verb Tense

Verb tense tells when an action takes place. There are three types of verb tenses, and they each have a specific job to do. You need to know about the different verb tenses so you can use verbs correctly and explain your thoughts clearly.

THE SIMPLE TENSES: PRESENT, PAST, AND FUTURE

First we will focus on the simple tenses, which are the ones you already know best. The simple tenses are the present tense, the past tense, and the future tense.

PRESENT TENSE

The present tense is used for actions that are happening now, actions that occur repeatedly, and general truths, which are statements that are always true.

Use this tense to show:

1. an action is happening now
2. an action happens repeatedly
3. a general truth

Pat <u>likes</u> to run and play games.
I <u>jog</u> three miles every day.
The sky <u>is</u> blue.

Examples:

1. Beth and Phil <u>study</u> hard in school. (happening now)
2. Debby <u>balances</u> her checkbook each month. (happens repeatedly)
3. Newborns <u>cry</u>. (general truth)

As you can see, the present tense uses the plain form of a regular verb or its -*s* form, which actually ends in s or -*es*. See more on verb agreement on pages 78–86.

PAST TENSE

The past tense simply shows that an action happened in the past. To form the past tense, add -*ed* to the plain form of regular verbs.

Note: Regular verbs follow a pattern to form different tenses. Irregular verbs do not follow the same pattern. See more on irregular verbs on pages 66–76.

Examples:

PAST TENSE = PLAIN VERB FORM + ED
1. Judy campaign<u>ed</u> in the last election.
2. Scott wash<u>ed</u> the car yesterday.

FUTURE TENSE

The future tense shows that an action will happen in the future. To form the future tense, use the helping verb *will* and the plain form of the verb.

Examples:

FUTURE TENSE = WILL + PLAIN VERB FORM
1. She <u>will finish</u> her work tomorrow.
2. They <u>will walk</u> ten miles to raise money for charity.

SIMPLE TENSES		
Past	**Present**	**Future**
walked	walk(s)	will walk
helped	help(s)	will help
washed	wash(es)	will wash

HINTS ABOUT TIME

A sentence often has words that show when the action happened. Look for words that signal a specific time (see the box that follows) and for other verbs that may give a clue.

Examples:

1. <u>Yesterday</u>, I weeded the garden and planted flowers.
2. <u>Now</u> we need new tires for the car.
3. We will be in New York <u>soon</u>.

SIGNAL WORDS FOR SIMPLE TENSES
yesterday
last year
last week
today
now
soon
tomorrow
next week
every day
many times
often
usually

EXERCISE 1: Underline the correct verb for each of the following sentences.

1. Kerry (baked, bakes, will bake) cookies every Monday.

2. Last week, I (helped, help, will help) my mom in the yard and (played, play, will play) ball with my friends.

3. Nate (received, receive, will receive) his last paycheck next Monday.

4. He (started, starts, will start) school next fall.

5. Yesterday, Blake (ripped, rips, will rip) a hole in his jacket while working on the car.

6. Tomorrow night, the news (showed, shows, will show) the new bear cub at the zoo.

7. Flowers (bloomed, bloom, will bloom) in the spring.

8. My dad (exploded, explode, will explode) with anger when he noticed the dent in the car.

9. She often (rowed, rows, will row) the boat all the way to the island.

10. Last night at the party, Rita (raved, raves, will rave) about the dessert.

Answers are on page 282.

Remember these <u>facts about simple tenses</u>:

- The present tense is used for actions that are happening now, actions that occur repeatedly, and general truths. (walk, walks, watch, watches)
- The past tense shows that an action happened in the past. (walked, watched)
- The future tense shows that an action will happen in the future. (will walk, will watch)
- Often a sentence has words that show when the action happened. (soon, yesterday, next week)

PERFECT TENSES

The perfect tenses show an action finished before a certain time or another action. Keep in mind, perfect means "completed." Thus, the perfect tenses show when something was or will be completed.

PRESENT PERFECT TENSE

The present perfect tense shows actions that started in the past and continue into the present. It also shows actions that have just finished. We form the present perfect tense by using *have* or *has* and the *-ed* form of the verb.

he, she, it +has + work<u>ed</u>
I, you, we, they + have + work<u>ed</u>
He <u>has worked</u> hard on this project since 1994.
They <u>have worked</u> to clean the landfill.

Examples:

PRESENT PERFECT TENSE = HAVE OR HAS + -ED FORM
1. I <u>have lived</u> in Maine for three years.
This action started in the past and continues into the present.
2. Jeff <u>has answered</u> every letter.
This action just finished.

PAST PERFECT TENSE

The past perfect tense shows that an action was finished before a specific time in the past. It also shows that one action was completed before another action. This tense is formed by using *had* with the *-ed* form of the verb.

I, you, he, she, it, we, they + had + work<u>ed</u>
She <u>had worked</u> until nine o'clock last night.
They <u>had worked</u> in Bosnia before the war began.

Examples:

PAST PERFECT TENSE = HAD + -ED FORM
1. He <u>had trained</u> in America before the 1996 Olympics.
This action was finished before a specific time in the past.
2. We <u>had climbed</u> down the mountain before the snow fell.
This action was finished before another action in the past.

THE FUTURE PERFECT TENSE

The future perfect tense shows an action that will be finished by a specific time in the future. It also shows that an action will be completed before another action. It is formed by using the helping verbs *will* and *have* and the *-ed* form of the verb.

FUTURE PERFECT TENSE

I, you, she, he, it, we, they + will have + work<u>ed</u>
By 2 o'clock tomorrow, I <u>will have worked</u> 24 hours straight.
By next spring, we <u>will have worked</u> on six different projects.

Examples:

FUTURE PERFECT TENSE = WILL HAVE + -ED VERB FORM
1. We <u>will have finished</u> the report by Friday.
   The action will be completed by a specific time in the future.
2. Before they move to New York, he <u>will have retired</u> from the company.
   The action will be completed before another action.

HINTS ABOUT TIME

Some words signal the perfect tenses. Keep in mind, the perfect tenses are used to show that an action was or will be completed before a specific time or action. Look for words that signal a specific time. See the examples in the box.

SIGNAL WORDS FOR PERFECT TENSES

already
before
by
for
just
last
next
since

Examples:

1. I have *just* learned about the storm.
2. He has made plans *already*.
3. *Before* she finished the book, she had heard about the ending.

4. *Since last* year, we have saved money.
5. *For* the past month, I have worked late.
6. *By next* week, he will have cleaned his room.

EXERCISE 2: Circle words that tell you when the action happened in each sentence. Then underline the correct verb tense. Pay attention to the different signal words.

1. Before running for office last year, Joel (considered, has considered, had considered) all of his options.

2. By tomorrow, Pam (has completed, completed, will have completed) the contract.

3. Since last week, Mark (is jogging, has jogged, will jog) every day.

4. Hien (will study, studies, has studied) already for the test.

5. Kerry, Jack, and Joseph (finish, are finishing, will have finished) their swim lessons by next spring.

6. John and Tricia already (have painted, paint, will paint) their new house.

7. Before July 4, 1776, few people in the New World (dream, have dreamed, had dreamed) of creating a new nation.

8. By 2050, people (travel, are traveling, will have traveled) to new planets.

9. Before they built the new building last year, Pete's company (destroys, had destroyed, will have destroyed) the old complex.

10. By next fall, Sue (applies, has applied, will have applied) to four colleges.

Answers are on page 282.

Remember these <u>facts about perfect tenses</u>:

• Perfect means "completed." The perfect tenses show that an action was or will be completed before a specific time or action.

- The present perfect tense shows actions that started in the past and continue into the present and actions that have just finished (have worked).
- The past perfect tense shows that an action was finished before a specific time or another action in the past (had worked).
- The future perfect tense shows an action that will be finished by a specific time or another action in the future (will have worked).
- Signal words will help you decide when the different tenses should be used.

CONTINUING TENSES

The continuing tenses are also called the progressive tenses because they show an action in progress.

PRESENT CONTINUING TENSE

The present continuing tense shows an action that is going on now.

> I + am + work<u>ing</u>
> he, she, it + is + work<u>ing</u>
> we, you, they + are + work<u>ing</u>
> I <u>am working</u> late today.
> She <u>is working</u> hard on the project.
> They <u>are working</u> to end world hunger.

Examples:

PRESENT CONTINUING TENSE = AM, IS, OR ARE + -ING VERB FORM
1. He <u>is running</u> away from me.
2. I <u>am watching</u> them play in the water.
3. We <u>are writing</u> letters to our friends.

As you can see, we form the present continuing tense by using the *-ing* form of the verb and *am*, *is*, or *are* as helping verbs.

PAST CONTINUING TENSE

The past continuing tense shows an action that was going on for some time in the past.

> I, he, she, it + was + work<u>ing</u>
> we, you, they + were + work<u>ing</u>
> I <u>was working</u> on my pilot's license.
> We <u>were working</u> on the new uniforms.

Examples:

PAST CONTINUING TENSE = WAS OR WERE + -ING VERB FORM
1. They <u>were planning</u> to go on a trip to Mexico.
2. Bob and Colleen <u>were working</u> towards retirement.
3. She <u>was thinking</u> about buying a new bike.

We form the past continuing tense by using the *-ing* verb form and *was* or *were* as helping verbs.

FUTURE CONTINUING TENSE

The future continuing tense shows action that will be going on in the future.

> I, he, she, it, we, you, they + will be + work<u>ing</u>
> I <u>will be working</u> on my new diet.
> You <u>will be working</u> on your resume.

Examples:

FUTURE CONTINUING TENSE = WILL BE + -ING VERB FORM
1. After this game, the team <u>will be training</u> for the World Cup.
2. He <u>will be playing</u> his new songs on tour.
3. I <u>will be asking</u> many questions during the meeting.

As you can see, the future continuing tense is formed by using the *-ing* verb form and the helping verbs *will be.*

EXERCISE 3: For each sentence, circle words that show when the action occurs and underline the correct verb tense.

1. Right now I (was working, am working, will be working) on my rough draft.

2. Yesterday, we (were watching, are watching, will be watching) the football game on TV.

3. Next year, they (were living, are living, will be living) in Colorado.

4. We (were shoveling, are shoveling, will be shoveling) snow all day last Friday.

5. Next fall, Nga and Van (were playing, are playing, will be playing) on a different soccer team.

6. This morning, the dogs (were barking, are barking, will be barking) so loudly they woke up the whole family.

7. Next spring, he still (was studying, is studying, will be studying) to get his degree.

8. James (was trying, is trying, will be trying) to calm the baby all morning yesterday.

9. In the spring next year, you (were struggling, are struggling, will be struggling) to save money.

10. At present, they (were putting, are putting, will be putting) new shingles on the roof.

Answers are on page 282, 283

Remember these facts about the continuing tenses:

- The continuing tenses show action in progress.
- The present continuing tense shows an action that is going on now (is working).
- The past continuing tense shows an action that was going on for some time in the past (was working).
- The future continuing tense shows action that will be going on in the future (will be working).

Irregular Verbs

Most verbs follow a pattern when they change tenses. Verbs that do not follow this pattern are called irregular verbs. You already know many irregular verbs.

REGULAR VERBS		
Verb	Past Tense	Past Participle
want live	wanted lived	wanted lived

The past participle is used for the perfect tenses. (I have wanted. She had lived.)

Examples:

Note the irregular verbs in the following paragraph.

Yesterday, Ken ran out of the house on the way to work and forgot his wallet. Luckily, he found money in his coat pocket to pay the tolls. His boss paid for a cup of coffee, and his friends bought him lunch. By the afternoon, Ken had gotten help from everyone in the office.

The good news is that you already know many irregular verbs; the bad news is that you will have to learn the ones you do not know. Focus on the plain form, the past tense, and the past participle, which is used for the perfect tenses.

COMMON IRREGULAR VERBS
YOU MUST LEARN THESE!

Present	Past	Past Participle
am, is, are	was, were	been
bring, brings	brought	brought
buy, buys	bought	bought
come, comes	came	come
do, does	did	done
go, goes	went	gone
has, have	had	had
run, runs	ran	run
see, sees	saw	seen

The past participle is used for the perfect tenses. (I <u>have brought</u>. She <u>had seen</u>.)

EXERCISE 4: Cover the box on irregular verbs with a piece of paper and complete the following chart. After you have tried all of the verbs, check your work. Continue to work on verbs that are difficult.

SAMPLE: *see* Last week I <u>saw</u>
         This week I have <u>seen</u>

1. *be* Last week I _____.
    This week I have _____.

2. *be* Last week they _____.
    This week they have _____.

3. *bring* Last week I _____.
    This week I have _____.

4. *buy* Last week I _____.
    This week I have _____.

5. *come* Last week I _____.
    This week I have _____.

6. *do* Last week I _____.
    This week I have _____.

7. *go* Last week I _____.
    This week I have _____.

8. *have* Last week I _____.
    This week I have _____.

9. *run* Last week I _____.
    This week I have _____.

10. *see* Last week I _____.
    This week I have _____.

Answers are on pages 283.

EXERCISE 5: For each sentence, underline the correct verb form.

1. I have (see, saw, seen) many people try to jump over that fence.

2. Yesterday, Russ (go, went, gone) for a walk to clear his mind.

3. Chris and Tom have (runs, ran, run) almost ten miles.

4. Have you (comes, came, come) here to ask me a question?

5. He has (do, did, done) many great things for the community.

6. Have you (buy, buys, bought) presents for everyone?

7. We have (have, has, had) a great vacation!

8. Who (bring, brings, brought) the donuts to the office last Friday?

9. For the past two weeks, she has (is, was, been) upset about her job.

10. The gusty winds and heavy rain (come, comes, came) quickly last night.

Answers are on page 283.

ONE LETTER CHANGES

Some irregular verbs change form by simply changing one letter. Look at the examples in the box.

ONE LETTER CHANGES		
Present	Past	Past Participle
begin, begins	began	begun
dig, digs	dug	dug
drink, drinks	drank	drunk
ring, rings	rang	rung
shrink, shrinks	shrank	shrunk
sing, sings	sang	sung
sink, sinks	sank	sunk
swim, swims	swam	swum
win, wins	won	won

The past participle is used for the perfect tenses. (I <u>have begun</u>. She <u>had won</u>.)

EXERCISE 6: Cover the box on irregular verbs with a piece of paper and complete the following chart. After you have tried all of the verbs, check your work. Continue to work on verbs that are difficult.

SAMPLE: *win* Last week I <u>won.</u>
             This week I have <u>won.</u>

1. *begin* Last week I _____.
   This week I have _____.

2. *dig* Last week I _____.
   This week I have _____.

3. *drink* Last week I _____.
   This week I have _____.

4. *ring* Last week I _____.
   This week I have _____.

5. *shrink* Last week I _____.
   This week I have _____.

6. *sing* Last week I _____.
   This week I have _____.

7. *sinks* Last week I _____.
   This week I have _____.

8. *swim* Last week I _____.
   This week I have _____.

9. *win* Last week I _____.
   This week I have _____.

Answers are on page 283.

EXERCISE 7: For each sentence, underline the correct verb form.

1. After we brought home the tree, we (dig, dug) a hole for it in the back yard.

2. By nine o'clock tomorrow, we will have (begin, began, begun) the new project.

3. Have you ever (win, won) a close game?

4. Our doorbell (ring, rang, rung) late last night.

5. In the past year, I have (shrink, shrank, shrunk) many shirts in the wash.

6. Chau had (drink, drank, drunk) two glasses of water before the race.

7. Have you (sing, sang, sung) before a large group of people?

8. Last night Joe (sings, sang, sung) a song that was on the radio.

9. Yesterday, Hoa finally (begins, began, begun) the book she bought for her trip.

10. Fakrah has (wins, win, won) every match that she has entered.

Answers are on page 284.

ENDINGS WITH N OR EN

Many irregular verbs have *n* or *en* endings in their past participle form. Look at the examples in the box.

ENDINGS WITH N OR EN		
Present	Past	Past Participle
break, breaks	broke	broken
choose, chooses	chose	chosen
drive, drives	drove	driven
eat, eats	ate	eaten
fall, falls	fell	fallen
forget, forgets	forgot	forgotten
freeze, freezes	froze	frozen
get, gets	got	gotten
give, gives	gave	given
grow, grows	grew	grown
know, knows	knew	known
ride, rides	rode	ridden
speak, speaks	spoke	spoken
take, takes	took	taken
tear, tears	tore	torn
wear, wears	wore	worn
write, writes	wrote	written

The past participle is used for the perfect tenses. (I <u>have worn</u>. She <u>had grown</u>.)

EXERCISE 8: Cover the box on irregular verbs with a piece of paper and complete the following chart. After you have tried all of the verbs, check your work. Continue to work on verbs that are difficult.

SAMPLE: *write* Last week I <u>wrote</u>
  This week I have <u>written</u>

1. *break* Last week I _____.
   This week I have _____.

2. *choose* Last week I _____.
   This week I have _____.

3. *eat* Last week I _____.
   This week I have _____.

4. *fall* Last week I _____.
   This week I have _____.

5. *freeze* Last week I _____.
   This week I have _____.

6. *get* Last week I _____.
   This week I have _____.

7. *give* Last week I _____.
   This week I have _____.

8. *grow* Last week I _____.
   This week I have _____.

9. *know* Last week I _____.
   This week I have _____.

10. *ride* Last week I _____.
    This week I have _____.

11. *speak* Last week I _____.
    This week I have _____.

12. *take* Last week I _____.
    This week I have _____.

13. *tear* Last week I _____.
    This week I have _____.

14. *wear* Last week I _____.
    This week I have _____.

15. *write* Last week I _____.
    This week I have _____.

Answers are on pages 284.

EXERCISE 9: For each sentence, underline the correct verb form.

1. Carl had (break, broke, broken) the window while playing ball in the house.

2. By nine o'clock last night, the coach had (choose, chose, chosen) the starting lineup for the game.

3. We all (eat, ate, eaten) pumpkin pie at Thanksgiving last year.

4. Rich (fall, fell, fallen) into the pool yesterday.

5. Have you (give, gave, given) Beth a gift for her birthday?

6. Many times she has (speak, spoke, spoken) about her childhood.

7. Jean's parents (take, took, taken) the car keys away from her this morning.

8. I have just (write, wrote, written) mom a letter.

9. Jane (know, knew, known) all of the answers on the test yesterday.

10. Steve has (ride, rode, ridden) his bike to work every day for the past month.

Answers are on page 284.

MORE IRREGULAR VERBS, PART I

	IRREGULAR VERBS	
Present	**Past**	**Past Participle**
arise, arises	arose	arisen
bid, bids	bid	bid
bite, bites	bit	bitten, bit
blow, blows	blew	blown
build, builds	built	built
burst, bursts	burst	burst
catch, catches	caught	caught
cost, costs	cost	cost
cut, cuts	cut	cut
draw, draws	drew	drawn

EXERCISE 10: Cover the boxes on irregular verbs with a piece of paper and complete the following chart. After you have tried all of the verbs, check your work. Continue to work on verbs that are difficult.

SAMPLE: *eat* Last week I <u>ate</u>.
              This week I have <u>eaten</u>.

1. *arise* Last week I _____.
This week I have _____.

2. *bid* Last week I _____.
This week I have _____.

3. *bite* Last week I _____.
This week I have _____.

4. *blow* Last week I _____.
This week I have _____.

5. *build* Last week I _____.
This week I have _____.

6. *burst* Last week I _____.
This week I have _____.

7. *catch* Last week I _____.
This week I have _____.

8. *cost* Last week I _____.
This week I have _____.

9. *cut* Last week I _____.
This week I have _____.

10. *draw* Last week I _____.
This week I have _____.

Answers are on page 284, 285.

MORE IRREGULAR VERBS, PART II

<table>
<tr><td colspan="3" align="center">**IRREGULAR VERBS**</td></tr>
<tr><td>Present</td><td>Past</td><td>Past Participle</td></tr>
<tr><td>dream, dreams</td><td>dreamed, dreamt</td><td>dreamed, dreamt</td></tr>
<tr><td>feed, feeds</td><td>fed</td><td>fed</td></tr>
<tr><td>feel, feels</td><td>felt</td><td>felt</td></tr>
<tr><td>fight, fights</td><td>fought</td><td>fought</td></tr>
<tr><td>find, finds</td><td>found</td><td>found</td></tr>
<tr><td>flee, flees</td><td>fled</td><td>fled</td></tr>
<tr><td>fly, flies</td><td>flew</td><td>flown</td></tr>
<tr><td>hang, hangs (an object)</td><td>hung</td><td>hung</td></tr>
<tr><td>hang, hangs (a person)</td><td>hanged</td><td>hanged</td></tr>
<tr><td>hear, hears</td><td>heard</td><td>heard</td></tr>
</table>

EXERCISE 11: Cover the box on irregular verbs with a piece of paper and complete the following chart. After you have tried all of the verbs, check your work. Continue to work on verbs that are difficult.

SAMPLE: *eat* Last week I <u>ate</u>.
This week I have <u>eaten</u>.

1. *dream* Last week I _____.
This week I have _____.

2. *feed* Last week I _____.
This week I have _____.

3. *feel* Last week I _____.
This week I have _____.

4. *fight* Last week I _____.
This week I have _____.

5. *find* Last week I _____.
This week I have _____.

6. *flee* Last week I _____.
This week I have _____.

7. *fly* Last week I _____.
This week I have _____.

8. *hang* (an object) Last week I
_____.
This week I have _____.

9. *hang* (a person) Last week I
_____.
This week I have _____.

10. *hear* Last week I _____.
This week I have _____.

Answers are on pages 285.

MORE IRREGULAR VERBS, PART III

<table>
<tr><td colspan="3" align="center">**IRREGULAR VERBS**</td></tr>
<tr><td>Present</td><td>Past</td><td>Past Participle</td></tr>
<tr><td>hide, hides</td><td>hid</td><td>hidden</td></tr>
<tr><td>hold, holds</td><td>held</td><td>held</td></tr>
<tr><td>hurt, hurts</td><td>hurt</td><td>hurt</td></tr>
<tr><td>keep, keeps</td><td>kept</td><td>kept</td></tr>
<tr><td>lay, lays</td><td>laid</td><td>lain</td></tr>
<tr><td>lead, leads</td><td>led</td><td>led</td></tr>
<tr><td>leave, leaves</td><td>left</td><td>left</td></tr>
<tr><td>let, lets</td><td>let</td><td>let</td></tr>
<tr><td>lie, lies</td><td>lay</td><td>lain</td></tr>
<tr><td>lose, loses</td><td>lost</td><td>lost</td></tr>
</table>

EXERCISE 12: Cover the box on irregular verbs with a piece of paper and complete the following chart. After you have tried all of the verbs, check your work. Continue to work on verbs that are difficult.

SAMPLE: *eat* Last week I <u>ate</u>.
          This week I have <u>eaten</u>.

1. *hide* Last week I _____.
   This week I have _____.

2. *hold* Last week I _____.
   This week I have _____.

3. *hurt* Last week I _____.
   This week I have _____.

4. *keep* Last week I _____.
   This week I have _____.

5. *lay* Last week I _____.
   This week I have _____.

6. *lead* Last week I _____.
   This week I have _____.

7. *leave* Last week I _____.
   This week I have _____.

8. *let* Last week I _____.
   This week I have _____.

9. *lie* Last week I _____.
   This week I have _____.

10. *lose* Last week I _____.
    This week I have _____.

Answers are on page 285.

MORE IRREGULAR VERBS, PART IV

IRREGULAR VERBS		
Present	**Past**	**Past Participle**
make, makes	made	made
meet	met	met
pay	paid	paid
prove	proved	proved, proven
put, puts	put	put
read, reads	read	read
rise, rises	rise	risen
say, says	said	said
set, sets	set	set
shoot, shoots	shot	shot

EXERCISE 13: Cover the box on irregular verbs with a piece of paper and complete the following chart. After you have tried all of the verbs, check your work. Continue to work on verbs that are difficult.

SAMPLE: *eat* Last week I <u>ate</u>.
          This week I have <u>eaten</u>.

1. *make* Last week I _____.
   This week I have _____.

2. *meet* Last week I _____.
   This week I have _____.

3. *pay* Last week I _____.
   This week I have _____.

4. *prove* Last week I _____.
   This week I have _____.

5. *put* Last week I _____.
   This week I have _____.

6. *read* Last week I _____.
This week I have _____.

7. *rise* Last week I _____.
This week I have _____.

8. *say* Last week I _____.
This week I have _____.

9. *set* Last week I _____.
This week I have _____.

10. *shoot* Last week I _____.
This week I have _____.

Answers are on page 285.

MORE IRREGULAR VERBS, PART V

IRREGULAR VERBS		
Present	Past	Past Participle
sit, sits	sat	sat
slide, slides	slid	slid
spend, spends	spent	spent
stand, stands	stood	stood
strike, strikes	struck	struck
teach, teaches	taught	taught
tell, tells	told	told
think, thinks	thought	thought
understand, understands	understood	understood

EXERCISE 14:   Cover the box on irregular verbs with a piece of paper and complete the following chart. After you have tried all of the verbs, check your work. Continue to work on verbs that are difficult.

SAMPLE: *eat* Last week I <u>ate</u>.
           This week I have <u>eaten</u>.

1. *sit* Last week I _____. This week I have _____.

2. *slide* Last week I _____.
This week I have _____.

3. *spend* Last week I _____.
This week I have _____.

4. *stand* Last week I _____.
This week I have _____.

5. *strike* Last week I _____.
This week I have _____.

6. *teach* Last week I _____.
This week I have _____.

7. *tell* Last week I _____.
This week I have _____.

8. *think* Last week I _____.
This week I have _____.

9. *understand* Last week I
_____.
This week I have _____.

Answers are on page 285, 286.

EXERCISE 15: Underline the correct verb form for each sentence.

1. Last week I (fly, flew, flown) across the Atlantic Ocean for the first time.

2. Over the weekend, Hoa (hung, hanged) pictures in her dorm room to make it feel more like home.

3. On the way home to Maine last week, Bruce (blew, blown) a tire on his truck.

4. Has Mary (hear, heard) any more news about her lost dog?

5. Katie (fight, fought) hard to become mayor.

6. Katherine (drew, drawn) a picture of the house yesterday.

7. By dinner time, Russell had (build, built) a fort with all the wood he collected.

8. Carlos had (hid, hidden) all of his toys from his little sister.

9. Have you (understand, understood) any of the teacher's lessons?

10. During the thunderstorm, the tall oak tree fell down and (strike, struck) my car.

Answers are on pages 286.

Remember these <u>facts about irregular verbs</u>:

- Irregular verbs need to be memorized.
- Some irregular verbs simply change one letter (sing, sang, sung).
- Many irregular verbs have *n* or *en* endings in their past participle form (break, broke, broken).

Troublesome Verbs

Lie-lay, sit-set, and *rise-raise* are irregular verbs that often cause trouble. The words have different meanings, but their tenses often look and sound alike. Nonetheless, these verbs have different jobs, and they are used for a specific reason. For example, *lie, sit,* and *rise* are used when the subject of the sentence moves. These verbs do not have objects.

THE SUBJECT MOVES FOR LIE, SIT, AND RISE

Present Tense	Past Tense	Past Participle	Definition
lie	lay	lain	to recline
sit	sat	sat	to rest
rise	rose	risen	to stand

Remember, these verbs do not have objects.

Examples:

LIE
1. He <u>lies</u> down every afternoon to take a short nap. *Present Tense*
2. When I came home, the dog <u>lay</u> on the front porch. *Past Tense*
3. For the past week, Jake has <u>lain</u> on the couch because of his bad back. *Past Participle*

SIT
4. The baby <u>sits</u> up now without help. *Present Tense*
5. The cat <u>sat</u> in the tree for hours watching the birds at the feeder. *Past Tense*
6. By Monday night, we will have <u>sat</u> in the car for over twelve hours. *Past Participle*

RISE
7. Jane <u>rises</u> every morning to the smell of coffee and eggs. *Present Tense*
8. Last night, Ed <u>rose</u> quickly from bed to answer the front door. *Past Tense*
9. Since Tuesday, I have <u>risen</u> before five in the morning. *Past Participle*

EXERCISE 16: Cover the box on lie, sit, and rise with a piece of paper and complete the following chart. After you have tried all of the verbs, check your work. Continue to work on verbs that are difficult.

1. *lie* Last week I _____.
   This week I have _____.

2. *sit* Last week I _____.
   This week I have _____.

3. *rise* Last week I _____.
   This week I have _____.

Answers are on page 286.

Lay, set, and raise have different meanings, and they always have an object of the verb. For these verbs, the subject handles something.

THE SUBJECT HANDLES SOMETHING FOR LAY, SET, AND RAISE

Present Tense	Past Tense	Past Participle	Definition
lay	laid	laid	to place
set	set	set	to place
raise	raised	raised	to lift,
			to grow,
			to increase

Remember, these verbs must have an object.

Examples:

LAY
1. Every holiday, Kim <u>lays</u> a wreath in honor of her mother. *Present Tense*
2. Yesterday, I <u>laid</u> three small boxes by the door. *Past Tense*
3. By Thursday, the crew will have <u>laid</u> two tons of concrete. *Past Participle*

SET
4. Every morning, she <u>sets</u> tea out for her guests. *Present Tense*
5. Last night, Joe <u>set</u> a log on the fire. *Past Tense*
6. For the past few days, he has <u>set</u> the dirty dishes in the sink. *Past Participle*

RAISE
7. Sayre often <u>raises</u> her hand to ask questions. *Present Tense*
8. Tai <u>raised</u> the flag last Friday. *Past Tense*
9. Sun has <u>raised</u> sheep over the past few years. *Past Participle*

EXERCISE 17: Cover the box on lay, set, and raise with a piece of paper and complete the following chart. After you have tried all of the verbs, check your work. Continue to work on verbs that are difficult.

Note that these sentences have an object of the verb.

1. *lay* Last week I _____ a book.
   This week I have _____ a book.

2. *set* Last week I _____ a book.
   This week I have _____ a book.

3. *raise* Last week I _____ a book. This week I have _____ a book.

Answers are on page 286.

EXERCISE 18: Underline the correct verb to complete each sentence.

1. Jong (rises, raises) early every morning and jogs before work.

2. Do you know where I (set, sat) my car keys?

3. Rose (lay, laid) her notes on your desk before she left the office.

4. We have (set, sat) in the same seats for the past three games.

5. By noon on Monday, I will have (lain, laid) in bed for four days.

6. Madge has (raised, risen) flowers for years.

7. Yesterday, I (lay, laid) down for just a few minutes.

8. Last Friday, José (rose, raised) quickly and left the meeting when he heard the news.

9. Jill had (set, sat) all of the gifts under the tree before midnight.

10. The workers will have (lain, laid) the new roof on the house by noon on Tuesday.

Answers are on page 286.

✐   Remember these <u>facts about troublesome verbs</u>:

- *Lie-lay*, *sit-set*, and *rise-raise* have different jobs.
- When *lie*, *sit*, or *rise* is used in a sentence, the subject of the sentence moves. These verbs do not have objects.
- When *lay*, *set*, or *raise* are used in a sentence, the subject handles something. These verbs always have objects.

In this chapter you have learned:

☐ How to form the present, past, and future tenses (pages 61, 62)

☐ How to form the perfect tenses (pages 63–65)

☐ How to form the continuing tenses (pages 65, 66)

☐ How to form the tenses for irregular verbs (pages 67–74)

☐ How to form the tenses for troublesome verbs (pages 74–76)

Review sections that are difficult for you.

Chapter Review

EXERCISE 1: Read the paragraph. Then underline the correct verb tense for each sentence. Pay attention to the different time clues.

Yesterday I (decided, decide, will decide) to change my study habits. I (wanted, want, will want) to be more successful in school. I always (worked, work, will work) hard, but my hard work does not pay off. I (studied, study, will study) differently from now on. Tomorrow, I will go to my teacher, and I (asked, ask, will ask) her for advice. Then I (listed, list, will list) all of the changes that I will make. I will put that list on my desk, and I (looked, look, will look) at it at night when I study. The list (frustrated, frustrate, will frustrate) me sometimes, but I know it will help me in the long run. If I (improved, improve, will improve) my skills now, I (studied, study, will study) better in the future.

Answers are on page 286.

EXERCISE 2:   Read the paragraph. For each sentence, underline the correct verb form.

Brie has (go, went, gone) through a major change. Last year, she (is, are, was) in terrible shape. She could not run a mile, and she (has, have, had) bad eating habits. Recently Brie has (is, was, been) training for a triathlon. For the past six months, she has (go, went, gone) to the gym every day. In February, she (see, sees, saw) a great bike in a store window, and she (buy, buys, bought) it. Now she rides her bike and (ran, runs, run) as often as she can. I (see, sees, saw) her last week, and I (do, did, done) not even know her. She (is, was, been) so different now. She (came, come, comes) up to me and introduced herself. This new lifestyle has (is, was, been) good for her.

Answers are on page 287.

EXERCISE 3: For each of the following sentences, the verb is in parentheses. Write the correct form of the verb in the space provided.

1. Fakrah is _____ harder now in her new job. (work)

2. If I had _____ what this place was really like, I never would have moved here. (know)

3. Will Becky be _____ before a large group of people? (speak)

4. After the snowfall yesterday, Kelly _____ down the big hill in her backyard. (slide)

5. Are we _____ the race? (win)

6. The man who robbed the bank _____ on foot. (flee)

7. This morning we were _____ about buying a new car. (think)

8. One day last winter, a bat _____ down our chimney and around the house. (fly)

9. Yesterday, the puppy _____ under the woodpile, and no one could find him. (hide)

10. Over the past two weeks, we have _____ four games that we should have won. (lose)

11. They _____ the wrong person for the crime. (hang)

12. The bride and groom will be _____ thank you notes for months. (write)

13. Jesse often _____ into town on a big, white horse. (ride)

14. The deer had _____ the hunter one long look before it ran away. (give)

15. Kyle and his dad have not _____ to the race track for over three years. (go)

16. The horse _____ on the rocky ledge and scared its rider. (stumble)

17. By next week, she will have _____ ten lessons to improve her golf game. (take)

18. Last Friday, the choir _____ in a concert for the whole town. (sing)

19. Before the big game, she had _____ four glasses of water to combat the heat. (drink)

20. Will she have _____ over a mile by this afternoon? (swim)

21. Last night we were _____ about moving to a new home. (talk)

22. The doorbell _____ often on Halloween last year. (ring)

23. She _____ from bed this morning to answer the phone. (arise)

24. Our boss _____ only five people to travel with her last week. (choose)

25. Who _____ all of these pages out of my book yesterday? (tear)

Answers are on pages 287.

Subject-Verb Agreement

4

In this chapter you will learn:

☐ How to form singular and plural verbs (pages 78, 79)

☐ How to create the singular and plural forms of *be* and *have* (pages 79, 80)

☐ How to work with difficult subjects (pages 80, 81)

☐ How to work with a different word order (pages 81, 82)

☐ How to work with indefinite pronouns (pages 82–84)

☐ How to work with compound subjects (pages 84, 85)

☐ How to work with linking verbs (page 85)

You write to get a message to the reader. Therefore, you need to make sure that the subject and the verb in each sentence send the same message. This is called subject-verb agreement.

Guidelines

Present tense verbs can be singular or plural. Make most verbs singular by adding *-s* or *-es*.

 Note:

SINGULAR - one (she, it, dog)

PLURAL - more than one (we, they, dogs)

Examples:

PLURAL	SINGULAR VERBS
run	runs
wash	washes
They run every day.	She runs every day.
They wash cars.	She washes cars.

Examples:

PLURAL	SINGULAR
1. wait	waits
2. see	sees
3. catch	catches
4. watch	watches

PLURAL

1. The workers <u>wait</u> for their paychecks.
2. They <u>see</u> the fireworks.
3. Kate and Bruce <u>catch</u> a cold every winter.
4. Pete and Sue <u>watch</u> football games on weekends.

SINGULAR

1. The worker wait<u>s</u> for her paycheck.
2. He see<u>s</u> the fireworks.
3. Kate catch<u>es</u> a cold every winter.
4. Pete watch<u>es</u> football games on weekends.

PRONOUNS

The pronouns *I* and *you* do not follow this pattern. When the subject of the sentence is *I* or *you*, the verb does not have an *-s* or *-es*.

PRONOUNS AND VERBS

WE, THEY, I, YOU, HE, SHE, IT
want   want<u>s</u>
wash   wash<u>es</u>

Examples:

PRONOUNS AND VERBS
1. I <u>wait</u> for my friend.
2. I <u>catch</u> a cold every winter.
3. You <u>wait</u> for your friend.
4. You <u>catch</u> a cold every winter.

EXERCISE 1:   Underline the verb form that agrees with the subject.

1. Her dry skin (itch, itches) in the morning.

2. You (read, reads) to your children every night.

3. I (look, looks) out the window often to check on the weather.

4. The players (practice, practices) hard to win more games.

5. They (think, thinks) about selling the land.

6. Ted (want, wants) to find a new job.

7. The children (open, opens) many gifts during the holidays.

8. The peaches (fall, falls) to the ground when they are too ripe.

9. Kay (wear, wears) some of her mother's earrings.

10. The girls (dress, dresses) their dolls with old baby clothes.

Answers are on page 287, 288.

👉 Remember these <u>facts about subject-verb agreement</u>:

- Make most verbs singular by adding an *-s* or *-es*. (He walk<u>s</u>. She watch<u>es</u>.)
- When the subject is *I* or *you*, the verb does not have an *-s* or *-es*. (I walk.)

Special Situations

BE AND HAVE

Be and *have* are irregular verbs. Nonetheless, the basic rules for verbs still work. The singular forms do end in *-s*, and the plural forms do not end in *-s*.

Examples:

BE (PRESENT TENSE)
1. Tara <u>is</u> a great soccer player.
2. He <u>is</u> a great soccer player.
3. Matt and Katie <u>are</u> great soccer players.
4. They <u>are</u> great soccer players.

HAVE (PRESENT TENSE)
1. Shantae <u>has</u> many ideas.
2. He <u>has</u> many ideas.
3. Kay and Tom <u>have</u> many ideas.
4. They <u>have</u> many ideas.

When the subject is *I* or *you*, the verb does not have an *-s*.

Examples:

BE (PRESENT TENSE)
1. I <u>am</u> a great lacrosse player.
2. You <u>are</u> a great lacrosse player.

HAVE (PRESENT TENSE)
1. I <u>have</u> many ideas.
2. You <u>have</u> many ideas.

Unlike other verbs, *be* has a singular and a plural form in the past tense.

Examples:

BE (PAST TENSE)
1. I <u>was</u> a member of the soccer team.
2. Lee <u>was</u> a member of the soccer team.
3. You <u>were</u> a member of the soccer team.
4. Khan and Vicki <u>were</u> members of the soccer team.

BE

PRESENT TENSE
I ↔ am
he, she, it ↔ is
you, we, they ↔ are

PAST TENSE
I, he, she, it ↔ was
you, we, they ↔ were

HAVE

I, you, we, they ↔ have
he, she, it ↔ has

EXERCISE 2: For each of the following sentences, underline the correct verb form.

1. Yesterday, we (was, were) in the store when we heard the fire alarms.

2. Megan (has, have) more money now that she is working.

3. The children (has, have) new toys.

4. They (is, are) the best cookies that I have ever had.

5. He (is, am) the new mayor in town.

6. (Are, Is) you sure that the movie starts at 7 o'clock?

7. Last week, the boys (were, was) playing in the mud down by the river.

8. I (has, have) enough money for the train and a cup of coffee.

9. Steve (is, am) a foot taller than his younger brother.

10. (Is, Are) the last flight to New York about to leave?

Answers are on pages 288.

☞ Remember these <u>facts about *be* and *have*</u>:

- The singular forms of *be* and *have* end in *-s*. (She <u>is</u>. She <u>has</u>.)

- The plural forms do **not** end in *-s*. (They <u>are</u>. They <u>have</u>.)

- *I* and *you* have their own rules. (I <u>am</u>. You <u>are</u>. I <u>have</u>. You <u>have</u>.)

- *Be* has two forms of the past tense. (He <u>was</u>. They <u>were</u>.)

DIFFICULT SUBJECTS

Some subjects are harder to find than others. For example, sometimes prepositional phrases separate the subject and the verb. In Chapter 2, you learned to cross out prepositional phrases in order to find the different parts of the sentence. This method will help you now, as well.

Examples:

1. The student ~~with the big backpack and heavy books~~ earns very good grades.
2. The boxes ~~under the ledge near the door~~ are full.
3. Marie, ~~along with her sisters~~, went to the play last night.

Sometimes other words that describe the subject are located between the subject and the verb. These words usually are set off by commas, *that*, or *which*. They do not change the relationship between the subject and the verb. Focus only on the subject and the verb—not the words in between.

**HOW TO FIND
DIFFICULT SUBJECTS**

1. Cross out prepositional phrases.
2. Find the subject.
3. Select the verb that agrees with the subject.
4. Beware of words that are set off by commas, *that*, or *which*.

Examples:

1. The <u>bleachers</u>, *freshly painted and ready for the big game*, <u>were</u> full of people.
2. The <u>trees</u> *that are full of color* <u>are</u> my neighbor's.
3. My <u>bike</u>, *which needs new tires*, <u>is</u> in the shop.

Some words make a subject appear to be plural. See the box below.

> *Note:* The following words may make a subject seem to be plural.
>
> besides
> as well as
> along with
> with
> together with
> in addition to
> *Make sure you follow the steps for difficult subjects.*

Examples:

1. Raj, *along with two friends*, is late for work.
2. The first floor, *in addition to the basement and the driveway*, was destroyed by the flood.
3. The teacher, *as well as her students*, likes the new classroom.

Remember, you must cross out prepositional phrases and focus only on the subject and the verb.

EXERCISE 3: Underline the correct verb for each sentence. Make sure that you focus on the subject and the verb, not the words in between.

1. The horse that jumped over four fences (is, are) in the lead.
2. The crate of apples (sit, sits) next to the pears.
3. Juan, together with his brothers, (work, works) at the paper mill.
4. The fence in the backyard by the barn (need, needs) a repair.
5. Rose, along with her children, (was, were) at the mall today.
6. The desk that has two chairs (is, are) mine.
7. The plants on the shelf over by the window (has, have) died.
8. The workers with long trips home (like, likes) to leave early on Fridays.

9. Nga's salary, as well as her benefits, (increase, increases) every fall.
10. The haunted house, full of rats and bats, (scare, scares) many people at night.

Answers are on page 288.

Remember these <u>facts about difficult subjects</u>:

- Focus only on the subject and the verb.
- Cross out prepositional phrases and beware of words that are set off by commas, *that*, or *which*.
- Some words may make a subject seem plural (besides, as well as, along with, together with, in addition to). If you cross out prepositional phrases, these words will not be a problem for you.

DIFFERENT WORD ORDER

Sometimes the subject is difficult to find because it follows the verb. Questions and sentences that begin with *here* or *there* often have the verb before the subject. To find the subject more easily, rephrase the sentence. Rewrite questions as statements and reword sentences that begin with *here* or *there*.

Examples:

ORIGINAL
SENTENCE: Here are the tickets for the show.

NEW
SENTENCE: The tickets for the show are here.

ORIGINAL
SENTENCE: Do <u>you</u> build roads and bridges?

NEW
SENTENCE: <u>You</u> do build roads and bridges.

ORIGINAL
SENTENCE: There are many reasons.

NEW
SENTENCE: Many reasons are there.

Once you find the subject, you can make sure that the subject and the verb agree.

EXERCISE 4: For each of the following sentences, underline the correct verb.

1. Where (is, are) my shoes?

2. There (is, are) two reasons for your success.

3. Do you (want, wants) more sugar for your coffee?

4. There (go, goes) Khan.

5. Where (is, are) Joe going on his trip?

6. What (is, are) you doing with my new coat?

7. Here (is, are) the horse from the stables across the road.

8. (Do, Does) your mother still drive to the store every day?

9. How (do, does) you win every time you play chess?

10. (Do, Does) Chad believe in ghosts?

Answers are on page 288.

 Remember, rephrase sentences that have a different word order. Rewrite questions as statements and reword sentences that begin with *here* or *there*.

INDEFINITE PRONOUNS

Indefinite pronouns make vague references. They do not refer to specific persons, places, or things. These pronouns are divided into three groups, which determine whether they are singular or plural.

SINGULAR PRONOUNS

Some indefinite pronouns are always singular. (See the following box.) These pronouns can be identified by their endings: *one*, *body*, and *thing*.

PRONOUNS THAT ARE ALWAYS SINGULAR

someone
somebody
something
anyone
anybody
anything
everyone
everybody
everything
no one
nobody
nothing
one
each (one)
either (one)
neither (one)

Examples:

1. <u>Everyone</u> in the office <u>thinks</u> the air is too cold.
2. <u>Nothing</u> <u>beats</u> coming home after a hard day at work.
3. <u>Everybody</u> on the team <u>is</u> ready for the last game.

EXERCISE 5: Underline the correct verb form.

1. Nobody (want, wants) to go to the movies with me.

2. (Does, Do) anyone need a ride to work?

3. Neither (likes, like) the new color of the house.

4. (Has, Have) everybody found a partner for the dance?

5. Each (knit, knits) a new sweater in the fall.

6. No one (care, cares) enough about morals today.

7. Either (is, are) a great plan for the old building on Main Street.

8. Somebody (cut, cuts) a hole in my newspaper every day.

9. (Does, Do) anybody know who broke mom's vase?

10. Something (needs, need) to be done about the broken glass in the play-ground.

Answers are on page 288.

PLURAL PRONOUNS

Other indefinite pronouns are always plural. (See the box below.) These words are easy because they appear plural.

> ### PRONOUNS THAT ARE ALWAYS PLURAL
>
> several
> few
> both
> many

Examples:

1. <u>Several</u> of the boys <u>need</u> new books.
2. <u>Both</u> of the captains <u>want</u> to hold a team meeting.
3. <u>Many</u> of the children <u>run</u> to catch the bus.

SINGULAR OR PLURAL PRONOUNS

A few pronouns can be singular or plural depending on the sentence. (See the box that follows.) For these pronouns, you must look at the prepositional phrase that follows. If the object of the preposition is plural, so is the verb. Likewise, if the object of the preposition is singular, the verb is singular.

> ### PRONOUNS THAT ARE SINGULAR OR PLURAL
>
> some
> all
> any
> most
> none
>
> *Use the prepositional phrase that follows.*

Examples:

1. <u>None</u> of the <u>teachers</u> want to go on strike. *None* refers to *teachers*, which is plural. The verb must be plural.
2. <u>All</u> of the <u>house</u> is destroyed. *All* refers to *house*, which is singular. The verb must be singular.
3. <u>Most</u> of the <u>money</u> was stolen. *Most* refers to *money*, which is singular. The verb must be singular.
4. <u>Some</u> of the <u>cars</u> were damaged in the accident. *Some* refers to *cars*, which is plural. The verb must be plural.

EXERCISE 6: For each of the following sentences, underline the correct verb.

1. Some of my friends (is, are) going out to dinner.

2. Several of my peers (want, wants) to change how they live their lives.

3. All of my change (falls, fall) out of my wallet when I open my purse.

4. (Do, Does) any of your brothers need a new coat?

5. Most of my time (is, are) spent work-ing on the new project.

6. None of my siblings (is, are) going to work in my dad's company.

7. (Does, Do) a few of your shirts need to be washed?

8. (Is, Are) most of your gifts wrapped?

9. Many of my socks (has, have) holes.

10. Both of the coaches (think, thinks) that they will win the big game tonight.

Answers are on page 289.

Remember these <u>facts about indefinite pronouns</u>:

- Pronouns that end in *-one,- body*, or *-thing* are always singular (someone, somebody, something, no one, nobody, nothing).
- Some pronouns are always plural (several, few, both, many).
- A few pronouns can be singular or plural depending on the sentence (some, all, any, most, none). You must look at the prepositional phrase that follows to choose the correct verb.

COMPOUND SUBJECTS

Some sentences use conjunctions (and, or, nor) to combine two or more subjects that are equally important. These combinations are called compound subjects. When *and* is used, the subjects act together. For compound subjects joined by *and*, use the plural form of the verb.

COMPOUND SUBJECTS

CONJUNCTION	VERB
and	plural
or, nor	agrees with the closest subject

Bob <u>and</u> Chris <u>are</u> good students.
Neither Bob <u>nor</u> Chris <u>is</u> a good student.
Either Chris <u>or</u> the boys <u>are</u> good students.
Either the boys <u>or</u> Chris <u>is</u> a good student.

Examples:

1. Jim *and* Alice <u>think</u> the price is too high.
2. The doctor *and* her staff <u>work</u> to keep health care costs down.

When *or* or *nor* is used, the subjects act separately. For compound subjects joined by *or* or *nor*, use the verb that agrees with the closest subject. To follow this rule easily, underline the subject that is closest to the verb.

Examples:

1. Every day, my mom *or* my <u>dad drives</u> to town to pick up the paper.
2. Rosa *or* the <u>children rake</u> the leaves in the fall.
3. Neither my sister *nor* my <u>brothers want</u> to go to Maine for the summer.
4. Neither my brothers *nor* my <u>sister wants</u> to go to Maine for the summer.

Note that changing the order of the subjects can alter the verb, as well.

EXERCISE 7: For each of the following sentences, underline the correct verb.

1. The tiger or the bear (growl, growls) at me every time I go to the zoo.

2. The chef and the waiters (work, works) hard all week.

3. Neither the coach nor his players (know, knows) how tough this game will be.

4. Red, blue, and yellow (is, are) primary colors.

5. The doctor and the nurses (think, thinks) that the boy will be just fine.

6. Carl or his sisters (join, joins) the family for dinner each Sunday.

7. The cats or the dog (knock, knocks) my plants over when I leave the house.

8. The cold air, snow, and high winds (make, makes) this a harsh winter.

9. Neither the flowers nor the tree (flourish, flourishes) in this bad weather.

10. The teacher or the students (erase, erases) the wrong answers and write the correct ones.

Answers are on page 289.

☞ Remember these <u>facts about compound subjects</u>:

• For compound subjects joined by *and*, use the plural form of the verb. (The TV <u>and</u> the VCR <u>are</u> on.)

• For compound subjects joined by *or* or *nor*, use the verb that agrees with the closest subject. (The dog or the <u>cows</u> <u>are</u> in the barn. The cows or the <u>dog</u> <u>is</u> in the barn.)

LINKING VERBS

Linking verbs connect the subject to subject complements, words that rename or describe the subject. Do not let subject complements confuse you. When you write, make sure the verb agrees with the subject of the sentence.

Examples:

1. <u>Hard work</u> and <u>discipline</u> <u>are</u> the key to success. *Hard work* and *discipline* are the subjects. The verb must be plural.

2. <u>The</u> <u>key</u> to success <u>is</u> hard work and discipline. *The key* is the subject. The verb must be singular.

EXERCISE 8: Underline the correct verb form for each sentence.

1. A great athlete (is, are) focused and dedicated.

2. Cars (was, were) a passion for Nate.

3. His main interest (is, are) sports.

4. A lovely sight in the fall (is, are) the trees with their leaves changing color.

5. The trees with their leaves changing color (is, are) a lovely sight in the fall.

6. His main concern when he goes to work (is, are) crazy drivers.

7. Nga's best idea for the store (is, are) more shelves.

8. A bigger backstop and more bleachers (was, were) Khan's idea.

9. A nicer sign or more ads (was, were) Beth's plan for a better image.

10. More voter turnout and better polls (was, were) the key for the campaign.

Answers are on page 289.

☞ Remember, make sure that the verb agrees with the <u>subject</u> of the sentence.

In this chapter you have learned:

☐ How to form singular and plural verbs (pages 78, 79)

☐ How to create the singular and plural forms of *be* and *have* (pages 79, 80)

☐ How to work with difficult subjects (pages 80, 81)

☐ How to work with a different word order (pages 81, 82)

☐ How to work with indefinite pronouns 82–84)

☐ How to work with compound subjects 84, 85)

☐ How to work with linking verbs (page 85)

Review sections that are difficult for you.

Chapter Review

EXERCISE 1: Underline the correct form of the verb.

1. The bag of balls (was, were) on the bench when we pulled out of the parking lot.

2. Every day, someone (forgets, forgot) to pick up the trash that is left behind.

3. All of my peers (is, are) moving to the new office.

4. Everyone (wants, want) a new desk, except for me.

5. The manager and her workers (thinks, think) the new team approach will work well.

6. The sitter or the children (needs, need) to close the gate in the yard.

7. Most of my money (is, are) packed in my suitcase.

8. Her idea (is, are) long skirts in wild colors.

9. The drums or the flute (was, were) playing the wrong music.

10. The stores in the mall or the new shop around the corner (has, have) the book you need.

11. She or I (has, have) the new teacher for math.

12. The coat that doesn't match any of my outfits (is, are) in the closet downstairs.

13. The fire hydrant down the street by Beth's trees (is, are) leaking.

14. My shoes, polished and ready to wear, (has, have) not been out of my closest in ages.

15. Grandma, along with her friends, (plays, play) bridge each week.

16. There (was, were) five tickets for the show on the table.

17. (Does, Do) you know the name of the new girl?

18. Both of my legs (is, are) tired from my long run this morning.

19. None of the change (is, are) left in my coat pocket.

Answers are on pages 289, 290.

EXERCISE 2: Read the following passage and find nine (9) errors in subject-verb agreement. Cross out the wrong verb and write the correct verb in the margin.

Health care is a tough issue for many people these days. Everybody want to have the best care at the lowest cost. Yet, poor people and ill people lack the health care that they need. The problem are high costs and scanty coverage. Neither medicine nor doctors is affordable for many people. Every year politicians, looking for votes and full of hot air, promises to improve health care, but nothing seems to change.

Even the thought of choosing a health plan is hard for some. In our office alone, there is five different health plans. My boss, along with some others, belong to an HMO. Many of the other employees see private doctors. Yet, no one is happy. The forms that we all complete seems endless. Few of the doctors is available when we need them, and the cost keeps rising. Better health plans is a great idea, but who knows how to improve them? Somebody is going to find a solution to this problem someday, but it will not be soon enough.

Answers are on page 290, 291.

Pronouns

In this chapter you will learn:

- ☐ How to use the subjective case (nominative case) (pages 87–89)
- ☐ How to use the objective case (pages 89–91)
- ☐ How to use the possessive case (pages 91, 92)
- ☐ How to use *who* and *whom* (pages 92–94)
- ☐ How to use reflexive or intensive pronouns (pages 94, 95)
- ☐ How to use pronouns in comparison (pages 95, 96)
- ☐ How to make pronouns agree (pages 97, 98)

Pronouns (I, you, he, she, it, we, they, me, him, her, us, them, who, whom, whoever, whomever) substitute for nouns and work as nouns in a sentence. Because pronouns have specific jobs, they are divided into cases or groups. Think of each case as a family of pronouns. This chapter will teach you about the different cases, so you will use the right pronoun for each job.

> ⇨ **Warning!**
>
> We often hear pronouns used incorrectly. What sounds right may be wrong. As you go through this chapter, read the examples and correct answers aloud many times. Also, practice using pronouns properly when you speak. If you speak correctly, you will be more likely to write correctly.

CASES

Subjective Case	Objective Case	Possessive Case
I	me	my, mine
you	you	your, yours
he	him	his
she	her	her, hers
it	it	its
we	us	our, ours
they	them	their, theirs
who	whom	whose
whoever	whomever	—

Subjective Case (Nominative Case)

The pronouns in the subjective case (I, you, he, she, it, we, they, who, whoever) have two main jobs. They are used for the subject of a sentence and for subject complements.

Examples:

1. <u>They</u> are best friends. *subject*
2. Kim and <u>I</u> are going out for pizza. *subject*
3. <u>She</u> and <u>he</u> left the price tags on their gifts. *subject*
4. It was only <u>he</u> at the door. *subject complement*
5. The teacher of the year is <u>Seon</u> or <u>she</u>. *subject complement*

Note that compound subjects or compound subject complements follow the same rule. If compound parts confuse you, write two separate sentences and then choose the correct pronoun.

Examples:

1. <u>Kathy</u> and <u>I</u> are going to buy bikes.
   <u>Kathy</u> is going to buy a bike. <u>I</u> am going to buy a bike.
2. <u>She</u> and <u>he</u> went for a picnic in the park on Sunday.
   <u>She</u> went for a picnic in the park. <u>He</u> went for a picnic in the park.
3. The top-rated doctors are <u>Khan</u> and <u>she</u>.
   The top-rated doctor is <u>Khan</u>. The top-rated doctor is <u>she</u>.

EXERCISE 1: For each sentence, underline the correct pronoun.

1. (She, Her) and Russ are moving into their new house today.

2. (They, Them) will have a lot of work to do in the next few days.

3. Rhea and (I, me) will bring dessert on Thursday.

4. (He, Him) and Nancy will provide most of the food and drinks.

5. The best person for the job is (he, him).

6. (He, Him) and (she, her) are Native Americans.

7. Is (she, her) the world class painter?

8. (She, Her) and John will bring the children with them.

9. The workers from the store are (they, them).

10. Which actress is (she, her)?

Answers are on page 291.

APPOSITIVES AND THE SUBJECTIVE CASE

Some sentences have a word or a group of words with similar jobs next to each other. These words are called appositives, and they often are separated by commas.

> ### APPOSITIVES
>
> A word or group of words next to each other with similar jobs
> <u>Kay</u>, <u>a key player</u>, is injured.
> <u>Pete</u> <u>the butcher</u> sells the best meat in town.

Examples:

1. The track <u>coach</u>, <u>Ms. Ngyun</u>, has a great program.
2. <u>Jahye</u>, <u>the world class runner</u>, is racing in New York.
3. <u>The situation in Bosnia</u>, <u>a major world issue</u>, fills the nightly news.

When an appositive refers to the subject, use the subjective case.

Examples:

1. Only <u>two people</u>, <u>she</u> and <u>he</u>, complained.
2. <u>The best workers</u>, <u>you</u> and <u>he</u>, earned a bonus.

If appositives confuse you, try writing two separate sentences. This will help you choose the correct pronoun more easily.

Examples:

1. Only <u>two people</u>, <u>she</u> and <u>he</u>, complained.
   Only <u>two people</u> complained. Only <u>she</u> and <u>he</u> complained.
2. <u>The best workers</u>, <u>you</u> and <u>he</u>, earned a bonus.
   <u>The best workers</u> earned a bonus. <u>You</u> and <u>he</u> earned a bonus.

SUBJECTIVE CASE

(I, you, he, she, it, we, they, who, whoever)

1. Subjects
2. Subject Complements
3. Appositives that refer to subjects

He and <u>I</u> finished our game.
The best plumber is <u>she</u>.
Two lawyers, <u>she</u> and <u>he</u>, argued for hours.

EXERCISE 2: Underline the correct pronoun for each of the following sentences.

1. The top two swimmers, (she, her) and Van, will advance to the finals.

2. Two construction crews, Bell and (they, them), bid the last contract.

3. Two soldiers, (she, her) and (he, him), were sent to the front line.

4. The mayor, (he, him) in the corner, will speak at the town meeting.

5. The last farmers in town, Jeff and (she, her), had to sell their land.

6. Only two members of Congress, (she, her) and (he, him), want the reforms.

7. Ken and (she, her), the first two customers, got free gifts from the store.

8. The only honest politicians, (he, him) and (I, me), are leaving office.

9. Two country singers, Reba and (she, her), have great voices.

10. (She, her), the top athlete, will compete in college.

Answers are on page 291.

Remember these <u>facts about the subjective case</u>:

- The subjective case is simply a group of pronouns with similar jobs (I, you, he, she, it, we, they, who, whoever). Think of these pronouns as a family that works together.

- The subjective case is used for subjects, subject complements, and appositives that refer to subjects.

- The subjective case also is used for compound subjects and compound subject complements.

- If compound parts or appositives confuse you, write two sentences and then choose the correct pronoun.

Objective Case

The pronouns in the objective case (me, you, him, her, it, us, them, whom, whomever) have two main jobs. They are used for the object of a verb and the object of a preposition.

Examples:

1. The host presented <u>him</u> to the guests at the party. *object of the verb*
2. The store owner handed <u>her</u> and <u>him</u> to the police. *object of the verb*
3. My wife gave <u>me</u> new hockey skates. *object of the verb*
4. Our boss gave <u>him</u> and <u>me</u> a raise for our hard work. *object of the verb*
5. It was a great honor for <u>us</u>. *object of the preposition*
6. My mom sat between <u>him</u> and <u>me</u>. *object of the preposition*

As you can see, compound objects follow the same rule. If compound objects confuse you, focus on one part of the object at a time.

Examples:

1. Rick drove <u>him</u> and <u>me</u> to the mall. Rick drove <u>him</u> to the mall. Rick drove <u>me</u> to the mall.
2. The judge gave <u>her</u> and <u>him</u> a tough sentence.
The judge gave <u>her</u> a tough sentence.
The judge gave <u>him</u> a tough sentence.

Many people use pronouns with prepositions incorrectly. As a result, what sounds right often is wrong. The following activity will help you practice using pronouns correctly.

Activity: Add each of the prepositions listed below to the following sentences and read the sentences aloud.

The bird flew _____ you and me.

The bird flew _____ him and her.

Prepositions that are used often with pronouns:

above
after
among
around
at
behind
between
beyond
by
for
from
like
near
over
past
to
towards
unlike
with

OBJECTIVE CASE

(me, you, him, her, it, us, them, whom, whomever)

1. Object of the verb
2. Object of the preposition
3. An appositive that refers to an object

That ball hit <u>him</u> hard!
The lawyer gave <u>me</u> a bill.
Dad built a tree house for <u>us</u>.

EXERCISE 3: For each sentence, underline the correct pronoun.

1. The little girl with the hose sprayed (I, me) with cold water.

2. The manager promised (her, him) and (I, me) a good job.

3. Congress sent (he, him) a bill on welfare reform.

4. Right now, this is the best choice for (we, us).

5. Did you give (he, him) and (she, her) enough paint to finish the job?

6. I want this secret to stay between you and (I, me).

7. Why did Nga tell (he, him) and (she, her) that story?

8. Two actors from the movie were sitting behind Dade and (I, me).

9. The press caught Di and (he, him) off guard.

10. Tyrone wrote his last novel about him and (she, her).

Answers are on page 291.

APPOSITIVES AND THE OBJECTIVE CASE

Appositives are words or groups of words with similar jobs that are next to each other in a sentence. When an appositive refers to an object in the sentence, use the objective case.

Examples:

1. Blair thanked two people, <u>him</u> and <u>her</u>.
   Him and her refers to the object of the verb, *two people.*
2. Our boss gave the best workers, <u>you</u> and <u>me</u>, two tickets.
   You and me refers to an object of the verb, *best workers.*

If appositives confuse you, try writing two separate sentences. This will help you choose the correct pronoun more easily.

Examples:

1. Blair thanked two people, <u>him</u> and <u>her</u>.
   Blair thanked <u>two people</u>. Blair thanked <u>him</u> and <u>her</u>.

2. Our boss gave <u>the best workers</u>, <u>you</u> and <u>me</u>, two tickets.
Our boss gave <u>the best workers</u> two tickets. Our boss gave <u>you</u> and <u>me</u> two tickets.

EXERCISE 4: Underline the correct pronoun(s) for each of the following sentences.

1. The singer brought two people, Anne and (she, her), up on the stage.

2. The team chose the player of the year, (I, me).

3. Yu Lin bought her best friends, you and (I, me), nice gifts.

4. The program gave two troubled kids, Carlos and (I, me) a chance.

5. Ingrid sent her sisters, you and (I, me), flowers.

6. Taxes are a burden for (I, me), a hard worker.

7. Dr. Koo gave her nurses, Jane and (I, me), a lot of grief.

8. Ty tipped the waiters, Fred and (he, him), too much.

9. The mentors helped two students, Ian and (I, me), learn more.

10. Leaving home was hard for one person, (I, me).

Answers are on page 291.

☞ Remember these <u>facts about the objective case</u>:

• The objective case is simply a group of pronouns with similar jobs (me, you, him, her, it, us, them, whom, whomever). Think of these pronouns as a family that works together.

• The objective case is used for an object of the verb, an object of a preposition, and an appositive that refers to an object.

• Compound objects follow the same rules.

• If appositives or compound objects confuse you, write two sentences and then choose the correct pronoun.

Possessive Case

Possessive pronouns have three main jobs. You already know two jobs well. Possessive pronouns show ownership of a noun, and they substitute for a noun.

Examples:

1. <u>My</u> dog ate <u>their</u> wedding cake.
2. <u>His</u> car is parked in <u>her</u> parking space.
3. The bike in the garage is <u>mine</u>.
4. <u>Theirs</u> is the yard with the tall grass and unkempt garden.

Keep in mind, possessive pronouns never have an apostrophe.

POSSESSIVE PRONOUNS WITH SPECIAL NOUNS

Some verbs that end in *-ing* act like nouns.

Examples:

1. We will not have time for <u>swimming</u> and <u>sailing</u>.
Swimming and *sailing* are nouns, and they work as objects of the preposition *for.*
2. Nate never tried <u>skating</u>.
Skating is a noun, and it works as an object of the verb.
3. Anh's <u>driving</u> makes me nervous.
Driving is a noun, and it works as the subject of the sentence. *Anh's* is an adjective that describes *driving.*

Possessive pronouns are used with verbs that end in *-ing* and act like nouns. The pronouns work as adjectives.

Examples:

1. <u>Your</u> hiking in the Alps is dangerous.
Hiking is a noun and the subject of the sentence. *Your* is an adjective that describes *hiking.*

2. I can't hear <u>his</u> singing.
Singing is a noun and the object of the verb. *His* is an adjective that describes *singing*.

3. There is no excuse for <u>their</u> lying.
Lying is a noun and the object of the preposition. *Their* is an adjective that describes *lying*.

POSSESSIVE CASE

(my, mine, your, yours, his, her, hers, its, our, ours, their, theirs, whose)

1. Before a noun to show ownership
2. Before an "*-ing* " verb that is used as a noun
3. Substitute for a noun

This is <u>his</u> briefcase.
<u>Her</u> sleeping in class is a big problem.
That book is not <u>hers</u>.

Possessive pronouns never have an apostrophe.

EXERCISE 5: Underline the correct pronoun for each of the following sentences.

1. The red backpack with black handles is (her's, hers).

2. (Me, My) mom and dad want to see us for the holidays.

3. The high winds and driving rain flooded (he, his) basement and destroyed (her, hers) patio.

4. (He, Him, His) chewing with his mouth open is vulgar.

5. I need to find my ticket, but he has (his', his).

6. (They, Their) lived in Guam, France, and Greece when she was in the military.

7. If he wants to be a pro golfer, he will have to improve (he, him, his) putting.

8. That is a nice table, but (it's, its) finish is fading in the sun.

9. Jihye has her own car, but she wants (their's, theirs).

10. Before Shantae runs for office, he will have to improve (he, him, his) speaking.

Answers are on pages 291, 292.

👉 Remember these <u>facts about the possessive case</u>:

- The possessive case is simply a group of pronouns with similar jobs (my, your, his, her, its, our, their, whose, mine, yours, his, hers, ours, theirs, whose). Think of these pronouns as a family that works together.

- Possessive pronouns show ownership of nouns and substitute for nouns. (<u>Her</u> book. The book is <u>hers</u>.)

- Possessive pronouns are used with verbs that end in *-ing* and act like nouns. The pronouns function as adjectives. (<u>Her</u> sleeping is a problem.)

- Possessive pronouns never have an apostrophe.

Who and Whom

Who and *whoever* are part of the subjective case. They work as subjects and subject complements. On the other hand, *whom* and *whomever* are part of the objective case. They work as objects of prepositions and objects of verbs. The *m's* in *who<u>m</u>* and *hi<u>m</u>* will help you keep the pronoun family together.

Examples:

1. <u>Who</u> caught the fly ball?   <u>He</u> caught the fly ball? *subject*
2. The best lawyer in town is <u>who</u>? The best lawyer in town is <u>he</u>? *subject complement*
3. The FBI charged <u>whom</u> with the crime? The FBI charged <u>him</u> with the crime? *object of the verb*
4. The clerk gave <u>whom</u> the money? The clerk gave <u>him</u> the money? *object of the verb*

5. Jake bought this gift for <u>whom</u>?
   Jake bought this gift for <u>him</u>?
   object of the preposition

Unfortunately, not all sentences are this easy. For example, questions that begin with *who* or *whom* often confuse students. Rewording these questions can make them easier.

Examples:

1. <u>Whom</u> do you want for the band?
   You do want <u>whom</u> for the band.
   object of the verb
2. <u>Whom</u> did you send cards to? You did send cards to <u>whom</u>. *object of the preposition*

EXERCISE 6: For each sentence underline the correct pronoun.

1. (Who, Whom) asked for more food?

2. Lee gave money to (who, whom)?

3. (Who, Whom) was elected president in Haiti?

4. (Who, Whom) should we send to the training program?

5. Cal gave (who, whom) the game ball?

6. (Who, Whom) did Brazil defeat to win the World Cup in 1994?

7. (Who, Whom) will be hurt by the new law?

8. (Whoever, whomever) thought we would travel to the moon?

9. The volunteers at the shelter help (whoever, whomever).

10. (Who, Whom) did Jack pay?

Answers are on page 292.

Some sentences have clauses, which are groups of words with a subject and a predicate. Clauses can act like nouns, verbs, and adjectives. They also can work as any part in the sentence. (See more on clauses in Chapter 7.) Note the clauses in the following examples.

 Note: A *clause* is a group of words within a sentence that has a subject and a predicate. Clauses can act like nouns, verbs, and adjectives, and they can work as any part of the sentence.

Examples:

1. The guard knew <u>who escaped</u>.
   Who escaped is a clause. *Who* is the subject of the clause, and *escaped* is the verb. The entire clause acts like a noun and is the object of the verb in the sentence. It answers the question, the guard knew who or what?
2. <u>Whoever built this road</u> deserves an award.
   Whoever built this road is the subject of the sentence. It answers the question who or what deserves? In the clause, *whoever* is the subject, *built* is the verb, and *this road* is the object of the verb.
3. The man <u>who filed an appeal</u> won his case.
   Who filed an appeal is an adjective that describes *the man*. It answers the question which man? In the clause, *who* is the subject, *filed* is the verb, and *an appeal* is the object of the verb.
4. She will give the job to <u>whomever her boss recommends</u>.
   Whomever her boss recommends is the object of the preposition *to*. It answers the question to whom or what? In the clause, *her boss* is the subject, *recommends* is the verb, and *whomever* is the object of the verb.

Clauses often start with *who*, *whom*, *whoever*, and *whomever*. In these sentences, the choice between *who* and *whom* or *whoever* and *whomever* depends on how the pronoun works in the clause. When the pronoun is the subject of the clause, use *who* or *whoever*. When the pronoun is an object in the clause, use *whom* or *whomever*. Sometimes rewording the sentence or the clause will help.

Examples:

1. The exiles helped <u>whoever fled Cuba</u>.
   Whoever is the subject of the clause.

2. Rhea gave <u>whomever she met</u> a warm smile.
   Whomever is the object of the verb in the clause. Rewording the clause may help. *She met whomever.*

3. <u>Whoever brings a weapon to school</u> will be expelled.
   Whoever is the subject of the clause.

4. We often are judged by <u>whom we befriend.</u>
   Rewording the clause may help. *We befriend whom. Whom* is the direct object of the clause.

5. <u>Who</u> do you think <u>is the best actor</u>?
   Rewording the sentence may help. You do think *who is the best actor. Who* is the subject of the clause.

WHO, WHOM, WHOEVER, AND WHOMEVER

WHO AND WHOEVER
subject
subject complement

WHOM AND WHOMEVER
object of the verb
object of preposition

If a sentence has a clause, the choice between *who* and *whom* or *whoever* and *whomever* depends on how the pronoun functions in the clause.

EXERCISE 7: For each sentence, underline the correct pronoun.

1. The donor gave his blood to (whoever, whomever) had the greatest need.

2. The person (who, whom) granted the money did not give her name.

3. The person (who, whom) we just met has been here before.

4. Three people saw (who, whom) took the new sign on Main Street.

5. (Whoever, Whomever) committed the war crimes in Bosnia will be brought to trial.

6. Dr. Hawk treats children (who, whom) are injured.

7. Kate will give the bonus to (whoever, whomever) she chooses.

8. (Whoever, Whomever) wins the war will have to rebuild the nation.

9. I did not see (who, whom) she saved from the burning car.

10. Many people (who, whom) come to America work hard to learn English.

Answers are on page 292.

Remember these <u>facts about who and whom</u>:

- *Who* is part of the subjective case, and *whom* is part of the objective case.

- *Who* and *he* have the same jobs. Likewise, *whom* and *him* have the same jobs.

- When the pronoun is the subject of a clause, use *who* or *whoever*. When the pronoun is an object of a clause, use *whom* or *whomever*.

- Rewording a sentence or clause may help you choose the correct pronoun.

Special Situations

REFLEXIVE OR INTENSIVE PRONOUNS

Reflexive or intensive pronouns are pronouns that end with *-self* or *-selves* (himself, themselves). Usually these pronouns are used to show that someone did something alone or to himself.

EXAMPLES OF REFLEXIVE OR INTENSIVE PRONOUNS

myself
yourself
himself
herself
itself
ourselves
yourselves
themselves

Examples:

1. Jay built the house <u>himself</u>.
   Jay built the house without any help.
2. Nasser hit <u>himself</u> with the car door.
   Nasser performed the action and received it.

A reflexive pronoun must refer to another noun or pronoun in the sentence. When you use reflexive pronouns, think of a mirror. To see <u>yourself</u> in the mirror, <u>you</u> must stand in front.

Examples:

Right: <u>Katy</u> traveled the world by <u>herself</u>.
   <u>Katy</u> <u>herself</u> traveled the world.
Wrong: <u>Herself</u> traveled the world.
Right: Lee sent letters to Kim and <u>me</u>.
Wrong: Lee sent letters to Kim and <u>myself</u>.
Right: The finalists were Tisha, Li, and <u>I</u>.
Wrong: The finalists were Tisha, Li, and <u>myself</u>. Remember, *were* is a linking verb. The pronoun should be in the subjective case.
Right: <u>I</u> bumped <u>myself</u> on the head.
Wrong: <u>I</u> bumped <u>me</u> on the head.

⇨ *Note:* A reflexive pronoun must refer to another noun or pronoun in the sentence. To see <u>yourself</u> in the mirror, <u>you</u> must stand in front.

EXERCISE 8:   Decide whether or not the underlined pronoun is used correctly. If the pronoun is correct, write a *C* in the space provided. If the pronoun is incorrect, write the correct pronoun in the space.

SAMPLE: Abdul sent cards to Jake and <u>myself</u>. <u>me</u>

1. Mom planned the whole trip <u>herself</u>. _____

2. <u>Itself</u> fell two stories to the ground below. _____

3. We surprised <u>ourselves</u> when we found a shortcut home. _____

4. You <u>yourself</u> need to get the job done. _____

5. The waiter spilled hot coffee on Megan, Mike, and <u>myself</u>. _____

6. They helped <u>themselves</u> raise money for the trip. _____

7. You cut <u>you</u> with the knife. _____

8. <u>Himself</u> sold the old car and bought a new one. _____

9. She <u>herself</u> paid for night school. _____

10. Rachel taught <u>herself</u> to read. _____

Answers are on pages 292, 293.

PRONOUNS IN COMPARISON

Sometimes we do not actually write all of the verbs in a sentence. For example, when we compare two people or things using *than* or *as*, the second verb often is left out of the sentence.

Examples:

1. Lee is <u>as</u> tall as I (am).
2. These children have better reading skills <u>than</u> they (do).

As you can see, the subject of the second verb is in the subjective case—even though the verb is implied. When you see a comparison with *than* or *as*, write in the second verb. Then choose the correct pronoun.

Examples:

1. Greg is faster than (he, him).
   Greg is faster than <u>he</u> is.
2. Your father is as upset as (me, I).
   Your father is as upset as <u>I</u> am.

EXERCISE 9: For each of the following sentences, underline the correct pronoun.

1. Mr. Pyo is as careful with the car as (I, me).

2. Sasha bikes more often than (her, she).

3. Shane skates as well as (he, him).

4. If we work hard, we can play as well as (them, they).

5. Beth and Phil are good athletes, but they are not better than (us, we).

6. Kyle runs less often than (him, he).

7. When they finish their dance lessons, they will be as good as (we, us).

8. The drummer in the band isn't any better than (me, I).

9. As an artist, Pam is much more creative than (her, she).

10. The umpire had a better view of the play than (him, he).

Answers are on page 293.

WE OR US WITH A NOUN

Sometimes the pronouns *we* and *us* appear right before a noun.

Examples:

1. The fans cheer hard for <u>us</u> athletes.
2. <u>We</u> <u>students</u> need to focus on our work.
3. They always need <u>us</u> workers.

The choice between *we* and *us* depends on the pronoun's job in the sentence. If it works like a subject, use *we.* If it works like an object, use *us.* When in doubt, simply cross out the noun and focus on the pronoun.

Examples:

1. The fans cheer hard for <u>us</u> ~~athletes~~.
2. We ~~students~~ need to focus on our work.

EXERCISE 10: For each of the following sentences, underline the correct pronoun.

1. (We, Us) children look forward to the holidays.

2. The owner gave a higher wage to (we, us) waiters.

3. How will (we, us) reporters know when you will take action?

4. (We, Us) parents must make sure that our children stay away from drugs.

5. Art and music classes are important for (we, us) students.

6. Are (we, us) workers in danger of losing our jobs?

7. (We, Us) voters must choose the best leaders for our country.

8. This memo is about (we, us) managers.

9. The road crew helped (we, us) commuters get to work in the snow.

10. When will he give (we, us) drivers a break?

Answers are on page 293.

✍ Remember these <u>facts about special situations</u>:

- A reflexive pronoun must refer to another noun or pronoun in the sentence.
- When you see a comparison with *than* or *as*, write in the second verb. Then choose the correct pronoun.
- If *we* or *us* appears right before a noun, cross out the noun and focus on the pronoun. If the pronoun works as a subject, use *we.* If it works as an object, use *us.*

Pronoun Agreement

Pronouns and their related nouns must send the same message. They must agree in number and gender.

Examples:

1. <u>Carl</u> brought <u>his</u> lunch.
   Carl and *his* show that the sentence is about one man.
2. <u>The students</u> are proud of <u>their</u> art.
   The students and *their* shows that the sentence is about more than one person.

Generally pronoun agreement is easy, but some situations need more thought.

PRONOUN AGREEMENT

1. Pronouns must agree in number and gender.
2. When *and* joins the related nouns, the pronoun is plural.
3. When *or* joins the related nouns, the pronoun agrees with the noun closest to the verb.
4. *One* shows that the sentence is about any individual.
5. Use the masculine form of pronouns when the related noun is masculine or feminine.

Examples:

1. <u>Miguel and Ria</u> planned <u>their</u> vacation.
   Miguel and Ria and *their* show that the sentence is about two people.
2. Either <u>the car or the trucks</u> blew <u>their</u> tires on the highway.
   Their agrees with the noun that is closest to the verb.
3. <u>One</u> must look both ways before <u>one</u> crosses the street.
   Many writers confuse *one* with *you.*
4. <u>Each</u> of the drivers maintains <u>his</u> own rig.
   His refers to *each.* (See indefinite pronouns on pages 82–84.)
5. <u>Some</u> of the women were upset about <u>their</u> wages.
   Their refers to *some* which is plural in this sentence. (See indefinite pronouns on page 82–84.)

EXERCISE 11: For each of the following sentences, underline the correct pronoun.

1. Juan or Carlos sends money to (his, their) family in Puerto Rico.

2. If one eats well, (one, you) will live a healthy life.

3. Few people think that (his, their) bad habits are easy to break.

4. Kerry and Katherine played well with (her, their) toys.

5. Many people try to save (his, their) money, but saving is hard work.

6. None of the pilots thought that (his, their) planes would go down.

7. Everyone wants (his, their) children to live a good life.

8. Each driver parks (his, their) car in the shade on hot days.

9. Nobody thinks (his, their) house will be robbed.

10. Several birds washed (his, their) feathers in the bath by my window.

Answers are on page 293.

✍ Remember pronouns must agree in number and gender with their related nouns.

RULES FOR PRONOUNS:

1. Think of each case as a family of pronouns. The subjective, objective, and possessive cases are simply groups of pronouns with similar jobs.
2. The subjective case is used for a subject, a subject complement, and an appositive that refers to a subject.
3. The objective case is used for an object of the verb, an object of the preposition, and an appositive that refers to an object.
4. Possessive pronouns show ownership of nouns and substitute for nouns. They also work with *-ing* verbs that act as nouns. (<u>Her</u> book. The book is <u>hers</u>. <u>Her</u> sleeping is a problem.)
5. Possessive pronouns never have apostrophes.
6. A reflexive pronoun must refer to another noun or pronoun in the sentence.
7. *Who* is part of the subjective case, and *whom* is part of the objective case.
8. *Who* and *he* have the same jobs. Likewise, *whom* and *him* have the same jobs.
9. Use *who* or *whoever* for the subject of a clause. Use *whom* or *whomever* for the object of a clause.
10. Pronouns and their related nouns must send the same message; they must agree in number and gender.

In this chapter you have learned:

☐ How to use the subjective case (nominative case) (pages 87–89)
☐ How to use the objective case (pages 89–91)
☐ How to use the possessive case (pages 91, 92)
☐ How to use *who* and *whom* (pages 92–94)
☐ How to use reflexive or intensive pronouns (pages 94, 95)
☐ How to use pronouns in comparison (pages 95, 96)
☐ How to make pronouns agree (pages 97, 98)

Review sections that are difficult for you.

Chapter Review

EXERCISE 1: Read each of the following sentences. If a pronoun is used incorrectly, circle it and write the correct pronoun in the space provided. If the sentence is correct, write no error. No sentence has more than one error.

SAMPLE: They gave free tickets to Rose and (I.) __me__

1. Who sent the e-mail to Jim and her? _____

2. Us coal miners need to earn higher wages. _____

3. When the phone rang, I thought it might be him. _____

4. Most blood donors give their blood to whoever needs it. _____

5. Two people, Mrs. Kim and her, welcomed us into their homes. _____

6. His running away from home was a sign that he needed help. _____

7. This judge is more strict than her. _____

8. Whom did we meet before we ate? _____

9. He said it was his bike, but I thought it was her's. _____

10. Drug use is rising among us teenagers. _____

11. He does not want to work as hard as her. _____

12. The medic tried to help whoever was hurt. _____

13. I tried to improve him singing, but he has a bad voice. _____

14. We women give our hearts to whomever we choose. _____

15. We must keep this secret between you and I. _____

16. We thanked Greg and him for their hard work. _____

17. Everyone wants their children to be happy. _____

18. The driver who ran his car into the wall was not hurt. _____

19. Dr. Lee loves to give advice to two people, you and I. _____

20. Some of the workers will get their overtime before long. _____

21. One must be ready for children before one becomes a parent. _____

22. Rosa wrote a note to her friend about you and me. _____

23. Coach Ngyun benched he and me because we missed practice. _____

24. Himself gave a raise to the wait staff. _____

25. Whomever gives them money will help stop heart disease. _____

Answers are on pages 293, 294.

EXERCISE 2: The following paragraph has seven incorrect pronouns. Cross out the wrong pronouns and write the correct ones in the margin.

Everybody who comes to America brings their hopes for a better life. For example, Juan and Rose always believed in the American dream. When they arrived, Juan and Rose promised to work hard for whomever gave them a job. Juan's brothers gave Rose and he money to get started, but it was not enough. Juan often thought that no person ever worked as hard as him. In time, life slowly improved for Rose and him. Them working for the future paid off. Before too long, they earned fair wages and provided a good home for their children. Juan told whoever he met about his new life. He was proud of himself. Us native-born Americans can learn a lot from these new arrivals.

Answers are on page 294.

SENTENCES

6

Phrases

In this chapter you will learn:

☐ What phrases are (page 103)

☐ How phrases work (page 103)

☐ How to use a phrase that works as a noun (pages 103, 104)

☐ How to use a phrase that works as an adjective (pages 104, 105)

☐ How to use a phrase that works as an adverb (page 105)

You are the boss, and words are your workers. A phrase is a group of words that work together to perform one job. Unlike other word groups, a phrase does not need a subject and a predicate.

Phrases can help you write more interesting sentences. In Chapter 4 you learned about verb phrases and prepositional phrases. This chapter will focus on phrases that work as nouns, adjectives, and adverbs.

Jobs for Phrases

A phrase can act like a noun, verb, adjective, or adverb in a sentence. It also can work as any part of a sentence. Even though a phrase does not need a subject and a predicate, it may include subjects, objects, adjectives and adverbs.

Examples:

1. <u>Wearing stripes and plaids</u> is not in fashion.
   Wearing strips and plaids acts as a noun. It is the subject in the sentence. What is not in fashion?

2. Dave wanted <u>to read a new book</u>.
   To read a new book acts as a noun. It is the object of the verb in the sentence. Dave wanted what?

3. This is one way <u>to live a good life</u>!
   To live a good life acts as an adjective. It describes what type of *way*.

4. It was unfair <u>to judge me</u>.
   To judge me acts as an adverb. It answers the question *how* for *unfair*.

Phrases That Work as Nouns

Phrases often work as nouns. In a sentence, these phrases can be subjects, objects, or subject complements.

Examples:

1. <u>To quit my job</u> was a bad idea.
   To quit my job is the subject of the sentence. It answers the question *what was a bad idea.*

2. <u>Eating fast food</u> makes me sick.
   Eating fast food is the subject of the sentence. It answers the question *what makes me sick.*

3. Sue wanted <u>to leave home</u>.
   To leave home is the object of the verb in the sentence. It answers the question *Sue wanted what.*

4. We like <u>shopping for clothes</u>.
   Shopping for clothes is the object of the verb. It answers the question *we like what.*

5. I worry about <u>working late at night</u>.
   Working late at night is the object of the preposition *about.*

6. The problem is <u>his wasting money on gambling</u>.
His wasting money on gambling is the subject complement. It renames *the problem*.

EXERCISE 1: For each of the following sentences, underline the phrase that works as a noun.

1. Sitting on the wall is dangerous.

2. Brie wrote a book on eating finger foods.

3. Rose recalls singing on the stage.

4. The goal was to trick us.

5. To read often is important.

6. Jan asked him to hire good workers.

7. Painting a huge sign is a great idea.

8. Pam often thinks about biking in Maine.

9. Russ enjoys running in the rain.

10. Sailing into the wind is hard.

Answers are on pages 294, 295.

✍ Remember these facts about <u>phrases that work as nouns</u>:

• A phrase is a group of words that work together to perform one job.

• A phrase does not need a subject and a predicate. However, it may include subjects, objects, adjectives, and adverbs.

• Phrases that work as nouns can be subjects, objects, or subject complements.

Phrases That Work as Adjectives

Some phrases work as adjectives. These phrases tell the size, shape, number, owner, or appearance of a noun or pronoun. Phrases that work as adjectives answer the following questions: How many? How much? Which one? What type? Whose?

➡ **Reminder**

Adjectives modify nouns. **How many? How much? Which one? What type? Whose?**

Adverbs modify verbs, adjectives, or other adverbs: **How? Where? When? Why? How often? How much?**

PHRASES THAT WORK AS ADJECTIVES

<u>Surprised by the noise</u>, Kate jumped.

We saw him <u>running from the police</u>.

When an adjective phrase begins a sentence, it modifies the first noun after the comma.

Examples:

1. <u>Annoyed by his boss</u>, José quit his job.
Annoyed by his boss describes *José*. The phrase is set off by a comma.

2. My mom saw Kay <u>driving home from work</u>.
Driving home from work describes *Kay*.

3. <u>Running down the road</u>, he was almost hit by a car.
Running down the road describes *he*. Again, the phrase is set off by a comma.

4. <u>Using her hands</u>, Hoa told a great story.
Using her hands describes *Hoa*.

When an adjective phrase begins a sentence, it is set off by a comma. The phrase always modifies the noun that is right after the comma.

EXERCISE 2: For each of the following sentences, underline the phrase that works as an adjective.

1. Angered by the vote, he lashed out at the school board.

2. Jack, thrilled with the news, ran to see his mom.

3. Sailing into the storm, the small boat capsized.

4. Nancy followed Russ driving into town.

5. The judge did not seem affected by his remarks.

6. Hunting in the woods, Pete lost track of time.

7. Joe, biking fast, passed his friends in the car.

8. Excited about Santa, Katherine could not eat breakfast.

9. We watched the clouds drifting in the sky.

10. The tree, decorated with lights, shined brightly in the night.

Answers are on page 295.

👉 Remember these <u>facts about phrases that work as adjectives</u>:

- A phrase is a group of words that work together to perform one job.

- A phrase does not need a subject and a predicate. However, it may include subjects, objects, adjectives, and adverbs.

- Phrases that work as adjectives tell the size, shape, number, owner, or appearance of a noun or pronoun.

- Phrases that work as adjectives answer the following questions about nouns or pronouns: How many? How much? Which one? What type? Whose?

- When an adjective phrase begins a sentence, it is set off by a comma. The phrase always modifies the noun that is right after the comma.

Phrases That Work as Adverbs

Sometimes phrases work as adverbs. They modify verbs, adjectives, and other adverbs in the sentence and answer the following questions: How? Where? When? Why? How often? How much?

Examples:

1. This truck is built <u>to drive in the snow</u>.
   To drive in the snow describes how the truck is built.

2. It is hard <u>to find good child care</u>.
   To find good child care acts like an adverb. It answers the question *how* for the adjective *hard*.

EXERCISE 3: For each of the following sentences, underline the phrases that work as adjectives.

1. We are anxious to finish the project.

2. It is unwise to answer that question.

3. Zach is scared to be home alone at night.

4. For adults, it is hard to balance work and family.

5. Athletes train daily to maintain their bodies.

Answers are on page 295.

👉 Remember these <u>facts about phrases that work as adverbs</u>:

- A phrase is a group of words that work together to perform one job.

- A phrase does not need a subject and a predicate. However, it may include subjects, objects, adjectives, and adverbs.

- Phrases that work as adverbs modify verbs, adjectives, and other adverbs.

- Phrases that work as adverbs answer the following questions: How? Where? When? Why? How often? How much?

In this chapter you have learned:

☐ What phrases are (page 103)

☐ How phrases work (page 103)

☐ How to use a phrase that works as a noun (pages 103, 104)

☐ How to use a phrase that works as an adjective (pages 104, 105)

□ How to use a phrase that works as an adverb (page 105)

Review sections that are difficult for you.

Chapter Review

EXERCISE 1: Underline the phrases in each of the following sentences. In the space provided, write whether the whole phrase is a noun, adjective, or adverb. Each sentence only has one phrase.

SAMPLE: <u>Flying into a storm</u>, the pilot was calm. <u>adjective</u>

1. Running errands keeps me busy. _____

2. Nga needs to write thank-you notes for the gifts. _____

3. I wanted him to leave the house before six o'clock. _____

4. Hurried by my friend, I did not enjoy the tour. _____

5. Sean enjoys playing ball with his friends. _____

6. Juan wants her to work more hours. _____

7. Waiting on tables is hard work. _____

8. Greg ran to the door to see his mom. _____

9. I wanted her to wash her hands before dinner. _____

10. Injured from the crash, Carlos could not move his right arm. _____

11. We saw a deer standing by the side of the road. _____

12. This car was designed to run on solar power. _____

13. The officer caught him running a red light. _____

14. The book forced me to think about my faults. _____

15. Running after the bus, he tripped and fell. _____

16. Skating on the pond was fun. _____

17. To travel abroad is just a dream for most people. _____

18. Educated by the warnings, Jill put her infant in the center of the back seat. _____

19. We almost left Grandma gathering flowers on the side of the road. _____

20. Leaving our homeland was very hard. _____

21. I thanked my mentor for helping me succeed. _____

22. A thief, armed with a gun, robbed the corner store. _____

23. Trained in CPR, Fred saves lives. _____

24. We want the sitter to watch the baby carefully. _____

25. Our boss wants her to keep costs down. _____

Answers are on pages 295, 296.

Clauses

In this chapter you will learn:

☐ What clauses are (page 107)

☐ The difference between independent and dependent clauses (pages 107, 108)

☐ How to use noun clauses (pages 108, 109)

☐ How to use adjective clauses (pages 109–111)

☐ How to use adverb clauses (pages 111, 112)

☐ When to use *who*, *which*, and *that* (pages 112, 113)

A clause is like a team of words. Each clause must have a subject and a verb, but it also may include objects, adjectives, and adverbs. The words on the team work together to send a message. Some clauses send complete messages on their own, while others need help to get the message to the reader. This chapter will teach you how to use clauses in sentences.

Independent and Dependent Clauses

Independent clauses can express a complete thought without any help. An independent clause could work as a sentence.

Examples:

The underlined words form independent clauses.

1. <u>Our boss announced the raise</u>, and <u>everyone cheered</u>.
2. Before Ruth opened the gift, <u>she read the card</u>.

3. <u>I ran to catch the train</u> when I heard the whistle.

A dependent clause has a subject and a predicate, but it does not express a complete thought. In order to send a message to the reader, it needs help from the other words in the sentence.

Examples:

The underlined words form dependent clauses.

1. <u>Whoever stole the book</u> should return it to the store.
2. <u>Whenever I study hard</u>, I do well on my tests.
3. Joe ate the pie <u>that I baked yesterday</u>.

 Note:

Independent Clauses express a complete thought and can work alone as sentences.

Dependent Clauses do not express a complete thought. They work as nouns, adjectives, and adverbs in a sentence.

Without help from other words, dependent clauses are meaningless. The reader needs more information to understand the message.

EXERCISE 1: Decide if the underlined words are independent or dependent clauses. Underline the correct answer.

1. After Brie spilled the milk, <u>I cleaned up the mess</u>. Independent/Dependent

2. <u>As long as I pay my bills on time</u>, the company should provide service. Independent/Dependent

3. Tougher laws went into effect, and <u>drunk driving arrests increased</u>. Independent/Dependent

4. Voters are tired of the tricks <u>that our leaders use</u>. Independent/Dependent

5. <u>No one cares</u> that the trains are full of spray paint. Independent/Dependent

6. Before Jong buys a car, <u>he makes sure that it will last a long time</u>. Independent/Dependent

7. Kim will have to save her money <u>until she pays off all of the loans</u>. Independent/Dependent

8. Cece prepared the food, and <u>Rich cleaned the house</u>. Independent/Dependent

9. The girl <u>who scored the last goal</u> is the best player on the team. Independent/Dependent

10. The school board knows <u>which parents want all-day kindergarten</u>. Independent/Dependent

Answers are on pages 296, 297.

☞ Remember these <u>facts about independent and dependent clauses</u>:

- A clause is simply a group of words with a subject and a predicate. The words in a clause work together to perform one job.
- Independent clauses can express a complete thought without any help.
- Dependent clauses need help from the other words in the sentence to express a complete thought.

Dependent Clauses

There are three types of dependent clauses: noun clauses, adjective clauses, and adverb clauses. In each case the clause, which has a subject and a predicate, acts like a single word.

NOUN CLAUSES

A noun clause is simply a team of words that acts like a noun. Thus, nouns, pronouns, and noun clauses have the same jobs in a sentence.

Examples:

1. <u>John</u> will win the game. <u>Whoever scores the most points</u> will win the game.
   John and *whoever scores the most points* are subjects. Who or what will win?
2. Tricia bought <u>a doll</u> for Kerry. Tricia bought <u>whatever was on sale</u> for Kerry.
   A doll and *whatever was on sale* are direct objects. Tricia bought whom or what?
3. We sent <u>Joseph</u> a gift. We sent <u>whoever was on the list</u> a gift.
   Joseph and *whoever was on the list* are indirect objects. We sent a gift to whom or what?
4. Biking is <u>exercise</u>. Biking is <u>what Jack enjoys</u>.
   Exercise and *what Jack enjoys* are subject complements.
5. My mom is upset about <u>my grades</u>. My mom is upset about <u>what happened today</u>.
   My grades and *what happened today* are objects of the preposition *about*. Mom is upset about whom or what?
6. My goal, <u>college</u>, is always on my mind. My goal, <u>that I go to college</u>, is always on my mind.
   College and *that I go to college* are appositives.

The whole clause works like one word and has one job in the sentence.

Certain words usually signal noun clauses. (See the list.) A noun clause includes the signal word, subject, verb, and objects or modifiers—if there are any. A noun clause works like one word. First, find the signal word, subject, and verb. Then, search for objects and modifiers.

SIGNAL WORDS FOR NOUN CLAUSES

who
which
that
whose
what
whom
whichever
whomever
whoever
whatever

Noun clauses usually begin with one of these signal words.

Examples:

CLAUSE = SIGNAL WORD + SUBJECT + VERB + OBJECTS + MODIFIERS

1. No one knew <u>that she was a famous writer</u>.
   That is the signal word, *she* is the subject, and *was* is the verb of the clause. *Famous* modifies *writer*.
2. <u>Whoever sold you this car</u> lied about its safety.
   Whoever is the signal word and the subject of the clause. *Sold* is the verb in the clause. *You* and *car* are objects of the verb in the clause.
3. I will do <u>whatever is best for my family</u>.
   Whatever is the signal word and the subject of the clause. *Is* is the verb in the clause, and *best* is a subject complement. *For my family* is a prepositional phrase that works as an adverb and describes *best*.

EXERCISE 2: Underline the noun clauses in the following sentences.

1. We discussed what happened in the store.
2. Nga is who will win the race today.

3. They will give the prize to whoever walks through the door.
4. We must decide which person is guilty.
5. The judge did not know whose story was true.
6. What the customer wanted was not on the menu.
7. Carlos will give the job to whomever his boss wants.
8. Jim knew that the house needed some repairs.
9. I will send whoever feels lonely a card.
10. Whoever needs food or shelter can get help from the church.

Answers are on page 297.

 Remember these <u>facts about noun clauses</u>:

- A noun clause is simply a team of words that acts like a noun.
- Certain words usually signal noun clauses: who, which, that, whose, what, whom, whichever, whomever, whoever, and whatever.
- A noun clause includes not only the signal word, subject and verb, but also objects or modifiers—if there are any.

ADJECTIVE CLAUSES

An adjective clause is simply a team of words that acts like an adjective. Thus, adjective clauses answer the following questions about nouns: How many? How much? Which one? What type? Whose? The whole clause works like one word.

> *Note:*
>
> If the clause works like a noun, it's a noun clause. Likewise, if the clause works like an adjective, it's an adjective clause.

Examples:

1. The <u>stomach</u> flu makes many people sick. The flu, <u>which is caused by a virus</u>, makes many people sick.
   Stomach and *which is caused by a virus* describe *flu*. They answer the question *what type*.
2. The <u>brave</u> man deserves an award. The man <u>who saved Khan's life</u> deserves an award.
   Brave and *who saved Khan's life* describe *man*. They answer the question *which one*.
3. <u>Lee's</u> drugstore is going out of business. The drugstore <u>that Lee owns</u> is going out of business.
   Lee's and *that Lee owns* describe *drugstore*. They answer the question *whose*.
4. Our boss fired the <u>corrupt</u> workers. Our boss fired the workers <u>whom he did not trust</u>.
   Corrupt and *whom he did not trust* describe *workers*. They answer the question *which ones*.

Certain words usually signal adjective clauses (see the box). Adjective clauses work like one word. First, find the signal word, subject, and verb. Then look for objects and modifiers. Adjective clauses should be next to the words that they describe.

SIGNAL WORDS FOR ADJECTIVE CLAUSES

who
whose
whom
which
that

Adjective clauses usually begin with one of these words.

Examples:

CLAUSE = SIGNAL WORD + SUBJECT + VERB + OBJECTS + MODIFIERS

1. The flu, <u>which is caused by a virus</u>, makes many people sick.
   Which is the signal word and the subject of the clause. *Is caused* is the verb of the clause. *By a virus* is a prepositional phrase that works like an adverb.
2. The man <u>who saved Khan's life</u> deserves an award.
   Who is the signal word and the subject of the clause. *Saved* is the verb in the clause, and *Khan's life* is the object of the verb in the clause.
3. The drugstore <u>that Lee owns</u> is going out of business.
   That is the signal word. *Lee* is the subject of the clause, and *owns* is the verb in the clause.
4. Our boss fired the workers <u>whom he did not trust</u>.
   Whom is the signal word and the object of the verb in the clause. *He* is the subject of the clause, and *did trust* is the verb in the clause. *Not* is an adverb.

EXERCISE 3: For each of the following sentences, underline the adjective clause.

1. The victim whose face is etched in my mind survived.

2. The team wants to build a new stadium that will hold more fans.

3. The person who finds a cure for AIDS will be a hero to some people.

4. My parents bought the dog that I saw in the pet store.

5. The Speaker of the House should be a person whose record is spotless.

6. Tom wants to hire the man whom he met on the plane.

7. The drivers who work overtime earn a lot of money.

8. Lisa will choose a day-care center, which will care for all three children.

9. She will charge the person whose hand went through the glass.

10. We will stop by the food store, which will have meat for dinner.

Answers are on page 297.

 Remember these <u>facts about adjective clauses</u>:

- An adjective clause is simply a team of words that acts like an adjective.
- Certain words usually signal adjective clauses: who, whose, whom, which, and that.
- An adjective clause includes not only the signal word, subject, and verb, but also objects and modifiers—if there are any.

An adjective clause should be next to the word it describes.

ADVERB CLAUSES

An adverb clause is simply a team of words that works like an adverb. Thus, adverb clauses answer the following questions about verbs, adjectives, or adverbs: How? Where? When? Why? How often? How much? The whole clause works like one word.

Examples:

1. Russell broke the window <u>yesterday</u>. Russell broke the window <u>when he banged the door</u>.
   Yesterday and *when he banged the door* tell *when* Russell broke the window.
2. Katherine plays with Brie <u>nicely</u>. Katherine plays with Brie <u>as if they were sisters</u>.
   Nicely and *as if they were sisters* tell *how* Katherine plays with Brie.

3. Ruth <u>often</u> cares for her niece. Ruth cares for her niece <u>whenever her sister needs help</u>.
   Often and *whenever her sister needs help* tell *how often* Ruth cares for her niece.
4. Russ <u>almost</u> paid the bank. Russ paid the bank <u>as much as he could afford</u>.
   Almost and *as much as he could afford* tell *how much* Russ paid the bank.

Certain words usually signal adverb clauses. An adverb clause works like one word. First find the signal word, subject, and verb. Then, look for objects and modifiers.

SIGNAL WORDS FOR ADVERB CLAUSES

after
although
as
as though
as long as
as much as
as soon as
as if
because
before
even though
if
in order that
now that
once
rather than
since
provided that
so that
than
though
unless
until
when
whenever
where
whereas
wherever
while

Adverb clauses usually will begin with one of these words.

Examples:

CLAUSE = SIGNAL WORD + SUBJECT + VERB + OBJECTS + MODIFIERS

1. Russell broke the window <u>when he banged the door</u>.
   When is the signal word. *He* is the subject in the clause, and *banged* is the verb in the clause. *The door* is the object of the verb in the clause.

2. Katherine plays with Brie <u>as if they were sisters</u>.
   As if signals an adverb clause. *They* is the subject in the clause, and *were* is the verb in the clause. *Sisters* is a subject complement in the clause.

3. Ruth cares for her niece <u>whenever her sister needs help</u>.
   Whenever is the signal word. *Her sister* is the subject in the clause, and *needs* is the verb in the clause. *Help* is the object of the verb in the clause.

4. Russ paid the bank <u>as much as he could afford</u>.
   As much as signals an adverb clause. *He* is the subject in the clause, and *could afford* is the verb in the clause.

EXERCISE 4: Underline the adverb clauses in the following sentences.

1. After I paid off all my debts, I felt a sense of relief.

2. We need to call the landlord before the cold weather comes.

3. Some schools offer aid provided that the students earn good grades.

4. As long as Rose works two jobs, Juan will have to do more house-work.

5. Salma will plant her garden wherever the soil and sunlight are good.

6. Nasser will go to work as soon as he completes high school.

7. Look both ways before you cross the street.

8. Even though Kate is smart, she still needs to work hard.

9. If I don't pass this test, I will not get my driver's license.

10. We have plenty of food and drinks unless more people come.

Answers are on pages 297, 298.

✍ Remember these <u>facts about adverb clauses</u>:

- An adverb clause is simply a clause that works as an adverb.
- Certain words signal adverb clauses (see page 111).
- Adverb clauses include not only the signal word, subject, and verb, but also objects and modifiers—if there are any.

WHO, WHICH, AND THAT

Who, which, and *that* have specific jobs. Use *who, whom,* or *whose* when you write about a person. Likewise, use *which* and *that* when you write about things or animals.

WHO, WHICH, AND THAT	
Signal Words:	**Job:**
Who, Whom, Whose	People
Which	Things and animals (nonrestrictive clauses)
That	Things and animals (restrictive clauses)

The man <u>who</u> sold me the house.
The horse <u>that</u> won the race.
My car, <u>which</u> I drive to work, needs new tires.

Examples:

1. Lee, <u>who</u> earned a big raise, has worked here for years.
2. The deer <u>that</u> eat my flowers come from the park.

3. Nick's bike, <u>which</u> is falling apart, should be fixed.

RESTRICTIVE AND NONRESTRICTIVE CLAUSES

Some clauses have more important jobs than others. For example, some adjective clauses simply give more information while other adjective clauses help identify the noun. A clause that helps to identify a noun is called a restrictive clause.

Examples:

RESTRICTIVE CLAUSES
1. The doctor <u>who performed my surgery</u> was great.
There are many doctors. *Who performed my surgery* restricts the noun and tells which doctor was great.
2. The light <u>that burned out</u> needs to be replaced.
There are many lights. *That burned out* restricts the noun and tells which light needs to be replaced.

NONRESTRICTIVE CLAUSES
3. My house, <u>which I just painted</u>, is in great shape.
The fact that the house was painted is not important. The reader knows which house it is, *my house.*

Restrictive clauses do not have commas. The clause is so important that it cannot be separated from the noun. When you have a restrictive clause for an animal or a thing, use *that* as the signal word.

 Note:

Restrictive clauses give key information that cannot be separated from the noun. Do **not** use **commas** for restrictive clauses. Use **that** as the signal word.

EXERCISE 5: Underline the correct signal word for the following sentences.

1. The lawyer (who, which) took my case is an old friend.

2. The geese (who, that) live in the park damage the grass.

3. Doug's barn, (which, that) needs repair, is partly on my land.

4. Lynne, (who, which) is my parents' friend, lives in New York.

5. Khan wants to find a job (which, that) will pay him more money.

6. Ahmed needs a friend (that, whom) he can trust.

7. Lung cancer, (that, which) kills many people, often can be prevented.

8. I told Dave a joke (which, that) he had not heard before.

9. Some soldiers (that, who) went to the Persian Gulf War are sick.

10. Joe wants to buy a dog (that, which) will be good with children.

Answers are on page 298.

MISSING THAT'S

When *that* is used as a signal word for clauses, it is sometimes left out of the sentence. If you keep in mind that a clause works like one word, you will find the whole clause.

Examples:

1. Jill said <u>(that) he is nice</u>.
Jill said what? *(That) he is nice* is a noun clause and the object of the verb.
2. I need the letter <u>(that) you sent me</u>.
(That) you sent me is an adjective clause that modifies *letter.*
3. Miguel left early <u>so (that) he would get to work on time</u>.
So (that) he would get to work on time is an adverb clause that tells *why* Miguel left early.

EXERCISE 6: Underline each clause in the following sentences.

1. We got a loan for a house we knew we could afford.

2. Ramla runs so she can lose a few extra pounds.

3. Our boss thinks her staff is working hard.

4. Jihye put a fence around the pool so no one will get hurt.

5. Kim insists we stay for lunch.

6. Congress passed a bill we knew would hurt the poor.

7. Ty thinks he will to go to college.

8. Shane searched for a snack he could eat quickly.

9. Tobacco causes diseases we don't know how to cure.

10. Greg bought a repellent so he can keep the deer out of the garden.

Answers are on page 298.

Remember these <u>facts about *who*, *which*, and *that*</u>:

- Use *who*, *whom*, or *whose* when you write about a person.
- Use *which* and *that* when you write about things or animals.
- Restrictive clauses help identify the noun, and they do not have commas.
- Use *that* for a restrictive clause that refers to an animal or thing.
- Sometimes when *that* is used as a signal word, it is left out of the sentence.

In this chapter you have learned:

- ☐ What clauses are (page 107)
- ☐ The difference between independent and dependent clauses (pages 107, 108)
- ☐ How to use noun clauses (pages 108, 109)
- ☐ How to use adjective clauses (pages 109–111)
- ☐ How to use adverb clauses (pages 111, 112)
- ☐ When to use *who*, *which*, and *that* (pages 112, 113)

Review sections that are difficult for you.

Chapter Review

EXERCISE 1: The following sentences have phrases and clauses that are underlined. Decide whether the word group works as a noun, adjective, or adverb. Write your answer in the space provided.

SAMPLE: Adverb <u>As soon as I finish this book</u>, I will go for a jog.

1. _____ <u>Working in the yard</u>, Nate cut his hands on some bushes.

2. _____ Food experts say <u>that we should eat five fruits and vegetables a day</u>.

3. _____ Blair will eat <u>whatever is on the menu</u>.

4. _____ The next president needs <u>to bring ethics to the White House</u>.

5. _____ You need to see your doctor <u>before you start exercising</u>.

6. _____ <u>To enter a marathon</u> takes courage.

7. _____ Thän wanted <u>to stay after school for extra help</u>.

8. _____ I will drive you to work <u>provided that you buy me coffee and a paper</u>.

9. _____ <u>Flying a kite</u> is fun.

10. _____ <u>If Ben does not learn to control his temper</u>, he will get himself in trouble.

11. _____ <u>His driving in the snow</u> upsets Jan.

12. _____ The social worker wanted <u>Anne to get a job in retail</u>.

13. _____ I understand <u>that you want to learn about cars</u>.

14. _____ A store owner caught the thief <u>running away from the scene</u>.

15. _____ <u>What José needs</u> is a nice long trip to a resort.

16. _____ Sal spent weekends with his dad <u>after his parents divorced</u>.

17. _____ <u>Racing to catch the train</u>, Paula locked her keys in the car.

18. _____ Kay was inspired by the women <u>whom she helped</u>.

19. _____ <u>As soon as there is a cure for the common cold</u>, we will stop sneezing.

20. _____ <u>Troubled by the flu</u>, Fran missed most of the play.

21. _____ Rita needs <u>to work harder</u>.

22. _____ The waiter <u>who spilled wine on my dress</u> said that he was sorry.

23. _____ The new store <u>that is on Elm Street</u> sells good clothes.

24. _____ I am worried about <u>driving to New York</u>.

25. _____ Please come see us <u>whenever you are in town</u>.

26. _____ <u>While we were at the bus stop</u>, a car jumped the curb.

27. _____ <u>Whoever wants to earn more money</u> can work over-time.

28. _____ When I was on the beach I could feel the sun <u>burning my skin</u>.

29. _____ Manuel wants <u>to be the best student in his class</u>.

30. _____ <u>Tired from the trip</u>, Al went straight to bed.

Answers are on pages 298, 299.

MECHANICS

8

End Marks and Commas

In this chapter you will learn:

☐ When to use periods, question marks, and exclamation points (pages 119–121)

☐ How to use commas with independent clauses and items in a series (pages 121, 122)

☐ How to use commas with adjectives (page 122)

☐ How to use commas with nonrestrictive words, phrases, and clauses (pages 122, 123)

☐ How to use commas with opening words, phrases, and clauses (pages 123, 124)

☐ How to use commas with quotation marks (pages 124, 125)

☐ How to use commas with interrupters (page 125)

☐ How to use commas with dates, addresses, and long numbers (page 126)

☐ How to use commas to prevent misreading (page 127)

Punctuation marks are like road signs. They tell the reader where to go and how to get there. If you want the reader to go in the right direction, you need to use the correct signs. Otherwise, the reader and your message will be lost. The next two chapters will teach you how to use punctuation marks correctly. As you read the chapters, keep in mind that each punctuation mark is used for specific reasons.

End Marks

All end marks appear at the end of the sentence.

Period
1. a statement
2. a polite command
3. an indirect question

Question mark
1. a direct question

Exclamation point
1. an emotional command
2. a statement that needs emphasis
3. emotional interjections (Wow!)

End marks are like stop signs. They end sentences and tell the reader to stop—for a moment. There are three different types of end marks: periods (.), question marks (?), and exclamation points (!).

PERIODS

Periods have three basic jobs; they end statements, polite commands, and indirect questions. A statement is a sentence that gives information. A polite command kindly tells someone what to do. An indirect question is a question that has been reworded or is not meant to be answered.

Examples:

1. We need to learn more about science.
   This statement gives information.
2. Please call me before noon.
   This polite command kindly asks someone to call.
3. The judge asked him why he was late for court.
   This indirect question rewords the judge's question.
4. Our teacher wondered who would finish the test first.
   This indirect question is not meant to be answered.

QUESTION MARKS

Question marks end sentences that ask questions. These sentences are called direct questions because they ask for something specific.

 Note:

Question marks and exclamation points work alone. They are not used with other end marks or commas.

Examples:

1. How does the government spend so much money?
   This question asks for specific information.
2. Whom should we hire to replace Kim?
   This question asks for a specific person.
3. Jake asked, "Who will be the new track coach?"
   This question is quoted directly.

EXCLAMATION POINTS

Exclamation points show emotion. Use an exclamation point after emotional commands, statements, and interjections (Wow!).

 Note:

An **interjection** is one word that bursts with emotion. It can begin a sentence or stand alone. Hey! No! Wow! Ouch!

Examples:

1. Ted shouted, "Watch out!"
   This command shows emotion.
2. This is a great game!
   This statement shows emotion.
3. Ouch! That hurt!
   Ouch! is an emotional interjection. *That hurt* is a statement that needs emphasis.

Keep in mind, exclamation points should be used rarely. In addition, they should not be used with other end marks or commas.

EXERCISE 1: Write the correct end mark in the space provided.

1. Change the oil in your car every three months or three thousand miles _____
2. When will you finish that book _____
3. Leave me alone _____
4. The plumber asked me how long the sink has been leaking _____
5. Hey _____ I am not done yet!
6. Pat wondered who watered her plants while she was gone _____
7. Please print your name _____
8. Look at me when I talk to you _____
9. What kind of cake do you want for the party _____
10. Many adults take classes at night _____

Answers are on page 299.

Remember these <u>facts about end marks</u>:

- End marks are punctuation marks that end sentences.
- Periods end statements, polite commands, and indirect questions.
- Question marks end sentences that ask direct questions.
- Exclamation points end emotional commands, statements, and interjections (Wow!).
- Exclamation points should not be used with other end marks or commas.

Commas

Commas are like speed bumps. When they are properly placed, the reader slows down at the right time. However, when they are misplaced, the reader becomes frustrated and the message is lost. Commas are used to separate words, phrases, and clauses. They are used for specific jobs that are listed in the following box.

THE MAIN USES OF COMMAS

1. separate independent clauses that are joined by coordinating conjunctions (and, but, so)
2. separate items in a series (three or more items)
3. set apart appositives, phrases, and clauses that are not necessary
4. set apart opening words, phrases, and clauses
5. separate adjectives that describe the same noun
6. separate a speaker from a quotation
7. punctuate dates, addresses, and numbers
8. prevent misreading

Use commas only for specific jobs.

INDEPENDENT CLAUSES AND ITEMS IN A SERIES

Commas are used before conjunctions to separate independent clauses. Commas also are used to separate items in a series. A series, which has three or more items, can include nouns, verbs, modifiers, and phrases.

Examples:

1. Beth wants to relax more, but she needs to work two jobs.
   The comma separates two independent clauses that are joined by a coordinating conjunction. It is placed before the conjunction.
2. She packed shorts, jeans, and a skirt for the trip.
   The comma separates nouns in a series.
3. I coughed, sneezed, and shivered all day.
   The comma separates verbs in a series.
4. My clothes are old, tattered, and boring.
   The comma separates modifiers in a series.
5. The dog ran under the fence, through the garden, and into the park.
   The comma separates phrases in a series.

▷ *Note:*

A comma is <u>not</u> placed after the last item in the series.

EXERCISE 2: Write commas where they are needed in the following sentences. Some sentences may not need commas.

1. Kim wants to travel with her family but they cannot afford to take a trip this year.

2. Meg bought clothes toys and food for the children at the shelter.

3. The sitter cares for four children during the day and goes to school at night.

4. She sang danced and acted like the star of the show.

5. The house was big well kept and costly.

6. I will work longer hours and Fred will help more at home.

7. Jong missed his train yet he did not call for a ride.

8. The gloves hats and scarves make a mess in the hall closet.

9. They played all day and laughed all night.

10. The trial will be delayed so both sides will have more time to gather evidence.

Answers are on pages 299, 300.

ADJECTIVES

Commas are used instead of *and* to separate adjectives that describe the same noun or pronoun. First, find which word is being described. Then, decide if the adjectives are equally important. If they are, insert a comma between them.

Examples:

1. Her thoughtful, caring friends helped her with her problems.
   Thoughtful and *caring* describe *friends*, and they are equally important. If you reversed the adjectives, the sentence would have the same meaning.
2. The soft, white, billowy clouds drifted in the sky.
   Soft, *white*, and *billowy* are adjectives that describe *clouds*. They are equally important. If you reversed the adjectives, the sentence would have the same meaning.
3. Ray's red sports car needs repairs.
   Ray's, *red* and *sports* are adjectives that describe *car*, but they are not equally important. If you reversed the adjectives, the sentence would not have the same meaning.

Commas are not used when numbers combine with adjectives.

Example:

The four rusty buckets are full of junk. *Four* and *rusty* are adjectives that describe buckets, but numbers do not follow the rule for adjectives.

EXERCISE 3: Place commas where they are needed in the following sentences. Some sentences will not need commas.

1. The clear blue sky did not have a cloud.

2. Three soup bowls need to be cleaned.

3. Thick black smoke from the fire filled the room.

4. Dr. Lee's shiny new dental chair scares many patients.

5. They searched the woods for five straight days.

6. The new brick building will be our town hall.

7. Fresh white paint will help the shabby old shelves.

8. The old bathroom sink is cracked.

9. It is hard to find good low-cost health care.

10. We filled six large bags with sand.

Answers are on page 300.

NONRESTRICTIVE WORDS, PHRASES, AND CLAUSES

Nonrestrictive words, phrases, and clauses are like extras; they add to the sentence, but they are not necessary. Without the word group, the sentence still makes sense. Nonrestrictive word groups are set apart with commas. (See more on nonrestrictive and restrictive clauses on page 113.)

Examples:

1. Sean, a struggling artist, needs money.
   The commas set apart the appositive, *a struggling artist*. The appositive is nonrestrictive, because it is not important. Without *a struggling*

artist, the reader still knows who needs money, and the sentence makes sense.

2. The band, tired from the concert, took a break.
Tired from the concert is a nonrestrictive phrase that describes *band*. Without *tired from the concert*, the sentence still makes sense.

3. Vera, who is a great athlete, plays many sports.
Who is a great athlete is a nonrestrictive clause that describes *Vera*. Without *who is a great athlete* the reader knows who plays many sports, and the sentence makes sense.

Restrictive words, phrases, and clauses do not have commas. They are so important that they cannot be separated from the noun.

Examples:

1. The philosopher Socrates taught by asking questions.
Socrates is an appositive that is restrictive. If *Socrates* were deleted, the reader would not know who taught by asking questions, and the sentence would not make sense.

2. The laws against drug use are being questioned.
Against drug use is a phrase that is restrictive. If the phrase were deleted, the reader would not know which laws are being questioned.

3. The books that we returned today were due last week.
That we returned today is a clause that is restrictive. If the clause were deleted, the reader would not know which books were due.

EXERCISE 4: Place commas where they are needed in the following sentences. Some sentences do not need commas.

1. Ty weary from the long trip drank coffee to wake himself.

2. The waiter who spilled soup down my back still got a tip.

3. The hiker cold and alone tried to find help.

4. Nate a lawyer has won some hard cases.

5. The artist Renoir painted many works.

6. Judge Car who is on my case is strict.

7. The judge who is on my case is strict.

8. The ratings that are used for TV shows are vague.

9. Jake tired of reading the same books went to the library to find something new.

10. *Cheers* a great show aired for many years.

Answers are on pages 300, 301.

OPENING WORDS, PHRASES, AND CLAUSES

Commas are used after opening words, phrases, and clauses. These word groups begin sentences, and they usually work as adjectives or adverbs. Interjections that are not emotional also are set apart by commas.

Examples:

1. Unfortunately, we need to train more workers.
The comma sets apart *unfortunately*, an opening word that works as an adverb.

2. Tired, Lee went straight to bed.
The commas set apart *tired*, an opening word that works as an adjective and describes Lee.

3. No, I do not want to go to the movies.
The comma sets apart *no*, an opening word that is an unemotional interjection.

4. Joe, will you get the phone for me?
The comma sets apart *Joe*, an opening word. *Joe* is a direct address because someone is speaking right to him.

5. Beaten by the wind, the old tree fell down.
   The comma sets apart *beaten by the wind*, an opening phrase that describes the tree.
6. To accept the award, Jan flew to Maine.
   The comma sets apart *to accept the award*, an opening phrase.
7. When we cut coupons, we save money.
   The comma sets apart *when we cut coupons*, an opening clause.
8. Before you fix the lights, turn off the power.
   The comma sets apart *before you fix the lights*, an opening clause.

EXERCISE 5: Place commas where they are needed in the following sentences. Some sentences may not need commas.

1. After the rain came the streams overflowed and the streets flooded.

2. Yes I will work a few extra hours.

3. Once the food arrives we can serve the children.

4. Bob leave the flashlight in the car.

5. Scared of the wind and noise Rick hid under the bed during the storm.

6. As soon as we get to the beach I will jump in the water.

7. Between the seat and the door of the car Rita found some loose change.

8. I checked the lights and turned down the heat before we left.

9. Juan did you learn to swim when you were a child?

10. For example some movies have good soundtracks.

Answers are on page 301.

QUOTATIONS

Commas are used to separate speakers from quotations. Commas are placed right after the "talking" word (said, whispered, shouted, announced, etc.) and inside the quotation marks.

Examples:

1. The boss said, "A few workers will be laid off."
   The comma is placed right after *said*.
2. "A few workers will be laid off," the boss said.
   The comma is placed inside the quotation mark.
3. "A few workers will be laid off," the boss said, "because the strike lasted so long."
   This quotation is divided into two parts. The commas are placed inside the quotation mark and after *said*.

Commas are not used when the speaker follows a quotation that ends with a exclamation point or question mark.

Examples:

1. "Look out!" the foreman called.
   Do not use a comma to set apart the speaker. Exclamation marks work alone.
2. "Why do I have to do the dishes?" her son moaned.
   Do not use a comma to set apart the speaker. Question marks work alone.

EXERCISE 6: Place commas where they are needed in the following sentences. Some sentences do not need commas.

1. He sang "We shall be free."

2. "It's just a job" Tom said "I need the money."

3. "Watch your language!" my mom scolded.

4. "Once we finish this project" he said "I will take a few days off."

5. "When can we go home?" Jane asked.

6. Ned shouted "We need to win this game!"

7. "When I was a boy" he declared "I had to walk to school in the snow."

8. "The ballot is stronger than the bullet" Abraham Lincoln said.

9. "Why will they fire so many work-ers?" Rose asked.

10. "Stay out of the water!" the lifeguard yelled.

Answers are on page 301.

INTERRUPTIONS

Sometimes the flow of the sentence is interrupted by a word or group of words. Direct addresses, words that connect ideas, and words that explain things often interrupt sentences. Commas separate these words from the rest of the sentence so that the reader will not get confused. If the interruption causes the reader to pause, use commas.

COMMON INTERRUPTERS

I believe
therefore
perhaps
I think
however
in fact
I hope
for example
also
of course
nonetheless
too
by the way
on the other hand

Examples:

1. Will you, Jen, buy milk on your way home from work?
   Jen is a direct address that interrupts the flow of the sentence.
2. We will, however, discuss this problem at a later date.
   However interrupts the sentence and tells the reader to pause.

3. The judge, in fact, delayed our case.
   In fact interrupts the sentence and connects ideas.
4. My main concern, besides paying too much, is finding the right car.
   Besides paying too much interrupts the sentence and provides explanation.

Keep in mind, commas are like speed bumps. In each case above, the commas tell the reader to pause so that the meaning of the sentence will be clear.

EXERCISE 7: Place commas where they are needed in the following sentences. Some sentences may not need commas.

1. The best sales I think are at the malls.

2. Are you sure Jeff that this car is safe?

3. Meat on the other hand should be refrigerated right away.

4. Singers who top the charts can make a lot of money.

5. Sue in fact works hard to save money.

6. You along with your doctor need to take care of your health.

7. Her wrist that had the cast is pale.

8. I hope Kay that we can hire more waiters.

9. The judge ruled of course that Dale should stand trial.

10. Surgeons besides making a lot of money earn respect.

Answers are on page 302.

DATES, ADDRESSES, AND LONG NUMBERS

Commas are used to punctuate dates and addresses. Note the rules in the box that follows.

PLACE A COMMA

1. between the date and the year.
2. after a day, date, and year that is used in a sentence.
3. between items in an address—except for the state and zip code.
4. at the end of an address that is used in a sentence.
5. between a city and state and after the state.
6. in long numbers after every three numbers counting from the right (1,000,000).

If a specific date is not given, do not use a comma.

Examples:

1. May 28, 1992
   A comma is placed between the date and the year.
2. On January 17, 1991, the air war against Iraq began.
   When a date is used in a sentence, an additional comma is placed after the year.
3. Monday, March 11, 1996, was the day my daughter was born.
   A comma is placed after the day, the date, and the year.
4. Send your comments to 55 Lake Drive, Portland, Maine 09845.
   A comma is placed between items in the address—except for the state and zip code.
5. Use Box 10, Red Bank, New Jersey, for all letters.
   A comma is placed between items and at the end of the address.

If a specific date is not given, do not use a comma.

Examples:

1. June 1990
   No comma is used.
2. Spring 1910
   No comma is used.

Commas are used to divide long numbers into groups of three. Place a comma after every three numbers counting from the right.

Examples:

1. A mile is 5,280 feet.
2. Many houses in this town cost over $200,000.

EXERCISE 8: Place commas where they are needed in the following sentences. Some sentences may not need commas.

1. On December 7 1941 the Japanese bombed Pearl Harbor.

2. We sent all of the cards to 10 King Street Wilton Maine 12543.

3. Many babies were born in September 1996, nine months after the big snow storm.

4. Carl spent over $40000 for that car.

5. We may have some bad luck on Friday May 13.

6. Please send our mail to Box 12 Rush New York 54693 after June 4 1997.

7. The moon is about 240000 miles from the earth.

8. I arrived in Glens Falls New York at three o'clock.

9. Sayre will have the book done by June 1997.

10. On Friday March 15 Ruth will have her birthday party.

Answers are on page 302.

PLACEMENT OF COMMAS TO PREVENT MISREADING

Commas force readers to pause so that they will understand a sentence.

Examples:

1. At seven people will start to arrive.
   At seven, people will start to arrive.
   Without the comma, the reader may think that the sentence is about seven people.
2. Soon after she bought the dress.
   Soon after, she bought the dress.
   Without the comma, the reader may wonder what happened soon after she bought the dress.

EXERCISE 9: Place commas in the following sentences to prevent misreading.

1. To Jen Laura was a great friend.

2. In baseball fans are a key part of the game.

3. For some dogs help cure loneliness.

4. Before nine guests had to leave.

5. Though sad Meg put a smile on her face for all to see.

Answers are on pages 302, 303.

Remember these <u>facts about commas</u>:

- Commas tell the reader to slow down.
- Commas separate words, phrases, and clauses. They should be used for specific jobs. (See the chart on page 121.)

In this chapter you have learned:

☐ How to use periods, question marks, and exclamation points (pages 119–121)

☐ How to use commas with independent clauses and items in a series (pages 121, 122)

☐ How to use commas with adjectives (page 122)

☐ How to use commas with nonrestrictive words, phrases, and clauses (pages 122, 123)

☐ How to use commas with opening words, phrases, and clauses (pages 123, 124)

☐ How to use commas with quotation marks (pages 124, 125)

☐ How to use commas with interrupters (page 125)

☐ How to use commas with dates, addresses, and long numbers (page 126)

☐ How to use commas to prevent misreading (page 127)

Review sections that are difficult for you.

Chapter Review

EXERCISE 1: Add end marks and commas where they are needed.

Looking for a job is hard but there are ways to get help Most people will change jobs many times during their life so it is important to learn job-search skills Where can you get these skills The public library has helpful books articles and computer programs. High schools and colleges have career counselors who aid students in the job market For a fee employment services will help workers find jobs in a particular field There even is information on-line So if resumes applications and interviews are in your future get the help you need Make this job search your last one

Answers are on page 303.

EXERCISE 2: Add end marks and commas where they are needed.

Every year children are injured by accidents that could have been prevented Even before a baby is brought home from the hospital parents should do a safety check What should parents inspect Cribs playpens and highchairs must meet federal safety guidelines Car seats which are crucial should fit securely in the back seat of the car Small objects medicines knives cleaning products and cords must be kept out of reach Bathtubs toilets and buckets should be off-limits; children in fact can drown in only a few inches of water If parents inspect their homes carefully they can prevent many accidents Safe homes save lives.

Answers are on pages 303, 304.

EXERCISE 3: Add end marks and commas where they are needed.

I went to a concert with some friends last night and we had a great time As we walked through the gate a man shouted "I have front row seats!" to my friend Sean We bought the tickets ordered some food and made ourselves comfortable After the first song Jack yelled "This band is awesome!" The lead singer looked down at us and mouthed, "What did you say" Jack was too embarrassed to repeat what he yelled so I did. Do you believe that they invited me up on stage "Just my luck" Jack said "I get their attention and you go up on stage" "Remember I got these seats" Sean remarked By the end of the concert there were no hard feelings. We had too much fun to hold grudges.

Answers are on page 304.

More Punctuation

In this chapter you will learn:

☐ How to use semicolons (pages 129–131)
☐ How to use colons (pages 131, 132)
☐ How to use apostrophes (pages 132–135)
☐ How to use quotation marks (pages 135–138)

Now that you know about end marks and commas, it's time to learn about more forms of punctuation. Keep in mind, punctuation marks are like road signs; each mark has specific jobs.

Semicolons (;)

Semicolons have two jobs. Semicolons join independent clauses, and they separate items in a series. Use a semicolon, instead of a coordinating conjunction, to join independent clauses that are closely related. Likewise, use a semicolon to join independent clauses that already contain commas or are particularly long.

THE MAIN USES OF THE SEMICOLON

1. joins independent clauses in a sentence
2. separates items in a series

INDEPENDENT CLAUSE, AND INDEPENDENT CLAUSE

OR

INDEPENDENT CLAUSE; INDEPENDENT CLAUSE

Examples:

1. Some people worship often; others do not.
   Both independent clauses are closely related. The semicolon is used instead of a comma and a conjunction. *Some people worship often, but others do not* also would make sense.
2. Hank Aaron, who played with the Braves, broke Babe Ruth's record for home runs; no one thought that record would be broken.
   The first clause has commas that could be confusing, so a semicolon is used to join the independent clauses.
3. We ordered more food, drinks, and supplies than last time; we still did not have enough.
   The first clause has commas that could be confusing, so a semicolon is used to join the independent clauses.

Generally, semicolons are not used with the conjunctions *and*, *but*, *for*, or *nor*. However, sometimes semicolons make sentences with conjunctions easier to read. If an independent clause is long or it has commas that could be confusing, use a semicolon with the conjunction.

Examples:

1. The home that we wanted to buy was sold over the weekend to a nice couple from Maine; but we will find another house.
   The first independent clause is long.

2. The river flooded our home, destroyed our crops, and killed our cows; but we will survive.

The first independent clause is long, and it has commas that could be confusing.

Conjunctive adverbs are like matchmakers; they form relationships between two independent clauses. Semicolons are placed before conjunctive adverbs, and commas are placed after them.

COMMON CONJUNCTIVE ADVERBS

anyway
besides
however
instead
likewise
meanwhile
nonetheless
now
still
then
thus

Examples:

INDEPENDENT CLAUSE;
CONJUNCTIVE ADVERB,
INDEPENDENT CLAUSE

1. We wanted to go to the beach; instead, we stayed home.
Instead forms a relationship between the two independent clauses.
2. For years people thought that smoking was safe; now, we know that it causes cancer.
Now forms a relationship between the two independent clauses.
3. When the doctor told Jay to lose weight, Jay fussed; however, the doctor was right.
However forms a relationship between the two independent clauses.

EXERCISE 1: Place semicolons and commas where they are needed in the following sentences. Some sentences may not need more punctuation.

1. Many people went home when the team started to lose the true fans stayed until the end.
2. Fakih saved enough money to buy a nice house now he can afford to live in a great town.
3. Ann took the children to the playground and pushed them on the swings.
4. Many women who have small children work full time others stay home.
5. When she was young, Heidi ran in road races to stay in shape but she preferred biking.
6. Iron pills can poison children therefore adults must store the pills safely.
7. The detective searched the crime scene, traced phone calls, and questioned suspects but no arrests have been made.
8. When the news called for snow, we were ready for a bad rush hour however the snow never came.
9. Garth sang for hours and the crowd cheered.
10. When we went on the boat, we wore lifejackets the water was rough, and we are not good swimmers.

Answers are on pages 304, 305.

Semicolons also are used to separate items in a series. Use a semicolon, instead of a comma, when the items are long or they have commas.

Examples:

1. We invited Megan, Brie's sitter; Jim and Alice, Megan's parents; and the Dimmicks to the party.
Brie's sitter describes *Megan*. *Megan's parents* describes *Jim and Alice*. Without the semicolons, the reader would think that they were all different people.

2. He was not sure whether he should live with his parents, which would save money; rent an apartment, which would give him more freedom; or buy a townhouse, which would make him feel mature.
The items in the series are long, and they have commas. The semicolons help the reader separate the items.

EXERCISE 2: Place semicolons and commas where they are needed. Some sentences may not need more punctuation.

1. During the strike, the union negotiated the contract organized the picket lines, which no one crossed began a boycott and helped strikers with financial problems.

2. On our trip to Washington, D.C., I saw the White House, which I had seen before the Capitol, where they never seem to do any work and the Supreme Court.

3. Parents today can choose to stop work and stay home with their children to work from home to work part time, which some people prefer or to work full time.

4. People who want freedom, refugees, and entrepreneurs come to the United States to improve their lives.

5. Before Jane got to work, she walked the dog gave medicine to her son, who has a bad cold and went to school to drop off her daughter, who forgot to do her homework.

Answers are on page 305.

Remember these <u>facts about semicolons</u>:

- Use a semicolon, instead of a coordinating conjunction, to join independent clauses that are closely related.

- Use a semicolon to separate items in a series that are long or have commas.

- Place semicolons before conjunctive adverbs and commas after them.

- For long independent clauses or independent clauses with confusing commas, use a semicolon with the conjunction.

Colons (:)

THE MAIN USES OF THE COLON

1. introduces a list or series
2. introduces an explanation, summary, or quotation
3. ends a greeting in a business letter (Dear Sir:)
4. separates the hour and minutes for time (8:30)

COLONS IN SENTENCES

A colon sends a signal. It tells the reader that a list, explanation, summary, or long quotation will follow. When a colon is used in a sentence, it is placed after an independent clause.

Examples:

1. We ordered the following supplies: cups, napkins, forks, spoons, and knives.
The colon signals a list.
2. Nate was mad: his car was towed, and he had no way to get home.
The colon signals an explanation. The words that follow the colon tell why Nate was mad.
3. Russ gave a great speech: clear, brief, and lively.
The colon signals a summary. *Clear*, *brief*, and *lively* summarize why the speech was great.
4. Muhammad Ali has his own view of boxing: "It's just a job. Grass grows, birds fly, waves pound the sand. I beat people up."
The colon signals a long quotation.

> **Hint:** *The following, as follows,* and *these* often are used with colons to signal a list.

The words that follow the colon may or may not form an independent clause. This is one way that a colon is different from a semicolon.

Colons are like other punctuation marks: if they are not placed properly, the message will be lost. Do **not** place a colon between a linking verb and complement, an action verb and object, or a preposition and object.

Examples:

1. **Right:** The best desserts are ice cream sundaes, cheesecakes, and apple pies.
   Wrong: The best desserts are: ice cream sundaes, cheesecakes, and apple pies.
2. **Right:** There are a few ways to save for retirement, such as a 401k, an IRA, and a pension plan.
   Wrong: There are a few ways to save for retirement, such as: a 401k, an IRA, and a pension plan.

BUSINESS LETTERS AND TIME

A colon ends the greeting in a business letter, and it divides the hour and minutes for time.

Examples:

1. Dear Sir:
   The colon ends the greeting.
2. 9:30 am
   The colon divides the hour and minutes.

EXERCISE 3: Place colons where they are needed in the following sentences. Some sentences may not need colons.

1. Please check the following things gas, oil, tires, and wiper fluid.

2. The weather was great sunny, cool, and pleasant.

3. The best sports for children are T-ball, soccer, and basketball.

4. Ray was thrilled he earned a huge bonus and got a raise.

5. The store will be closed on the following days May 7, 8, and 9.

6. Franklin D. Roosevelt's words have been quoted often "Let me assert my firm belief that the only thing we have to fear is fear itself."

7. Dear Dr. Kim

8. We need to take care of some problems in the house, such as dirt, leaks, and mice.

9. The rule is simple don't talk when I am talking.

10. In small towns across the United States, strong values still matter hard work, honesty, and family.

Answers are on pages 305, 306.

 Remember these <u>facts about colons</u>:

- A colon (:) sends a signal: it tells the reader that a list, explanation, summary, or long quotation will follow.
- Use a colon after an independent clause in a sentence.
- A colon ends the greeting in a business letter. It also divides the hour and minutes for time.

Apostrophe (')

THE MAIN USES OF THE APOSTROPHE

1. shows possession
2. forms contractions

Possession

The apostrophe (') has specific jobs. First, the apostrophe shows ownership or possession.

Examples:

1. The teacher read <u>Carl's</u> essay to the class.
   Carl owns the essay.

2. The <u>children's</u> toys are all over the house.
   The children own the toys.

3. <u>Everyone's</u> goal is to finish this job.
   Everyone possesses the goal.

Look at the box below to see how nouns are made possessive.

USING APOSTROPHES (') FOR POSSESSION			
Noun:	**Add:**	**Examples:**	**Sentences:**
Singular noun	's	Charles + 's boy + 's	<u>Charles's</u> book won an award. The <u>boy's</u> shoes were lost.
Plural noun that does not end in -s	's	children + 's	The <u>children's</u> eyes were wide open.
Indefinite pronoun that does not end in -s	's	everyone + 's	<u>Everyone's</u> dream is to succeed.
Plural noun that does end in -s	'	nurses + ' hours + '	The <u>nurses'</u> shifts were changed. Many <u>hours'</u> work was wasted.

Possessive pronouns (his, her, theirs, its, ours, yours) never have apostrophes.

EXERCISE 4: In the space provided, write the possessive form of the word that is in parentheses.

1. (Lori) plane will land in a few hours. _____

2. We do not want to leave (anyone) things behind. _____

3. Both (lawyers) legal pads were filled with notes during the trial. _____

4. I don't like her plan, so let's go with (his). _____

5. The (voters) minds were made up long before the election. _____

6. The notebook must be (hers). _____

7. Make sure that (James) car has enough gas. _____

8. Check (children) toys to be sure that they are safe. _____

9. Why did they need to take (ours)?

10. The (baby) cries filled the house. _____

11. (Everybody) needs are different. _____

12. I am not sure if this car is (theirs). _____

13. A (year) work has gone into this project. _____

14. It was hard to judge the (people) mood during the debate. _____

15. (Jen Stephens) job keeps her busy. _____

Answers are on page 306.

There are some special situations for apostrophes. Note the rules in the box below.

SPECIAL SITUATIONS FOR POSSESSION

Situation: Compound word or word groups
Rule: Add -'s to the last word
Examples: My sister-in-law's taste in clothes is great. This is somebody else's problem.
Situation: Individual ownership with two or more
Rule: Add 's to each individual
Example: Mike's and Jim's cars are fast. (Each person has his own car. Note that *cars* is plural.
Situation: Joint ownership with two or more
Rule: Add 's to the last word
Example: Mom and dad's house sits on a hill. (They share the same house. Note that *house* is singular.)

EXERCISE 5: In the space provided, write the possessive form of the words that are in parentheses.

1. (Gale and Myleen) trip to Greece was cut short by the bad weather. _____

2. I will have my (step-sister) room when she goes to college. _____

3. (Kristin and Pat) son works after school. _____

4. (Kay and Phil) writing skills have helped them get great jobs. _____

5. My (brother-in-law) job is in New York. _____

6. (Brian, Rachel, Deena, and David) day-care center is near where I work. _____

7. My (mother-in-law) advice is helpful. _____

8. (Greg and Rye) bad habits got them in trouble. _____

9. The judge did not accept (Erin and Doris) reasons. _____

10. Someone stole (Rose and Juan) car from the lot. _____

Answers are on page 306.

CONTRACTIONS

Apostrophes also are used to form contractions. The apostrophe shows that one or more letters have been left out of the word. Note the common contractions that are listed in the box.

Many people confuse contractions with personal pronouns (their, its, your, whose). Keep in mind, personal pronouns show ownership, and they never have apostrophes.

COMMON CONTRACTIONS

Full Words	Contraction
did not	didn't
does not	doesn't
were not	weren't
can not	can't
could not	couldn't
is not	isn't
you are	you're
they are	they're
it is	it's
there is	there's
who is	who's
class of 1990	class of '90
of the clock	o'clock

Use contractions for speech and informal writing, but do not use them in formal writing.

Examples:

1. It's going to be a great day.
   It is going to be a great day.
2. Its blue cover is fading in the sun.
   Something owns a blue cover.
3. They're running to catch the bus.
   They are running to catch the bus.
4. Their tire is flat.
   They own a tire.

EXERCISE 6: Underline the correct word for each of the following sentences.

1. Fix (your, you're) hair before we go on stage.
2. (Whose, Who's) car did you borrow last night?
3. (It's, Its) a bad habit that you need to break.
4. (They're, Their) check bounced at the food store.
5. (Whose, Who's) the lead actor in this play?

6. I want to be sure that (you're, your) ready on time.
7. Jim just heard that (they're, their) moving.
8. Kay wants to ride her bike, but I need to fix (its, it's) back wheel.
9. (Whose, Who's) toys are out in the rain?
10. (It's, Its) a great day to go to the zoo.

Answers are on page 306, 307.

 Remember these <u>facts about apostrophes</u>:

- To show possession, add an apostrophe and an *s* ('s) to singular nouns, indefinite pronouns, and plural nouns that do not end in -*s*.
- To show possession, add an apostrophe (') to plural nouns that do end in -*s*.
- Possessive pronouns (his, her, theirs, its, ours, yours) never have apostrophes.
- Apostrophes form contractions. The apostrophe shows that one or more letters have been left out of a word.

Quotation Marks (" ")

THE MAIN USES OF QUOTATION MARKS

1. set off someone's exact words (direct quotations)
2. set off the title of something that is part of a larger work (song, short story, poem, essay, episode of a TV or radio program, part of a book)
3. set off special words

There are two types of quotations, direct and indirect. Direct quotations quote someone word-for-word. Indirect quotations tell what someone has said, but they do not use the person's exact words. Thus, indirect quotations often begin with *that.* Quotation marks are used only for direct quotations. They set the quotation apart from the rest of the sentence.

Examples:

1. Abraham Lincoln said, "In giving freedom to the slave, we assure freedom to the free."
   These are Lincoln's exact words. Direct quotations need quotation marks.
2. Lincoln said that when the slaves are free, we will all be free.
   Lincoln's words have been changed. Do not use quotation marks for indirect quotations. Note the quotation begins with *that.*
3. "Put all your eggs in one basket," Mark Twain wrote, "and — watch that basket."
   These are Mark Twain's exact words. Quotation marks are placed before and after each part of the quotation.

EXERCISE 7: Place quotation marks where they are needed. Some sentences may not need quotation marks.

1. Golf is good walk spoiled, said Mark Twain.

2. Our boss announced that we will have fewer hours this year.

3. I don't want much, he said, I just want to spend more time with my family.

4. I remain just one thing, and one thing only — and that is a clown, said Charlie Chaplin.

5. John said that he wants to take a trip to Greece.

6. The day has just begun, she sang.

7. He argued that we spent too much time on this project.

8. During the speech Barb whispered, If we all put our heads down, maybe he will stop talking, and we will go home.

9. Will Rogers said that he didn't know jokes, he just watched the government and reported the facts.

10. I need a break! he yelled.

Answers are on page 307.

LESSER TITLES AND DEFINITIONS

Use quotation marks to set off the title of something that is part of a larger work. For example, quotation marks are used for songs, short poems, and short stories because they are part of something larger. Quotation marks also are used for episodes of TV or radio programs, essays, articles in periodicals (magazines), and parts of books.

Examples:

1. "Friends in Low Places" Song title
2. "Great Men" by Ralph Waldo Emerson Short poem
3. "Courage" by John Galsworthy Short story
4. "The Man Who Made Things Happen" in *Golf Digest* Article in a periodical
5. "Faith" (Chapter 10 of *The Book of Virtues*) Part of a book

Quotation marks or italics may be used to set apart words that are being defined.

Example:

When I say "hurry," I mean come here right away.
Hurry is being defined.

EXERCISE 8: Place quotation marks where they are needed. Some sentences may not need quotation marks.

1. The article New Toys for Fishermen appeared in the last issue of *Field and Stream*.
2. Billy Joel's song Goodnight My Angel will put her to sleep.
3. Chapter 7 which is titled What We Live By made me think about many things in my life.
4. The Stone in the Road is a story that you will like.
5. In my view, discipline means setting limits.
6. Have you read the poem titled The Busy Man?

Answers are on page 307.

PUNCTUATION WITH QUOTATION MARKS

Keep in mind, punctuation marks are like road signs. If road signs are not placed in the right order, drivers get lost. The same is true with punctuation marks. When quotation marks are used with other forms of punctuation, you need to put the marks in the correct order. Note the rules that are listed.

1. Place **periods** and **commas inside** the quotation marks (." or ,")
2. Place **semicolons** and **colons outside** the quotation marks (": or ";)
3. If the **whole sentence** is a **question** or **exclamation**, place the question mark or exclamation point **outside** the quotation marks ("! or "?)
4. If **only** the **quotation** is a **question** or **exclamation**, place the question mark or exclamation point **inside** the quotation marks (!" or ?")
5. Question marks and exclamation points work alone. They are not used with other end marks or commas.

Examples:

1. Van yelled, "Ready or not, here I come."
The period is inside the quotation marks.
2. When she says we "will be here at 5 am sharp," she is serious.
The comma is inside the quotation marks.
3. For years Lee's teacher said, "whole language is the best way to teach reading"; now phonics is back.
The semicolon is outside the quotation marks.
4. There is one way to describe "downsizing": fewer people, more work.
The colon is outside the quotation marks.
5. "Do I have to?" she cried.
Only the quotation is a question. The question mark is inside the quotation marks, and it works alone.
6. Who asked, "Where can I find a good plumber"?
The whole sentence is a question. The question mark is outside the quotation marks, and it works alone.
7. That man called me "crazy"!
The whole sentence is an exclamation. The exclamation point is outside of the quotation marks, and it works alone.

EXERCISE 9: Insert quotation marks where they are needed in the following sentences. Make sure that all punctuation marks are placed correctly inside or outside the quotation marks.

1. They say, there are at least one thousand chips in every bag of cookies; but how do they know?
2. When he shouted, Ump, you are crazy! he was thrown out of the game.
3. Have you heard the song called The Dance on the radio?

4. When he asked, Why do teens join gangs? I did not know what to say.

5. The sign says, You must be as tall as my hand to go on this ride.

6. He shouted, You're out!

7. Are you sure he said, We need to hire four more drivers?

8. I now know the real meaning of taxes: watching someone else spend your money.

9. She said, We need to talk.

10. Jim screamed, I want to go home! as his mother pushed the cart through the store.

Answers are on page 307, 308.

Remember the following <u>facts about quotation marks ("   ")</u>:

- Quotation marks are used for direct quotations, lesser titles, and words that are being defined.

- Quotation marks set the quotation apart from the rest of the sentence.

- When quotation marks are used with other forms of punctuation, you need to put the marks in the correct order. (See the chart on page 137.)

In this chapter you have learned:

☐ How to use semicolons (pages 129–131)

☐ How to use colons (pages 131, 132)

☐ How to use apostrophes (pages 132–135)

☐ How to use quotation marks (pages 135–138)

Review sections that are difficult for you.

Chapter Review

EXERCISE 1: Add commas, semicolons, colons, and apostrophes where they are needed.

We have moved many times but moving does not get much easier with experience. When we search for a new home, we look for the following features an affordable house a nice neighborhood excellent schools and a good commute to work. Generally weve moved into homes that weve enjoyed but finding a nice home in a new town is hard. One needs to learn about the town which can vary from one neighborhood to another the schools which are different for every child and the surrounding area. The meetings with realtors seem endless however a good realtor can help make the move a little easier. Every move is hard its important to take the time to do it right.

Answers are on page 308.

EXERCISE 2: Add commas, semicolons, colons, apostrophes, and quotation marks where they are needed.

We promised to help celebrate Kathys birthday. Nonetheless, when we walked into the house I knew we were in trouble. As we strolled through the front door Ruth said, There must be thirty children here. Yeah Russ added and they're climbing the walls. We couldnt believe our eyes two adults were trying to entertain thirty six-year-olds without driving themselves crazy. It seemed impossible. Suddenly Joe yelled Toss me some eggs and he started to juggle. Ruth magic tricks also got their attention. Before long the children were spellbound, and the adults regained their sanity mission accomplished.

Answers are on pages 308, 309.

EXERCISE 3: Add commas, semicolons, colons, parentheses, apostrophes, and quotation marks where they are needed.

By now everyone knows that eating right and exercising are important however life is not that easy. Every time I see the doctor, she asks How often do you exercise? Not often enough I respond. People who travel struggle to find decent meals and a place to work out. Parents schedules are hectic work trips to the doctor soccer games PTA meetings. Students even have trouble fitting good food and exercise into their lives. We all need to step back and look at our priorities. If we dont take care of ourselves who will? Even though its hard we need to take the frustrations out of our lives and put the healthy habits back in.

Answers are on page 309.

Capitalization

In this chapter you will learn:

☐ When to capitalize letters (pages 140–143)

Capital letters talk to the reader; they say, "Look at me. I'm special." This chapter will teach you to use capital letters correctly so that you can get your message to the reader.

CAPITALIZE THE FOLLOWING:

1. the first word in a sentence
2. the pronoun *I*
3. major words in titles
4. proper nouns, which are names for specific people, places, or things
5. abbreviations for proper nouns

Capital letters are used for certain jobs. By now you know most of these jobs. For example, you know to capitalize the first word in a sentence and the pronoun *I*.

Examples:

1. <u>W</u>e need to improve our skills.
2. <u>W</u>here can <u>I</u> find a good job?

Quotations

When you quote someone, capitalize the first word of that person's sentence.

Example:

Hoa said, "<u>S</u>ome teachers want more students."

Titles

Capitalize major words in titles. Major words include the first and last word of the title. Do not capitalize articles (a, an, the), conjunctions (and, but, so), or prepositions (about, between, etc.) unless they are the first or last word of the title.

Examples:

1. Titles of books: *The Bridges of Madison County*, *Green Eggs and Ham*, *Winds of War*
2. Titles of songs: "Take It Easy," "Over There," "Where Do We Go from Here"

Capitalize the titles that appear before a person's name. If the title comes after a person's name, do not capitalize it.

Examples:

1. Dr. Kathy Hawkins
   Kathy Hawkins, a doctor
2. Senator Bob Dole
   Bob Dole, a senator
3. Professor Tran Lee
   Tran Lee, a professor

EXERCISE 1: For each of the following sentences, cross out letters that should be capitalized, and write the capital letter in the space above.

1. my boss said, "we need a longer lunch break. a half hour is not enough time."

2. I wrote a letter about health care to senator Robb, and i sent a copy to Vi Rus, my doctor.

3. Kate wants to take a class with Ted Jones, a professor with great teaching skills.

4. in her book, Jan wrote, "meeting friends is hard for some people."

5. dr. Seuss's book, *the cat in the hat*, is a big hit with children.

6. Susan said, "we get more conservative as we age."

7. Mark Beauchamp, our mayor, has done great things for this town.

8. The song "let's give them something to talk about" reminds me of you.

9. Some people want governor Weld and vice president Gore to run in the next election.

10. Ellen's music box plays "ring around the rosie."

Answers are on pages 309, 310.

Common Nouns and Proper Nouns

Common nouns are nouns that name general groups of people, places, or things (park, street, father, time). However, common nouns can be used as part of a name (Park Street, Father Time). Capitalize common nouns only when they are used to name specific people, places, or things.

Examples:

1. <u>Mother</u>, will you please sit with Brie?
   Mother is used as a name.
2. My <u>mother</u> will sit with Brie.
   My mother is not used as a name.
3. The food store is on <u>Main Street</u>.
   Main Street is the name of the street.

4. The food store is on the <u>main street</u> in town.
   Main street is not used as a name. It simply describes where the store is.
5. Four years ago, <u>Governor</u> Bill Clinton ran for <u>president</u>.
   Governor is a title. *President* is a position; it is not used to name anyone in particular.
6. Four years ago, a <u>governor</u> became <u>President</u> Bill Clinton.
   Governor is used to describe a position. *President* is used as a title before a name.

Proper nouns are nouns that name definite persons, places, or things (Michael J. Fox, New York City, Mount Rushmore). Capitalize proper nouns, but do not capitalize articles that appear before them.

PROPER NOUNS

Names of specific people, companies, or things
George Bush Pepsi Nobel Peace Prize

Geographic names
The United States Paris Cape of Good Hope Main Street the South (the place, not the direction)

Peoples and languages
American English Inca French Farsi

Religions, their worshippers, holy days, holy books, and holy beings
Judaism Jews Islam Muslims Christianity Christians Christmas Ramadan Yom Kippur Bible Koran Talmud God Yahweh Allah

Days of the week, months, holiday
Sunday March Labor Day

Historical events, periods, documents
Korean War the Ice Age the Bill of Rights

Government agencies, organizations, institutions
State Department Red Cross Fairfax High School First Baptist Church

Abbreviations of Proper Nouns
CIA (Central Intelligence Agency) CNN (Cable News Network) UN (United Nations)

EXERCISE 2:   Cross out letters that should be capitalized and write the capital letter in the space above.

1. On monday, hope church will open a new soup kitchen at park street and king street.

2. Blair high school held classes on veterans' day, but the students were off for labor day.

3. Christians read the bible, and jews read the talmud.

4. my mom came all the way from france to see me.

5. the purple heart and the bronze star are meaningful awards.

6. The renaissance was a time of great art and music.

7. Aunt Sue and uncle Peter are from the south, but they enjoyed traveling to vermont and new york.

8. Dad studied russian and spanish when he worked for the fbi.

9. Many lakes, such as lake champlain and squam lake, attract tourists in the summer.

10. Did you know that grandma liked nike's commercials that aired during the super bowl?

Answers are on page 310.

Remember these <u>facts about capitalization</u>:

• Capital letters are used for certain jobs.

• Capitalize the first word in a sentence, major words in titles, proper nouns, and the pronoun *I*.

• Capitalize a title that appears before a person's name.

• Capitalize common nouns only when they are used to name specific people, places, or things (Park Street).

In this chapter you have learned:

☐ When to capitalize letters (pages 140–143)

Review sections that are difficult for you.

Chapter Review

EXERCISE 1:   Capitalize as needed. Likewise, cross out capital letters where they don't belong.

Reading is part of life. we read road signs, recipes, directions, and newspapers daily. Your Mom may be able to prepare dinner without a recipe, but the rest of us depend on *Dinner in no time* or some other cookbook for help. Likewise, when we program the VCR, we read the directions. We check the paper for TV shows, such as *wings*, or special movies like *Twister*. At the health club, some people read the *New York Times* while they ride the bike. We even read our Junk mail. Reading doesn't just get us through the day; it opens up a whole new world.

Answers are on page 310, 311.

EXERCISE 2: Capitalize as needed. Likewise, cross out capital letters where they don't belong.

Art, music, and literature touch our lives. A french playwright said, "a work of art is above all an adventure of the mind." Some people travel the world to see great works, such as *David* or the *Mona lisa*. Other people simply go to the library or turn on the radio to find great works. Books, such as the *Road Less Traveled,* make us think about our lives. Songs, such as "My Hometown," describe our feelings. We all can't travel to see art from the renaissance or hear great music, but we can enjoy the simple works that reach us every day.

Answers are on page 311.

EXERCISE 3: Capitalize words as needed. Likewise, cross out capital letters where they don't belong.

No one likes going to the dentist, but my dentist is good. dr. Aldrege, whose office is on park street, has new issues of *Time* in her waiting room, and she is rarely late for an appointment. Her dental chair looks like the space shuttle Columbia, but she is great with my teeth. dr. Aldrege uses methods that the ada (American Dental Association) supports. When I leave her office, my teeth look and feel much better. I tell everyone, even my Dad, to go to dr. Aldrege. After all, going to the dentist does not have to be a bad experience.

Answers are on page 311.

Spelling

There are tricks that can make spelling easier. To become a good speller, you must decide which words are hard for you. Then, you need to create a plan to help yourself with those words. The best way to learn how to spell is to use your imagination. Words need to leave a mark in your memory. This chapter will teach you traditional spelling rules. It also will help you develop memory tricks for words that are used often.

Memory Marks

Memory marks, which are silly sayings, create a picture in your mind of the word spelled correctly. There are rules for spelling, but the rules do not always work. (See pages 151–154).

Many words simply have to be memorized. Memory marks can help you learn words that are hard for you. You must learn to spell the following words that are used often. See if the memory marks help.

Examples:

The underlined letters often cause problems with these words. When you read the memory marks, picture the words in your mind.

Word	Memory Mark
ache	a cold heart aches.
again	A again
among	only o among us
answer	we answer the phone
been	a bee has been here
beginning	three n's are beginning to grow two i's
break	we break bread when we eat
built	U and I built that house
business	bus in business to our store
busy	Y are U busy?
buy	U know Y I buy things
choose	choose between two o's (present tense)
chose	I chose the first o (past tense)
could	O U could not forget the L
country	your country counts on U
course	our math course
dear	use dear to address someone
every	very good every time
February	brr! February is cold!
forty	for forty years
friend	i before e except after c (see rule on page 152)
grammar	two m's got A's in grammar
guess	U guess first
half	half a liter
hear	you need an ear to hear
hour	our hour is up
loose	a goose is loose (not bound)
meant	the ant meant what it said
minute	U time the minute
piece	i before e except after c (see rule on page 152)
raise	I need a raise
says	say, "s"

separate	*r* sep<u>a</u>rates two *a*'s
should	*O U* sh<u>ou</u>ld not forget the *L*
tear	the t<u>ea</u>r on my <u>ear</u>
would	*O U* w<u>ou</u>ld not forget the *L*
trouble	*O U* are in tr<u>ou</u>ble
wear	w<u>ea</u>r <u>ear</u>muffs

EXERCISE 1: Cover the words listed above with a piece of paper. Underline the correct spelling in each of the following sentences. Hint: Think of the correct spelling before you look at the choices.

1. We wanted (seprate, separate, separet) checks for the meal.

2. She got a (tare, tair, tear) in her paper.

3. Lee asked his boss for a (raze, rase, raise).

4. Juan (would, woud, wold) love to take a trip.

5. Will you please (anser, ansir, answer) the door?

6. I am too (bizy, busy, bisy) to talk right now.

7. Laura and Joel are (begining, beginng, beginning) to like their new home.

8. Jen took many French (coarses, courses, corses) in school.

9. (February, Febuary, Feburary) in Maine is cold and snowy.

10. Did you know that Vera is almost (fourty, forty, fortie) years old?

11. We study (grammer, grammar, gramar) each year.

12. Kim takes the children to day care (evry, evrie, every) day.

13. He (built, bilt) the fence around his house.

14. Where have you (bin, been, ben)?

15. Suzanne and I have been (friends, freinds) since grade school.

16. The clock rings on the (our, hour, ore).

17. Yesterday, I (choose, chose, chos) new drapes for the house.

18. What are you going to (wear, where, ware) to the party?

19. Fran wants to start her own (bisness, buisness, business).

20. Wait, I need a (minit, minute, minnet) to get ready.

Answers are on pages 311.

Commonly Misspelled Words

The following lists have words that are frequently used and often misspelled. The letters that usually cause problems are underlined. Words with stars (*) have rules that may help. (See pages 151–154).
   Try this method to learn these words:

1. Take a piece of paper and fold it into three columns lengthwise.
2. Leave the first column blank. In the second column, write the spelling word.
3. In the third column write a memory mark. Make sure that your memory mark helps you with the difficult letters. Use sayings or pictures to make your mark.
4. Fold the paper so that you can only see your memory mark.
5. Practice spelling the words using your memory mark.
6. Have someone read you the words, so you can practice spelling them without looking at your memory mark.
7. Repeat steps 5 and 6 as needed.

Examples:

BLANK COLUMN	SPELLING WORD	MEMORY MARK
1.	would	O U would not forget the L
2.	trouble	O U are in trouble
3.	wear	we wear earmuffs

KEY WORDS (PART I)

Words that are starred (*) have spelling rules that apply to them. You may want to review the spelling rules before creating memory marks.

abi<u>li</u>ty	a<u>no</u>ther
ab<u>sen</u>ce	a<u>pp</u>ly
a_lot	a<u>pp</u>roval
a<u>cc</u>ept	ar<u>gu</u>ing
a<u>cc</u>ident	ar<u>gu</u>ment
accident<u>ally</u>	ar<u>ou</u>nd
add<u>ress</u>	artic<u>le</u>
a<u>cc</u>use	as<u>k</u>ed
a<u>cross</u>	ath<u>le</u>te
act<u>ually</u>	at<u>tem</u>pt
advert<u>ise</u>ment	atten<u>da</u>nce
advice	attention
a<u>gainst</u>	<u>A</u>ugust
all<u>owed</u>	a<u>u</u>thor
a<u>l</u>most	a<u>u</u>tumn
a<u>l</u>ready	avail<u>a</u>ble
a<u>l</u>together	* a<u>w</u>ful
am<u>ou</u>nt	a<u>w</u>kward
an<u>ge</u>l	bal<u>a</u>nce
an<u>gl</u>e	bal<u>loo</u>n

EXERCISE 2: Cover the words in the list above. Cross out words that are misspelled in the following sentences. Write the correct spelling in the space provided. Some sentences may not have any misspellings.

1. The hot-air baloon sailed across the sky and almost landed in a lake. _____

2. She is an athelete with a lot of ability. _____

3. The author did not get much attention from his first book because it was aweful. _____

4. Brian accidentally gave me the wrong adress. _____

5. Bob actually lost his ballance and fell against the fence. _____

6. An arguement between two drivers caused the accident on Main Street. _____

7. Chris did accuse me of not paying the right amont. _____

8. Even though it was awkward, Rachel did axcept her mother's advice. _____

9. Patrick asked if another crib were availible. _____

10. In August, we will aply for a mortgage and attempt to buy a home. _____

11. Attendence is already low this autumn. _____

12. Students who have aproval from their parents are allowed to go on the trip. _____

13. In the artical, Steve was arguing for town parks. _____

14. Altogether the angels add up to 180°. _____

15. There must be an angel around here. _____

Answers are on page 311.

MORE WORDS (PART II)

basic	* ceiling
* beautiful	cereal
because	certain
become	* chief
before	choice
being	cigarette
between	citizen
bicycle	climbed
bottle	clothes
brakes	coarse (rough)
breathe	coffee
bulletin	collect
buried	college
cafeteria	color
calendar	column
career	comfortable
* careful	committee
careless	common
carrying	company
category	completely

EXERCISE 3: Cover the words in the list above. Cross out words that are mis-spelled in the following sentences. Write the correct spelling in the space provided. Some sentences may not have any mis-spellings.

1. I go to college because I want a good carer. _____

2. Megan came into the cafeteria smoking a cigarrette and carrying a cup of coffee. _____

3. Before Cody goes to work, he has a basic breakfast with cereal, toast, and juice. _____

4. Beutiful clothes were buried in her closet. _____

5. The water bottle is between your bycicle and mine. _____

6. According to the calendar, Miquel will become a citisen in three weeks. _____

7. Mike climbed up the ladder to fix the cieling fan. _____

8. My teacher will want a certain coler for the bulletin board. _____

9. Be carefull! The brakes are not completely dry. _____

10. We all need to breath. _____

11. The chief wants to form a comittee. _____

12. A white colum is the best choice for the background of this painting. _____

13. Coarse sand fills the comon beach. _____

14. He was being careless when he slipped on the ice. _____

15. When I collect my pension from the compeny, I will live a comfortable life. _____

Answers are on page 312.

MORE WORDS (PART III)

compliment	doctor
confident	does
congratulate	dollar
* controlled	doubt
corner	dozen
cough	* dropped
counselor	dying
curtain	earliest
customer	early
daily	education
daughter	eighth
death	English
decide	enough
destroy	envelope
dictator	everybody
died	excellent
different	exercise
direction	expense
disease	experience
distance	extremely

EXERCISE 4: Cover the words in the list above. Cross out words that are misspelled in the following sentences. Write the correct spelling in the space provided. Some sentences may not have any misspellings.

1. Nga had to dicide which doctor to see about her cough. _____

2. My counselor wants me to take an English course to improve my edgecation. _____

3. My daghter does exercise daily. _____

4. Everybody wants to congradulate you for your excellent speech. _____

5. The customer spent only one doller in the store. _____

6. Joseph Stalin, a dictator, died a strange deth. _____

7. I dout we are going in the right direction. _____

8. There is enough distance between here and the cornor to park the car. _____

9. I am confidint that we can find a cure for this disease. _____

10. Greg had a bad experience in eith grade. _____

11. Joe gets to work extremely erly. _____

12. Kathy droped the envelope behind the curtain. _____

13. Russ had to fill out a dosen different expense reports before he could leave work. _____

14. The trees that were planted the earliest were diing. _____

15. Ruth wanted to complement the angry man who controlled himself well. _____

Answers are on page 312.

MORE WORDS (PART IV)

factory	holiday
finally	hoping
foreign	hospital
forth	hundred
forward	hurrying
four	immigrant
fourteen	increase
fourth	instead
future	interesting
gallon	individual
government	invitation
great	island
grocery	jewelry
guard	judgment
* handful	kindergarten
handle	kitchen
healthy	knife
heavy	knock
height	language
here	laugh

EXERCISE 5: Cover the words in the list above. Cross out words that are misspelled in the following sentences. Write the correct spelling in the space provided. Some sentences may not have any misspellings.

1. Put the nife back in the kitchen. _____

2. She was hoping to live on an iland in the future. _____

3. To an imigrant, our language is hard. _____

4. At fourteen, it is not helthy for her to carry such a heavy burden. _____

5. The goverment wants to increase the tax on a gallon of gas to four cents. _____

6. Kindergarden is a great place to laugh and play. _____

7. The guard in the hospital sees at least a hundred people a day. _____

8. Instead of enjoying the holliday, we were hurrying to the grocery store. _____

9. This is the first foriegn coin that I have found. _____

10. We finaly have an invitation to visit the factory. _____

11. Lee is an intresting individual. _____

12. Her judgment was hard to handle. _____

13. Tom picked up a forth handful of dirt. _____

14. I look forward to buying some nice jewlry. _____

15. At his height, it may be hard to nock on the door. _____

Answers are on pages 312.

MORE WORDS (PART V)

lesson	ocean
library	offer
license	officer
losing	operate
lying	opinion
maintenance	paid
marriage	parallel
match	pear
material	pencil
measure	people
misspelled	perform
medicine	period
movable	permanent
muscle	picture
neighbor	planning
neither	pocket
* niece	poison
ninety	politics
ninth	possible
noticeable	prejudice

EXERCISE 6: Cover the words in the preceding list. Cross out words that are misspelled in the following sentences. Write the correct spelling in the space provided. Some sentences may not have any misspellings.

1. They mispelled her last name on the marriage license. _____

2. Is it possible that the libarry books are due on the ninth? _____

3. She is planning a lesson on politics and prechudice. _____

4. If you don't measure your medecine correctly, you can poison yourself. _____

5. After losing the match, my neice cried. _____

6. Some people are paid to preform. _____

7. Let's go take a picture of the ocean. _____

8. My dad keeps a pensil in his pocket. _____

9. They want to operate on her mussle to prevent any permanent damage. _____

10. In my opinion, our nieghbor is lying about her age; she must be at least ninety years old. _____

11. Without the right material, we can't perform the maintenence. _____

12. Each officer has a movible radar gun. _____

13. I will offer you fifty cents for that pear. _____

14. For a long period of time, we were on parralel roads. _____

15. Neither spot on your shirt is notis-
    able. _____

Answers are on page 312.

MORE WORDS (PART VI)

presence	recipe
prescription	recognize
president	recommend
probably	referee
produce	reference
professor	refugee
promise	repeat
promptly	repetition
purpose	responsibility
quality	restaurant
quantity	safety
quarter	salary
quiet	sandwich
quizzes	schedule
realistic	scissors
realize	season
really	secretary
reason	sentence
* receipt	several
* receive	sheriff

EXERCISE 7: Cover the words in the list
above. Cross out words that are misspelled in the following sentences. Write
the correct spelling in the space provided.
Some sentences may not have any misspellings.

1. The sheriff does reccomend that we
   install safety locks. _____

2. During soccer season, our secretary
   is a referee for her son's league.
   _____

3. A refuge may leave his or her country for several reasons. _____

4. Our professor does grade quizzes
   and give them back to us promtly.
   _____

5. The reference section really is quiet.
   _____

6. You probly need fresh produce for
   this recipe. _____

7. He will reconize poor quality.
   _____

8. It is your responsability to create
   the work schedule and close the
   restaurant. _____

9. Pat did not realise that she needed a
   receipt for the scissors. _____

10. They promised to have my perscrip-
    tion ready by noon. _____

11. The president will probably repeat
    the same sentence many times in
    his speech. _____

12. On my salary, I can barely aford a
    sandwich. _____

13. Be relistic! A quarter will not buy
    much. _____

14. The purpose of this study is to see
    how repitition affects us. _____

15. A large quantity of goods was stolen
    in my presence. _____

Answers are on page 312.

MORE WORDS (PART VII)

shoulder	surround
signal	technical
soldier	telephone
sophomore	temperature
soul	temporary
source	tenant
special	terrible
speech	therefore
statue	together
stomach	tomorrow
* stopped	toward
straight	tries
strength	Tuesday
striking	twelve
studying	typical
succeed	unnecessary
success	until
summer	unusual
surely	* useful
surprise	vacuum

EXERCISE 8: Cover the words in the preceding list. Cross out words that are misspelled in the following sentences. Write the correct spelling in the space provided. Some sentences may not have any misspellings.

1. On Tuesday, Kay had a terrible stomache flu. _____

2. Tomorrow the solders will go straight into battle. _____

3. This special vacuum is usefull on the stairs. _____

4. Last summer we had high temperitures that were unusual. _____

5. His telephone call is a signal that we will meet at twelve. _____

6. A typical sophmore surely tries to fit in with the crowd. _____

7. We were allowed to stay here until the tenant stoped paying the rent. _____

8. Her speech was an unnecessary sirprise. _____

9. The sholder on the statue fell off. _____

10. When we were studying together, he wasn't a good sorce for help. _____

11. If you want to suceed, your soul needs to have strength. _____

12. Some people's success is only temporary. _____

13. I was surronded by technical people at the meeting. _____

14. Therefore, we were striking for a good reeson. _____

15. Run tward the house! _____

Answers are on page 312.

MORE WORDS (PART VIII)

val<u>ua</u>ble	We<u>d</u><u>nes</u>day
var<u>ied</u>	w<u>ei</u>rd
ve<u>ge</u>table	welfare
*v<u>ei</u>n	<u>while</u>
*v<u>iew</u>	wo<u>man</u>
visit<u>o</u>r	* wonderf<u>ul</u>
voi<u>ce</u>	written
w<u>ea</u>ther	* y<u>ie</u>ld

EXERCISE 9: Cover the words in the list above. Cross out words that are misspelled in the following sentences. Write the correct spelling in the space provided. Some sentences may not have any misspellings.

1. Vegtables are part of a varied diet. _____

2. On Wednesday the wether was wonderful. _____

3. Congress has written a bill that will change wellfare. _____

4. While I was waiting here, a woman with a wierd voice spoke with me. _____

5. That visitor may not veiw the house. _____

6. The treatment for my veins did yield valuble results. _____

Answers are on page 313.

Spelling Rules

There are many exceptions to spelling rules. Nonetheless, the rules can help with most words. Before you can learn spelling rules, you need to recognize vowels, consonants, prefixes, and suffixes. If you do not know these terms, check the box.

SPELLING RULES

1. *I* before *e* except after *c* or when sound like *ay* as in n<u>ei</u>ghbor or w<u>eigh</u>
2. words are too *full* to have two *L*'s on the end (wonder*ful*)
3. silent *e*'s leave endings with vowels (car<u>e</u> + ing = caring)
4. silent *e*'s like endings with consonants (car<u>e</u> + ful = car<u>e</u>ful)
5. silent *e*'s help soft *c*'s and *g*'s (courag<u>e</u> + ous = courageous)
6. If you add an ending other than *ing*, *Y*'s become *i*'s after consonants (bab<u>y</u> + es = bab<u>i</u>es, bab<u>y</u> + ing = bab<u>y</u>ing)
7. 1 syllable + 1 vowel = 2 consonants (sl<u>i</u>p + ed = slipped)
8. a prefix wants to be with the whole word (mis + spelling = misspelling)
9. *s* makes most nouns plural (toy + s = toys) *es* is used for nouns that end in *-s*, *-sh*, *-ch*, or *x*. (box + es = boxes, dish + es = dishes)

There are many exceptions to these guidelines, but they will still help.

KEY TERMS

vowel—one of these letters: a, e, i, o, u, and sometimes y
consonant—a letter of the alphabet that is not a vowel
syllable—part of a word that works together to form a sound (*For* has one syllable. *For/got* has two syllables, and *for/got/en* has three.)
prefix—letters that are placed on the front of a word to change its meaning
suffix—letters that are placed at the end of a word to change its meaning

S MAKES MOST NOUNS PLURAL

Adding an *s* to the singular form makes most nouns plural. *Es* is used for nouns that end in *-s*, *-sh*, *-ch*, or *x*.

Examples:

1. toy + s = toys
2. box + es = boxes
3. dish + es = dishes

I BEFORE *E*

One standard spelling rule says, "*I* before *e* except after *c* or when sounding like *ay* as in n<u>ei</u>ghbor or w<u>ei</u>gh." This rule works for many words.

Examples:

1. **I before *e*:**
   v<u>ie</u>w, ch<u>ie</u>f, qu<u>ie</u>t, y<u>ie</u>ld, n<u>ie</u>ce, f<u>ie</u>ld
2. **except after *c*:**
   c<u>ei</u>ling, rec<u>ei</u>pt, rec<u>ei</u>ve, conc<u>ei</u>t
3. **or when sounding like *ay* as in neighbor or weigh:**
   v<u>ei</u>n, <u>ei</u>ght, fr<u>ei</u>ght, sl<u>ei</u>gh

Note these exceptions: <u>ei</u>ther, n<u>ei</u>ther, for<u>ei</u>gn, h<u>ei</u>ght, w<u>ei</u>rd, s<u>ei</u>ze, caff<u>ei</u>ne. All of these words are spelled with *ei*. Try this silly sentence: In weird foreign lands, neither caffeine nor protein seizes either height or leisure.

EXERCISE 10: Cross out words that are misspelled and write the correct spelling in the space provided. Some sentences may not have any mistakes.

1. When I saw the two foxes, I could not beleive my eyes. _____

2. No one likes to pay taxs. _____

3. Did you recieve any bills in the mail? _____

4. She is weird when she has too much caffiene. _____

5. My neighbor has to fix the ceiling in his kitchen. _____

6. We have a great view of the field from these seates. _____

7. Busses are very quiet in the morning. _____

8. In many foreign nations, people eat a lot less protien than we do. _____

9. My friend tried to guess my wieght. _____

10. Some boates ran into the pier last week. _____

Answers are on page 313.

WORDS ARE TOO FULL TO HAVE TWO *L*'S ON THE END

When -*ful* is added to the end of a word, it only has one *l*.

Examples:

1. awful
2. wonderful
3. deceitful
4. doubtful
5. handful

SILENT *E*'S LEAVE ENDING WITH VOWELS

A silent *e* marks the end of a word and is not pronounced. Silent *e*'s leave endings with vowels. In other words, if the ending or suffix begins with a vowel (a, e, i, o, u), drop the silent *e*.

Examples:

1. move + able = movable
2. dare + ing = daring
3. response + ible = responsible

SILENT *E*'S LIKE ENDINGS WITH CONSONANTS

Silent *e*'s like endings with consonants. In other words, if the ending or suffix begins with a consonant, keep the silent *e*.

Examples:

1. move + ment = movement
2. wake + ful = wakeful
3. like + ly = likely
4. gentle + ness = gentleness

Some words simply drop the silent *e*. Learn these words.

Examples:

1. true + ly = truly
2. argue + ment = argument

SILENT *E*'S HELP SOFT *C*'S AND *G*'S

Sometimes the silent *e* changes the sound of a *c* or *g* so that these letters have a soft sound (like the *g* in *gel* or the *c* in *nice*) instead of a hard sound (like the *g* in *game* or the *c* in *cup*). Keep silent *e*'s that make a *c* or *g* soft.

Examples:

1. knowledge + able = knowledgeable
2. notice + able = noticeable
3. outrage + ous = outrageous

Y'S BECOME *I*'S AFTER CONSONANTS

A word that ends in *y* may change its spelling when an ending is added. If the *y* is right after a consonant, it changes to an *i* for most endings.

Examples:

1. carry + ed = carried
2. baby + es = babies
3. merry + ment = merriment

If the *y* is right after a vowel (a, e, i, o, u) or an -*ing* ending is added, keep the *y*.

Examples:

1. play + ed = played
2. obey + s = obeys
3. carry + ing = carrying

1 SYLLABLE
+ 1 VOWEL = 2 CONSONANTS

When an ending is added to a word with one syllable and one vowel right before the last consonant, double the last consonant.

Examples:

1. slip + ed = slipped
2. bat + ing = batting
3. run + ing = running

A PREFIX WANTS TO BE
WITH THE WHOLE WORD

When prefix is added to a word, do not delete any letters from the original word.

Examples:

1. mis + spelled = misspelled
2. un + necessary = unnecessary
3. dis + similar = dissimilar

EXERCISE 11: Add prefixes and suffixes as directed. Write the new word in the space provided.

1. move + ment = _____

2. meaning + full = _____

3. daze + ing = _____

4. love + able = _____

5. confuse + ed = _____
   his kitchen.

6. argue + ing = _____

7. advantage + ous = _____

8. marry + ed = _____

9. swim + ing = _____

10. notice + able = _____

11. stay + ed = _____

12. mis + state = _____

13. tip + ed = _____

14. like + ness = _____

15. un + natural = _____

16. bounty + full = _____

17. consume + able = _____

18. dis + service = _____

19. beautify + ing = _____

20. care + ing = _____

Answers are on page 313.

In this chapter you have learned:

☐ How to improve your spelling (pages 144, 145)

☐ Which words are often misspelled (pages 145–151)

☐ How to use spelling rules (pages 151–154)

Review sections that are difficult for you.

Chapter Review

EXERCISE 1: There are 10 spelling mistakes in the following paragraph. Cross out the incorrect words and write the correct spelling in the margin.

Each individual relaxes in a diferent way. Atheletes often exercise to work their mussles and reduce their tension. Cooks go the kichen to prepare favorite recipes. Dedicated shopers probably search the stores for bargains. Many people simply put on comfterble clothes and read a book or watch TV. How each person relaxes is not realy important. Evrybody who takes some time to unwind will be more helthy and successfull in the long run.

Answers are on page 313.

EXERCISE 2: There are 10 spelling mistakes in the following paragraph. Cross out the incorrect words and write the correct spelling in the margin.

In today's workforce, women have many different jobs. In the past, some women staied at home, worked in factry jobs, waited tables in resterants, or became secreteries. However, over the past fourty years women have taken on new roles; young girls now dream of becoming docters, lawyers, soldiers, and professors. The welfare reform bill has already opened up even more feilds to women. In an effort to leave welfare, some women have had valuble technical training. As a result of their education, these women have entered trades that were typicly controled by men. Female workers today have redefined success on the job.

Answers are on page 313.

Word Choice

In this chapter you will learn:

☐ Which words are often confused (pages 156–162)

☐ How to use these words correctly (pages 156–162)

Remember, you are the boss, and words are your workers. You need to choose the right word for the job. However, some words are easy to mix up. This chapter will teach you not only which words cause problems but also memory marks that may help you use these words correctly. Remember, a memory mark is a silly saying that helps you learn difficult words.

Use the following steps to learn these words:

1. Divide a sheet of paper into three columns lengthwise and label the columns as follows:

   Words
   Definitions
   Sentences
   Memory Marks

2. Make a list of the words that are hard for you. Include sentences and memory marks that help you understand the words. Even though the chapter provides many sample sentences and memory marks, you may want to create your own.

3. Complete the exercises and practice using the words in new sentences.

Commonly Confused Words

accept, except

accept is a verb that means "to receive something" or to "agree to something."
Memory Mark: I will <u>a</u>ccept <u>a</u> fortune.

except is usually a preposition that means "leaving out." *Memory Mark:* Everyone dies, <u>ex</u>cept Elvis.

affect, effect

affect is a verb that means "to influence" or "to cause a change."

effect is usually a noun that means "result."

Sample Sentences:

The frost will <u>affect</u> the apples.

The layoffs will have an <u>effect</u> on everyone.

already, all ready

already is an adverb that shows when something happened.

all ready means "everyone or everything was prepared."

Sample Sentences:

We <u>already</u> biked four miles.

We are <u>all ready</u> for dinner.

among, between

among is used for more than two things or persons.

between is used for only two things or persons.

Memory Mark: Be<u>tw</u>een is for <u>two</u>.

Sample Sentences:

We were <u>among</u> friends at the party.

I will choose <u>between</u> you and him.

amount, number

amount refers to something that can not be counted.

number refers to something that can be counted.

Sample Sentences:

She baked a large <u>amount</u> of dough. (We cannot count dough.)

She baked a large <u>number</u> of cookies. (We can count how many cookies were baked.)

as, like

as and **like** are used for comparisons.

as can work like a conjunction and precede a clause. *As* often is followed by a noun and a verb.

Memory Mark: As has two letters because it is followed by two things, a noun and a verb.

like is a preposition that is followed by a noun.

Sample Sentences:

She runs as fast <u>as</u> I do. (as + noun + verb)

She runs <u>like</u> a deer. (like + noun)

board, bored

board is a noun that means "piece of wood."

bored is the past tense of bore, a verb that means "to tire by being dull."

Sample Sentences:

The <u>board</u> needs paint.

Sue's job <u>bored</u> her.

borrow, lend

borrow means "to receive something that will be returned." The borrower is expected to give the item back.

lend means "to give something that will be returned."

Sample Sentences:

Laura <u>borrowed</u> a book from Jen.

Jen will <u>lend</u> Laura a book.

bring, take

bring means "to lead or carry." It is used when the action moves toward the speaker.

take means "to lead or carry." It is used when the action moves away from the speaker.

Sample Sentences:

<u>Bring</u> the books to me.

<u>Take</u> the books to them.

by, buy

by is a preposition.

buy is a verb that means "to purchase."

Sample Sentences:

We ran <u>by</u> the store. The book is <u>by</u> the lamp.

Where did you b<u>uy</u> those shoes?

capital, capitol, Capitol

capital means "the city that holds the state or national government." It also refers to wealth that is used for business.

capitol refers to the actual building where a state legislature meets.

Capitol (with a capital *c*) refers to the actual building where Congress meets.

Sample Sentences:

Salt Lake City is the <u>capital</u> of Utah.

This business has some <u>capital</u>.

The dome on the <u>Capitol</u> needs repair.

desert (verb), desert (noun), dessert

desert (verb) means "to leave or abandon," and the emphasis is on the second syllable (dî-zûrt´).

desert (noun) refers to dry, sandy regions that have few plants. The emphasis is on the first syllable (dèz´ert).

dessert refers to a sweet food that is served at the end of a meal.
Memory Mark: De<u>ss</u>ert has two *s*'s because we want <u>s</u>econd<u>s</u>.

Sample Sentences:

Did the soldier <u>desert</u> his post?

The Gobi <u>Desert</u> is in Asia.

He likes ice cream and pie for <u>dessert</u>.

emigrate, immigrate

emigrate means "to leave one country to settle permanently in another." A person who emigrates is called an emigrant.
Memory Mark: An <u>e</u>migrant <u>e</u>xits a country.

immigrate means "to enter a country that is not one's native land and settle there." A person who immigrates is called an immigrant.
Memory Mark: An <u>i</u>mmigrant goes <u>i</u>nto a country.

Sample Sentences:

Rosa did not want to <u>emigrate</u> from Spain.

The war in their native land forced Juan's family to <u>immigrate</u> to the United States.

fewer, less

fewer, like number, refers to things that can be counted.
Memory Mark: If you work <u>fewer</u> hours, you will earn <u>less</u> money.

less, like amount, refers to things that can not be counted.

Sample Sentences:

We have <u>fewer</u> cans of paint. You can count how many cans you have (1 can, 2 cans, etc.).

We have <u>less</u> paint. You can not count paint.

hear, here

hear is what we do with our ears.
Memory Mark: We h<u>ear</u> sounds with our <u>ears</u>.

here is a place.
Memory Mark: We put things <u>here</u> and <u>t</u>here.

EXERCISE 1: Underline the correct word in each of the following sentences.

1. Rick will (except, accept) the award for best actor.
2. The doctor (all ready, already) gave me a blood test.
3. Will this witness (affect, effect) the trial?
4. I sat (between, among) Wayne and Suzanne during the game.
5. She needs to copy a large (number, amount) of papers.
6. Jean sings (as, like) I do.
7. His speech (bored, board) some people.
8. Will you (borrow, lend) me ten dollars for the movies?
9. Please (take, bring) this note home to your parents.
10. I don't want to (by, buy) a new car now.
11. Trenton is the (capital, Capitol) of New Jersey.
12. Do you want some ice cream for (desert, dessert)?
13. We had to (emigrate, immigrate) from Cuba.
14. My doctor says I should eat (fewer, less) fat.
15. Did you (hear, here) the news?
16. A (desert, dessert) has few plants and little rainfall.
17. When did you (emigrate, immigrate) to the United States?
18. When I want to lose weight, I eat (fewer, less) sweets.
19. He will work (as, like) a dog to get this project done.
20. No one has a key to the safe, (accept, except) the owner.

Answers are on page 313.

More Words

hole, whole

hole is a noun that refers to an opening.

whole is an adjective that means complete or full.

Sample Sentences:

There is a <u>hole</u> in your shirt.
He ate the <u>whole</u> cake.

imply, infer

imply means "to hint or suggest something." If in doubt, try to substitute *hint* for *imply*.

infer means to find a hidden meaning in someone's words.

Sample Sentences:

Did you <u>imply</u> that I should eat less?
I <u>infer</u> from your words that you do not like him.

know, no

know is a verb that means "to understand."

no is a negative response or an adjective that means "not one."

Sample Sentences:

I <u>know</u> that you are upset with me.
<u>No</u>, I will not go out with you. There is <u>no</u> way.

learn, teach

learn means "to gain understanding or information."

teach means "to give understanding or information."

Sample Sentences:

He wants to <u>learn</u> about birds.
I will <u>teach</u> him about birds.

leave, let

leave means "to go out or to go away."

let means "to allow or to permit."

Sample Sentences:

She wants to <u>leave</u> the room.
<u>Let</u> her come in.

meat, meet

meat, a noun, is part of an animal that we eat.

Memory Mark: We <u>eat</u> <u>meat</u>.

meet, a verb, means "to get together or to join."

Sample Sentences:

What type of <u>meat</u> do you want for dinner?
We will <u>meet</u> at the station.

plain, plane

plain is an adjective that means "clear, pure, or simple."

plane can be an adjective or a noun. The adjective means "flat or level." The noun refers to an airplane, a flat surface, or a tool that is used to make things flat.

Sample Sentences:

I just want <u>plain</u> (pure) water.
The ocean is in <u>plain</u> (clear) view.
She could only afford <u>plain</u> (simple) clothes.
We need a <u>plane</u> (flat) surface to write.
This <u>plane</u> (airplane) flies to New York.
He used a <u>plane</u> (tool) to make the shelves.

principal (noun), principal (adjective), principle (noun)

principal (noun) is the head of a school.

Memory Mark: If you behave, the principal is your <u>pal</u>.

principal (adjective) means "main."

principle (noun) refers to a rule or law.

Sample Sentences:

Mrs. Bev is the <u>principal</u> at Fax High School.
The <u>principal</u> cause of the fire was bad wiring.
Our policy is based on sound <u>principles</u>.

quiet, quit, quite

quiet is an adjective that means "calm or not making a sound."

quit is a verb that means "to give up or leave."

quite is an adverb that means "really or to a degree."

Sample Sentences:

We are quiet in the library.
He will quit his job.
She is quite (to a degree) an athlete.
I am not quite (really) sure about this new plan.

stationary, stationery

stationary is an adjective that means "not moving."
Memory Mark: If you are station**a**ry, you **a**ren't going anywhere.

stationery is a noun that refers to writing paper, envelopes, and office supplies.
Memory Mark: We use station**e**ry to write l**e**tters.

Sample Sentences:

Riding the stationary bike is boring because the view doesn't change.
I need more stationery to write my letters.

sweat, sweet

sweat refers to the drops of water that form on our bodies when were are hot or exercising.

sweet refers to sugary foods that we eat.

Sample Sentences:

Running on a hot day makes me sweat.
We should not eat too many sweets.

their, there, they're

their shows possession.
Memory Mark: Their, there, and they're begin with *the*.

there is a place.
Memory Mark: There and here both refer to a place.

they're is a contraction for *they are*.

Sample Sentences:

Their new car is a blue sedan.
The book is over there on the shelf.
They're moving in June.

to, too, two

to can be preposition or part of a verb in its infinitive form.

too is an adverb that means "also or extremely."

two is the number *2*.

Sample Sentences:

He ran to the store (preposition).
She wanted to run (part of the infinitive *to run*).
I want to have dessert. Do you want dessert, too (also)?
He was driving too (extremely) fast on this road.
I need two new tires for my car.

weather, whether

weather refers to temperature, sunshine, rain, snow, etc.
Memory Mark: E**a**ch day the we**a**ther was nice.

whether shows options.

Sample Sentences:

What will the weather be today?
He did not know whether he should study for his test or go for a walk. (Option one is to study. Option two is to go for a walk.)

EXERCISE 2: Underline the correct word in each of the following sentences.

1. The (whole, hole) team will go to the game.

2. When I said that you look great today, I did not mean to (imply, infer) that you usually look bad.

3. Do you (know, no) how to fix a flat tire?

4. Please (teach, learn) me how to change the oil in my car.

5. We should not (let, leave) her walk home alone.

6. What type of (meet, meat) is in this dish?

7. She will wear a (plane, plain) shirt and jeans to the dance.

8. Smoking is the (principal, principle) reason for lung cancer.

9. People should be (quiet, quit, quite) in a movie theater.

10. How could you hit a (stationary, stationery) car?

11. The (sweet, sweat) from his body soaked right through his shirt.

12. I thought we parked the car (their, they're, there) by the light.

13. The lawyer is (to, two, too) confident that he will win this case.

14. Lee was not sure (weather, whether) he should clean the house or take a nap.

15. Juan wants to buy (to, two, too) more tickets for the show.

16. Are you sure (their, there, they're) done with dinner?

17. Shantae wants to (learn, teach) Tara a new dance.

18. From the president's speech, we can (imply, infer) that he wants Congress to take action.

19. Dee wants to (quiet, quit, quite) the team and focus on her schoolwork.

20. We need to order more (stationary, stationery) for the office.

Answers are on pages 313, 314.

In this chapter you have learned:

☐ Which words are often confused (pages 154–160)

☐ How to use these words correctly (pages 154–160)

Review sections that are difficult for you.

Chapter Review

EXERCISE 1:   The following paragraph has five (5) words that are used incorrectly. Cross out the wrong words and write the correct words in the margin.

Exercise is important, but less young Americans are staying fit. While some young adults and children have become quite active, to many have ignored their bodies. Stationery lifestyles cause health problems. However, a good diet with few sweats and a decent exercise program can favorably affect our health. Most people already know what they need to do to improve their fitness; their just not doing it. We Americans need to quit making excuses and start breaking a sweat. We can't all look like the top athletes, but we can have healthy lifestyles.

Answers are on page 314.

EXERCISE 2:   The following paragraph has five words that are used incorrectly. Cross out the wrong words and write the right words in the margin.

Buying a car takes time and effort. First, the buyer must teach about the different cars that are on the market and decide what type of car she wants. She may need to lend money and get insurance, two. After the preparations, the buyer and salesperson meat to agree upon a price. If the buyer already knows a lot about the car, she may get a better deal. After the sale, even more paperwork is done. Many people are glad when the hole process is finally over.

Answers are on page 314.

EXERCISE 3: The following paragraph has five words that are used incorrectly. Cross out the wrong words and write the right words in the margin.

The number of people emigrating to America has increased in recent years, but the challenges they face are still the same. When people leave there native land, they have to let family and friends behind. When they arrive here, their lives change forever. Weather or not they are skilled, many immigrants have to accept jobs with low wages. Most immigrants also have to learn a whole new language and culture. In spite of these hardships, many immigrants are quiet successful in America.

Answers are on page 314.

Units 1 Through 4

Overview

The setup for this practice section is similar to an actual GED exam. However, this practice section will test only what you learned in units 1 through 5. The actual GED exam will test all of the information in this book. (See the posttest on page 260.)

Directions

1. This practice test has five paragraphs with numbered sentences. The sentences may have errors, or they may be correct as written. First, read the paragraph. Then, answer the related questions. Choose the best answer for each question. The best answer should be consistent with the point of view and verb tense that is used throughout the paragraph.

2. Answer every question. If you are not sure of the answer, make a logical guess.

3. Write your answers to the questions on the answer grid. For each question, mark the number that matches the answer you chose.

ANSWER GRID

1. ① ② ③ ④ ⑤
2. ① ② ③ ④ ⑤
3. ① ② ③ ④ ⑤
4. ① ② ③ ④ ⑤
5. ① ② ③ ④ ⑤
6. ① ② ③ ④ ⑤
7. ① ② ③ ④ ⑤
8. ① ② ③ ④ ⑤
9. ① ② ③ ④ ⑤
10. ① ② ③ ④ ⑤
11. ① ② ③ ④ ⑤
12. ① ② ③ ④ ⑤
13. ① ② ③ ④ ⑤
14. ① ② ③ ④ ⑤
15. ① ② ③ ④ ⑤
16. ① ② ③ ④ ⑤
17. ① ② ③ ④ ⑤
18. ① ② ③ ④ ⑤
19. ① ② ③ ④ ⑤

20. ① ② ③ ④ ⑤
21. ① ② ③ ④ ⑤
22. ① ② ③ ④ ⑤
23. ① ② ③ ④ ⑤
24. ① ② ③ ④ ⑤
25. ① ② ③ ④ ⑤
26. ① ② ③ ④ ⑤
27. ① ② ③ ④ ⑤
28. ① ② ③ ④ ⑤
29. ① ② ③ ④ ⑤
30. ① ② ③ ④ ⑤
31. ① ② ③ ④ ⑤
32. ① ② ③ ④ ⑤
33. ① ② ③ ④ ⑤
34. ① ② ③ ④ ⑤
35. ① ② ③ ④ ⑤
36. ① ② ③ ④ ⑤
37. ① ② ③ ④ ⑤
38. ① ② ③ ④ ⑤

39. ① ② ③ ④ ⑤
40. ① ② ③ ④ ⑤
41. ① ② ③ ④ ⑤
42. ① ② ③ ④ ⑤
43. ① ② ③ ④ ⑤
44. ① ② ③ ④ ⑤
45. ① ② ③ ④ ⑤
46. ① ② ③ ④ ⑤
47. ① ② ③ ④ ⑤
48. ① ② ③ ④ ⑤
49. ① ② ③ ④ ⑤
50. ① ② ③ ④ ⑤
51. ① ② ③ ④ ⑤
52. ① ② ③ ④ ⑤
53. ① ② ③ ④ ⑤
54. ① ② ③ ④ ⑤
55. ① ② ③ ④ ⑤

Questions 1 through 11 refer to the following paragraph.

(1) For the past few decades, Americans neglect to save enough money. (2) People who struggle to pay their bills each month can't imagine saving a little extra for the future but they must. (3) A down payment for a home, college tuition, and retirement are major milestones in many peoples lives. (4) Likewise, a job loss or disability can be an awfull financial burden. (5) With discipline and careful financial planning, Americans can save more money. (6) First, they must create an emergency fund. (7) This fund holds enough money to cover expenses for three to six months. (8) Next, they should pay off credit card debts which have high interest rates. (9) Instead of saving for the future many people are trapped paying their bills. (10) The high interest rates for credit cards deplete potential savings. (11) Once an emergency fund is created and credit card debts are eliminated, Americans can focus on long-term goals such as a home, college or retirement. (12) Some financial planners offer free counseling that learns people to make saving a way of life.

1. Sentence 1: **For the past few decades, Americans <u>neglect</u> to save enough money.**

   Which of the following is the best way to write the underlined portion of the sentence? If you think the original is best, choose option (1).

   (1) neglect
   (2) will neglect
   (3) have neglected
   (4) will have neglected
   (5) had neglected

2. Sentence 2: **People who struggle to pay their bills each month can't imagine saving a little extra for the<u> future but</u> they must.**

   Which of the following is the best way to write the underlined portion of the sentence? If you think the original is the best way, choose option (1).

(1) future but
(2) future; But
(3) future. But
(4) future: but
(5) future, but

3. Sentence 3: **A down payment for a home, college tuition, and retirement are major milestones in many peoples lives**.

   What correction should be made to this sentence?

   (1) insert a comma after *retirement*
   (2) replace *are* with *is*
   (3) change the spelling of *college* to *colledge*
   (4) change the spelling of *peoples* to *people's*
   (5) no correction is necessary

4. Sentence 4: **Likewise, a job loss or disability can be an awfull financial burden.**

   What correction should be made to this sentence?

   (1) remove the comma after *likewise*
   (2) change the spelling of *awfull* to *awful*
   (3) insert a comma after *loss*
   (4) change the spelling of *disability* to *dissability*
   (5) no correction is necessary

5. Sentence 5: **With discipline and careful financial planning, Americans can save more money.**

   What correction should be made to this sentence?

   (1) remove the comma after *planning*
   (2) change the spelling of *careful* to *carful*
   (3) change the spelling of *Americans* to *Americans'*
   (4) insert a comma after *discipline*
   (5) no correction is necessary

6. Sentences 6 and 7: **First, they must create an emergency fund. This fund holds enough money to cover expenses for three to six months.**

   The most effective combination of sentences 6 and 7 would include which of the following words groups?

(1) fund, but holds
(2) fund, and which holds
(3) fund however holds
(4) fund, which holds
(5) fund, that holds

7. Sentence 8: **Next, they should pay off credit card debts which have high interest rates.**

   Which of the following is the best way to write the underlined portion? If you think the original is the best way, choose option (1).

   (1) debts which
   (2) debts, that
   (3) debts, which
   (4) debts. Which
   (5) debts: that

8. Sentence 9: **Instead of saving for the future many people are trapped paying their bills.**

   What correction should be made to this sentence?

   (1) insert comma after *future*
   (2) change the spelling of *trapped* to *traped*
   (3) change the spelling of *their* to *there*
   (4) replace *are* with *is*
   (5) no change is necessary

9. Sentence 10: **The high interest rates for credit cards deplete potential savings.**

   What correction should be made to this sentence?

   (1) change the spelling of *interest* to *intrest*
   (2) insert a comma after *cards*
   (3) replace *deplete* with *depletes*
   (4) insert *have* before *deplete*
   (5) no change is necessary

10. Sentence 11: **Once an emergency fund is created and credit card debts are eliminated, Americans can focus on long-term goals such as a home, college or retirement.**

    What correction should be made to this sentence?

    (1) change the spelling of *debts* to *dets*
    (2) remove the comma after *eliminated*
    (3) replace *can focus* with *focused*
    (4) insert a comma after *college*
    (5) no correction is necessary

11. Sentence 12: **Some financial planners offer free counseling that learns people to make saving a way of life.**
    What correction should be made to this sentence?

    (1) replace *learns* with *teaches*
    (2) insert a comma after *counseling*
    (3) replace *planners* with *planers*
    (4) replace *offer* with *offers*
    (5) no change is necessary

Questions 12 through 19 refer to the following paragraph.

(1) Families with young children have to make many difficult decisions about child care, work and lifestyle changes. (2) Many parents want to decrease their hours, work from home, or stop working altogether once their children are born. (3) Others want to continue working full time. (4) For single parents, the options are limited, Single parents often must work full time to provide for their families. (5) Likewise, many households depend on too incomes to pay the bills. (6) However, in some families the cost of child care, commuting, and services may outweigh the benefit of a second income. (7) In other situations, parents simply may want to be home while the children are young. (8) Parents need to evaluate their concerns carefully. (9) Parents have to make choices that will have a lasting influence on themselves and their children. (10) Fortunately, new opportunities for child care are emerging every day.

12. Sentence 1: **Families with young children have to make many difficult decisions about child care, work and lifestyle changes.**

    What correction should be made to this sentence?

(1) change the spelling of *difficult* to *dificult*
(2) remove the comma after *care*
(3) replace *have* with *has*
(4) insert a comma after *work*
(5) no correction necessary

13. Sentences 2 and 3: **Many parents want to decrease their hours, work from home, or stop working altogether once their children are born. Others want to continue working full time.**
The most effective combination of sentences 2 and 3 would include which of the following word groups?

(1) born, but others
(2) born, nonetheless others
(3) born; others
(4) born, which others
(5) no correction necessary

14. Sentence 4: **For single parents, the options are <u>limited. Single</u> parents often must work full time to provide for their families.**

Which of the following is the best way to write the underlined portion of the sentence? If you think the original is best, choose option (1).

(1) limited, single
(2) limited, and single
(3) limited, but single
(4) limited: Single
(5) limited; single

15. Sentence 5: **Likewise, many households depend on too incomes to pay the bills.**

What correction should be made to this sentence?

(1) remove the comma after *likewise*
(2) replace *too* with *two*
(3) replace *depend* with *depends*
(4) insert a comma after *incomes*
(5) no correction necessary

16. Sentence 6: **However, in some families the cost of child care, commuting, and services may outweigh the benefit of a second income.**

If you rewrote this sentence beginning with

The cost of child care, commuting, and services

the next words should be

(1) the benefit of
(2) some families
(3) may outweigh
(4) second income
(5) in however

17. Sentence 7: **In other situations, parents simply may want to be home while the children are young.**

What correction should be made to this sentence?

(1) insert a comma after *home*
(2) replace *to* with *too*
(3) remove the comma after *situations*
(4) change the spelling of *parents* to *parent's*
(5) no correction is necessary

18. Sentences 8 and 9: **Parents need to evaluate their concerns carefully. Parents have to make choices that will have a lasting influence on themselves and their children.**

The most effective combination of sentences 8 and 9 would include which of the following word groups?

(1) carefully and make choices
(2) concerns, lasting influence
(3) carefully, but parents
(4) concerns that will have
(5) carefully; however

19. Sentence 10: **Fortunately, new options for work and child care <u>emerged</u> every day.**

What is the best way to write the underlined portion of the sentence? If you think the original is best, choose option (1).

(1) emerged
(2) had emerged
(3) emerge
(4) will have emerged
(5) were emerging

Questions 20 through 27 refer to the following paragraph.

(1) Although federal income taxes get the most attention, state and local taxes play a role, to. (2) Where do the state and local governments get their money and how do they spend it? (3) States generated revenue through a variety of taxes. (4) Most states have income taxes, which bring in most of the revenue; sales taxes, which affect businesses as well as consumers, and property taxes. (5) Corporate income taxes, estate taxes, fees, and lisences also contribute to the coffers. (6) The state and local governments use they're funds to support many services. (7) Most of the money sustains the schools, public assistance, police and fire protection, legal system and highways. (8) Nobody want to pay taxes, but we do depend on the support that our tax dollars provide.

20. Sentence 1: **Although federal income taxes get the most attention, state and local taxes play a role, too.**

    What correction should be made to this sentence?

    (1) remove the comma after *attention*
    (2) insert a comma after *state*
    (3) change *attention* to *atention*
    (4) replace *to* with *too*
    (5) no correction is necessary

21. Sentence 2: **Where do the state and local governments get their money and how do they spend it?**

    What correction should be made to this sentence?

    (1) insert a comma after *money*
    (2) replace *their* with *there*
    (3) change the spelling of *governments* to *goverments*
    (4) replace *do* with *did*
    (5) no correction necessary

22. Sentence 3: **States generated revenue through a variety of taxes.**

    What correction should be made to this sentence?

    (1) change the spelling of *states* to *state's*
    (2) change the spelling of *through* to *threw*
    (3) insert a comma after *revenue*
    (4) replace *generated* with *generate*
    (5) no correction necessary

23. Sentence 4: **Most states have income taxes, which bring in most of the revenue; sales taxes, which affect businesses as well as consumers, and property taxes.**

    What correction should be made to this sentence?

    (1) change the spelling of *businesses* to *bisnisses*
    (2) replace *consumers, and* with *consumers; and*
    (3) change the spelling of *states* to *state's*
    (4) remove the comma after *taxes*
    (5) no correction necessary

24. Sentence 5: **Corporate income taxes, estate taxes, fees, and lisences also contribute to the coffers.**

    (1) remove the comma after *fees*
    (2) replace *contribute* with *contributes*
    (3) change the spelling of *lisences* to *licenses*
    (4) replace *too* with *to*
    (5) no correction necessary

25. Sentence 6: **The state and local governments use they're funds to support many services.**

    What correction should be made to this sentence?

    (1) insert a comma after *state*
    (2) replace *they're* with *their*
    (3) change the spelling of *services* to *servises*
    (4) change the spelling of *governments* to *goverments*
    (5) no correction necessary

26. Sentence 7: **Most of the money sustains the schools, public assistance, police and fire protection, legal system and highways.**

What correction should be made to this sentence?

(1) insert a comma after *system*
(2) insert a comma after *police*
(3) replace *sustains* with *sustain*
(4) change the spelling of *police* to *Police*
(5) no correction necessary

27. Sentence 8: **Nobody want to pay taxes, but we do depend on the support that our tax dollars provide.**
What correction should be made to this sentence?

(1) replace *depend* with *depends*
(2) remove the comma after *but*
(3) change the spelling of *dollars* to *dollar's*
(4) replace *want* with *wants*
(5) no correction necessary

Questions 28 through 36 refer to the next paragraph.

(1) Police Departments in major cities across the nation are taking new steps to fight crime. (2) In the past police officers focused on major crimes while letting minor offenses go unnoticed. (3) Now, they will be working harder to enforce all of the laws. (4) Traffic violations and crimes such as disorderly conduct, panhandling, loitering, and prostitution are getting much more atention. (5) When all laws are upheld the quality of life for the city improves. (6) Many police officials also believe that enforcing minor laws actually prevents major crimes from happening. (7) This approach has reduced crime in some cities but not everyone is happy. (8) The American Civil Liberties Union (ACLU), that works to protect people's rights, notes that complaints against officers have increased. (9) Nonetheless, the new focus on enforcing all laws probly will continue.

28. Sentence 1: **Police Departments in major cities across the nation are taking new steps to fight crime.**

What correction should be made to this sentence?

(1) change *are* to *were*
(2) change the spelling of *cities* to *cityes*
(3) insert a comma after *cities*
(4) change the spelling of *Departments* to *departments*
(5) no correction necessary

29. Sentence 2: **In the past police officers focused on major crimes while letting minor offenses go unnoticed.**
What correction should be made to this sentence?

(1) change the spelling of *officers* to *oficers*
(2) change the spelling of *unnoticed* to *unoticed*
(3) insert a comma after *past*
(4) change *focused* to *focus*
(5) no correction necessary

30. Sentence 3: **Now, they will be working harder to enforce all of the laws.**

What correction should be made to this sentence?

(1) change *will be* to *are*
(2) remove the comma after *now*
(3) change the spelling of *enforce* to *enforse*
(4) insert a comma after *harder*
(5) no correction necessary

31. Sentence 4: **Traffic violations and crimes such as disorderly conduct, panhandling, loitering, and prostitution are getting much more atention.**

What correction should be made to this sentence?

(1) insert a comma after *prostitution*
(2) change *are* to *were*
(3) remove the comma after *loitering*
(4) change the spelling of *atention* to *attention*
(5) no correction necessary

32. Sentence 5: **When all laws are upheld the quality of life for the city improves.**

What correction should be made to this sentence?

(1) change *improves* to *improved*
(2) insert a comma after *upheld*
(3) change *are* to *will be*
(4) insert a comma after *life*
(5) no correction necessary

33. Sentence 6: **Many police officials also believe that enforcing minor laws actually prevents major crimes from happening.**
What correction should be made to this sentence?

(1) change the spelling of *believe* to *beleive*
(2) replace *prevents* to *prevented*
(3) insert a comma after *laws*
(4) replace *police* with *Police*
(5) no correction necessary

34. Sentence 7: **This approach has reduced crime in some cities but not everyone is happy.**

What correction should be made to this sentence?

(1) replace *is* with *was*
(2) insert a comma after *cities*
(3) replace *has* with *have*
(4) change the spelling of *approach* to *aproach*
(5) no correction necessary

35. Sentence 8: **The American Civil Liberties Union (ACLU), that works to protect people's rights, notes that complaints against officers have increased.**

What correction should be made to this sentence?

(1) replace *that* with *which*
(2) remove the comma after *rights*
(3) replace *ACLU* with *aclu*
(4) replace *notes* to *will note*
(5) no correction necessary

36. Sentence 9: **Nonetheless, the new focus on enforcing all laws probly will continue.**

What correction should be made to this sentence?

(1) remove the comma after *nonetheless*
(2) change *will continue* to *continued*
(3) change the spelling of *probly* to *probably*
(4) change the spelling of *enforcing* to *enforsing*
(5) no correction necessary

Questions 37 through 45 refer to the following paragraph.

(1) Companies are developing computer software to meet varied intrests. (2) For years the market was dominated by business programs and computer games. (3) Now these software packages are making room for new products. (4) Traditional programs still are popular however encyclopedias, medical guides, and tutorials also line the shelves. (5) Software can't solve every problem. (6) Computer programs do help children with their homework and adults with their taxes. (7) Software can trace family roots, track finances, or created greeting cards. (8) The list of programs keeps growing. (9) Manufacturers have increased the number of computer users by making computers more accessible. (10) Software companies have tapped into this expanding market and have created programs that meet diffrent needs.

37. Sentence 1: **Companies are developing computer software to meet varied intrests**.

What correction should be made to this sentence?

(1) change the spelling of *companies* to *companys*
(2) insert a comma after *software*
(3) change the spelling of *intrests* to *interests*
(4) replace *developing* with *develop*
(5) no correction necessary

38. Sentence 2: **For years the market was dominated by business programs and computer games.**

If you rewrote sentence 2 beginning with

Business programs and computer games

the next word should be

(1) market
(2) for
(3) was
(4) years
(5) dominated

39. Sentence 3: **Now these software packages <u>are making</u> room for new products.**
Which of the following is the best way to write the underlined portion of the sentence? If you think the original is best, choose option (1).

(1) are making
(2) will make
(3) have been making
(4) made
(5) had made

40. Sentence 4: **Traditional programs still are <u>popular however encyclopedias, medical guides, and</u> tutorials also line the shelves.**

Which of the following is the best way to punctuate the underlined portion of this sentence? If you think the original is the best way, choose option (1).

(1) popular however encyclopedias, medical guides, and
(2) popular; however, encyclopedias, medical guides, and
(3) popular: however, encyclopedias, medical guides, and
(4) popular, however encyclopedias; medical guides; and
(5) popular, however ; encyclopedias, medical guides, and

41. Sentences 5 and 6: **Software can't solve every problem. Computer programs do help children with their homework and adults with their taxes.**

The most effective combination of sentences 5 and 6 would include which of the following word groups?

(1) homework, and computer
(2) homework; or computer
(3) homework; nonetheless, computer
(4) homework, so computer
(5) homework; therefore, computer

42. Sentence 7: **Software can trace family roots, track finances, or created greeting cards.**

Which of the following corrections should be made to this sentence?

(1) remove the comma after *finances*
(2) replace *trace* with *traces*
(3) insert a comma after *family*
(4) replace *created* with *create*
(5) no correction necessary

43. Sentence 8: **The list of programs <u>keeps</u> growing.**

Which of the following is the best way to write the underlined portion of the sentence? If you think that the original is the best way, choose option (1).

(1) keeps
(2) is keeping
(3) kept
(4) had kept
(5) keep

44. Sentence 9: **Manufacturers have increased the number of computer users by making computers more accessible.**

If you rewrote sentence 9 beginning with

By making computers more accessible,

the next word should be

(1) increased
(2) computer
(3) users
(4) have
(5) manufacturers

45. Sentence 10: **Software companies have tapped into this expanding market and have created programs that meet diffrent needs.**

Which of the following corrections should be made to this sentence?

(1) insert a comma after *market*
(2) replace *meet* with *meat*
(3) change *created* to *create*
(4) change the spelling of *diffrent* to *different*
(5) no correction necessary

Questions 46 through 55 refer to the following paragraphs.

(1) Many factors have contributed to America's current educational crises, however, one characteristic clearly marks a successful school—parental involvement. (2) When parents participate regularly in school activities children excel. (3) Active parents send a clear message to their children. (4) Education matters. (5) They work with teachers to reinforce key values and to develop confident eager learners. (6) Involved parents understand the concerns of there local schools, and they address problems quickly.

(7) Many educators which stress parental involvement have developed innovative ways to get parents into the schools. (8) Conferences, meetings, and atheletic events are scheduled at night so that working parents can attend. (9) Some schools encourage parents to attend classes, eat lunch, and go on field trips with their children. (10) Parents pledge to volunteer during the school year and to assist whomever needs help. (11) While some people wait for the federal government to help Americas schools, others work to improve the schools now.

46. Sentence 1: **Many factors have contributed to America's current educational <u>crises, however, one</u> characteristic clearly marks a successful school— parental involvement.**

    What is the best way to write the underlined portion of this sentence? If you think the original is the best, choose option (1).

    (1) crises, however, one
    (2) crises, however. One
    (3) crises; however, one
    (4) crises: however one
    (5) crises: However one

47. Sentence 2: **When parents participate regularly in school activities children excel.**

    What correction should be made to this sentence?

(1) change the spelling of *activities* to *activitys*
(2) insert a comma after *activities*
(3) change *excel* to *excels*
(4) replace *regularly* with *regular*
(5) no correction necessary

48. Sentences 3 and 4: **Active parents send a clear message to their children. Education matters.**
    The most effective combination of sentences 3 and 4 would include which of the following word groups?

    (1) children: education
    (2) children; however, education
    (3) children, and
    (4) children; nonetheless
    (5) children, but

49. Sentence 5: **They work with teachers to reinforce key values and to develop confident eager learners.**

    (1) change the spelling of *confident* to *confidant*
    (2) insert a comma after *values*
    (3) replace *work* with *worked*
    (4) insert a comma after *confident*
    (5) no correction necessary

50. Sentence 6: **Involved parents understand the concerns of there local schools, and they address problems quickly.**

    What correction should be made to this sentence?

    (1) remove the comma after *schools*
    (2) change the spelling of *there* to *their*
    (3) replace *parents* with *parents'*
    (4) replace *quickly* with *quick*
    (5) no correction necessary

51. Sentence 7: **Many educators which stress parental involvement have developed innovative ways to get parents into the schools.**

    What correction should be made to this sentence?

    (1) insert a comma after *educators*
    (2) replace *have developed* with *will have developed*
    (3) replace *which* with *who*

(4) change the spelling of *involvement* to *involvment*

(5) no correction necessary

52. Sentence 8: **Conferences, meetings, and atheletic events are scheduled at night so that working parents can attend.**
What correction should be made to this sentence?

(1) remove the comma after *meetings*
(2) change the spelling of *atheletic* to *athletic*
(3) replace *are* with *were*
(4) change the spelling of *scheduled* to *schedualed*
(5) no correction necessary

53. Sentence 9: **Some schools encourage parents to attend classes, eat lunch, and go on field trips with their children.**

What correction should be made to this sentence?

(1) remove the comma after *lunch*
(2) change the spelling of *field* to *feild*
(3) insert a comma after *parents*
(4) change the spelling of *their* to *they're*
(5) no correction necessary

54. Sentence 10: **Parents pledge to volunteer during the school year and to assist whomever needs help.**

What correction should be made to this sentence?

(1) replace *whomever* with *whoever*
(2) insert a comma after *year*
(3) change the spelling of *Parents* to *Parents'*
(4) insert a comma after *assist*
(5) no correction necessary

55. Sentence 11: **While some people wait for the federal government to help Americas schools, others work to improve the schools now.**

What correction should be made to this sentence?

(1) remove the comma after *schools*
(2) change the spelling of *federal* to *fedral*
(3) insert a comma after *wait*
(4) change the spelling of *Americas* to *America's*
(5) no correction necessary

Answers are on pages 314–317.

typographic the spelling of motion-ment to inclement.
(5) no correction necessary

53. Sentence 5: Conferences, meet-ings, and athletic events are scheduled at night so that work-ing parents can attend.
What correction should be made to this sentence?
(1) remove the comma after meetings
(2) change the spelling of athletic to athlete
(3) replace are with were
(4) change the spelling of scheduled to scheduled
(5) no correction necessary

54. Sentence 6: Some schools encourage parents to attend classes, eat lunch, and go on field trips with their children.
What correction should be made to this sentence?
(1) remove the comma after lunch
(2) change the spelling of field to feild
(3) insert a comma after parents
(4) change the spelling of their to there
(5) no correction necessary

54. Sentence 10: Parents pledge to volunteer during the school year and to assist wherever needs help.
What correction should be made to this sentence?
(1) replace someone with another
(2) insert a comma after help
(3) change the spelling of pledge to Parents
(4) insert a comma after year
(5) no correction necessary

55. Sentence 11: While some people wait for the federal government to help America's schools, others work to improve the schools now.
What correction should be made to this sentence?
(1) remove the comma after schools
(2) change the spelling of federal to Federal
(3) insert a comma after until
(4) change the spelling of America's to America's
(5) no correction necessary

Answers are on pages 314–317.

SENTENCES AND PARAGRAPHS

Writing Clear Sentences

In this chapter you will learn:

- ☐ How to use conjunctions (pages 179, 180)
- ☐ How to write sentences with parallel structure (pages 180–182)
- ☐ How to write sentences that are balanced (pages 182–184)
- ☐ How to keep the verb tense consistent (pages 184–186)
- ☐ How to avoid misplaced modifiers (pages 186, 187)
- ☐ How to avoid dangling modifiers (page 187–189)
- ☐ How to keep pronouns consistent (page 189)
- ☐ How to rewrite sentences (pages 190–191)
- ☐ How to combine sentences (pages 191–196)

As a writer, you need to be sure that you express your thoughts clearly. Writing sentences is like giving someone directions. Sometimes what is obvious to you may not be so plain to the reader. This chapter will help you send a clear message. It also will teach you to express ideas in many different ways.

Conjunctions

Conjunctions join words, phrases, and clauses. However, not all conjunctions are the same. Each one has a specific job, as noted in the following box.

CONJUNCTIONS

Conjunctions	Jobs
and	adds two equal statements
but, yet	shows a difference, a contrast, or something unexpected or shows an option or choice
nor	shows that neither option or choice is good
for, so	show why something happens, connect cause and effect

Place a comma before a conjunction that joins two independent clauses.

Examples:

1. Dee worked two jobs, <u>and</u> she raised three children.
   Both clauses are equal. If *she raised three children* came first, the sentence would have the same meaning.
2. Kim wants to help her son with his homework, <u>but</u> she doesn't know how to read.
   The reader assumes that Kim can read. *But* shows that the second clause is unexpected.

3. Jong won the lottery, <u>or</u> he got a huge raise.
Or shows an option, the lottery *or* a raise.

4. Jack worked overtime, <u>so</u> he could pay off his loans.
Why did Jack work overtime? So he could pay off his loans. *So* shows why something happens.

5. Lee broke his arm, <u>yet</u> he still enjoyed his birthday.
Yet means nonetheless. In spite of his broken arm, Lee enjoyed his birthday.

EXERCISE 1: Write an appropriate conjunction in the space provided. Some sentences have more than one correct answer.

1. Claire moved out of her apartment, _____ she bought a house.

2. Lou wanted to buy a new car, _____ he saved his money.

3. Snakes are not cuddly pets, _____ some people love them.

4. Many people order pizza for the Super Bowl, _____ they prepare food before the game.

5. Yang is a great cook, _____ she does not like to have friends over for dinner.

6. Kyle worked hard in school, _____ he could get a good job after graduation.

7. Tim liked soccer, _____ he became a good player.

8. Nu worked hard to save her money, _____ she could retire early.

9. After high school, students often go to college, _____ they go to work.

10. Kira came to this country as an adult, _____ she learned English as quickly as she could.

Answers are on page 317.

☞ Remember these <u>facts about conjunctions:</u>

- Conjunctions join words, phrases, and clauses.
- Each conjunction has a specific job.
- A comma should be placed before a conjunction that joins two clauses.

Parallel Structure

In sentences, parallel structure means that words with similar jobs have the same form. Sentences with parallel structure are clear and easy to read. Check for parallel structure every time you have items in a series.

CHECKLIST FOR PARALLEL STRUCTURE

☐ Find the items in a series, which may be adjectives, nouns, verbs, adverbs, or prepositional phrases.

☐ Make sure each item is in the same form.

Examples:

VERBS IN A SERIES

1. **Wrong**
The boss who <u>praises</u> workers, <u>giving</u> raises, and <u>allows</u> vacations should have a good staff.
Giving is not in the same form as *praises* and *allows*.
Right
The boss who <u>praises</u> workers, <u>gives</u> raises, and <u>allows</u> vacations should have a good staff.
Praises, *gives*, and *allows* are in the same form.

ADJECTIVES IN A SERIES

2. **Wrong**
The resort has <u>good</u> food, <u>live</u> entertainment, and a pool <u>that is heated</u>.

Good, *live*, and *that is heated* all work like adjectives, but they are not in the same form. *That is heated* is an adjective clause.

Right

The resort has good food, live entertainment, and a heated pool. *Good*, *live*, and *heated* are in the same form.

ADVERBS IN A SERIES

3. **Wrong**

Parents must teach values to their children consciously, openly, and with consistence.
Consciously, *openly*, and *with consistence* all work like adverbs, but they are not in the same form. *With consistence* is a prepositional phrase.

Right

Parents must teach values to their children consciously, openly, and consistently.
Consciously, *openly*, and *consistently* are in the same form.

PHRASES IN A SERIES

4. **Wrong**

Next month, our friends will decide to buy a car, to save their money, or go on a trip.
To buy and *to save* are infinitives. *Go* is not in the same form.

Right

Next month, our friends will decide to buy a car, to save their money, or to go on a trip.
To buy, *to save*, and *to go* are in the same form.

PREPOSITIONAL PHRASES

5. **Wrong**

When you wash the car, clean under the hood, cleaning behind the wheels, and between the doors.
Under the hood, *behind the wheels*, and *between the doors* are prepositional phrases that work like adverbs. They tell where *you* should clean. *Cleaning*, which is unnecessary in this sentence, makes the phrases not parallel.

Right

When you wash the car, clean under the hood, behind the wheels, and between the doors.

The phrases *under the hood*, *behind the wheels*, and *between the doors* are in the same form.

EXERCISE 2: Underline the words or groups of words that are not parallel. Write the correct, parallel structure in the space provided.

1. Nate dressed up because he wanted to charm his girlfriend, to impress his friends, and please his parents.

_____

_____

_____

2. Food that was free, great music, and good weather made the state fair a big hit.

_____

_____

_____

3. People should save their money carefully, regularly, and with knowledge.

_____

_____

_____

4. Tran who wants a quiet, bright place that is relaxing to study needs to look hard.

_____

_____

_____

5. When you go to the food store, drive through town, over the bridge, and drive past the town pool.

_____

_____

6. Before they admitted that nicotine is addictive, cigarette manufacturers ignored scientific research, testified before Congress, and fighting lawsuits against them.

_____

_____

_____

7. Many people in the community volunteer happily, repeatedly, and with kindness.

_____

_____

_____

8. Many students look for a college with a good reputation, athletic programs, and a tuition that is reasonable.

_____

_____

_____

9. Various books, on-line computers, and materials that are for children help the public libraries attract many different people.

_____

_____

_____

10. Athletes who want a large, open gym that is well designed should go to the health club around the corner.

_____

_____

Answers are on pages 317, 318.

Remember these <u>facts about parallel structure</u>:

- Words with the same job should be in the same form.
- Check for parallel structure whenever you have items in a series.

Balanced Structure

Sentences need balance. Words that have similar jobs in a sentence should be in the same form.

Examples:

1. **Wrong**
   Pete argued that <u>playing sports</u> is better than <u>someone who watches TV</u>.
   The sentence compares playing sports with watching TV. Both groups of words should be in the same form.
   Right
   Pete argued that <u>playing sports</u> is better than <u>watching TV</u>.
   Both groups of words are in the same form.

2. **Wrong**
   Ty worked <u>quickly</u> and <u>with skill</u>.
   Quickly and *with skill* both work like adverbs, but they are not in the same form.
   Right
   Ty worked <u>quickly</u> and <u>skillfully</u>.
   Both adverbs are in the same form.

COMPOUND PARTS

Often sentences that are not balanced need to be rewritten with compound parts.

Examples:

Wrong
I <u>buy gas</u> for the car once a week, and <u>the oil is changed by me</u> every three months.
The same person performs both actions.

Right
I <u>buy</u> gas for the car every week <u>and change</u> the oil every three months.
A compound verb, *buy and change*, gives the sentence balance. *I* performs both actions.

EXERCISE 3: Check for balance in each of the following sentences. If a sentence is not balanced, write a new, balanced sentence in the space provided. Each sentence has more than one correct answer.

1. The new player is tall and with athletic ability.

   _____

   _____

   _____

2. Running daily and to eat well are important for me.

   _____

   _____

3. Nate shops for food each week, and the laundry is done by him.

   _____

   _____

   _____

4. The coach thinks that playing well is more important than to win every game.

   _____

   _____

   _____

5. Matt works late, and dinner is prepared by him when he gets home.

   _____

   _____

   _____

6. Many doctors think that finding a cure for cancer is as important as research on heart disease.

   _____

   _____

   _____

7. In the city, many people argue that improving the schools is as important as to lower crime rates.

   _____

   _____

   _____

8. Tourists enjoy hearing the Cleveland Orchestra and to visit the Cleveland Museum of Art.

   _____

   _____

   _____

9. Ray fixed the car, and the deck was stained by him.

_____

_____

_____

10. Writing poetry and to compose music have some similarities.

_____

_____

_____

Answers are on page 318.

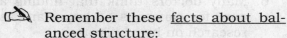 Remember these <u>facts about balanced structure</u>:

• Words that have similar jobs should be in the same form.

• Sentences that are not balanced may need to be rewritten with compound parts.

CONSISTENT VERB TENSE

The verb tense, which tells when something happens, generally should be the same throughout a sentence or paragraph.

Example:

Wrong
On Fridays, Wolf <u>went</u> for a stroll, and he <u>stops</u> by the bread store.
Both actions occur repeatedly on Fridays.
Went and *stops* should be in the present tense.

Right
On Fridays, Wolf <u>goes</u> for a stroll, and he <u>stops</u> by the bread store.
Wolf performs both actions repeatedly, so *goes* and *stops* are in the present tense.

EXERCISE 4: Choose the correct tense for the underlined verb. Write your answer in the space provided.

1. Every Friday, Jake orders pizza, and he <u>watched</u> a movie. _____

2. Next week, Kim will clean the basement, and she <u>cut</u> the lawn. _____

3. Lee bought a new computer and <u>will have moved</u> his office last month. _____

4. Next year, Congress <u>passed</u> a welfare reform bill, and the president will sign it. _____

5. On Monday, she walked into the store and <u>acts</u> like she owned the place. _____

6. Last week, leaders of the warring nations signed a peace treaty, and the fighting <u>ends</u>. _____

7. In the next few years, business leaders <u>invested</u> more money downtown and will bring more jobs to the region. _____

8. Jamestown, the first permanent English settlement in America, lures various tourists and <u>attracted</u> many historians every year. _____

9. In Haiti, a military group overturned the democratic government and <u>establishes</u> a dictatorship. _____

10. Chi's parents took her out of the public school and <u>teach</u> her at home last year. _____

Answers are on pages 318, 319.

SENTENCES WITH TWO CLAUSES

Sentences that have two clauses also have two verbs. For the sentence to be clear, the tense of each verb must show when the actions occurred. If you focus only on the subject and verb for each clause, you can choose the correct verb form more easily.

Examples:

1. **Wrong**

   After I <u>pay</u> my bills next week, I <u>put</u> more money in savings.

   After I pay, I put. *Put* should be in the future tense.

   Right

   After I <u>pay</u> my bills next week, I <u>will put</u> more money in savings.

   Now it is clear which action occurs first.

2. **Wrong**

   Whenever a comet <u>appears</u>, many people <u>bought</u> telescopes.

   Whenever a comet appears, people bought. Both actions occur at the same time. The verbs should be in the present tense.

   Right

   Whenever a comet <u>appears</u>, many people <u>buy</u> telescopes.

   Appears and *buy* are in the present tense. Both actions occur at the same time.

3. **Wrong**

   While Kay <u>was running</u> in the race, her children <u>will be cheering</u> for her.

   While Kay was running, the children will be cheering. Both actions occurred at the same time in the past.

   Right

   While Kay <u>was running</u> in the race, her children <u>cheered</u> for her.

   Was running is in the past continuing tense, which means that the action was going on for some time in the past. *Cheered* is in the past tense. Both actions occur at the same time.

   While Kay <u>was running</u> in the race, her children <u>were cheering</u> for her.

   Was running and *were cheering* are in the past continuing tense. Both actions occur at the same time in the past.

4. **Wrong**

   After Bob <u>retired</u> from work, he <u>sold</u> his house.

   Both events occurred in the past, but Bob sold his house after he had retired. The action that was com-

   pleted first must be in the past perfect tense.

   Right

   After Bob <u>had retired</u> from work, he <u>sold</u> his house.

   Had retired is in the past perfect tense because this action was completed before the house was sold.

⇨ **Reminder**

Perfect means "completed." The perfect tenses (had, has, have, or will have + verb) show that something was or will be completed before another action or time.

Past Perfect

She <u>had worked</u> until ten o'clock last night.

They <u>had lived</u> in New York before they moved to Maine.

Future Perfect

By noon, he <u>will have worked</u> for two days straight.

Before I change jobs next week, I <u>will have cleaned</u> out my office.

EXERCISE 5: Choose the correct tense for the underlined verb. Write your answer in the space provided.

1. After Shantae <u>won</u> the match, he waved to his dad in the stands. _____

2. When the weather reports predict snow, people <u>rushed</u> to the food store to buy milk and eggs. _____

3. If he doesn't return my calls soon, I <u>find</u> a new lawyer. _____

4. Because it will rain hard, the traffic <u>was</u> awful. _____

5. I washed the dishes while I <u>talk</u> on the phone. _____

6. Anne <u>won</u> the award if she gives a good speech. _____

7. Before my friends arrived last week, I <u>cleaned</u> the house. _____

8. After we <u>studied</u> for the test, we relaxed and watched a movie. _____

9. John <u>cooked</u> the food before the party next Sunday. _____

10. As soon as the check arrives, Han <u>put</u> it in a savings account. _____

Answers are on page 319.

☞ Remember these <u>facts about consistent verb tense</u>:

- Generally, the verb tense should be the same throughout a sentence or paragraph.
- In a complex sentence (1 independent clause + 1 dependent clause), each verb must show when the actions occurred.

Misplaced Modifiers

A misplaced modifier is like a letter that is sent to the wrong person. When modifiers are misplaced, the meaning of the sentence is lost. To keep sentences clear, always place modifiers near the words that they describe.

Examples:

1. **Wrong**
   After we searched for a sitter, we found a nice woman to care for our children <u>frantically</u>.
   Will the sitter care for the children frantically, or did we search frantically?
   Right
   After we <u>frantically</u> searched for a sitter, we found a nice woman to care for our children.
   Frantically describes how *we* searched.

2. **Wrong**
   Rachel wanted to buy a safe car <u>with a child on the way</u>.
   Does the car have a child on the way?
   Right
   <u>With a child on the way</u>, Rachel wanted to buy a safe car.
   With a child on the way describes *Rachel*, first noun after the comma.

3. **Wrong**
   Our coach yelled at the umpire <u>who rarely loses his temper</u>.
   Does the coach or the umpire rarely lose his temper?
   Right
   Our coach, <u>who rarely loses his temper</u>, yelled at the umpire.
   Who rarely loses his temper describes *coach*.

EXERCISE 6: Rewrite the following sentences so that the meaning is clear. Some questions have more than one possible answer.

1. Air bags and seat belts can save lives used properly.

   _____

   _____

   _____

2. Children often watch TV until their parents come home after school.

   _____

   _____

   _____

3. Homes are being moved to higher ground with flood damage.

   _____

   _____

   _____

4. The working poor often can not afford good health care struggling to pay the bills.

   _____

   _____

   _____

5. I called in sick to work tired from the flu.

   _____

   _____

   _____

6. Lim found a good plumber to fix his sink unintentionally.

   _____

   _____

   _____

7. Dr. Tim tells people to eat a low-fat diet and exercise with weight problems.

   _____

   _____

   _____

8. Some people are frustrated with HMOs who want to choose their own doctors.

   _____

   _____

   _____

9. The Chair of the Federal Reserve will raise interest rates concerned about the risk of inflation.

   _____

   _____

   _____

10. Trained to help the visually impaired, some people use dogs.

   _____

   _____

   _____

Answers are on pages 319, 320.

Dangling Modifiers

A dangling modifier has nothing to describe. It is like a letter without an address. You must reword the sentence to give the modifier meaning.

Examples:

1. **Wrong**
   <u>Driving to the store</u>, a horse ran across the road.
   Was the horse driving? *Horse* is the first noun after the comma.
   Right
   When we were <u>driving to the store</u>, a horse ran across the road.
   In this sentence, *driving* is the main verb in the verb phrase *were driving*. *To the store* is a prepositional phrase that shows where we were driving. The sentence is clear.
2. **Wrong**
   <u>Sailing on the lake</u>, a beautiful sunset filled the sky.
   Was the sunset sailing on the lake? *Sunset* is the first noun after the comma.

Right

While we were <u>sailing on the lake</u>, a beautiful sunset filled the sky.

In this sentence, *sailing* is the main verb in the verb phrase *were sailing*. *On the lake* is a prepositional phrase that shows where we were sailing.

EXERCISE 7: Rewrite the following sentences so that the meaning is clear. Each question has more than one correct answer.

1. While climbing up the mountain face, my foot slipped.

   _____

   _____

   _____

2. Searching for clues to the crime, the police car was stolen.

   _____

   _____

3. Tired and hungry, our museum tour ended.

   _____

   _____

4. Checking my watch, the sun came out from behind the clouds.

   _____

   _____

   _____

5. Frustrated with campaign funding, reform bills quickly passed through Congress.

   _____

   _____

   _____

6. After checking all the numbers, Kim's tax return was mailed to the IRS.

   _____

   _____

   _____

7. With steady hours and good pay, Ty searched the want ads for a job.

   _____

   _____

   _____

8. Running to catch the bus, my briefcase spilled all over the sidewalk.

   _____

   _____

   _____

9. Angered by the slow response, the ambulance finally arrived at the scene.

   _____

   _____

   _____

10. Fresh off the delivery truck, the salesperson showed us the new cars.

_____

_____

_____

Answers are on pages 320, 321.

✍ Remember these <u>facts about modifiers</u>:

- Always place modifiers near the words that they describe.
- Sentences with misplaced or dangling modifiers must be reworded.

Consistent Pronouns

Pronouns substitute for nouns. When you write, make sure the reader clearly understands to whom or what the pronoun refers.

Examples:

1. **Wrong**
   When <u>I</u> am on the highway, the crazy drivers upset <u>you</u>.
   Is the sentence about *I* or *you*?
   Right
   When <u>I</u> am on the highway, the crazy drivers upset <u>me</u>.
   The sentence is clearly about *I*.
2. **Wrong**
   The staff asked me about a new software <u>program</u> that has great graphics. <u>They</u> should help with the new account.
   Does *they* refer to the program, the graphics, or the staff?
   Right
   The staff asked me about a new software <u>program</u> that has great graphics. <u>It</u> should help with the new account.
   The second sentence is clearly about the program.

EXERCISE 8: Underline the pronoun that needs to be changed in each of the following sentences. Write the correct pronoun in the space provided.

1. Doctors must graduate from medical school, serve as residents, and pass the boards before you set up a practice. _____

2. Before Ms. Tran hired the new clerks, they interviewed each person. _____

3. Many companies expect their employees to pass a drug test. Persons who fail them may lose their jobs. _____

4. Our food store caters to busy lives. They open early, close late, and carry prepared meals. _____

5. When the school board members announced the budget cut, it was on local TV. _____

6. Jill learned CPR during her first aid classes. They helped when her father had a heart attack.

   _____

7. When Kathy took karate classes, they learned a lot about self-defense. _____

8. Before one interviews for a job, you need to learn about the company.

   _____

9. Soon after Glen traveled to Japan, he was hit by a terrible earthquake.

   _____

10. In 1846, James Smithson's fortune helped form the Smithsonian Institution. Today, he operates many museums in Washington, DC.

    _____

Answers are on page 321.

✍ Remember, pronouns should clearly refer to a specific person or thing.

Rewriting Sentences

Rewriting sentences is like reorganizing a closet. Using the same space, you need to reorganize the items effectively. The GED will test your ability to rewrite sentences. Although the words may change, the meaning of the new sentence must be the same.

STEPS FOR REWRITING SENTENCES

1. Find the main idea(s).
2. Find the relationship between ideas.
3. Rewrite the sentence. (Some words may be changed or omitted in the new sentence.)
4. Make sure that the new sentence sends the same message as the original.
5. Check the grammar in the new sentence.

Examples:

1. **Original Sentence**
   The store was flooded by shoppers with bags in hand.
   New Sentence
   Shoppers with bags in hand flooded the store.
2. **Original Sentence**
   Children's toys, car seats, and cribs are safer because of federal safety guidelines.
   New Sentence
   Federal safety guidelines have made children's toys, car seats, and cribs safer.
   Practice will make rewriting sentences easier.

EXERCISE 9: Rewrite the following sentences as directed. Some sentences have more than one correct answer.

1. Hunters slaughter elephants whose ivory tusks are valuable.
   Rewrite the sentence beginning with <u>Because ivory tusks are valuable</u>

   _____

   _____

2. Wildlife groups work hard to save the endangered species, but some animals may not survive.
   Rewrite the sentence beginning with <u>Although wildlife groups work hard to save</u>

   _____

   _____

3. Children are affected by the violence that they see on TV.
   Rewrite the sentence beginning with <u>TV violence</u>

   _____

   _____

4. Car owners must be prepared to spend a lot of money: gas, maintenance, and insurance are expensive.
   Rewrite the sentence beginning with <u>Gas, maintenance, and insurance are expensive</u>

   _____

   _____

5. Back support is important whenever one lifts something heavy.
   Rewrite the sentence beginning with <u>Whenever one lifts something heavy</u>

   _____

   _____

6. Sometimes persons are infected by rabid animals.
   Rewrite the sentence beginning with
   <u>Rabid animals</u>

   _____

   _____

7. Some persons earn bad credit ratings because they do not pay their bills on time.
   Rewrite the sentence beginning with
   <u>Because they do not pay</u>

   _____

   _____

8. Financial planners help people with bad debts.
   Rewrite the sentence beginning with
   <u>People with bad debts</u>

   _____

   _____

9. Over time, alcoholism can destroy the liver and other organs.
   Rewrite the sentence beginning with
   <u>The liver and other organs</u>

   _____

   _____

10. Jim and Pat saved money each year so their child would go to college.
    Rewrite the sentence beginning with
    <u>Because their child</u>

    _____

    _____

Answers are on page 321.

 Remember, when rewriting a sentence, the new sentence must have the same meaning as the original.

Combining Sentences

The GED will ask you to combine two sentences and form one new sentence. Combining sentences also is like reorganizing a closet. However, you generally need to send the same message with fewer words.

COMBINING SENTENCES PART I

One way to combine sentences is to use connectors. Coordinating conjunctions (and, but, nor, or), conjunctive adverbs (therefore, now), and semicolons connect independent clauses. Sentences are combined in different ways to keep the original meaning. Note the jobs for connectors that are listed below.

CONNECTORS		
Coordinating Conjunctions	**Conjunctive Adverbs**	**Job**
and	also, likewise, moreover, besides, in addition, furthermore	add two equal statements
but, yet	nonetheless, however, still, instead, nevertheless, though, although	show a difference, a contrast, or something unexpected
for, so	thus, therefore, consequently	show why something happens, connect cause and effect
or	_____	show an option or choice
nor	_____	show that neither option or choice is good

Conjuctive adverbs now, next, then, finally, and meanwhile show when something happens.

A semicolon (;) shows that the two statements are related.

Insert a comma before a coordinating conjunction (, but).

Insert a semicolon before and a comma after a conjunctive adverb (; however,).

Examples:

1. **Original Sentences**
   Tran wants to get her eyes checked. She needs new glasses.
   Both statements are related.
   New Sentence
   Tran wants to get her eyes checked; she needs new glasses.
   The semicolon (;) shows that both ideas are related.

2. **Original Sentences**
   Phil wants to buy a house. He can not afford a down payment.
   These sentences show a difference or contrast. There is a contrast between what Phil wants and what he can afford.
   New Sentence
   Phil wants to buy a house, but he can not afford a down payment.
   But shows that there is a contrast between the two statements.
   Phil wants to buy a house; however, he can not afford a down payment.
   However also shows a contrast between the two statements.

3. **Original Sentences**
   Juan's car would not start. He had to walk to work.
   These sentences show a cause and an effect. The first sentence tells why Juan had to walk to work.
   New Sentence
   Juan's car would not start, so he had to walk to work.
   So shows that there is a cause and an effect.
   Juan's car would not start; therefore, he had to walk to work.
   Therefore also shows that there is a cause and an effect.

EXERCISE 10: Combine the sentences in each of the following exercises. First, join the sentences using a coordinating conjunction. Then, combine the sentences using a conjunctive adverb. Write the connecting words and the correct punctuation in the space provided.

SAMPLE: We bought a lot of food at the store. We forgot to buy milk.

a. We bought a lot of food at the store, but we forgot to buy milk.
b. We bought a lot of food at the store; however, we forgot to buy milk.

1. Kay was struggling to pay her bills. She took an extra job on weekends.
   a. Kay was struggling to pay her bills _____ she took an extra job on weekends.
   b. Kay was struggling to pay her _____ she took an extra job on weekends.

2. Han wants to let her daughter play outside. There is too much violence in their neighborhood.
   a. Han wants to let her daughter play outside _____ there is too much violence in their neighborhood.
   b. Han wants to let her daughter play outside _____ there is too much violence in their neighborhood.

3. Tim drops Greg off at day-care in the morning. Shavone picks Greg up after work.
   a. Tim drops Greg off at day-care in the morning _____ Shavone picks Greg up after work.
   b. Tim drops Greg off at day-care in the morning _____ Shavone picks Greg up after work.

4. Ray wants to star in the school play. He has not learned his lines.
   a. Ray wants to star in the school play _____ he has not learned his lines.
   b. Ray wants to star in the school play _____ he has not learned his lines.

5. Eve wants to learn a new software program by Friday. She needs to prepare for her presentation, which is tomorrow.
   a. Eve wants to learn a new software program by Friday _____ she needs to prepare for her presentation, which is tomorrow.
   b. Eve wants to learn a new software program by Friday _____ she needs to prepare for her presentation, which is tomorrow.

6. Credit card debt can destroy a family's finances. It is better to buy only what one can afford to pay in cash.
   a. Credit card debt can destroy a family's finances _____ it is better to buy only what one can afford to pay in cash.
   b. Credit card debt can destroy a family's finances _____ it is better to buy only what one can afford to pay in cash.

7. Most people know the dangers of smoking. Teenage tobacco use continues to increase.
   a. Most people know the dangers of smoking _____ teenage tobacco use continues to increase.
   b. Most people know the dangers of smoking _____ teenage tobacco use continues to increase.

8. Politicians keep talking about cutting government spending. Few people want to give up the government services that they use.
   a. Politicians keep talking about cutting government spending _____ few people want to give up the government services that they use.
   b. Politicians keep talking about cutting government spending _____ few people want to give up the government services that they use.

9. The tax code in America is complex. Many Americans must pay a professional to do their taxes.
   a. The tax code in America is complex _____ many Americans must pay a professional to do their taxes.
   b. The tax code in America is complex _____ many Americans must pay a professional to do their taxes.

10. Ray needs more training for his job. He is taking a computer class on weekends.
    a. Ray needs more training for his job _____ he is taking a computer class on weekends.
    b. Ray needs more training for his job _____ he is taking a computer class on weekends.

Answers are on pages 321, 322.

COMBINING SENTENCES PART II—USING PHRASES OR DEPENDENT CLAUSES

Sometimes you will use phrases or dependent clauses to combine two sentences. Most sentences will be related in one of five ways: time, additional information, contrast, comparison, or cause and effect. After you have found the relationship between the two sentences, write a new sentence that sends the same message. Note that some words may be changed or deleted to make the new sentence clear.

Examples:

TIME

1. **Original Sentences**
   The shop opened at ten o'clock. Customers filed though the doors.
   The two sentences are related by time.
   New Sentence
   When the shop opened at ten o'clock, customers filed through the doors.
   When signals a clause that works like an adverb. The clause answers the question when.

2. **Original Sentences**
   The train rates change. They drop after rush hour.
   The sentences are related by time. The second sentence tells when the rates change.
   New Sentence
   After rush hour, the train rates drop.

After rush hour is an introductory phrase that tells when the rates drop.

ADDITIONAL INFORMATION

3. **Original Sentences**
   Some cars are easy targets for thieves. They are stolen more often than other cars.
   These sentences are related by additional information. The second sentence describes *cars.*
   New Sentence
   Some cars that are easy targets for thieves are stolen more often than others.
   That signals a dependent clause that works like an adjective. *That are easy targets for thieves* describes *cars.*

CONTRAST

4. **Original Sentences**
   Most people know that seat belts save lives. Many drivers still do not wear them.
   These sentences show a contrast. There is a difference between what people know and what they do.
   New Sentence
   Although most people know that seat belts save lives, many drivers still do not wear them. *Although* signals a dependent clause that works like an adverb. It also shows a contrast.

COMPARISON

5. **Original Sentences**
   Greg likes to visit the zoo. Vera likes the zoo as much as Greg.
   New Sentence
   Greg likes to visit the zoo as much as Vera does.

CAUSE AND EFFECT

6. **Original Sentences**
   Industrial waste poured in rivers for years. We need to spend time and money cleaning up the environment.
   These sentences show cause and effect. The first sentence explains the cause, and the second sentence shows the effect.

New Sentence

Because industrial waste poured into rivers for years, we have to spend time and money cleaning up the environment.

Because signals a dependent clause that works like an adverb. The clause answers the question why.

COMMON SIGNAL WORDS FOR CLAUSES

Time: after, when, whenever, once, before, since, until, while

Additional Information: who, whose, whom, which, that

Contrast: although, though, even though

Comparison: as if, as well as, as much as

Cause and Effect: because, so that

EXERCISE 11: For each question, combine the sentences using phrases or dependent clauses. Write the new sentence in the space provided. There is more than one correct answer for each question.

1. Matt's mom came home from work. He was excited to see her.

_____

_____

_____

2. We were sitting at the stoplight, and we could hear music blaring from another car. The car was across the street.

_____

_____

_____

3. Salma had a bad cold. Salma's mother could not leave her at day-care.

_____

_____

_____

4. Anh finished his test in less than thirty minutes. He did not have many correct answers.

_____

_____

_____

5. The lights on a school bus flash. Cars must stop so that students can exit the bus safely.

_____

_____

_____

6. Nathan paints landscapes well. Kayla can paint them just as well.

_____

_____

_____

7. The tornado whipped through the town. People huddled in their basements hoping they would be safe.

_____

_____

_____

8. Very few people voted in the primary elections. The elections will determine the Republican candidates.

_____

_____

_____

9. Wolf wanted to swim to cool off from the hot weather. The water in the pool was too cold.

_____

_____

_____

10. Many people in the Midwest desperately need flood relief. The politicians promised to give the relief a month ago.

_____

_____

_____

Answers are on pages 322, 323.

In this chapter you have learned:

☐ How to use conjunctions (pages 179, 180)

☐ How to write sentences with parallel structure (pages 180–182)

☐ How to write sentences that are balanced (pages 182–184)

☐ How to keep the verb tense consistent (pages 184–186)

☐ How to avoid misplaced modifiers (pages 186, 187)

☐ How to avoid dangling modifiers (pages 187–189)

☐ How to keep pronouns consistent (page 189)

☐ How to rewrite sentences (pages 190–191)

☐ How to combine sentences (pages 191–196)

Review sections that are difficult for you.

Chapter Review

EXERCISE 1: Read the paragraphs and answer the questions that follow.

Items 1 through 11 refer to the following paragraphs.

(1) Across the nation, developers are discovering rural areas and create new communities. (2) Where farms and orchards once stood, townhouses and strip malls now dominate the land. (3) Although these new developments delight some people, they frustrate others. (4) New housing changes property values, crowds schools, and local services are burdened.

(5) Some government leaders are working hard to balance the need for more housing with the desire to preserve a rural setting. (6) In Montgomery County, Maryland, county leaders established a preservation project. (7) The project protects over 93,000 acres of land from development. (8) Many people want the preservation project to continue, but others want it to end. (9) Farmers, who own much of the land, are losing money that is preserved. (10) Meanwhile, developers want to use the land to create new housing, office space, and stores for retail. (11) They insist that effective use of the land could bring jobs and money to the county. (12) This debate will rage for years between developers and preservationists.

1. Sentence 1: **Across the nation, developers are discovering rural areas and create new communities.**

   What is the best way to write the underlined portion of the sentence? If you think the original is the best way, choose option (1).

(1) areas, and create
(2) areas will create
(3) areas and creating
(4) areas; create
(5) areas and had created

2. Sentence 2: **Where farms and orchards once stood, townhouses and strip malls now dominate the land.**

   If you rewrote the sentence beginning with

   Townhouses and strip malls

   the next word should be

   (1) land
   (2) farms
   (3) where
   (4) now
   (5) once

3. Sentence 3: **Although these new developments delight some people, they frustrate others.**

   If you rewrote the sentence beginning with

   These new developments delight some people

   The next word(s) should be

   (1) , but
   (2) , nor
   (3) ; now,
   (4) ; therefore,
   (5) , so

4. Sentence 4: **New housing changes property values, crowds schools, and local services are burdened.**

   Which of the following is the best way to write the underlined portion of the sentence? If you think that the original is best, choose option (1).

   (1) local services are burdened.
   (2) local services are burdening.
   (3) burdening local services.
   (4) burdened local services.
   (5) burdens local services.

5. Sentence 5: **Some government leaders are working hard to balance the need for more housing with the desire to preserve a rural setting.**

What correction should be made to this sentence?

(1) insert a comma after *housing*
(2) replace *are working* with *worked*
(3) insert a comma after *leaders*
(4) move *with the desire* after *setting*
(5) no correction necessary

6. Sentences 6 and 7: **In Montgomery County, Maryland, county leaders established a preservation project. The project protects over 93,000 acres of land from development.**

   The most effective combination of sentences 6 and 7 would include which of the following word groups?

   (1) ; however, the
   (2) , but the
   (3) which protects
   (4) who protects
   (5) ; nonetheless, the

7. Sentence 8: **Many people want the preservation project to continue, but others want it to end.**

   If you rewrote sentence 8 beginning with

   Although many people

   The next word(s) should be

   (1) however
   (2) it
   (3) but
   (4) others
   (5) want

8. Sentence 9: **Farmers, who own much of the land, are losing money that is preserved.**

   What correction should be made to this sentence?

   (1) move *that is preserved* after *land*
   (2) remove the comma after *Farmers*
   (3) insert a comma after *money*
   (4) change *own* to *owns*
   (5) no correction necessary

9. Sentence 10: **Meanwhile, developers want to use the land to create new housing, office space, and stores for retail.**

   What correction should be made to this sentence?

(1) remove the comma after *mean-while*
(2) remove the comma after *space*
(3) change *stores for retail* to *retail stores*
(4) change *want* to *wants*
(5) no correction necessary

10. Sentence 11: **They insist that effective use of the land could bring jobs and money to the county.**

What correction should be made to this sentence?

(1) insert a comma after *jobs*
(2) change *they* to *it*
(3) change *insist* to *insists*
(4) move *to the county* after *land*
(5) no correction necessary

11. Sentence 12: **This debate will rage for years between developers and preservationists.**

What correction should be made to this sentence?

(1) insert a comma after *developers*
(2) move *between developers and preservationists* after *debate*
(3) change *rage* to *rages*
(4) move *for years* after *developers*
(5) no correction necessary

Answers are on pages 323, 324.

EXERCISE 2: Read the paragraphs and answer the questions that follow.

Questions 1 through 9 refer to the following paragraphs.

(1) Home parties are making a comeback. (2) These parties are used to sell products. (3) In the traditional home party, a sales representative invites people to purchase goods with friends and neighbors while socializing. (4) Tupperware has sold its products through home parties for years, but now many different companies use this technique to market their goods. (5) At home parties today, sales representatives peddle everything from baskets to computers.

(6) This sales trend has developed for a number of reasons. (7) The trend started in the early nineties. (8) Many parents became sales representatives to supplement their family income. (9) Busy lifestyles have encouraged some people to shop in these social settings. (10) Likewise, an increasing inventory of goods have made home parties more inviting. (11) Whatever the reason, this is a trend that will continue.

1. Sentences 1 and 2: **Home parties are making a comeback. These parties are used to sell products.**

The most effective combination of sentences 1 and 2 would include which of the following word groups?

(1) comeback, but
(2) comeback; however,
(3) parties that are used
(4) home, which parties are
(5) Although home parties are

2. Sentence 3: **In the traditional home party, a sales representative invites people to purchase goods with friends and neighbors while socializing.**

What correction should be made to this sentence?

(1) insert a comma after *friends*
(2) move *with friends and neighbors* after *socializing*
(3) remove the comma after *party*
(4) replace *invites* with *invited*
(5) replace *socializing* with *socializes*

3. Sentence 4: **Tupperware has sold its products through home parties for years, but now many different companies use this technique to market their goods.**

If you rewrote this sentence beginning with

Although Tupperware has sold its products through home parties for years

The next word(s) should be

(1) use this
(2) , but now
(3) ; however, now
(4) , now many
(5) because many

4. Sentence 5: **At home parties today, sales representatives peddle everything from baskets to computers.**

    What correction should be made to this sentence?

    (1) remove the comma after *today*
    (2) replace *parties* with *party's*
    (3) insert a comma after *baskets*
    (4) replace *peddle* with *will peddle*
    (5) no correction necessary

5. Sentences 6 and 7: **This sales trend has developed for a number of reasons. The trend started in the early nineties.**

    The most effective combination of these sentences would include which of the following word groups?

    (1) trend, which started
    (2) reasons, but
    (3) reasons; therefore,
    (4) Even though this sales
    (5) reasons, so the

6. Sentence 8: **Many <u>parents became sales</u> representatives to supplement their family income.**

    Which of the following is the best way to write the underlined portion of the sentence? If you think that the original is best, choose option (1).

    (1) parents became sales
    (2) parents, became sales
    (3) parents will become sales
    (4) parents' became sales
    (5) parents have become

7. Sentence 9: **Busy lifestyles have encouraged some people to shop in these social settings.**

    If you rewrote this sentence beginning with

    <u>Some people</u>

    The next word(s) would be

    (1) , and
    (2) ; nonetheless
    (3) have been encouraged
    (4) lifestyle
    (5) , so busy

8. Sentence 10: **Likewise, an increasing inventory of goods have made home parties more inviting.**

    What correction should be made to this sentence?

    (1) remove the comma after *likewise*
    (2) replace *parties* with *party's*
    (3) insert a comma after *goods*
    (4) replace *have* with *has*
    (5) no correction necessary

9. Sentence 11: **Whatever the reason, this is a trend that will continue.**

    What correction should be made to this sentence?

    (1) remove the comma after *reason*
    (2) replace *is* with *was*
    (3) replace *that* with *which*
    (4) replace *will continue* with *continued*
    (5) no correction necessary

Answers are on page 324.

Writing Paragraphs

In this chapter you will learn:

☐ How to write a topic sentence (pages 201–203)

☐ How to write supporting details (pages 203–206)

☐ How to vary sentences (pages 206–208)

☐ How to use specific words (pages 208, 209)

Paragraphs are like scenes from a movie. Each paragraph focuses on one topic. Together, paragraphs present all of the information to the reader.

Topic Sentences

A topic sentence is like a movie preview. It summarizes the paragraph and tells the reader what to expect. Every sentence in the paragraph must be related to the topic sentence. In most paragraphs, the topic sentence is the first sentence.

Examples:

1. <u>Children are fascinated by animals.</u> From infancy onward, children enjoy seeing animals in zoos, farms, pet shops, and parks. Books and videos about animals also stimulate a child's interest. Some children prefer soft, cuddly animals, such as rabbits; others are attracted to monkeys, elephants, and even snakes. Clearly, creatures large and small capture children's attention.

2. <u>Campaign finance reform has become a major issue since the last election.</u> Fund-raising abuses by both major parties have alarmed voters. Unfortunately, many Americans do not trust political leaders to fix the system. Why should they? Everyone seems to benefit from fund-raising abuses—except the American public.

TOPIC SENTENCE
1. Summarizes the paragraph
2. Relates to every sentence in the paragraph
3. Pulls all of the information together
4. Usually begins the paragraph

EXERCISE 1: On a separate sheet of paper write topic sentences for each of the following paragraphs. Make sure that every sentence in the paragraph is related to the topic sentence. Each question has more than one correct answer.

1. _____

_____

Dan insists that he is working hard, but his grades have dropped. He is often late to class, and he has been disciplined many times by his teacher. Dan rarely does any homework. Even his track coach has noticed a change. If Dan turns himself around soon, he will still be able to pursue his college dreams.

2. _____

_____

Farms and homes were destroyed. Roads and bridges were washed away. Our town has had many floods, but most people cannot remember the last time that the river was this high. In spite of the devastation, the townspeople will rebuild on this land. These families have lived here for generations.

3. _____

Many parents want their children to be involved in several different activities. These parents believe that active children are less likely to get into trouble. However, this belief can be taken to an extreme. These days, even young children have full schedules. By the end of the week, some parents and children are exhausted.

4. _____

_____

Just a few years ago, few people knew much about aggressive driving. Now it is a national problem. Drivers who ignore the speed limit, run red lights, and recklessly pass other cars are causing numerous fatal accidents. Like drunk drivers, aggressive drivers pose a risk for everyone on the road.

5. _____

_____

In France, strict labor laws make it difficult for companies to lay off workers. Although this may sound great, it actually hurts the economy. Because French businesses are unable to close factories or relocate workers, they lose money. Many French companies simply cannot compete with other international businesses. As a result, France has a high unemployment rate, which just keeps growing.

6. _____

_____

No one expected that two feet of snow would fall on April 1, but it did. Schools, roads, and airports closed. Trains stopped in their tracks, and people were left without power for days. It took some time for life to get back to normal. This was one April Fool's joke that we could have done without.

7. _____

_____

Appendicitis can be devastating. Initially, patients experience abdominal pain, nausea, and a fever. However, within twelve hours the pain becomes more intense in the lower right side, and the abdomen swells. Anyone who experiences these symptoms should contact a doctor.

8. _____

_____

For years, children took their first few steps in walkers, which are baby seats with wheels. Now many pediatricians speak out against walkers. Every year thousands of children are injured while using these toys. Often these injuries occur when the child falls down a flight of stairs. Some of the accidents are even fatal. Walkers, which were once a right of passage, have become a genuine safety concern.

9. _____

_____

Americans used to enjoy steaks regularly. A steak on the grill in the summertime was almost an American tradition. Now, Americans consume much less red meat. Fish and poultry have become more popular. While some people avoid meat for health reasons, others are simply looking for less expensive meals.

10. _____

_____

Girls and boys enjoy watching bulldozers, excavators, and dump trucks working the land. Perhaps they are attracted to the size of the equipment or the noise that it makes. Whatever the reason, few children can stroll by a construction site without stopping.

Answers are on page 325.

Remember these <u>facts about topic sentences</u>:

- Topic sentences summarize the paragraph and tell the reader what to expect.
- Every sentence in a paragraph must relate to the topic sentence.

Supporting Details

Supporting details are like the actors' lines in a film. The topic sentence summarizes the paragraph, and the supporting details provide more specific information. Remember, every sentence in the paragraph must be related to the topic sentence.

Example:

Children are fascinated by animals. <u>From infancy onward, children enjoy seeing animals in zoos, farms, pet shops, and parks. Books and videos about animals also stimulate a child's interest. Some children prefer soft, cuddly animals, such as rabbits; others are attracted to monkeys, elephants, and even snakes. Clearly, creatures large and small capture children's attention.</u>

In this paragraph, every sentence supports the idea that children are fascinated by animals.

TEST FOR SUPPORTING DETAILS

1. Find the topic sentence.
2. Read each supporting detail along with the topic sentence.
3. Decide if each supporting detail agrees with the topic sentence.

Example:

In the following paragraph, one sentence is not related to the topic sentence.

Fireworks can be very dangerous when they are not handled properly. Many children and young adults are injured by fireworks every year. Guns are also dangerous for children. Because of the danger, fireworks are illegal in some states. However in many areas of the country, fireworks are easy to get. If parents allow their children to use fireworks, they must provide constant supervision.

TOPIC SENTENCE: Fireworks can be very dangerous when they are not handled properly. Clearly this paragraph is about the danger of fireworks.

MISPLACED SENTENCE: Guns are also dangerous for children. This sentence has nothing to do with the danger of fireworks.

EXERCISE 2: Read the topic sentences and supporting details that follow. If a supporting detail does not agree with the topic sentence, write an *X* in the space provided.

1. TOPIC SENTENCE: Searching for a new job requires a lot of hard work and patience.

   SUPPORTING DETAILS:

   _____ a. Job applicants have to write many letters and research companies.

   _____ b. Completing applications and going on interviews takes time.

_____ c. In some areas of the country, few jobs are available.

_____ d. Congress recently increased the minimum wage.

_____ e. Many people have to look for a new job while they are still working.

2. TOPIC SENTENCE: Soccer has become a popular sport in America.

SUPPORTING DETAILS:

_____ a. Unlike baseball, every child has a chance to participate actively in soccer.

_____ b. Many colleges have worked hard to develop their soccer programs for both men and women.

_____ c. Leg injuries are common in many sports.

_____ d. Some soccer leagues can not keep up with the demand for new teams, equipment, and playing fields.

_____ e. Lacrosse is also very popular in some areas.

3. TOPIC SENTENCE: Americans need to take food poisoning seriously.

SUPPORTING DETAILS:

_____ a. Many Americans eat too much.

_____ b. Some cases of food poisoning are fatal.

_____ c. Everyone should take precautions to make sure that food is safe to eat.

_____ d. Food poisoning affects thousands of people every year.

_____ e. In England, mad cow disease poisoned the beef and sickened several people.

4. TOPIC SENTENCE: More Americans are investing in mutual funds than ever before.

SUPPORTING DETAILS:

_____ a. Baby boomers are using mutual funds to save for retirement.

_____ b. People in their twenties and thirties use mutual funds to save for a home or their children's education.

_____ c. Many people prefer mutual funds to individual stocks, which demand more research and attention.

_____ d. It is important to save money for the future.

_____ e. Some new investors may not realize that mutual funds can be risky investments.

5. TOPIC SENTENCE: A good baby-sitter is hard to find.

SUPPORTING DETAILS:

_____ a. Many people simply are not interested in caring for young children.

_____ b. Other jobs offer higher wages and better benefits.

_____ c. Some local hospitals offer baby-sitting classes that teach teenagers to care for young children.

_____ d. Parents are having fewer children these days.

_____ e. Instead of hiring a sitter, many parents simply choose to stay home.

Answers are on pages 325, 326.

DEVELOPING SUPPORTING DETAILS

Good supporting details are critical. Without them, a paragraph is pointless. The topic sentence provides a preview, but the supporting details give the key information. These details may include examples, facts, and opinions.

DEVELOPING SUPPORTING DETAILS

Type	Description	Examples
Example	An example is someone or something that supports your ideas. Think of specific people, events, activities, or explanations that illustrate your thoughts.	In my family, TV time is restricted to one hour a day. While some people simply watch the news or sports, others tune into daytime drama or talk shows.
Fact	A fact is something that can be proved true. Think of information from the news, magazines, or books.	Most Americans watch some television every day.
Opinion	An opinion is one's view on an issue. Although an opinion can not be proved or disproved, someone can agree or disagree with it. Focus on your thoughts and feelings about the topic.	People should turn off the TV and start doing more positive things.

Example:

TV viewing habits vary greatly. Most Americans watch some television every day (fact). While some people simply watch the news or sports, others tune into daytime drama or talk shows (example and fact). In my family, TV time is restricted to one hour a day (example). My friends, however, are allowed to watch as much television as they want (example). As a result, they often watch TV for almost five hours a day (example and fact). People should turn off the television and start doing more positive things (opinion).

A good paragraph has <u>at least</u> three sentences with supporting details. These sentences may include examples, facts, or opinions.

EXERCISE 3: For each topic sentence, write three supporting details. Include one example, one fact, and one opinion. Make sure each detail relates to the topic sentence. Each question has more than one correct answer.

1. Movie rentals are a major form of entertainment.

EXAMPLE: _____

_____

FACT: _____

_____

OPINION: _____

_____

2. Amusement parks are fun for the whole family.

EXAMPLE: _____

_____

FACT: _____

_____

OPINION: _____

_____

3. Parenting is exciting, but it is also hard work.

EXAMPLE: _____

_____

FACT: _____

_____

OPINION: _____

_____

4. Exercise and good nutrition are important.

EXAMPLE: _____

_____

FACT: _____

_____

OPINION: _____

_____

5. Many Americans do not save enough money.

EXAMPLE: _____

FACT: _____

_____

OPINION: _____

_____

Answers are on page 326.

☞ Remember these <u>facts about supporting details</u>:

- Supporting details provide specific information about the topic sentence.
- Each supporting detail must relate to the topic sentence.
- A paragraph should have <u>at least</u> three sentences with supporting details.
- Supporting details may be examples, facts, or opinions.

Sentence Variety

Sentences are like food; variety is key. In the last chapter, you learned to rewrite sentences. Now it is time to use what you have learned in a new way. Paragraphs need to have sentences with different lengths and styles. Note how frustrating it is to read a paragraph without a variety of sentences.

Example:

WITHOUT SENTENCE VARIETY

Americans take space travel for granted these days. We know astronauts can travel to the moon. We use space satellites daily. We often do not pay attention when a space shuttle launches. We are not even excited about Americans living on a Russian space station. Maybe future space missions will generate more enthusiasm.

This paragraph needs help. Too many sentences begin with *we*, and most sentences are simple sentences. Note the improvements that follow:

WITH SENTENCE VARIETY

Americans take space travel for granted these days. We know astronauts can travel to the moon, and we use space satellites daily. When a space shuttle launches, few people pay attention. Even Americans living on a Russian space station does not excite many people. Maybe future space missions will generate more enthusiasm.

A few simple changes can make a big difference.

EXERCISE 4: Improve each of the following paragraphs by rewriting the underlined sentences. You may change the sentence length or style, but you must keep the message the same. Each question has more than one correct answer.

1. Technology changes very quickly. Twenty-five years ago a costly fax machine would fill an entire room. <u>It would take ten minutes to transmit one page. That page would be hard for the recipient to read. Some fax machines are now the size of a large book. They can send multiple pages in minutes.</u> By next year, fax machines will be smaller, faster, and cheaper.

_____

_____

_____

_____

_____

2. Many young athletes dream of turning professional. <u>They often focus on improving their athletic ability. They neglect their education. Very few athletes turn pro. Those who do often have short careers.</u> Athletes need an excellent education so that they will be prepared for whatever the future brings.

_____

_____

3. Early science education is getting more attention. Television programs such as *The Magic School Bus* and *Bill Nye, the Science Guy* interest children at a young age. <u>More schools are introducing science topics to students who are in elementary school. Second and third graders now learn about basic biology. They also learn about physics.</u> Future scientists will spring from these new educational efforts.

_____

_____

_____

_____

_____

_____

4. Computers have created new privacy issues. <u>Many features make computers helpful and easy to use. These same features often expose private information. People use computers for banking and investments. Hackers enter their files and learn personal information.</u> Computer users need to protect their privacy.

_____

_____

_____

_____

_____

5. When buying a car, you need to follow several steps. <u>Obviously, you will need to check the car carefully. You may want to hire a good mechanic to inspect the car for you. You need to get insurance. You may need to arrange for a loan</u>. Once all the arrangements are made, simply drive your new car home.

_____

_____

_____

_____

Answers are on pages 326, 327.

 Remember, paragraphs need sentences with different lengths and styles.

Specific Words

Use words that leave an image in the reader's mind. Sometimes changing one or two words in a sentence can make a big difference.

Examples:

Changing the verb does not change the meaning of the sentence. In each case, Tim went to the store. However, the various verbs leave different images in the reader's mind.
1. Tim <u>walked</u> to the store.
2. Tim <u>rushed</u> to the store.
3. Tim <u>limped</u> to the store.
4. Tim <u>skipped</u> to the store.
5. Tim <u>ran</u> to the store.

Specific words throughout a paragraph create a clear mental picture.

Example:

WITHOUT SPECIFIC WORDS

We **go** downtown **often** to visit the shops, get something to eat, and enjoy different events. The local bakery offers free slices of **good** bread. Sylvana's, a restaurant, has **great** food and a **nice** atmosphere. On Friday nights, there are free concerts on the town green. Most of the bands play **good** music. The downtown area has something for everyone.

WITH SPECIFIC WORDS

We **stroll** downtown **weekly** to visit the shops, get something to eat, and enjoy different events. The local bakery offers free slices of **soft, warm** bread. Sylvana's, a **Greek** restaurant, has **healthy, inexpensive** food and a **relaxing** atmosphere. On Friday nights, there are free concerts on the town green. Most of the bands play **upbeat** music. The downtown area has something for everyone.

Remember, you want to create an image in the reader's mind. Describe how things look, smell, taste, and feel. Likewise, answer the questions *why*, *when*, and *how*. Why is something good or bad? When does an event occur? How is an action done?

EXERCISE 5: For each sentence, think of three or more words that could replace the underlined word without changing the basic meaning of the sentence. Write your answers in the space provided. There is more than one correct set of answers.

1. Phebe <u>said</u>, "This class is boring."
   _____

2. We had a <u>good</u> day. _____

3. We saw a <u>big</u> cow in the road.
   _____

4. This is a <u>small</u> problem for us.
   _____

5. Today is a <u>bad</u> day. _____

6. The food was <u>great</u>. _____

7. The truck <u>hit</u> the car. _____

8. The waves <u>landed</u> on the beach. _____

9. I go to the food store <u>often</u>. _____

10. The traffic was <u>annoying</u>. _____

Answers are on page 327.

✍ Remember to use words that create an image in the reader's mind.

CHECKLIST FOR PARAGRAPHS

☐ Does the paragraph have a good topic sentence?

☐ Does the paragraph have <u>at least</u> three sentences with supporting details?

☐ Do all of the supporting details relate to the topic sentence?

☐ Does the paragraph have sentences with different lengths and styles?

☐ Do the verbs and adjectives create an image in the reader's mind?

In this chapter you have learned:

☐ How to write a topic sentence (pages 201–203)

☐ How to write supporting details (pages 203–206)

☐ How to vary sentences (pages 206–208)

☐ How to use specific words (pages 208, 209)

Review sections that are difficult for you.

Chapter Review

EXERCISE 1: Each paragraph below needs a topic sentence. Write a topic sentence in the space provided. Each question has more than one possible answer.

1. _____

   _____

A recent study by the National Institute of Child Health and Human Development focused on young children in day care. According to the study, children in good day care programs learn to speak and think as well as children who are cared for by their mothers. However, the research also showed that very young children who are in day care for many hours each week have weaker bonds with their mothers. As day care becomes increasingly popular, researchers will continue to study how day care affects children and their parents.

2. _____

   _____

Many roads and bridges in our country have not been well maintained. Routine maintenance is expensive, but necessary. Large, dangerous potholes are damaging cars and causing accidents. Aging structural supports are weakening bridges and endangering motorists. We need to focus on making roads and bridges safe for everyone.

3. _____

   _____

The associations regulate solicitation. Homeowners' associations set standards for landscaping, maintenance, and additions to homes. They even decide what color paint may be used for each house. Some homeowners like the structure of associations; others think that the associations are too heavy handed.

4. _____

_____

The longer days make it easier for people to get outside after work or school. Green grass and flowers add color to the landscape. Everyone finally gets a chance to open their windows and enjoy the fresh air. Even spring cleaning lifts some people's spirits.

5. _____

Some people save a little bit of money from each paycheck. Others write a check for savings when they pay the rent or mortgage. A few people put money in savings before they pay their bills. Whatever the technique, it is important to create a good savings account.

6. _____

_____

When children are young, they want to do many things when they grow up. A child may insist that she wants to be a doctor, a dancer, and an artist. Unfortunately as children age, these wonderful dreams often fade away. Parents and teachers need to work hard to keep children's dreams alive so that today's children will be tomorrow's leaders.

7. _____

_____

Major purchases, such as cribs, strollers, and high chairs, are expensive. Even disposable items are costly. Formula for babies can cost $150 dollars a month. Diapers cost about $600 a year. Parents need to be prepared for the financial responsibilities of having children.

8. _____

_____

TV sets, radios, and telephones have more features than they had years ago. Likewise, answering machines, VCRs, and microwaves are common in homes today. Many older Americans think that these objects are luxuries and a waste of money. To younger generations, however, these items seem necessary for everyday life.

9. _____

_____

By law, school districts must provide transportation for their students. However, many parents on their way to work simply drive their children to school. As a result, school buses in many towns are almost empty. These empty buses cost taxpayers a lot of money. There must be a better way to provide transportation for the students.

10. _____

Most people have a favorite station on the radio. However, there are many other rhythms around us. Dishwashers and washing machines hum as they clean. Construction equipment beats out a rhythm. The wind whistles through the trees, and birds sing wonderful melodies. Once in a while, we should turn off our radios and listen to the other music in our lives.

Answers are on pages 327, 328.

EXERCISE 2: Add two supporting details to each of the following paragraphs. Write your answers in the space provided. Each question has more than one possible answer.

1. Maintaining a home takes a lot of work. Carpets need to be vacuumed. Floors must be washed, and bathrooms need to be cleaned regularly.

   a.

   b.

2. Biking is a great form of exercise. Some exercise programs are hard to learn, but most people already know how to ride a bike. Biking also does not need a lot of fancy equipment; any bike will work.

   a.

   b.

3. Pets become part of the family. Some pets protect the home while others simply provide friendship. When a pet dies, many people feel a great sense of loss.

   a.

   b.

4. Many different items travel through the mail. Bills and payments are just one form of mail. Advertisements and special offers, which are commonly called junk mail, fill mailboxes everywhere.

   a.

   b.

5. Fire engines capture children's attention. The lights and sirens are exciting for some children. Likewise, the size of the trucks and the powerful equipment interest others.

   a.

   b.

6. Computers have changed our lives. They help us get information faster and easier than ever before. Computers enable people to communicate around the world.

   a.

   b.

7. Many new services have developed to help people with their busy lives. Dry cleaners pick up clothes right where people work. Taxi services that are specially designed for busy parents transport children to various activities.

   a.

   b.

8. Parents can be involved in their children's education in many ways. Checking homework is just one way. Parents can take their children to museums, zoos, and aquariums, which stimulate learning.

   a.

   b.

9. Advertisers use many gimmicks to capture our attention. Catchy songs and slogans help us remember products. Clothing, such as T-shirts and hats, make the products seem fashionable.

   a.

   b.

10. There are many ways to save money. Cutting coupons can help reduce grocery bills. Turning off lights that are not being used can save on electricity.

    a.

    b.

Answers are on pages 328, 329.

THE GED ESSAY

Planning the Essay

In this chapter you will learn:

- ☐ How the Writing Skills Test, Part II is organized (page 215)
- ☐ How to manage your time (pages 215, 216)
- ☐ How to read the instructions (pages 216, 217)
- ☐ How to write a thesis statement (pages 218, 219)
- ☐ How to brainstorm (pages 219–221)
- ☐ How to create an outline (pages 223–228)

Essays are like exercise routines. To have a good workout, you need to warm up, exercise, and cool down. If you neglect any one of these stages, your workout will suffer. The same is true with an essay. To write a good essay, you need to plan, write, and revise. Writers who pay attention to each step in the process write stronger essays.

Overview of the Essay

In Part II of the GED Writing Skills Test, you will be asked to write an essay that explains your views on a certain topic. You will have 45 minutes to write the essay, which should be about 200 words long. You will not need to know any special information about the topic, but you will need to know how to write a clear, organized, well-developed essay.

Example:

ESSAY TOPIC

The telephone, which was invented in the 1870s, has become standard in most American homes. The telephone has improved our lives in many ways, but it also has had negative effects.

Write an essay of about 200 words that describes the effects that the telephone has had on modern life. You may describe the good effects, the bad effects, or both.

The essay will be scored holistically (see the grading chart that follows on page 250). In other words, the evaluators will look at your essay as a whole; they will focus mostly on how well you explain your ideas. A few minor errors will not drastically affect your score. Nonetheless, it is important to check your writing carefully. If misspellings and grammatical errors make your essay hard to understand, you will earn a lower score.

Time Management

The following chapters will teach you how to write a solid five-paragraph essay. Writing a good essay includes more than just putting words on paper. There are three important steps to the writing process: planning, writing, and revising. Taking the time to complete each step will help you write a better essay.

You will have 45 minutes to complete the essay. The following chart suggests how your time should be divided.

TIME MANAGEMENT

Planning (10 Minutes)
1. Read the instructions and the topic.
2. Write a thesis statement.
3. Brainstorm.
4. Create an outline.

Writing (25 Minutes)
1. Review your notes.
2. Write an introduction, body, and conclusion.

Revising (10 Minutes)
1. Compare your essay and notes.
2. Check and revise for the information: organization, content, and clarity.
3. Check and revise for the rules: grammar, usage, mechanics, spelling, and capitalization.

 Remember these <u>facts about the essay</u>:

- You will have 45 minutes to write an essay that should be about 200 words.
- Even though your essay will be graded holistically, you should pay attention to grammar and spelling.
- There are three steps to writing a good essay: planning, writing, and revising.
- Allow about 10 minutes for planning, 25 minutes for writing, and 10 minutes for revising.

Understanding Instructions

The basic instructions for the essay question are always the same. You will be expected to do the following:

1. Read the entire question carefully.
2. Plan your response before you write.
3. Write only about the assigned topic.
4. Make notes on the blank pages of the test booklet or scratch paper. Your notes will not be scored.
5. Write your essay on the separate answer sheet.
6. Carefully read your essay and make changes that will improve it.
7. Use correct paragraphing, sentence structure, spelling, usage, punctuation, and capitalization.
8. Use a ballpoint pen and write legibly.

 Note:

You <u>must</u> write about the assigned topic. Essays that are on a different topic cannot be scored. As a result, a Writing Skills Test composite score will not be reported.

The essay will have specific instructions that tell you about the topic. These instructions use signal words that tell you how to write the essay. Note the signal words that are listed in the box.

SIGNAL WORDS FOR ESSAY TOPICS	
Signal Words:	**Write About:**
describe effects	causes and effects, or simply effects
support your view, state your opinion, support your opinion	your thoughts on the issue
discuss how or why, explain how or why, tell how or why, describe how or why	reasons for an issue, steps to take, or information about a topic

The instructions will remind you to use specific examples to support your ideas.

EXERCISE 1: Read each essay topic. Underline the signal words that tell you how to write the essay. In the space provided, write how the essay should be written.

SAMPLE:

ESSAY TOPIC: For decades health experts have stated that good nutrition and a balanced diet are important. Many Americans have ignored these warnings. Instead, fast food and snacks have become regular parts of our diets.

Why don't Americans eat healthier meals? In a composition of about 200 words, <u>explain why</u> good eating habits are hard to find. Use specific examples to support your views.

WRITE ABOUT: <u>reasons why many Americans don't eat healthy meals</u>

1. ESSAY TOPIC: In the 1970s and 1980s, women with young children entered the workforce in record numbers. In recent years, more parents have decided to stay home while their children are young. Some parents have even started home-based businesses so that they can work and be home with their children.

   Should both parents work or should one stay home with the children? In a composition of about 200 words, state your opinion. Use specific examples to support your views.

   WRITE ABOUT: _____

2. ESSAY TOPIC: Even though the legal age for drinking was increased from eighteen to twenty-one, many minors still drink alcohol. Teenage alcohol abuse is a serious problem.

   Should responsible teenagers be allowed to drink alcohol or should more efforts be made to stop teenage drinking? In a composition of about 200 words, tell how teenage alcohol use should be handled. Use specific examples to support your views.

   WRITE ABOUT: _____

3. ESSAY TOPIC: The television has become standard in most American homes. It has improved our lives in many ways, but it has also had negative effects.

   Write an essay of about 200 words that describes the effects that the television has had on modern life. You may describe the good effects, the bad effects, or both. Use specific examples to support your views.

   WRITE ABOUT: _____

4. ESSAY TOPIC: Homelessness has been a problem for years. Shelters, soup kitchens, and counseling centers are often overwhelmed by the number of people who need help.

   In an essay of about 200 words, describe how homeless persons should be helped. Include specific details and good examples.

   WRITE ABOUT: _____

5. ESSAY TOPIC: A driver's license is a rite of passage for many people. They use their cars to go to school, work, and social events. Inexperienced drivers, however, cause a high percentage of automobile accidents.

   In an essay of about 200 words, explain how new drivers should be taught before they get a license. Include good examples and specific details.

   WRITE ABOUT: _____

Answers are on page 329.

☞ Remember these <u>facts about the instructions</u>:

- Carefully read all of the instructions before you begin the essay.
- Look for signal words that will tell you how to write about the topic.

Thesis Statements

The thesis statement is like an arrow that points a lost writer in the right direction. In an essay, the thesis statement summarizes what you want to write and organizes your thoughts.

Examples:

ESSAY TOPIC:

The telephone, which was invented in the 1870s, has become standard in most American homes. The telephone has improved our lives in many ways, but it has also had negative effects.

Write an essay of about 200 words that describes the effects that the telephone has had on modern life. You may describe the good effects, the bad effects, or both.

1. THESIS STATEMENT ➡ <u>The tele-phone has helped people in many ways</u>. According to the thesis statement, the essay will be about the benefits of the telephone.
2. THESIS STATEMENT ➡ <u>Although the telephone has been beneficial in some ways, it has had many negative effects</u>. This essay will be about the good effects and bad effects of the telephone, but it will emphasize the bad effects.

The thesis statement of an essay depends on the writer's thoughts. Some writers like to brainstorm before writing a thesis statement. If this may describe you, read the next section before completing Exercise 2.

 Hint: Do not use the phrases "In my opinion," "I believe," or "I think." Simply state your thoughts.

WRONG: In my opinion, the telephone has been beneficial.

RIGHT: The telephone has been beneficial.

EXERCISE 2: Read each essay topic. Underline the signal words that tell you how to write the essay. In the space provided, write your thesis statement for the essay. Each question has more than one correct answer.

1. ESSAY TOPIC: In the 1970s and 1980s, women with young children entered the workforce in record numbers. In recent years, more parents have decided to stay home while their children are young. Some parents have even started home-based businesses so that they can work and be home with their children.

   Should both parents work or should one stay home with the children? In a composition of about 200 words, state your opinion. Use specific examples to support your views.

   THESIS STATEMENT ➡ _____

   _____

2. ESSAY TOPIC: Even though the legal age for drinking was increased from eighteen to twenty-one, many minors still drink alcohol. Teenage alcohol abuse is a serious problem.

   Should responsible teenagers be allowed to drink alcohol or should more efforts be made to stop teenage drinking? In a composition of about 200 words, tell how teenage alcohol use should be handled.

   THESIS STATEMENT ➡ _____

   _____

3. ESSAY TOPIC: The television has become standard in most American homes. It has improved our lives in many ways, but it has also had negative effects.

   Write an essay of about 200 words that describes the effects that the television has had on modern life. You may describe the good effects, the bad effects, or both.

THESIS STATEMENT ➡ _____

_____

4. ESSAY TOPIC: Homelessness has been a problem for years. Shelters, soup kitchens, and counseling centers are often overwhelmed by the number of people who need help.

In an essay of about 200 words, describe how homeless persons should be helped.

THESIS STATEMENT ➡ _____

_____

5. ESSAY TOPIC: A driver's license is a rite of passage for many people. They use their cars to go to school, work, and social events. Inexperienced drivers, however, cause a high percentage of automobile accidents.

In an essay of about 200 words, explain how new drivers should be taught before they get a license.

THESIS STATEMENT ➡ _____

_____

Answers are on page 329.

☞ Remember these <u>facts about the thesis statement</u>:

- The thesis statement summarizes what you want to write.
- The thesis statement should point your thoughts in the right direction.

Brainstorming

Brainstorming is like emptying all of your thoughts on a piece of paper. When you brainstorm, do not worry about grammar or spelling; simply write your ideas as quickly as you can. In addition, do not separate the good ideas from the bad ones; let them all spill out. A "bad" idea may actually help you think of more good information.

Example:

ESSAY TOPIC:
The telephone, which was invented in the 1870s, has become standard in most American homes. The telephone has improved our lives in many ways, but it has also had negative effects.

Write an essay of about 200 words that describes the effects that the telephone has had on modern life. You may describe the good effects, the bad effects, or both.
THESIS STATEMENT ➡ <u>The telephone has helped people in many ways, but it also has drawbacks</u>.

BRAINSTORMING
GOOD EFFECTS:
call in emergency, talk to friends, touch-tone phones are easy to dial, keep in touch with family that is far away, easier than writing a letter, cell phones are portable, can talk anytime, can talk and do other things, check on older relatives and neighbors, keep people connected with world, with an answering machine a phone can take messages
DRAWBACKS:
bills, expensive, more than one in some homes, employers can contact you at home, interruptions at dinner, calls in the middle of the night, don't always want to talk to other people

After you have emptied all of your thoughts, cross out the ones that you do not want to include.

Example:

BRAINSTORMING
GOOD EFFECTS:
call in emergency, talk to friends, ~~touch-tone phones are easy to dial~~, keep in touch with family that is far away, easier than writing a letter, ~~cell phones are portable~~, can talk anytime, can talk and do other things, call stores to see if they are open, call movie theaters to see what is playing, check on older relatives and neighbors, keep people connected with world, with an answering machine a phone can take messages

DRAWBACKS:
bills, expensive, ~~more than one in some homes~~, employers can contact you at home, interruptions at dinner, calls in the middle of the night, don't always want to talk to other people

The crossed-out items are true, but they are not related to the topic.

> ➡ *Hint:* To get your thoughts flowing, ask yourself the following questions about the topic: How? When? Where? What? Who?

EXERCISE 3: Brainstorm ideas for each of the following topics. Try to come up with at least 10 ideas. Write your thoughts in the space provided. Each question has many possible answers.

1. ESSAY TOPIC: In the 1970s and 1980s, women with young children entered the workforce in record numbers. In recent years, more parents have decided to stay home while their children are young. Some parents have even started home-based businesses so that they can work and be home with their children.

   Should parents work or stay home with their children? In a composition of about 200 words, state your opinion. Use specific examples to support your views.

   BRAINSTORM:

2. ESSAY TOPIC: Even though the legal age for drinking was increased from eighteen to twenty-one, many minors still drink alcohol. Teenage alcohol abuse is a serious problem.

   Should responsible teenagers be allowed to drink alcohol or should more efforts be made to stop teenage drinking? In a composition of about 200 words, tell how teenage alcohol use should be handled.

   BRAINSTORM:

3. ESSAY TOPIC: The television has become standard in most American homes. It has improved our lives in many ways, but it has also had negative effects.

   Write an essay of about 200 words that describes the effects that the television has had on modern life. You may describe the good effects, the bad effects, or both.

   BRAINSTORM:

4. ESSAY TOPIC: Homelessness has been a problem for years. Shelters, soup kitchens, and counseling centers are often overwhelmed by the number of people who need help.

   In an essay of about 200 words, describe how homeless persons should be helped.

   BRAINSTORM:

5. ESSAY TOPIC: A driver's license is a rite of passage for many people. They use their cars to go to school, work, and social events. Inexperienced drivers, however, cause a high percentage of automobile accidents.

   In an essay of about 200 words, explain how new drivers should be taught before they get a license.

   BRAINSTORM:

Answers are on pages 329, 330.

EXERCISE 4: Now go back over each question in Exercise 3 and cross out ideas that you will not use.

☞ Remember these <u>facts about brainstorming</u>:

- While brainstorming, do not be critical of your thoughts; let them all spill out.
- After you have brainstormed, cross out ideas that you will not use.
- Try to come up with <u>at least</u> ten good ideas.

Organizing the Information

After you have brainstormed and crossed out irrelevant information, you need to separate your thoughts into main ideas and details. Main ideas work like boxes that group the details together. Eventually, main ideas will become topic sentences for your paragraphs.

Example:

ESSAY TOPIC:
The telephone, which was invented in the 1870s, has become standard in most American homes. The telephone has improved our lives in many ways, but it has also had negative effects.

Write an essay of about 200 words that describes the effects that the telephone has had on modern life. You may describe the good effects, the bad effects, or both.

1. MAIN IDEA: Telephones help people stay in touch
   DETAILS: talk to friends, keep in touch with family that is far away, check on older relatives and neighbors, keep people connected with world

2. MAIN IDEA: Telephones are practical
   DETAILS: call in emergency, easier than writing a letter, can talk anytime, with an answering machine a phone can take messages

3. MAIN IDEA: Phone calls can be annoying and expensive
DETAILS: bills, employers can contact you at home, interruptions at dinner, calls in the middle of the night, don't always want to talk to other people

EXERCISE 5: Group the following details according to a main idea. When you are finished, you should have three groups: A, B, and C. For the first group of details that belong together, write an *A* in the space provided. For the second group of details, write a *B*, and for the third group, write a *C*.

1. ESSAY TOPIC: Many high schools across the country have made community service a graduation requirement. Students are expected to volunteer for a certain number of hours each year. Students who do not volunteer will not earn a diploma. People who support community service requirements believe that the students become better citizens. Opponents do not want schools to force students to work for free.

Should high schools have community service requirements? In a composition of about 200 words, state your opinion. Use specific examples to support your views.

THESIS STATEMENT ➡ High schools should require community service because it helps students become more thoughtful, responsible citizens.

_____ students can volunteer in programs that interest them

_____ teenagers become more interested in community issues

_____ students can learn about careers that might interest them

_____ students help in nursing homes and day-care centers

_____ community service improves many students' self-esteem

_____ students learn to work with other adults

_____ teens work as tutors and hospital aides

_____ students learn how important it is to volunteer

_____ when people volunteer as teens, they are more likely to volunteer as adults

_____ students can learn important job skills

_____ students clean roadways and improve playgrounds

_____ high school community service programs have made students more active in college volunteer programs

Now that you have grouped the information, write a main idea for each group.

A. _____

B. _____

C. _____

Answers are on page 330.

Remember these facts about organizing the information:

- Separate your thoughts into main ideas and details.
- Main ideas will eventually become topic sentences for your paragraphs.
- The details will become the supporting details for your topic sentences.

Outlines

Our minds are like computers; everybody is wired a little differently. What works well for some writers will not work for others. Before you can learn how to organize the information for your essay, you need to know how your mind works.

OUTLINE OPTIONS

Thinking Style: Do you like structured, organized lists? Do you like to organize your thoughts in nice, neat packages? Are you comfortable with standard outlines?
Try: Standard Outlines

Thinking Style: Do you like lists that are flexible? Do you want your more important thoughts to stand out on the piece of paper? Do you think that standard outlines are okay, but hard to use?
Try: T-lists

Thinking Style: Do you dislike lists? Do you prefer to write your ideas in different places on the paper? Are standard outlines frustrating?
Try: Webs

If you are not sure how your mind works, try each method and see which one is best for you.

STANDARD OUTLINE

A standard outline is a structured way to organize your thoughts. It uses letters and numbers to show the difference between main ideas and supporting details. Use Roman numerals (I, II, III) for main ideas and capital letters (A, B, C) for supporting details. Use Arabic numerals (1, 2, 3) to list minor details or examples.

Example:

ESSAY TOPIC:
The telephone, which was invented in the 1870s, has become standard in most American homes. The telephone has improved our lives in many ways, but it has also had negative effects.

Write an essay of about 200 words that describes the effects that the telephone has had on modern life. You may describe the good effects, the bad effects, or both.

THESIS STATEMENT ➡ The telephone has helped people in many ways, but it also has drawbacks.

I. Help people stay in touch
   A. Talk to friends
   B. Keep in touch with family that is far away
   C. Check on older relatives and neighbors
   D. Keep people connected with world

II. Telephones are practical
   A. Easier than writing a letter
      1. Takes less time
      2. Can just pick up the phone and talk anytime
      3. Can talk and do other things
   B. With an answering machine a phone can take messages
      1. People can always get in touch
      2. Won't miss important information
   C. Call in emergency

III. Phone calls can be annoying and expensive
   A. Bills
   B. Employers can contact you at home
   C. Don't always want to talk to other people
      1. Interruptions at dinner
      2. Calls in the middle of the night

A standard outline easily flows into an essay. Each Roman numeral becomes a topic sentence, and each capital letter becomes a supporting detail.

EXERCISE 6: In the space provided, organize the following details into a standard outline. You may use the groups and main ideas that you created in Exercise 5.

THESIS STATEMENT ➡ High schools should require community service because it helps students become more thoughtful, responsible citizens.

_____ students can volunteer in programs that interest them

_____ teenagers become more interested in community issues

_____ students can learn about careers that might interest them

_____ students help in nursing homes and day-care centers

_____ community service improves many students' self-esteem

_____ students learn to work with other adults

_____ teens work as tutors and hospital aides

_____ students learn how important it is to volunteer

_____ when people volunteer as teens, they are more likely to volunteer as adults

_____ students can learn important job skills

_____ students clean roadways and improve playgrounds

_____ high school community service programs have made students more active in college volunteer programs

STANDARD OUTLINE:

Answer is on pages 330, 331.

T-LIST

A T-list is like an standard outline with a twist. For a T-list, the paper is divided into two columns. Main ideas are listed on the left side, and supporting details are listed on the right.

Example:

ESSAY TOPIC:
The telephone, which was invented in the 1870s, has become standard in most American homes. The telephone has improved our lives in many ways, but it has also had negative effects.

Write an essay of about 200 words that describes the effects that the telephone has had on modern life. You may describe the good effects, the bad effects, or both.
THESIS STATEMENT ➡ The telephone is helpful in many ways, but it also has drawbacks.

Main Ideas	Details
Help people stay in touch	➡ *Talk to friends* ➡ *Keep in touch with family that is far away* ➡ *Check on older relatives and neighbors* ➡ *Keep people connected with world*

Telephones are practical	➡ *Easier than writing a letter*
	    Takes less time
	    Can just pick up the phone and talk
	➡ *Can talk and do other things*
	➡ *With an answering machine a phone can take messages*
	    People can always get in touch
	    Won't miss important information
	➡ *Call in emergency*

Phone calls can be annoying and expensive	➡ *Bills*
	➡ *Employers can contact you at home*
	➡ *Don't always want to talk to other people*
	    Interruptions at dinner
	    Calls in the middle of the night

Many people prefer T-lists to outlines for three reasons. When using a standard outline, writers worry too much about the numbers and letters; they get distracted from the information. It is easier to add new thoughts to a T-list. In addition, by just looking at a T-list, one can tell what is important.

When you write your essay, the main ideas that are listed on the left become topic sentences, and the details that are listed on the right become supporting details.

EXERCISE 7: In the space provided, organize the following information into a T-list. You may use the groups and main ideas that you created in Exercise 5.

THESIS STATEMENT ➡ High schools should require community service because it helps students become more thoughtful, responsible citizens.

_____ students can volunteer in programs that interest them

_____ teenagers become more interested in community issues

_____ students can learn about careers that might interest them

_____ students help in nursing homes and day-care centers

_____ community service improves many students' self-esteem

_____ students learn to work with other adults

_____ teens work as tutors and hospital aides

_____ students learn how important it is to volunteer

_____ when people volunteer as teens, they are more likely to volunteer as adults

_____ students can learn important job skills

_____ students clean roadways and improve playgrounds

_____ high school community service programs have made students more active in college volunteer programs

T-LIST:

WEBS

Webs for taking notes are like spider webs: everything is connected by common threads. Webs are great if you like to organize information visually.

First, place your thesis statement in a circle in the middle of the paper. Then write your main ideas in circles that surround your thesis statement. Finally, make your supporting details branch off of your main ideas. (See page 227.)

Example:

THESIS STATEMENT ➡ The telephone has helped people in many ways, but it also has drawbacks.

Answer is on page 331.

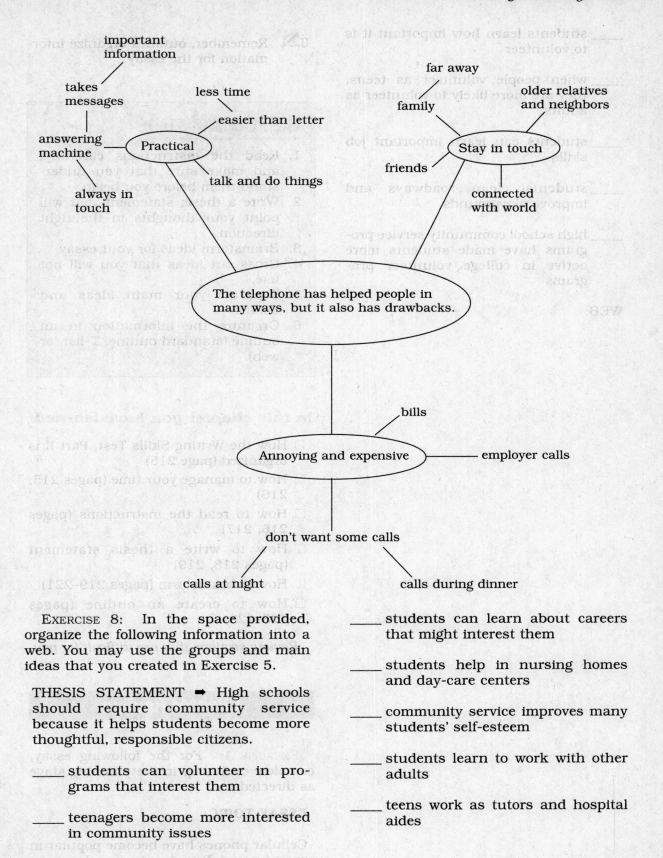

EXERCISE 8: In the space provided, organize the following information into a web. You may use the groups and main ideas that you created in Exercise 5.

THESIS STATEMENT ➡ High schools should require community service because it helps students become more thoughtful, responsible citizens.

_____ students can volunteer in programs that interest them

_____ teenagers become more interested in community issues

_____ students can learn about careers that might interest them

_____ students help in nursing homes and day-care centers

_____ community service improves many students' self-esteem

_____ students learn to work with other adults

_____ teens work as tutors and hospital aides

_____ students learn how important it is to volunteer

_____ when people volunteer as teens, they are more likely to volunteer as adults

_____ students can learn important job skills

_____ students clean roadways and improve playgrounds

_____ high school community service programs have made students more active in college volunteer programs

WEB:

Answer is on page 332.

Remember, outlines organize information for the essay.

THE PLANNING STAGE

1. Read the instructions carefully, and make sure that you understand them before you begin.
2. Write a thesis statement that will point your thoughts in the right direction.
3. Brainstorm ideas for your essay.
4. Cross out ideas that you will not use.
5. Separate your main ideas and details.
6. Organize the information in an outline (standard outline, T-list, or web).

In this chapter you have learned:

☐ How the Writing Skills Test, Part II is organized (page 215)
☐ How to manage your time (pages 215, 216)
☐ How to read the instructions (pages 216, 217)
☐ How to write a thesis statement (pages 218, 219)
☐ How to brainstorm (pages 219–221)
☐ How to create an outline (pages 223–228)

Review sections that are difficult for you.

Chapter Review

EXERCISE 1: For the following essay, complete each step in the planning stage as directed.

ESSAY TOPIC:

Cellular phones have become popular in recent years. Now people can always be just a phone call away from family, friends, and work. For some, cellular phones are beneficial; others are concerned about the negative effects.

Write a composition of about 200 words that describes both the positive and negative effects of cellular phones on modern life. Use specific examples.

Part A: Write the signal words and a thesis statement in the spaces provided.

SIGNAL WORDS _____

THESIS STATEMENT ➡ _____

_____

Answers are on page 332.

Part B: Brainstorm ideas for the essay. Make sure that you have <u>at least</u> 10 good ideas. After brainstorming, cross out ideas that you will not use.

Part C: Separate your thoughts into groups with main ideas. Then, organize your thoughts into an outline. Use either a standard outline, T-list, or web.

Answers are on page 333.

EXERCISE 2: For the following essay, complete each step in the planning stage as directed.

ESSAY TOPIC:

Good public schools are important in our society. Unfortunately, many children in America do not receive the education that they need and deserve. As a nation, we must work together to improve America's schools.

Answers are on pages 332, 333.

In a composition of about 200 words, tell how public education in America can be improved.

Part A: Write the signal words and a thesis statement in the spaces provided.

SIGNAL WORDS _____

THESIS STATEMENT ➡ _____

_____

Answers are on page 333.

Part B: Brainstorm ideas for the essay. Make sure that you have <u>at least</u> 10 good ideas. After brainstorming, cross out ideas that you will not use.

Answers are on pages 333, 334.

Part C: Separate your thoughts into groups with main ideas. Then, organize your thoughts into an outline. Use either a standard outline, T-list, or web.

Answers are on page 334.

Writing the Essay

In this chapter you will learn:

- ☐ How to organize a five-paragraph essay (page 231)
- ☐ How to write the introductory paragraph (pages 231–234)
- ☐ How to write the body paragraphs (pages 234–236)
- ☐ How to use transitional words and phrases (pages 236–238)
- ☐ How to write the concluding paragraph (pages 238–241)

Remember, essays are like exercise routines. A good workout includes a warm-up, an exercise, and a cool down. The writing stage of essay writing is like the exercise phase of a workout. Now that your mind is warmed up from the planning stage, you can actually write your essay.

During this stage, do not worry about spelling, punctuation, or grammar. You can correct your mistakes later. First let the information flow. Then write about your ideas. After you have completed the first two steps, revise your work.

Overview

Now it is time to learn how to write a five-paragraph essay. Each paragraph in the essay has a job. Note the jobs that are listed in the following box.

THE FIVE-PARAGRAPH ESSAY

Introductory Paragraph
Provides background material
Gives the essay direction
Includes the thesis statement

Body Paragraph 1
Develops the thesis statement
Includes a topic sentence
Includes supporting details

Body Paragraph 2
Develops the thesis statement
Includes a topic sentence
Includes supporting details

Body Paragraph 3
Develops the thesis statement
Includes a topic sentence
Includes supporting details

Concluding Paragraph
Summarizes the essay
Provides an insightful statement

Writing the Introductory Paragraph

The introductory paragraph is like an advertisement for a movie. It grabs the reader's attention. An advertisement does not show all the good scenes or tell the ending of a film. Likewise, a good introduction does not provide details about the topic. Instead, it encourages the reader to continue.

INTRODUCTORY PARAGRAPH

1. Review your outline and thesis statement.
2. Write 1–2 general sentences about the topic.
3. Write 1–2 more specific sentences about the topic.
4. Write your thesis statement.

Your introductory paragraph should move from general information to more specific material. You may write your thesis statement anywhere in the introduction. However, if you write the thesis statement last, it will help point your thoughts in the right direction.

Example:

ESSAY TOPIC
The telephone, which was invented in the 1870s, has become standard in most American homes. The telephone has improved our lives in many ways, but it has also had negative effects.

Write an essay of about 200 words that describes the effects that the telephone has had on modern life. You may describe the good effects, the bad effects, or both.

INTRODUCTORY PARAGRAPH

Throughout history, new inventions have changed people's lives. Inventions often make our lives easier or our work more productive. Sometimes, however, they seem to make life more difficult. The telephone is one invention that has had mixed results. The telephone is helpful in many ways, but it also has drawbacks.

The introduction starts off with a general statement about all inventions and ends with a thesis statement about the positive and negative effects of the telephone. The reader clearly knows what to expect from this essay.

EXERCISE 1: Read each essay topic. Review the thesis statements that you wrote on pages 218, 219 and the information that you brainstormed on pages 220, 221. Then write an introductory paragraph for each topic. Each question has more than one correct answer.

1. ESSAY TOPIC: In the 1970s and 1980s, women with young children entered the workforce in record numbers. In recent years, more parents have decided to stay home while their children are young. Some parents have even started home-based businesses so that they can work and be home with their children.

   Should both parents work or should one stay home with the children? In a composition of about 200 words, state your opinion. Use specific examples to support your views.

INTRODUCTORY PARAGRAPH:

_____

_____

_____

_____

_____

_____

_____

_____

_____

_____

_____

_____

2. ESSAY TOPIC: Even though the legal age for drinking was increased from eighteen to twenty-one, many minors still drink alcohol. Teenage alcohol abuse is a serious problem.

Should responsible teenagers be allowed to drink alcohol or should more efforts be made to stop teenage drinking? In a composition of about 200 words, tell how teenage alcohol use should be handled.

INTRODUCTORY PARAGRAPH:

_____

_____

_____

_____

_____

_____

_____

_____

_____

3. ESSAY TOPIC: The television has become standard in most American homes. It has improved our lives in many ways, but it also has had negative effects.

Write an essay of about 200 words that describes the effects that the television has had on modern life. You may describe the good effects, the bad effects, or both.

INTRODUCTORY PARAGRAPH:

_____

_____

_____

_____

_____

_____

_____

_____

4. ESSAY TOPIC: Homelessness has been a problem for years. Shelters, soup kitchens, and counseling centers are often overwhelmed by the number of people who need help.

In an essay of about 200 words, describe how homeless persons should be helped.

INTRODUCTORY PARAGRAPH:

_____

_____

_____

_____

_____

_____

_____

_____

5. ESSAY TOPIC: A driver's license is a rite of passage for many people. They use their cars to go to school, work, and social events. Inexperienced drivers, however, cause a high percentage of automobile accidents.

In an essay of about 200 words, explain how new drivers should be taught before they get a license.

INTRODUCTORY PARAGRAPH:

_____

_____

_____

_____

_____

_____

_____

_____

_____

_____

Answers are on pages 335.

 Remember, these <u>facts about the introductory paragraph</u>:

- The introductory paragraph provides background material and the thesis statement.
- Start the introductory paragraph with general information and end with more specific material.
- Make your thesis statement the last sentence in the paragraph.

Body Paragraphs

Paragraphs are like scenes from a movie. Each paragraph focuses on one topic. Together, the paragraphs present all of the information to the reader. Once you have organized your thoughts into an outline, the body paragraphs are fairly easy to write. The main ideas in your outlines become topic sentences for the paragraphs. Likewise, the details for each main idea become the supporting details for each paragraph.

The topic sentence can be placed anywhere in the paragraph. However, if you write the topic sentence first, it will direct your thoughts. In addition, it will be easier to check that every supporting detail relates to the topic sentence.

THE BODY PARAGRAPHS

1. Review your outline and thesis statement.
2. Choose the order for your main ideas.
3. Focus on one main idea at a time.
4. Rewrite the main idea as a topic sentence.
5. Rewrite the details as supporting sentences.
6. Add more information as needed.

Example:

THESIS STATEMENT ➡ The telephone is helpful in many ways, but it also has drawbacks.

Telephones help people communicate with family, friends, and the world. With telephones, people can keep in touch with family members who may be across town or across the country. Phones help friends communicate, and they help people check on older relatives or neighbors who may need assistance. For some people in remote areas, telephones provide a connection to the outside world.

Telephones are practical. Making a phone call is easier than writing a letter. In much less time, you can pick up the phone and talk with a friend. While talking on the phone, you can do other things, such as dishes or laundry. If you have an answering machine, people can always get in touch—even if you are not home. Thus, you will not miss important information. In an emergency, a telephone can get you help quickly.

Although telephones are helpful in many ways, phone calls can be expensive and annoying. Monthly bills, which are based on the calls you make, can be costly. In addition, telephones help people contact you—even when you do not want them to call. For example, an employer can call you at home. Likewise, people call during dinner or in the middle of the night.

The writer added some information that was not in the outline. If new thoughts come to you while you are writing, include them.

 Remember

It is important to add specific examples and details to support your thoughts. Ask yourself the following questions to get your thoughts flowing about the topic: How? When? Where? What? Who? Why?

EXERCISE 2: Read the essay topic. Review the brainstorming that you did on page 220 and write an outline in the space provided. Then write the body paragraphs for this topic. If you need more space for your writing, use an additional sheet of paper. Each question has more than one correct answer.

ESSAY TOPIC: The television has become standard in most American homes. It has improved our lives in many ways, but it also has had negative effects.

Write an essay of about 200 words that describes the effects that the television has had on modern life. You may describe the good effects, the bad effects, or both. Use specific examples to support your views.

OUTLINE:

BODY PARAGRAPHS:

_____

_____

_____

_____

_____

_____

_____

_____

_____

_____

_____

_____

_____

_____

_____

_____

_____

_____

_____

_____

_____

_____

_____

Answers are on page 335.

Transitions

When a movie jumps from one scene to another, the story is hard to follow. The same is true with an essay. When you write, you need to make sure that your writing flows smoothly. Transitional words and phrases will help your thoughts flow.

TRANSITIONS BETWEEN SENTENCES

Transitional words and phrases form connections; they show the relationship between one thought and another. You may use transitional words in the beginning or middle of a sentence. Wherever they are located, transitional words should be set apart with commas.

TRANSITIONAL WORDS AND PHRASES

Transitions: also, in addition, likewise, too, furthermore
Job: connect similar ideas

Transitions: because, as a result, therefore, thus, so that, consequently

Job: connect a cause to an effect

Transitions: for instance, for example, such as

Job: connect specific examples to a general idea

Transitions: although, even though, instead, however, yet, on the other hand, nonetheless

Job: connect ideas that are different

Transitions: first, second, next, then, later, after, now

Job: connects ideas according to time

Examples:

1. Running regularly can improve your muscle tone and help you lose weight. <u>Likewise</u>, biking provides many health benefits.
Likewise shows that biking and running have similar benefits.

2. Smokers suffer from many different smoking-related illnesses. <u>For example</u>, lung cancer kills many Americans every year.

   For example shows that lung cancer is a smoking-related illness.

3. We need to eat a variety of foods to get the nutrients that our bodies need. Junk food, <u>however</u>, has no nutritional value.

   However shows that there is a difference between what our bodies need and what junk food provides.

4. Children have been killed by airbags in cars. <u>As a result</u>, parents are told that all children under twelve should sit in the back seat of a car.

   As a result shows that there is a cause and effect relationship between the two sentences.

5. <u>First</u>, melt the butter and add the spices. <u>Then</u>, brush the mixture on the fish. <u>Finally</u>, broil the fish for five or six minutes.

   First, *then*, and *finally* show when the different tasks should be completed.

EXERCISE 3: Read the sentence pairs below. Then write an appropriate transitional word or phrase in the space provided. Include the correct punctuation. Each question has more than one correct answer.

1. His new book is full of suspense and intrigue. The violence _____ is overwhelming.

2. Many species are protected by the Endangered Species Act. _____ the snail darter and the spotted owl have been protected for years.

3. The move from middle school to high school is difficult for some students. _____ the transition from high school to college is challenging.

4. _____ find a spot where the fish are biting. _____ make a few casts and reel in some dinner.

5. Many people can not afford to go to college or a vocational school. _____ many students do not get the education that they need.

6. We wanted to go to a fancy restaurant downtown. _____ we went to a fast food place around the corner.

7. For years women were expected to stay home and raise children. _____ they have many options for their careers and their families.

8. Many immigrants work hard to start a new life in America. Some adults _____ work two or three jobs to provide for their families.

9. We thought that we were buying the home of our dreams. _____ what we bought was one big nightmare.

10. Children need immunizations for protection from serious diseases. _____ many children in America are not immunized properly.

Answers are on page 336.

TRANSITIONS BETWEEN PARAGRAPHS

Transitional words and phrases are also used to connect paragraphs.

Example:

Even though health clubs can provide a great workout, I prefer exercising outdoors. Health clubs can be expensive. On the other hand, for the cost of a pair of running shoes I can get all the exercise I need. Likewise, I do not need to drive to a health club or workout during certain times of the day. Instead, I can walk out my front door and exercise wherever or whenever I want.

I do not want to exercise with other people. I am around many people all day. When I work out, I want to be alone so that I have some time to myself. I also like to exercise by myself so that I can set my own pace; I do not like being rushed or slowed down. Health clubs are great for a lot of people, but for me the best workouts are outdoors.

Both paragraphs show the advantages of exercising outside instead of in a health club. Each of the following transitions could be used to show this relationship:

1. <u>In addition</u>, I do not want to exercise with other people.
2. <u>Likewise</u>, I do not want to exercise with other people.
3. <u>Furthermore</u>, I do not want to exercise with other people.
4. I <u>also</u> do not want to exercise with other people.

EXERCISE 4: After you have read the following essay, underline the transitional words that will connect the ideas effectively.

Over the past ten years, computer use has increased significantly. Like many inventions, computers have changed our lives. Although computers have had some negative effects, most of the changes have been positive.

1. (Likewise, For example) computers help us communicate faster and easier. Computer networks help coworkers, family members, and friends send e-mail or faxes. 2. (As a result, Nonetheless) people who used to drive to an office can now use their computers to telecommute. 3. (Likewise, Instead) companies can use computers to hold meetings without actually getting people together in the same room.

4. Computers (however, also) help people learn more easily. Computer programs can teach everything from Spanish to anatomy. Computers give students individualized instruction; each student can learn the material at his or her own pace. 5. (In addition, Therefore) through the world-wide web, computer users can tour museums or foreign countries.

6. (On the other hand, For instance) computers isolate people. Some people play computer games rather than socializing with others. Students use computers to get class notes without ever actually going to class. 7. (Likewise, Thus) employees who work from home may never even meet their coworkers.

Computers have had positive and negative effects. Computers have improved communication and made learning easier, but they also have isolated people. 8. (Nonetheless, Because) they will continue to be an important invention.

Answers are on page 336.

Remember these <u>facts about the body paragraphs</u>:

- Each body paragraph should have one topic sentence and <u>at least</u> three sentences with supporting details.
- Use your outline as a guide for writing the body paragraphs.
- Use transitional words and phrases to show the relationship between ideas. Transitional words can connect sentences and paragraphs.

Concluding Paragraph

The conclusion is like a quick review of your essay. It summarizes your main points and ends with an insightful statement.

WRITING A CONCLUDING PARAGRAPH

1. Review your essay.
2. In 1 sentence, rewrite your thesis statement.
3. In 1–2 sentences, summarize your topic sentences.
4. In 1–2 sentences, write a general statement about the topic.

> ➡ *Hint:*
> You should rewrite your thesis statement. However, if you cannot think of a new sentence, write *clearly* in front of your original thesis statement.

Example:

Clearly, the telephone can be both beneficial and frustrating. Telephones help people communicate, and they have many practical uses. However, they also are expensive and annoying. Like many inventions, the telephone is a great tool when it is used wisely.

EXERCISE 5: Read the thesis statement and topic sentences for each question. Then write a concluding paragraph for each item. If you need more space, use an additional sheet of paper. Each question has more than one correct answer.

1. THESIS STATEMENT: Parents should do what is best for their children.

TOPIC SENTENCES:

1. Many parents need to work to support their families financially.

2. On the other hand, it is hard for working parents to provide the emotional support that young children demand.

3. Fortunately, there are many ways that parents can work and provide for their families.

_____

_____

_____

_____

_____

2. THESIS STATEMENT: As a nation, we must work harder to stop teenage drinking.

TOPIC SENTENCES:

1. Parents, schools, and the media need to teach teenagers about the dangers of alcohol.

2. In addition, teenagers need positive activities that will steer them away from alcohol.

3. Teenagers also need to be held responsible for their actions.

_____

_____

_____

_____

_____

_____

_____

_____

_____

3. THESIS STATEMENT: Televisions have helped Americans learn more about themselves and the world.

TOPIC SENTENCES:

1. Educational programs teach everything from English to ancient history.

2. Television programs create a common culture in America because many Americans watch the same shows.

3. Televisions help people feel connected with the rest of the world.

_____

_____

_____

_____

_____

_____

_____

_____

_____

_____

4. THESIS STATEMENT: There are many ways to help homeless people.

TOPIC SENTENCES:

1. Charities, private individuals, and government services need to coordinate their efforts to help the homeless.

2. In particular, we need to provide more counseling services and training programs.

3. In addition, shelters and soup kitchens need to focus on helping homeless children.

_____

_____

_____

_____

_____

_____

_____

5. THESIS STATEMENT: Drivers need to experience many different driving situations before they earn a license.

TOPIC SENTENCES:

1. Driver training programs should include more practice driving.

2. Likewise, licenses for new drivers should have restrictions.

3. In addition, drivers should have to drive well in different conditions to pass the test.

_____

_____

_____

_____

_____

_____

_____

_____

_____

_____

_____

_____

_____

_____

Answers are on page 337.

☞ Remember, the concluding paragraph summarizes the main points in the essay.

In this chapter you have learned:

☐ How to organize a five-paragraph essay (page 231)

☐ How to write the introductory paragraph (pages 231–234)

☐ How to write the body paragraphs (pages 234–236)

☐ How to use transitional words and phrases (pages 236–238)

☐ How to write the concluding paragraph (pages 238–241)

Review sections that are difficult for you.

Chapter Review

EXERCISE 1: Read the essay topic. Review the thesis statement that you wrote on pages 228, 229 and the outline that you created on page 229. Then write a five-paragraph essay. If you need more space, use an additional sheet of paper. Each question has more than one correct answer.

ESSAY TOPIC

Cellular phones have become popular in recent years. Now people can always be just a phone call away from family, friends, and work. For some, cellular phones are beneficial; others are concerned about the negative effects.

Write a composition of about 200 words that describes both the positive and negative effects of cellular phones on modern life. Use specific examples.

_____

_____

_____

_____

_____

_____

_____

_____

_____

_____

_____

_____

_____

_____

_____

_____

_____

_____

_____

_____

_____

_____

_____

_____

_____

_____

_____

_____

_____

_____

_____

_____

_____

_____

_____

_____

_____

Answers are on page 337.

EXERCISE 2:   Read the essay topic. Review the thesis statement and the outline that you created on page 230. Then write a five-paragraph essay. If you need more space, use an additional sheet of paper. Each question has more than one correct answer.

ESSAY TOPIC

Good public schools are important in our society. Unfortunately, many children in America do not receive the education that they need and deserve. As a nation, we must work together to improve America's schools.

In a composition of about 200 words, tell how public education in America can be improved.

_____

_____

_____

_____

_____

_____

_____

_____

_____

_____

_____

_____

_____

_____

_____

_____

_____

_____

_____

_____

_____

_____

Answers are on page 338.

Revising the Essay

In this chapter you will learn:

☐ How to check the information in your essay (pages 243–245)

☐ How to check grammar, usage, mechanics, spelling, and capitalization in your essay (pages 245, 246)

☐ How to make corrections in your essay (page 245)

Keep in mind, essays are like exercise routines. A good workout includes three stages: a warm-up, an exercise, and a cool down. The revision stage of essay writing is like the cool down phase of a workout. During this stage, review your work and make necessary changes.

The revision stage has two main steps. In the first step, focus on the information in your essay. In the second step, concentrate on the rules: grammar, usage, mechanics, spelling, and capitalization. Once you have finished both steps, your essay will be complete.

 Note:

Even though the revision stage focuses on corrections, you may make changes at any point in the writing process. If you notice an error, fix it.

Step One: The Information

ORGANIZATION, CONTENT, AND CLARITY

The first step focuses on the information in your essay. Are your thoughts well organized? Did you include good information to support your ideas? Is the information clearly presented? The checklist that follows will give you a systematic way to review your essay.

CHECKLIST FOR INFORMATION

ORGANIZATION

☐ Does the introductory paragraph have a thesis statement that gives the essay direction?

☐ Does each body paragraph have a topic sentence and supporting details?

☐ Does each body paragraph relate to the thesis statement?

☐ Does the concluding paragraph summarize the main points of your essay?

CONTENT

☐ In each paragraph, do the supporting details relate to the topic sentence?

☐ Does the essay include all appropriate information from the outline?

☐ Does each body paragraph have at least three sentences with supporting details?

CLARITY

☐ Is each idea clearly written?

☐ Do transitional words connect the information smoothly?

☐ Does the essay have different types of sentences?

After you have reviewed the information, make necessary corrections. Add supporting details, and reword awkward sentences. Likewise, cross out material that is not related to the topic.

HOW TO MAKE CORRECTIONS:

1. Cross out unwanted words with a single line.
2. Use a caret (^) or asterisk (*) to insert words or sentences.
3. Use the margins or spaces between lines to add ideas or make corrections.
4. Use the symbol ¶ to show that a paragraph should be indented.
5. Rewrite any section that is too sloppy to read.

Do not rewrite your whole essay unless it is absolutely necessary.

Example:

New inventions are created every day. Often they make our lives easier, but sometimes they can be frustrating.

for instance,
The cellular phone, ^ has changed the way people communicate. However not all of the changes have been helpfull. Cellular phones have had positive and negative effects on modern life.

For example,
^ cellular phones help people stay in touch with family, friends, and employers. If a child has a problem, he or she can always call a parent. Some children regularly call their parents after school. ~~Parents want to be sure that their children are safe.~~ Likewise, adults can call home or work when they is going to be late.

Cellular phones also are convenient. It is easy to make a phone call in an emergency. Many people keep the phones in their cars but others take them jogging, biking, or walking to make themselves feel safer. Cell phones also are more convenient than pay phones; sometimes it is hard to find a pay phone that works.

Nonetheless, cellular phones do have drawbacks. Some studies show that cell phone use while driving actually causes accidents. Even basic cellular phone rates can be expensive, and other people can listen into your conversations.

In addition, cell phones may make it to easy for people to contact you; there are times when you do not want phone calls.

Clearly, cellular phones have affected our lives in positive and negative ways. Even though cell phones are helpful and convenient, they do cause some problems. Like many inventions, cell phones can make our lives easier. ~~After all, computers have made our lives easier.~~ We simply need to use them wisely.

The writer crossed out information that was not related to the topic and added transitional words to the first and second paragraphs. She also added a supporting detail to the fourth paragraph.

EXERCISE 1: Revise the following essay using these steps:

1. Read the essay once.
2. Read the essay a second time while completing the checklist for information.
3. Make necessary changes in the margins or spaces between the lines. You may need to cross out some material and add new sentences.

CHECKLIST FOR INFORMATION

ORGANIZATION
- [ ] Does the introductory paragraph have a thesis statement that gives the essay direction?
- [ ] Does each body paragraph have a topic sentence and supporting details?
- [ ] Does each body paragraph relate to the thesis statement?
- [ ] Does the concluding paragraph summarize the main points of your essay?

CONTENT
- [ ] In each paragraph, do the supporting details relate to the topic sentence?
- [ ] Does the essay include all appropriate information from the outline?
- [ ] Does each body paragraph have <u>at least</u> three sentences with supporting details?

CLARITY

☐ Is each idea clearly written?

☐ Do transitional words connect the information smoothly?

☐ Does the essay have different types of sentences?

Public education is an important part of American society. Many public schools in America do not educate children well. As a result, too many students do not have the skills that they need.

First, parents and educators need to set higher expectations for students. Children learn more when they are challenged. High school students should take at least three years of English, math, science, social studies, and physical education. Courses for high school students should prepare them for college, job training, or both.

Likewise, parents need to get more involved in the schools and show their children that education matters. Parents should attend parent-teacher conferences and volunteer in the schools. Parents must improve their own education to show their children that learning does not stop at the school door.

The community also needs to support the local schools. Community leaders can donate equipment to the schools and arrange more after-school activities for students. Often teachers live in the community. Adults in the community can serve as mentors for students. The community as a whole can work together to make sure that school buildings are well maintained.

Higher standards, greater parental involvement, and more local support can make the public schools more successful. If we work together, public schools can help students develop their skills and achieve their dreams.

Answers are on pages 338, 339.

Step Two: The Rules

GRAMMAR, USAGE, MECHANICS, SPELLING, AND CAPITALIZATION

The second step, which is often called editing or proofreading, focuses on the rules of English. Are pronouns and verbs used correctly? Are punctuation marks used properly? Are words spelled correctly? The checklist that follows will give you a systematic way to review your essay.

CHECKLIST FOR RULES

☐ Is every sentence a complete sentence?

☐ Are pronouns and verbs used correctly?

☐ Are punctuation marks used correctly?

☐ Are words spelled correctly?

☐ Are words capitalized correctly?

Example:

Now, the writer has completed the second step with the essay on cellular phones. Note the corrections that are in color.

New inventions are created every day. Often they make our lives easier, but sometimes they can be frustrating.

for instance,
The cellular phone, ^ has changed the way people communicate. However not all of the
helpful
changes have been ~~helpfull~~. Cellular phones have had positive and negative effects on modern life.

For example, cellular
^ ~~Cellular~~ phones help people stay in touch with family, friends, and employers. If a child has a problem, he or she can always call a parent. Some children regularly call their parents after school. ~~Parents want to be sure that their children are safe.~~ Likewise, adults can call
are
home or work when they ~~is~~ going to be late.

Cellular phones also are convenient. It is easy to make a phone call in an emergency. Many people keep cell phones in their cars but others take them jogging, biking, or walking to make themselves feel safer. Cellular phones also are more convenient than pay phones; sometimes it is hard to find a pay phone that works.

Nonetheless, cellular phones do have drawbacks. Some studies show that cell phone use while driving actually causes accidents. Even basic cellular phone rates can be expensive, and other people can listen into your conversations. In addition, cell phones may
                                too
make it ~~to~~ easy for people to contact you; there are times when you do not want phone calls.

Clearly, cellular phones have affected our lives in positive and negative ways. Even though cell phones are helpful and convenient, they do cause some problems. Like many inventions, cell phones can make our lives easier. ~~After all, computers have made our lives easier.~~ We simply need to use them wisely.

EXERCISE 2: Revise the following essay using these steps.

1. Read the essay once.
2. Read the essay a second time while completing the checklist for rules.
3. Make necessary changes in the margins or spaces between the lines.

CHECKLIST FOR RULES

☐ Is every sentence a complete sentence?
☐ Are pronouns and verbs used correctly?
☐ Are punctuation marks used correctly?
☐ Are words spelled correctly?
☐ Are words capitalized correctly?

Throughout history, new inventions have changed peoples lives. Inventions often make our lives easier or our work more productive. Sometimes, however, they seem to make life more difficult. The telephone is one invention that has had mixed results. The telephone is helpful in many ways but it also has drawbacks.

Telephones help people communicate with family, friends, and the world. With telephones, people can keep in touch with family members who may be across town or across the country. phones help friends communicate, and they help people check on older relatives or neighbors who may need assistance. Telephones a connection to the outside world.

Telephones are practical. Making a phone call is easier than writing a letter. In much less time, you can pick up the phone and talk with a freind. While talking on the phone, you can do other things, such as dishes or laundry. In an emergency, a telephone can get you help quickly.

Although telephones are helpful in many ways, phone calls can be expensive and annoying. Monthly bills which are based on the calls you make can be costly. In addition, telephones help people contact you—even when you do not want them to call. For example, an employer can call you at home. Likewise, people call during dinner or in the middle of the night.

Clearly, the telephone can be both beneficial and frustrating. Telephones help people communicate and they have many practical uses. However, they also are expensive and annoying. Like many inventions, the telephone is a great tool when it is used wisely.

Answers are on page 339.

EXERCISE 3: Revise the following essay using these steps:

1. Read the essay once.
2. Read the essay a second time while completing the checklist for information and rules.
3. Make necessary changes in the margins or spaces between the lines. You may need to cross out some material and add new sentences.

CHECKLIST FOR INFORMATION AND RULES

ORGANIZATION

- ☐ Does the introductory paragraph have a thesis statement that gives the essay direction?
- ☐ Does each body paragraph have a topic sentence and supporting details?
- ☐ Does each body paragraph relate to the thesis statement?
- ☐ Does the concluding paragraph summarize the main points of your essay?

CONTENT

- ☐ In each paragraph, do the supporting details relate to the topic sentence?
- ☐ Does the essay include all appropriate information from the outline?
- ☐ Does each body paragraph have <u>at least</u> three sentences with supporting details?

RULES

- ☐ Is every sentence a complete sentence?
- ☐ Are pronouns and verbs used correctly?
- ☐ Are punctuation marks used correctly?
- ☐ Are words spelled correctly?
- ☐ Are words capitalized correctly?

Many people are active in volunteer activities. These projects not only get people involved in they're communities, but also help people in need. Some people want to make community service a high school graduation requirement; others think that schools should not force students to "volunteer." High schools should require community service because it helps students become more thoughtful, responsible adults.

Students discover different careers that might intrest them such as medicine or teaching. Students also learn to work with adults. Teens develop important job skills that will help them in the future. They learn to be on time, to follow directions, and to complete projects.

Students also get involved in many different types of community service. Teenagers can choose volunteer programs that interest them.

Likewise, when students are involved in community service, they develop into more active confident adults. Community service improves students self-esteem. People who volunteer as teens more likely to volunteer as adults. High school community service programs have made students more active in college volunteer programs. In addition, teenagers who are involved in community programs are more interested in local issues.

Clearly, community service can be an important part of one's high school education. Community service programs positively effect students not only when they are teens, but also when they become adults.

Answers are on pages 339, 340.

In this chapter you have learned:

- ☐ How to check the information in your essay (pages 243–245)
- ☐ How to check grammar, usage, mechanics, spelling, and capitalization in your essay (pages 245, 246)
- ☐ How to make corrections in your essay (page 245)

Review sections that are difficult for you.

Chapter Review

In Chapter 16, you wrote about the following essay topics. Use the checklist for information and the checklist for rules to revise your essays. Share your revised essay with a teacher or another student.

ESSAY TOPIC 1:

Cellular phones have become popular in recent years. Now people can always be just a phone call away from family, friends, and work. For some, cellular phones are beneficial; others are concerned about the negative effects.

Write a composition of about 200 words that describes both the positive and negative effects of cellular phones on modern life. Use specific examples.

ESSAY TOPIC 2:

Good public schools are important in our society. Unfortunately, many children in America do not receive the education that they need and deserve. As a nation, we must work together to improve America's schools.

In a composition of about 200 words, tell how public education in America can be improved.

Evaluating the Essay

In this chapter you will learn:

☐ How essays are scored (pages 249, 250)

☐ What you can do to improve your essay score (pages 251–254)

Two GED evaluators will read your essay once and score it holistically. The evaluators will focus mostly on your ability to support a good, clear thesis statement. Even though a few minor errors will not significantly affect your score, check your writing carefully. If misspellings and grammatical errors make your essay hard to understand, you will earn a lower score.

GED Essay Scoring Guide

Copyright © 1987, GED Testing Service Papers will show <u>some or all</u> of the following characteristics.

Upper-half papers have a clear, definite purpose pursued with varying degrees of effectiveness. They have a structure that shows evidence of some deliberate planning. The writer's control of the conventions of Standard Written English (spelling, punctuation, grammar, word choice, and sentence structure) ranges from a score of fairly reliable at 4 to confident and accomplished at 6.

6 The *6 paper* offers sophisticated ideas within an organizational framework that is clear and appropriate for the topic. The supporting statements are particularly effective because of their substance, specificity, or illustrative quality. The writing is vivid and precise, although it may contain an occasional error in the conventions of Standard Written English.

5 The *5 paper* is clearly organized with effective support for each of the writer's major points. While the writing offers substantive ideas, it lacks the fluency found in the 6 paper. Although there are some errors, the conventions of Standard Written English are consistently under control.

4 The *4 paper* shows evidence of the writer's organization plan. Support, though adequate, tends to be less extensive or effective than that found in the 5 paper. The writer generally observes the conventions of Standard Written English. The errors that are present are not severe enough to interfere significantly with the writer's main purpose.

Lower-half papers either fail to convey a purpose sufficiently or lack one entirely. Consequently, their structure ranges from rudimentary at 3, to random at 2, to absent at 1. Control of the conventions of Standard Written English tends to follow the same gradient.

3 The *3 paper* usually shows some evidence of planning, although the development is insufficient. The supporting statements may be limited to a listing or a repetition of ideas. The 3 paper often demonstrates repeated weakness in the conventions of Standard Written English.

2 The *2 paper* is characterized by a marked lack of organization or inadequate support for ideas. The development is usually superficial or unfocused. Errors in the conventions of Standard Written English may seriously interfere with the overall effectiveness of this paper.

1 The *1 paper* lacks purpose or development. The dominant feature is the absence of control of structure of the conventions of Standard Written English. The deficiencies are so severe that the writer's ideas are difficult or impossible to understand.

* An asterisk code is reserved for papers that are blank, illegible, or written on a topic other than the one assigned. Because these papers cannot be scored, a Writing Skills Test composite score cannot be reported.

SCORING CHART

For some students, a chart is easier to understand. Each column shows the characteristics of a particular essay.

EVALUATING THE ESSAY

Essay Scoring Chart

	6	5	4	3	2	1
Organization	Excellent organization	Very good organization	Some organization	Some organization, but not enough	Very little organization	No organization
Content	Plenty of specific supporting details for each major point	Good supporting details for each major point	Fair supporting details	Few supporting details, may be repetitive	Very few supporting details, ideas are not explained	No supporting details
Clarity	Clear, smooth writing	Clear writing	Mostly clear writing	Often unclear writing	Usually unclear writing	Unclear writing
Rules	An occasional minor error	A few errors, but they are minor	Some errors, main points somewhat hard to understand	Many errors, main points somewhat hard to understand	Numerous errors, ideas hard to understand	Numerous errors, ideas almost impossible to understand

An asterisk (*) is for papers that are blank, illegible, or on topic that is different from the assigned topic. These papers can not be scored; therefore, a Writing Skills Test composite score cannot be reported.

Example:

ESSAY TOPIC

Faced with budget problems, many schools across the country have reduced or eliminated programs for art, music, and athletics. Many people feel that these programs are part of a quality education. Others believe that the programs are luxuries that we cannot afford when money is tight.

How important are these programs? In a composition of about 200 words, state your view. Use specific examples.

SAMPLE ESSAY

Programs for art, music, and athletics are important. These programs help keep some students in school. Even if schools don't have a lot of money, they should keep art, music, and athletics.

Many students like art, music, and sports. Even people who don't want to go to school like going to these classes. They get bored in there other classes, but in these classes they get to do things that they want to do. These classes are more relaxed then other classes.

In these programs students learn things that they can't learn in there other classes. Some people work hard in school so they can stay in these programs. Art, music, and athletics help people become better students.

In my opinion, programs for art, music, and athletics should not be cut. Students need these programs.

This essay probably would receive a 3. It has some organization, but it does not have enough supporting details. Some sentences are repetitious. In addition, there are a few errors—mostly in word choice.

Your Turn

The following pages have sample essays for you to evaluate. Use the Checklist for Evaluating an Essay and the Scoring Chart as guides. After you have evaluated the essays independently, have a teacher or student review the scores that you assigned. Follow these steps:

1. Read the essay once to get an over-all impression.
2. Read the essay a second time to evaluate the information. Complete the first three sections of the checklist.
3. Read the essay a third time to evaluate how well it follows the rules. Complete the last section of the checklist.
4. Review your answers to the checklist. Look on the chart to find the numbered column that best describes the essay. Assign an essay score.

ESSAY TOPIC

Faced with budget problems, many schools across the country have reduced or eliminated programs for art, music, and athletics. Many people feel that these programs are part of a quality education. Others believe that the programs are luxuries that we can not afford when money is tight.

How important are these programs? In a composition of about 200 words, state your view. Use specific examples.

SAMPLE ESSAY 1:

I think that art, music, and sports are important. Kids like them. They are a lot easier than other classes. They are more relaxing. You get to do things that you like to do and you can have fun. These classes teach students things that they can't learn in there other classes. Some students are really intrested in these classes. They may want to be artists, musisians or atheletes. When they get older. If these classes are cut some kids won't want to go to school. Schools should cut other things that aren't as important.

CHECKLIST FOR EVALUATING AN ESSAY

ORGANIZATION

☐ Does the introductory paragraph have a thesis statement that gives the essay direction?

☐ Does each body paragraph have a topic sentence and supporting details?

☐ Does each body paragraph relate to the thesis statement?

☐ Does the concluding paragraph summarize the main points of the essay?

CONTENT

☐ In each paragraph, do the supporting details relate to the topic sentence?

☐ Does the essay include all appropriate information from the outline?

☐ Does each body paragraph have <u>at least</u> three sentences with supporting details?

CLARITY

☐ Is each idea clearly written?

☐ Do transitional words connect the information smoothly?

☐ Does the essay have different types of sentences?

THE RULES

☐ Is every sentence a complete sentence?

☐ Are pronouns and verbs used correctly?

☐ Are punctuation marks used correctly?

☐ Are words spelled correctly?
☐ Are words capitalized correctly?
SCORE
O *   O 1   O 2   O 3   O 4   O 5   O 6

SAMPLE ESSAY 2:

Art! everybody like art. Music to and sports. Long time ago people think that artrists are famous like monet and now they want to not spend money on art classes. Even music classes. Where will all the new artrists come from? Oh no! who will paint pictures and make music? We need sports to. Some kids, they liked sports. where will they play? what will they did if they don't play sports? who will played on pro teams? These classess keep kids off drugs. big problem. Theyll do more drugs. Keep art and music in school. Sports to! Kids want to go to school and go to these classess and learn lots about art and music. Some kids wont go. who will teach them? Art is great!

CHECKLIST FOR EVALUATING AN ESSAY

ORGANIZATION

☐ Does the introductory paragraph have a thesis statement that gives the essay direction?
☐ Does each body paragraph have a topic sentence and supporting details?
☐ Does each body paragraph relate to the thesis statement?
☐ Does the concluding paragraph summarize the main points of the essay?

CONTENT

☐ In each paragraph, do the supporting details relate to the topic sentence?
☐ Does the essay include all appropriate information from the outline?
☐ Does each body paragraph have <u>at least</u> three sentences with supporting details?

CLARITY

☐ Is each idea clearly written?
☐ Do transitional words connect the information smoothly?
☐ Does the essay have different types of sentences?

THE RULES
☐ Is every sentence a complete sentence?
☐ Are pronouns and verbs used correctly?
☐ Are punctuation marks used correctly?
☐ Are words spelled correctly?
☐ Are words capitalized correctly?
SCORE
O *   O 1   O 2   O 3   O 4   O 5   O 6

SAMPLE ESSAY 3:

Schools should work hard to keep their art, music, and athletic programs.

Art, music, and athletics are important for many students. Some enjoy the more relaxed atmosphere that these classes offer because it is different than their other classes. Other students want to learn more about these subjects so that they can study them in college or use them for jobs. For some students, these classes are the only reason they want to go to school. Schools that cut these classes may end up with a higher dropout rate.

These programs give students a better education. They learn to be creative, to appreciate other people's skills, to relax, to explore, and to take care of their health. They also learn to think better. For example, students who are involved in music often do well in math.

Some schools may want to cut these programs because they don't have enough money, but they should cut something else instead, like Spanish or something. Art, music, and athletics are important in the schools. They make education more interesting.

CHECKLIST FOR EVALUATING AN ESSAY

ORGANIZATION

☐ Does the introductory paragraph have a thesis statement that gives the essay direction?
☐ Does each body paragraph have a topic sentence and supporting details?
☐ Does each body paragraph relate to the thesis statement?
☐ Does the concluding paragraph summarize the main points of your essay?

CONTENT

- ☐ In each paragraph, do the supporting details relate to the topic sentence?
- ☐ Does the essay include all appropriate information from the outline?
- ☐ Does each body paragraph have <u>at least</u> three sentences with supporting details?

CLARITY

- ☐ Is each idea clearly written?
- ☐ Do transitional words connect the information smoothly?
- ☐ Does the essay have different types of sentences?

THE RULES

- ☐ Is every sentence a complete sentence?
- ☐ Are pronouns and verbs used correctly?
- ☐ Are punctuation marks used correctly?
- ☐ Are words spelled correctly?
- ☐ Are words capitalized correctly?

SCORE

O *   O 1   O 2   O 3   O 4   O 5   O 6

SAMPLE ESSAY 4:

Schools have many different programs. Some give extra help to students, and others make school more interesting. However, when money is tight, some programs have to be eliminated. The art, music, and athletics programs should not be cut.

Art, music, and athletics add variety to the school day. These classes are set up differently than other subjects. Most art classes, for example, are less structured than math or science. In physical education classes students are active; they do not have to sit in seats for the entire period. Some students need these subjects so that they can get through the rest of the day.

Art, music, and athletics also are an important part of an education. These classes help students learn more about different types of art and music. Otherwise the only music some students would hear would be on the radio. Athletics help students learn more about their bodies and how to keep themselves healthy. Through these programs, students learn more about themselves and the world around them.

These programs help students develop a variety of skills. Some people use these skills to pursue hobbies such as photography and drawing. Others play in bands or sell paintings to earn money. Through sports, students develop athletic skills that they can use there entire lives.

Art, music, and athletics are an important part of our schools. These educational programs add variety to the school day. They also help students develop useful skills.

CHECKLIST FOR EVALUATING AN ESSAY

ORGANIZATION

- ☐ Does the introductory paragraph have a thesis statement that gives the essay direction?
- ☐ Does each body paragraph have a topic sentence and supporting details?
- ☐ Does each body paragraph relate to the thesis statement?
- ☐ Does the concluding paragraph summarize the main points of your essay?

CONTENT

- ☐ In each paragraph, do the supporting details relate to the topic sentence?
- ☐ Does the essay include all appropriate information from the outline?
- ☐ Does each body paragraph have <u>at least</u> three sentences with supporting details?

CLARITY

- ☐ Is each idea clearly written?
- ☐ Do transitional words connect the information smoothly?
- ☐ Does the essay have different types of sentences?

THE RULES

- ☐ Is every sentence a complete sentence?
- ☐ Are pronouns and verbs used correctly?
- ☐ Are punctuation marks used correctly?
- ☐ Are words spelled correctly?
- ☐ Are words capitalized correctly?

SCORE

O *   O 1   O 2   O 3   O 4   O 5   O 6

SAMPLE ESSAY 5:

School leaders always have to make difficult decisions when budgets are tight. Some programs are easy to eliminate, but most are hard to cut. No one wants to lose a good program. The art, music, and athletic programs should not be reduced because they are too important.

Art, music, and athletics often attract students' attention. Many students struggle in their academic classes. For these children, other programs provide a break and an opportunity to develop skills that they enjoy using. In the early years, these programs are a good, easy way to learn about something new. As students grow, however, the classes become an important part of the school day. Some students would not even attend school if programs in art, music, and athletics were eliminated.

When students learn about art, music, and athletics, they have a more general education. They learn to be more creative, innovative, and daring. They learn more about themselves, other people, and other cultures. Through sports, students learn to keep their bodies healthy. Students may even find good role models. According to some studies, these classes actually help students do better in other subjects such as math, science, and English. Without these programs, one's education is limited.

The special programs help students interact better. In some schools, students are grouped in academic classes according to their abilities. They often spend most of the school day with the same students. In the special programs, however, students are more likely to be mixed together. Therefore, they learn to get along with a variety of people, and they learn that everybody has different talents.

Clearly, art, music, and athletic programs are necessary. These programs interest students and develop their general education. In addition, these programs help students interact better. Most budget decisions are hard, but this is one choice that is easy to make.

CHECKLIST FOR EVALUATING AN ESSAY

ORGANIZATION
- ☐ Does the introductory paragraph have a thesis statement that gives the essay direction?
- ☐ Does each body paragraph have a topic sentence and supporting details?
- ☐ Does each body paragraph relate to the thesis statement?
- ☐ Does the concluding paragraph summarize the main points of your essay?

CONTENT
- ☐ In each paragraph, do the supporting details relate to the topic sentence?
- ☐ Does the essay include all appropriate information from the outline?
- ☐ Does each body paragraph have <u>at least</u> three sentences with supporting details?

CLARITY
- ☐ Is each idea clearly written?
- ☐ Do transitional words connect the information smoothly?
- ☐ Does the essay have different types of sentences?

THE RULES
- ☐ Is every sentence a complete sentence?
- ☐ Are pronouns and verbs used correctly?
- ☐ Are punctuation marks used correctly?
- ☐ Are words spelled correctly?
- ☐ Are words capitalized correctly?

SCORE

O * O 1 O 2 O 3 O 4 O 5 O 6

In this chapter you have learned:

- ☐ How essays are scored (pages 249, 250)
- ☐ What you can do to improve your essay score (pages 251–254)

Review sections that are difficult for you.

Chapter Review

In Chapter 16 you wrote about the topics that are listed below. Evaluate your essays using the Checklist for Evaluating an Essay and the Scoring Chart as guides. After you have evaluated the essays independently, have a teacher or student review the scores that you assigned. Follow these steps:

1. Read the essay once to get an overall impression.
2. Read the essay a second time to evaluate the information. Complete the first three sections of the checklist.
3. Read the essay a third time to evaluate how well it follows the rules. Complete the last section of the checklist.
4. Review your answers to the checklist. Look on the chart to find the numbered column that best describes the essay. Assign an essay score.

ESSAY TOPIC 1:

Cellular phones have become popular in recent years. Now people can always be just a phone call away from family, friends, and work. For some, cellular phones are beneficial; others are concerned about the negative effects.

Write a composition of about 200 words that describes both the positive and negative effects of cellular phones on modern life. Use specific examples.

ESSAY TOPIC 2:

Good public schools are important in our society. Unfortunately, many children in America do not receive the education that they need and deserve. As a nation, we must work together to improve America's schools.

In a composition of about 200 words, tell how public education in America can be improved.

Practice Essays

Overview

This practice section includes one essay with step-by-step instructions that guide you through the writing process. It also includes simulated tests that you should complete independently.

 Note:

The practice topics are similar to real GED essay topics. In order to maintain the integrity of the test, actual GED essays are not published.

GUIDED SAMPLE ESSAY

This practice essay is designed to guide you through the entire writing process. Before you begin the essay, make sure that you have plenty of scratch paper and a copy of the answer sheet on page 259. Do not time yourself for this particular essay.

Directions

1. Read the entire question carefully.

2. Plan your response before you write.

3. Write only about the assigned topic. You will receive no credit for writing on a different topic.

4. Make notes on scratch paper. Your notes will not be scored.

5. Write your essay on a copy of the answer sheet on page 259 or a separate sheet of paper.

6. Carefully read your essay and make changes that will improve it.

7. Use correct paragraphing, sentence structure, spelling, usage, punctuation, and capitalization.

8. Use a ballpoint pen and write legibly.

ESSAY TOPIC

For decades health experts have stated that good nutrition and a balanced diet are important. Many Americans have ignored these warnings. Instead, fast food and snacks have become major sources of nourishment.

Why don't Americans eat healthier meals? In a composition of about 200 words, explain why good eating habits are hard to find. Use specific examples to support your views.

STEP-BY-STEP INSTRUCTIONS

Check off each completed step.

Planning

☐ 1. Read the essay topic and underline the signal words that tell you how to write the essay. In the space provided, write your thesis statement.

Thesis Statement ➡ _____

_____

☐ 2. On a separate sheet of paper, brainstorm ideas for the essay. Make sure you have <u>at least</u> ten good ideas.

☐ 3. Separate your ideas into main ideas and details.

☐ 4. Organize your ideas into an outline. Use either a standard outline, T-list, or web.

Writing

☐ 5. Write your introductory paragraph.

  a. Review your outline.

  b. Write 1–2 general statements about the topic.

  c. Write 1–2 more specific statements about the topic.

  d. Write your thesis statement.

☐ 6. Write your body paragraphs.

  a. Review your outline and thesis statement.

  b. Choose the order for your main ideas.

  c. Focus on one main idea at a time.

  d. Rewrite the main idea as a topic sentence.

  e. Rewrite the supporting details as supporting sentences.

  f. Add more information as needed.

☐ 7. Write your conclusion.

  a. Review your essay.

  b. In 1 sentence, rewrite your thesis statement.

  c. In 1–2 sentences, summarize your topic sentences.

  d. In 1–2 sentences, write a general statement about the topic.

Revising

☐ 8. Complete the checklist and make changes as necessary.

CHECKLIST FOR EVALUATING AN ESSAY

ORGANIZATION

☐ Does the introductory paragraph have a thesis statement that gives the essay direction?

☐ Does each body paragraph have a topic sentence and supporting details?

☐ Does each body paragraph relate to the thesis statement?

☐ Does the concluding paragraph summarize the main points of your essay?

CONTENT

☐ In each paragraph, do the supporting details relate to the topic sentence?

☐ Does the essay include all appropriate information from the outline?

☐ Does each body paragraph have <u>at least</u> three sentences with supporting details?

CLARITY

☐ Is each idea clearly written?

☐ Do transitional words connect the information smoothly?

☐ Does the essay have different types of sentences?

THE RULES

☐ Is every sentence a complete sentence?

☐ Are pronouns and verbs used correctly?

☐ Are punctuation marks used correctly?

☐ Are words spelled correctly?

☐ Are words capitalized correctly?

Evaluating

☐ 9. Use the essay checklist and scoring chart on pages 250, 251 to evaluate your essay.

☐ 10. After you have evaluated your essay independently, have a teacher or student review your writing and the score that you assigned.

SIMULATED TESTS

For these tests, it is important to simulate the actual testing conditions as much as possible. For each essay, assemble your materials (pens, paper, etc.) before you begin, and set a timer for 45 minutes. Start the timer as soon as you begin reading the instructions.

After you have completed your essay, evaluate it. First, complete the evaluation process independently. Then, ask your teacher or another student to evaluate your essay.

➡ *Reminder:* Time Management

Planning (10 Minutes)

1. Figure out the instructions and the topic.
2. Write the thesis statement.
3. Brainstorm.
4. Create an outline.

Writing (25 Minutes)

1. Review your notes.
2. Write the introduction, body, and conclusion.

Revising (10 Minutes)

1. Compare your essay and notes.
2. Check and revise for the information: organization, content, and clarity.
3. Check and revise for the rules: grammar, usage, mechanics, spelling, and capitalization.

SAMPLE TEST A

Directions

Part II of the Writing Skills Test examines your ability to write well. In 45 minutes, write an essay on the assigned topic. Follow the steps below:

1. Read the entire question carefully.
2. Plan your response before you write.
3. Write only about the assigned topic. You will receive no credit for writing on a different topic.
4. Make notes on scratch paper. Your notes will not be scored.
5. Write your essay on a copy of the answer sheet on page 259 or a separate sheet of paper.
6. Carefully read your essay and make changes that will improve it.
7. Use correct paragraphing, sentence structure, spelling, usage, punctuation, and capitalization.
8. Use a ballpoint pen and write legibly.

ESSAY TOPIC

Many children look to athletes, actors, and musicians as role models. Others think that these people are simply entertainers, not role models.

What are the characteristics of a good role model? In a composition of about 200 words, state your opinion. Use specific examples to support your views.

SAMPLE TEST B

Directions

Part II of the Writing Skills Test examines your ability to write well. In 45 minutes, write an essay on the assigned topic. Follow the steps below:

1. Read the entire question carefully.
2. Plan your response before you write.
3. Write only about the assigned topic. You will receive no credit for writing on a different topic.
4. Make notes on scratch paper. Your notes will not be scored.
5. Write your essay on a copy of the answer sheet on page 259 or a separate sheet of paper.
6. Carefully read your essay and make changes that will improve it.

7. Use correct paragraphing, sentence structure, spelling, usage, punctuation, and capitalization.
8. Use a ballpoint pen and write legibly.

ESSAY TOPIC

Teenage violence is now a major problem in our society. Teenagers are committing more violent crimes than ever before. Some people want to punish teen offenders severely. Others want to create more programs to treat violent teens.

In a composition of about 200 words, describe what can be done to prevent teenage violence. Use examples to support your views.

ANSWER SHEET FOR PRACTICE ESSAYS

Name _____

Class _____

Date _____

Topic _____

Start Time _____

Finish Time _____

(Continue practice essay on additional sheets of paper)

Posttest

Directions

1. This test has paragraphs with numbered sentences. The sentences may have errors, or they may be correct as written. First read the paragraphs. Then answer the related questions. Choose the best answer for each question. The best answer should be consistent with the point of view and verb tense that is used throughout the paragraph.

2. Answer every question. If you are not sure of the answer, make a logical guess.

3. Allow yourself 75 minutes to answer the 55 questions. When time is up, underline the last item that you completed. Then complete the test. This will help you monitor your time for the actual GED test.

4. Write your answers to the questions on the answer grid. For each question, mark the number that matches the answer you chose.

5. After you have completed the test, check your answers and complete the Posttest Skills Chart to see which sections are difficult for you.

Example:

Sentence 1: **Parents need to give their children a lot of atention.**

What correction should be made to this sentence?

(1) replace *Parents* with *Parents'*

(2) change *their* to *there*

(3) replace *need* with *needed*

(4) change *atention* to *attention*

(5) no correction necessary

1. ① ② ③ ● ⑤

In this sentence, *attention* is spelled incorrectly.

ANSWER GRID

1. ① ② ③ ④ ⑤
2. ① ② ③ ④ ⑤
3. ① ② ③ ④ ⑤
4. ① ② ③ ④ ⑤
5. ① ② ③ ④ ⑤
6. ① ② ③ ④ ⑤
7. ① ② ③ ④ ⑤
8. ① ② ③ ④ ⑤
9. ① ② ③ ④ ⑤
10. ① ② ③ ④ ⑤
11. ① ② ③ ④ ⑤
12. ① ② ③ ④ ⑤
13. ① ② ③ ④ ⑤
14. ① ② ③ ④ ⑤
15. ① ② ③ ④ ⑤
16. ① ② ③ ④ ⑤
17. ① ② ③ ④ ⑤
18. ① ② ③ ④ ⑤
19. ① ② ③ ④ ⑤

20. ① ② ③ ④ ⑤
21. ① ② ③ ④ ⑤
22. ① ② ③ ④ ⑤
23. ① ② ③ ④ ⑤
24. ① ② ③ ④ ⑤
25. ① ② ③ ④ ⑤
26. ① ② ③ ④ ⑤
27. ① ② ③ ④ ⑤
28. ① ② ③ ④ ⑤
29. ① ② ③ ④ ⑤
30. ① ② ③ ④ ⑤
31. ① ② ③ ④ ⑤
32. ① ② ③ ④ ⑤
33. ① ② ③ ④ ⑤
34. ① ② ③ ④ ⑤
35. ① ② ③ ④ ⑤
36. ① ② ③ ④ ⑤
37. ① ② ③ ④ ⑤
38. ① ② ③ ④ ⑤

39. ① ② ③ ④ ⑤
40. ① ② ③ ④ ⑤
41. ① ② ③ ④ ⑤
42. ① ② ③ ④ ⑤
43. ① ② ③ ④ ⑤
44. ① ② ③ ④ ⑤
45. ① ② ③ ④ ⑤
46. ① ② ③ ④ ⑤
47. ① ② ③ ④ ⑤
48. ① ② ③ ④ ⑤
49. ① ② ③ ④ ⑤
50. ① ② ③ ④ ⑤
51. ① ② ③ ④ ⑤
52. ① ② ③ ④ ⑤
53. ① ② ③ ④ ⑤
54. ① ② ③ ④ ⑤
55. ① ② ③ ④ ⑤

Questions 1 through 10 refer to the following paragraph.

(1) Home schooling has become a popular trend throughout the United States in the last decade. (2) In the past, religious conservatives dominate the home-schooling movement. (3) Now, parents teach their children at home for a variety of resons. (4) Many parents of home-schooled children will be concerned that the public schools do not teach sound values. (5) Others are upset about drug use teen pregnancy and violence in the schools. (6) As a result, many families have decided that the public schools cannot be trusted with their childrens education. (7) Since 1990, the number of home-schooled children in kindergarten through twelfth grade has almost doubled to 500,000 students nationally. (8) As a result, special support groups, materials for teaching, and athletic organizations for home-schooled children have emerged. (9) At the same time, home-schooled children have enrolled in various Colleges and Universities. (10) Although home-schooling is not suitable for many families, it is an increasingly popular choice for some parents.

1. Sentence 1: **Home schooling has become a popular trend throughout the United States in the last decade.**

   If you rewrote sentence 1 beginning with

   In the last decade,

   the next words should be

   (1) has become
   (2) a popular trend
   (3) the United States
   (4) home schooling
   (5) trend throughout

2. Sentence 2: **In the past, religious conservatives dominate the home-schooling movement.**

   What correction should be made to this sentence?

   (1) change *dominate* to *dominated*
   (2) replace *religious* with *religis*
   (3) change *conservatives* to *Conservatives*
   (4) insert a comma after *home*
   (5) no correction necessary

3. Sentence 3: **Now, parents teach their children at home for a variety of resons.**

   What correction should be made to this sentence?

   (1) remove the comma after *now*
   (2) replace *their* with *they're*
   (3) replace *resons* with *reasons*
   (4) replace *teach* with *learn*
   (5) no correction necessary

4. Sentence 4: **Many parents of home-schooled children will be concerned that the public schools do not teach sound values.**

   What correction should be made to this sentence?

   (1) replace *will be* with *are*
   (2) insert a comma after *concerned*
   (3) replace *parents* with *parent's*
   (4) replace *do* with *did*
   (5) no correction necessary

5. Sentence 5: **Others are upset about drug use teen pregnancy and violence in the schools.**

   Which of the following is the best way to write the underlined portion of this sentence? If you think that the original is best, choose option (1).

   (1) drug use teen pregnancy and violence
   (2) drug use, teen pregnancy, and violence
   (3) drug use, teen pregnancy, and violence,
   (4) drug use teen pregnancy, and violence
   (5) drug use; teen pregnancy, and violence

6. Sentence 6: **As a result, many families have decided that the public schools cannot be trusted with their childrens education.**

What correction should be made to this sentence?

(1) replace *their* with *there*
(2) change *families* to *family's*
(3) remove the comma after *result*
(4) replace *childrens* with *children's*
(5) no correction necessary

7. Sentence 7: **Since 1990, the number of home-schooled children in kindergarten through twelfth grade has almost doubled to 500,000 students nationally.**

If you rewrote this sentence beginning with

Nationally since 1990, the number of home-schooled children

the next words would be

(1) has almost
(2) in kindergarten through
(3) almost doubled
(4) to 500,000 students
(5) twelfth grade has

8. Sentence 8: **As a result, special support groups, materials for teaching, and athletic organizations for home-schooled children have emerged.**

Which of the following is the best way to write the underlined portion of this sentence? If you think that the original is best, choose option (1).

(1) special support groups, materials for teaching, and athletic organizations
(2) special support groups; materials for teaching; and athletic organizations
(3) special support groups, teaching materials, and athletic organizations
(4) special, support groups; materials for teaching; and athletic organizations
(5) special support groups, materials for teaching, and athletic organizations,

9. Sentence 9: **At the same time, home-schooled children have enrolled in various Colleges and Universities.**

What correction should be made to this sentence?

(1) replace *Colleges and Universities* with *colleges and universities*
(2) remove the comma after *time*
(3) change *have enrolled* to *will enroll*
(4) insert a comma after *Colleges*
(5) no correction necessary

10. Sentence 10: **Although home schooling is not suitable for many families, it is an increasingly popular choice for some parents.**

If you rewrote sentence 10 beginning with

Home schooling is not suitable

the next words should be

(1) for many families, and it
(2) for many families; therefore, it
(3) for many families; however, it
(4) for many families, because it
(5) for many families. Since it

Questions 11 through 20 refer to the following paragraphs.

(1) At the same time that adult smoking has declined teenage smoking has increased. (2) Teenagers are smoking not only cigarettes, but also cigars. (3) Many teens argue that they smoke because of peer pressure others insist that they simply like to smoke. (4) Unfortunately, the nicotine in cigarettes are addictive for many people. (5) Thus, teens which start smoking are likely to continue their habit into adulthood.

(6) Across the nation, various efforts to stop teenage smoking is now underway. (7) People who want to buy tobacco products may soon have to show photo identification. (8) This identification proves they are at least 18 years old. (9) Persons who sell tobacco products to them may be punished more severely. (10) Likewise, vending machines may no longer be accessible to teenage smokers. (11) These actions will not eliminate teenage smoking but they should stop some teens from picking up a dangerous habit.

11. Sentence 1: **At the same time that adult smoking has declined teenage smoking has increased.**

    What correction should be made to this sentence?

    (1) replace *has increased* with *will have increased*
    (2) replace *has declined* with *will decline*
    (3) insert a comma after *declined*
    (4) replace *increased* with *increeed*
    (5) no correction necessary

12. Sentence 2: **Teenagers are smoking not only cigarettes, but also cigars.**

    What correction should be made to this sentence?

    (1) replace *Teenagers* with *Teenagers'*
    (2) remove the comma after *cigarettes*
    (3) replace *cigarettes* with *cigarets*
    (4) change *are smoking* to *will smoke*
    (5) no correction necessary

13. Sentence 3: **Many teens argue that they smoke because of peer <u>pressure others insist</u> that they simply like to smoke.**

    Which of the following is the best way to write the underlined portion of this sentence? If you think that the original is best, choose option (1).

    (1) pressure others insist
    (2) pressure; others insist
    (3) pressure. And others insist
    (4) pressure because others insist
    (5) pressure others, insist

14. Sentence 4: **Unfortunately, the nicotine in cigarettes are addictive for many people.**

    What correction should be made to this sentence?

    (1) remove the comma after *Unfortunately*
    (2) move *for many people* after *nicotine*
    (3) replace *are* with *is*
    (4) replace *cigarettes* with *Cigarettes*
    (5) no correction necessary

15. Sentence 5: **Thus, teens which start smoking are likely to continue their habit into adulthood.**

    What correction should be made to this sentence?

    (1) replace *their* with *they're*
    (2) remove the comma after *thus*
    (3) replace *are* with *is*
    (4) replace *which* with *who*
    (5) no correction necessary

16. Sentence 6: **Across the nation, various efforts to stop teenage smoking is now underway.**

    What correction should be made to this sentence?

    (1) replace *is* with *are*
    (2) remove the comma after *nation*
    (3) insert a comma after *smoking*
    (4) change *efforts* to *eferts*
    (5) no correction necessary

17. Sentences 7 and 8: **People who want to buy tobacco products may soon have to show photo identification. This identification proves they are at least 18 years old.**

    The most effective combination of sentences 17 and 18 would include which of the following words?

    (1) but
    (2) that
    (3) who
    (4) when
    (5) because

18. Sentence 9: **Persons who sell tobacco products to them may be punished more severely.**

    What correction should be made to this sentence?

    (1) change *sell* to *sold*
    (2) insert a comma after *Persons*
    (3) replace *may be* with *were*
    (4) replace *them* with *underage smokers*
    (5) no correction necessary

19. Sentence 10: **Likewise, vending machines may no longer be accessible to teenage smokers.**

What correction should be made to this sentence?

(1) remove the comma after *Likewise*
(2) change *smokers* to *smokers'*
(3) replace *be* with *were*
(4) change *vending machines* to *Vending Machines*
(5) no correction necessary

20. Sentence 11: **These actions will not eliminate teenage smoking but they should stop some teens from picking up a dangerous habit.**

    What is the best way to write the underlined portion of the sentence? If you think that the original is correct, choose option (1).

    (1) smoking but they
    (2) smoking. But they
    (3) smoking, but they
    (4) smoking; but, they
    (5) smoking: but they

Questions 21 through 29 refer to the following paragraph.

(1) In the past decade, Doctors have emphasized the importance of good prenatal care. (2) Even before women become pregnant, she should consider prenatal treatment. (3) Many doctors prescribe vitamins to women that want to have children. (4) During checkups throughout the pregnancy, the developing baby's health and the mother's condition are monitored by doctors. (5) Doctors listen to the baby's heartbeat and observe it's growth. (6) Physicians focus on the mother's nutrition exercise and emotional well-being. (7) They also taught expectant parents about childbirth and newborn care. (8) Women generally deliver healthier babies who have good prenatal care. (9) As a result prenatal care should be part of every woman's pregnancy.

21. Sentence 1: **In the past decade, Doctors have emphasized the importance of good prenatal care.**

    What correction should be made to this sentence?

(1) change *Doctors* to *doctors*
(2) remove the comma after *decade*
(3) replace *have emphasized* with *will emphasize*
(4) insert a comma after *good*
(5) no correction necessary

22. Sentence 2: **Even before women become pregnant, she should consider prenatal treatment.**

    What correction should be made to this sentence?

    (1) remove the comma after *pregnant*
    (2) replace *become* with *became*
    (3) insert a comma after *prenatal*
    (4) replace *she* with *they*
    (5) no correction necessary

23. Sentence 3: **Many doctors prescribe vitamins to women that want to have children.**

    What correction should be made to this sentence?

    (1) change *prescribe* to *perscribe*
    (2) replace *that* with *who*
    (3) insert a comma after *women*
    (4) change *doctors* to *doctors'*
    (5) no correction necessary

24. Sentence 4: **During checkups throughout the pregnancy, the developing baby's health and the mother's condition are monitored by doctors.**

    If you rewrote sentence 4 beginning with

    During checkups throughout the pregnancy, doctors

    the next words would be

    (1) condition are
    (2) baby's health
    (3) monitor the
    (4) mother's condition
    (5) monitored by

25. Sentence 5: **Doctors listen to the baby's heartbeat and observe it's growth.**

    What correction should be made to this sentence?

(1) replace *baby's* with *babies*
(2) change *listen* to *listened*
(3) insert a comma after *heartbeat*
(4) replace *it's* with *its*
(5) no correction necessary

26. Sentence 6: **Physicians focus on the <u>mother's nutrition exercise and emotional well-being</u>.**
    What is the best way to write the underlined portion of the sentence? If you think that the original is best, choose option (1).

    (1) mother's nutrition exercise and emotional well-being
    (2) mothers nutrition exercise and emotional well-being
    (3) mother's nutrition; exercise; and emotional, well-being
    (4) mother's nutrition exercise, and emotional well-being
    (5) mother's nutrition, exercise, and emotional well-being

27. Sentence 7: **They also taught expectant parents about childbirth and newborn care.**

    What correction should be made to this sentence?

    (1) change *taught* to *teach*
    (2) replace *they* with *he*
    (3) insert a comma after *childbirth*
    (4) replace *parents* with *parent's*
    (5) no correction necessary

28. Sentence 8: **Women generally deliver healthier babies who have good prenatal care.**

    What correction should be made to this sentence?

    (1) move *who have good prenatal care* after *women*
    (2) change *babies* to *baby's*
    (3) replace *healthier* with *helthier*
    (4) change *deliver* to *delivers*
    (5) no correction necessary

29. Sentence 9: **As a result prenatal care should be part of every woman's pregnancy.**

    What correction should be made to this sentence?

    (1) replace *woman's* with *womans'*
    (2) change *every* to *evry*

(3) insert a comma after *result*
(4) replace *should be* with *was*
(5) no correction necessary

<u>Questions 30 through 35</u> refer to the following paragraph.

(1) The Marshall Plan, that was created by George C. Marshall, rebuilt Europe after World War II. (2) From 1948 to 1951, the United States gives money, goods, and services worth $13 billion to war-torn Western Europe. (3) In todays dollars, the plan would cost almost $88 billion.
(4) The Marshall Plan stimulated the economy in Europe and prevent the spread of communism. (5) American supplies helped provide food, reconstruct factories, and businesses were recreated. (6) As a result of the Marshall Plan Western Europe developed a stronger economy and became more unified.

30. Sentence 1: **The Marshall Plan, that was created by George C. Marshall, rebuilt Europe after World War II.**

    What correction should be made to this sentence?

    (1) change *World War II* to *world war II*
    (2) replace *that* with *which*
    (3) replace *was* with *is*
    (4) remove the comma after *Plan*
    (5) no correction necessary

31. Sentence 2: **From 1948 to 1951, the United States gives money, goods, and services worth $13 billion to war-torn Western Europe.**

    What correction should be made to this sentence?

    (1) remove the comma after *1951*
    (2) change *Western Europe* to *western Europe*
    (3) move *worth $13 billion* after *United States*
    (4) replace *gives* with *gave*
    (5) no correction necessary

32. Sentence 3: **In todays dollars, the plan would cost almost $88 billion.**

    What correction should be made to this sentence?

(1) remove the comma after *dollars*
(2) change *dollars* to *dollers*
(3) change *billion* to *Billion*
(4) replace *todays* with *today's*
(5) no correction necessary

33. Sentence 4: **The Marshall Plan stimulated the economy in Europe and prevent the spread of communism.** What correction should be made to this sentence?

    (1) replace *Plan* with *plan*
    (2) insert a comma after *Europe*
    (3) move *in Europe* after *prevent*
    (4) change *prevent* to *prevented*
    (5) no correction necessary

34. Sentence 5: **American supplies helped <u>provide food, reconstruct factories, and businesses were recreated.</u>**

    What is the best way to write the underlined portion of the sentence? If you think the original is best, choose option (1).

    (1) provide food, reconstruct factories, and businesses were recreated
    (2) provide food; reconstruct factories; and recreate businesses
    (3) provide food, reconstruct factories, and recreate businesses
    (4) provide food reconstruct factories and businesses were recreated
    (5) provide food, reconstruct factories. Businesses were recreated

35. Sentence 6: **As a result of the Marshall Plan Western Europe developed a stronger economy and became more unified.**

    What correction should be made to this sentence?

    (1) insert a comma after *Plan*
    (2) change *Western Europe* to *western europe*
    (3) insert a comma after *economy*
    (4) change *developed* to *develops*
    (5) no correction necessary

<u>Questions 36 through 46</u> refer to the following paragraphs.

(1) Many parents struggle for their children to install car seats safely. (2) However, a correctly, installed car seat can reduce the risk of death in an accident by 71 percent. (3) Parents must be carefull; they should follow the guidelines for car-seat safety.

(4) For each stage of development, there is different car seats. (5) Newborns should be placed in a rear-facing car seat until they are one year of age and at least 20 pounds. (6) After that stage, a child should sit in a forward-facing car seat which is designed for children between 20 and 40 pounds. (7) Children over 40 pounds should sit in a booster, which works with the seat belt in the car.

(8) Parents must regularly check to make sure that they are positioned properly. (9) They always should be placed in the back seat of the car. (10) In addition, car seats should be secured tightly to the car the seat should not move more than one inch when tugged. (11) Many local police departments will assist whomever needs help with car-seat installation.

36. Sentence 1: **Many parents struggle for their children to install car seats safely.**

    What correction should be made to this sentence?

    (1) insert a comma after *seats*
    (2) move *for their children* after *safely*
    (3) change *parents* to *parent's*
    (4) replace *their* with *they're*
    (5) no correction necessary

37. Sentence 2: **However, a correctly, installed car seat can reduce the risk of death in an accident by 71 percent.**

    What correction should be made to this sentence?

    (1) remove the comma after *correctly*
    (2) replace *accident* with *accidant*
    (3) change *percent* to *Percent*
    (4) insert a comma after *accident*
    (5) no correction necessary

38. Sentence 3: **Parents must be carefull; they should follow the guidelines for car-seat safety.**
What correction should be made to this sentence?

    (1) replace *they* with *them*
    (2) change *follow* to *follows*
    (3) change *carefull* to *careful*
    (4) replace *Parents* with *Parent's*
    (5) no correction necessary

39. Sentence 4: **For each stage of development, there is different car seats.**
What correction should be made to this sentence?

    (1) change *different* to *diffrent*
    (2) replace *there* with *their*
    (3) remove the comma after *development*
    (4) replace *is* with *are*
    (5) no correction necessary

40. Sentence 5: **Newborns should be placed in a rear-facing car seat until they are one year of age and at least 20 pounds.**

    What correction should be made to this sentence?

    (1) change *Newborns* to *Newborns'*
    (2) replace *pounds* with *Pounds*
    (3) insert a comma after *car seat*
    (4) replace *are* with *is*
    (5) no correction necessary

41. Sentence 6: **After that stage, a child should sit in a forward-facing car seat which is designed for children between 20 and 40 pounds.**

    What correction should be made to this sentence?

    (1) remove the comma after *stage*
    (2) replace *which* with *that*
    (3) replace *between* with *among*
    (4) insert a comma after *forward-facing*
    (5) no correction necessary

42. Sentence 7: **Children over 40 pounds should sit in <u>a booster, which works</u> with the seat belt in the car.**

What is the best way to write the underlined portion of the sentence? If you think that the original is best, choose option (1).

(1) a booster, which works
(2) a booster, that works
(3) a booster; which works
(4) a booster. Which works
(5) a booster; that works

43. Sentence 8: **Parents must regularly check to make sure that they are positioned properly.**
What correction should be made to this sentence?

(1) move *sure* after *check*
(2) change *check* to *checks*
(3) replace *they* with *car seats*
(4) move *regularly* after *to*
(5) no correction necessary

44. Sentence 9: **Car seats should be placed in the back seat of the car.**

What correction should be made to this sentence?

(1) move *of the car* after *back*
(2) change *should be placed* to *were placed*
(3) insert a comma after *seat*
(4) replace *car seats* with *car seats'*
(5) no correction necessary

45. Sentence 10: **In addition, car seats should be secured tightly <u>to the car the seat should</u> not move more than one inch when tugged.**

What is the best way to write the underlined portion of the sentence? If you think that the original is best, choose option (1).

(1) to the car the seat should
(2) to the car, but the seat should
(3) to the car; the seat should
(4) to the car, the seat should
(5) to the car; however, the seat should

46. Sentence 11: **Many local police departments will assist whomever needs help with car-seat installation.**

What correction should be made to this sentence?

(1) replace *whomever* with *whoever*
(2) change *police departments* to *Police Departments*
(3) insert a comma after *help*
(4) replace *needs* with *needed*
(5) no correction necessary

Questions 47 though 55 refer to the following paragraph.

(1) For years the american cancer society has warned people about the dangers of sun exposure. (2) Skin cancer, a deadly disease strikes thousands of Americans every year. (3) To prevent skin cancer, adults and children should apply sunscreen, wear hats, use sunglasses, and not spend too much time in the sun. (4) Many people unfortunately do not take these precautions. (5) Although most children wear sunscreen at the beach, less than 50 percent use them when they play outside or go to a park. (6) Likewise, only half of all parents apply sunscreen to themselves' regularly. (7) Besides skin cancer, sun exposure causes skin to prematurely age. (8) People often ignore these risks, which are well documented and highly publicized. (9) If Americans would change there habits, many skin problems could be prevented.

47. Sentence 1: **For years the american cancer society has warned people about the dangers of sun exposure.**

    What correction should be made to this sentence?

    (1) change *american cancer society* to *American Cancer Society*
    (2) replace *has* with *have*
    (3) change *years* to *year's*
    (4) insert a comma after *people*
    (5) no correction necessary

48. Sentence 2: **Skin cancer, a deadly disease strikes thousands of Americans every year.**

    What correction should be made to this sentence?

    (1) remove the comma after *cancer*
    (2) change *Americans* to *americans*
    (3) change *every* to *evry*
    (4) insert a comma after *disease*
    (5) no correction necessary

49. Sentence 3: **To prevent skin cancer, adults and children should apply sunscreen, wear hats, use sunglasses, and not spend too much time in the sun.**

    What is the best way to write the underlined portion of the sentence? If you think that the original is best, choose option (1).

    (1) apply sunscreen, wear hats, use sunglasses, and not spend too much time in the sun
    (2) apply sunscreen wear hats use sunglasses, and not spend too much time in the sun
    (3) apply sunscreen, wear hats, use sunglasses, and limit sun exposure
    (4) apply sunscreen; wear hats; use sunglasses; and limit sun exposure
    (5) apply Sunscreen; wear hats; use sunglasses; and not spend too much time in the sun

50. Sentence 4: **Many people unfortunately do not take these precautions.**

    What is the best way to write the underlined portion of the sentence? If you think that the original is best, choose option (1).

    (1) people unfortunately do
    (2) people, unfortunately, do
    (3) people; unfortunately, do
    (4) people. Unfortunately do
    (5) people, unfortunately do

51. Sentence 5: **Although most children wear sunscreen at the beach, less than 50 percent use them when they play outside or go to a park.**

    What correction should be made to this sentence?

    (1) replace *them* with *it*
    (2) remove the comma after *beach*
    (3) insert a comma after *outside*
    (4) change *wear* to *ware*
    (5) no correction necessary

52. Sentence 6: **Likewise, only half of all parents apply sunscreen to themselves' regularly.**

    What correction should be made to this sentence?

    (1) remove the comma after *Likewise*
    (2) change *half* to *haf*
    (3) insert a comma after *sunscreen*
    (4) change *themselves'* to *themselves*
    (5) no correction necessary

53. Sentence 7: **Besides skin cancer, sun exposure causes skin to prematurely age.**

    What correction should be made to this sentence?

    (1) remove the comma after *cancer*
    (2) change *causes* to *cause*
    (3) move *prematurely* after *age*
    (4) change *causes* to *cuzes*
    (5) no correction necessary

54. Sentence 8: **People often ignore these risks, which are well documented and highly publicized.**

    What correction should be made to this sentence?

    (1) remove the comma after *risks*
    (2) replace *which* with *who*
    (3) insert a comma after *documented*
    (4) replace *are* with *is*
    (5) no correction necessary

55. Sentence 9: **If Americans would change there habits, many skin problems could be prevented.**

    What correction should be made to this sentence?

    (1) change *Americans* to *Americans'*
    (2) replace *there* with *their*
    (3) remove the comma after *habits*
    (4) change *could* to *coud*
    (5) no correction necessary

    Answers are on pages 340–347.

Posttest Skills Chart

Directions:

Check your answers to the Posttest and circle the items that you got wrong. While studying for the actual GED test, focus particularly on the topics that are difficult for you.

TOPICS	QUESTION NUMBERS	PAGE REFERENCES
Parts of Speech		
Verbs	53	34–37
Verb Usage		
Verb Tense	2, 31	61–77
Subject-Verb Agreement		**78–86**
General Guidelines	39	78, 79
Special Situations	16	79–85
Pronouns		**87–98**
Possessive Case	25	91, 92
Who and Whom	46	92–94
Special Situations	52	94, 95
Pronoun Agreement	22, 51	97, 98
Clauses		**107–113**
Dependent Clauses		107, 108
Adjective Clauses	28	109–111
Who, Which, and That	23, 42	112, 113
Restrictive vs. Nonrestrictive Clauses	30, 41	113
End Marks and Commas		**119–128**
Commas		121
Independent Clauses and Items in a Series	5, 20, 26	121, 122
Adjectives	37	122
Nonrestrictive Words, Phrases, and Clauses	48	122, 123
Opening Words, Phrases, and Clauses	11, 29, 35	123, 124
Interruptions	50	125
Dates, Addresses, and Long Numbers		126
More Punctuation		**129–139**
Semicolons	13, 45	129–131
Apostrophes	6, 32	132–135
Capitalization		
Capitalization	9, 21, 47	140–143
Spelling		**140–155**
Most Common Errors	3	145–151
Spelling Rules	38	151–154

* No correction necessary for questions 12, 19, 40, 44, 54

Answers to Exercises

CHAPTER 1: PARTS OF SPEECH

EXERCISE 1: *pages 31, 32.*

1. SUBJECT: **The girl** PREDICATE: **ate a donut.**
2. SUBJECT: **Some people** PREDICATE: **cannot afford health care.**
3. SUBJECT: **Lions, tigers, elephants, and horses** PREDICATE: **perform tricks at the circus.**
4. SUBJECT: **Mr. Po** PREDICATE: **read the poem to the class.**
5. SUBJECT: **The flu** PREDICATE: **strikes many people in the winter.**
6. SUBJECT: **Some workers** PREDICATE: **have to develop their skills.**
7. SUBJECT: **Cal** PREDICATE: **caught the ball, ran to second base, and tagged the runner.**
8. SUBJECT: **Juan** PREDICATE: **dreams of playing in the pros.**
9. SUBJECT: **Parents** PREDICATE: **want decent jobs, safe streets, and good schools.**
10. SUBJECT: **Some people** PREDICATE: **come to America to start a new life.**

EXERCISE 2: *page 33.*

1. **manager, store** Both nouns follow *the*, which is an article.
2. **coach, Saul, medal** *The* is an article that comes before *coach*. *Saul* is a person's name. *A* is an article that comes before *medal*.
3. **judge, Chris, car** *A* is an article that comes before *judge*. *Chris* is a person's name. *The* is an article that comes before *car*.
4. **coffee, notebook** *The* comes before *coffee*. *Rita's* is an adjective that describes *notebook*.
5. **fire, house** *The* comes before *fire*. *Kim's* is an adjective that describes *house*. 6. **Sean, letters, computer** *Sean* is a person. *Three* is an adjective that describes how many *letters*. *The* is an article that comes before *computer*.
7. **Lynn, sitter, baby** *Lynn* is a person. *A* comes before *sitter*, and *the* comes before *baby*.
8. **Ty, job, hours, pay** *Ty* is a person. *A* comes before *job*. *Decent* describes *hours*, and *good* describes *pay*. *Hours* and *pay* are things.
9. **landlord, leaks, ceiling** *Paul's* is an adjective that describes *landlord*. *The* comes before *leaks* and *ceiling*.
10. **Students, success, school** *Students* are people. *Success* is an idea. *School* is a place.

EXERCISE 3: *page 34.*

1. **it** *It* substitutes for *the wallet*.
2. **whomever, they** *Whomever* is used because we do not know who will be questioned. *They* substitutes for FBI.
3. **Who** *Who* substitutes for the volunteer. The volunteer is unknown.
4. **himself, he** *Himself* and *he* refer to Nate.

5. **Everybody** *Everybody* substitutes for the people.
6. **They, themselves** *They* and *themselves* substitute for the people who were hurt on the field.
7. **I, this** *I* refers to a person. *This* refers to a thing.
8. **you, you** *You* refers to a person.
9. **It, her, herself** *It* refers to a thing. *Her* and *herself* refer to a person.
10. **Which** *Which* refers to a thing.

EXERCISE 4: *page 35.*

1. **linking verb** That band ↔ awful. *The band is awful* makes sense.
2. **linking verb** Juan ↔ in the hospital for days. *Juan was in the hospital for days* makes sense.
3. **action verb** Ahmed ... the hot sun on his back. *Ahmed was the hot sun on his back* does not make sense.
4. **linking verb** My soup ↔ salty. *My soup is salty* makes sense.
5. **action verb** She ... the flowers on the table. *She is the flowers on the table* does not make sense.
6. **action verb** Carl...three inches last year. *Carl was three inches last year* does not make sense.
7. **action verb** (You) ... the cheesecake. *(You) are the cheesecake* does not make sense.
8. **linking verb** After the lawsuit, Ray ↔ angry for months. *Ray was angry for months* does make sense.
9. **linking verb** Jill ↔ in the race. *Jill was in the race* does make sense.
10. **linking verb** We ↔ tired of his empty promises. *We were tired of his empty promises* does make sense.

EXERCISE 5: *page 36.*

1. VERB: **are** MAIN VERB: **are**
2. VERB PHRASE: **were arguing** MAIN VERB: **arguing**
3. VERB PHRASE: **could have eaten** MAIN VERB: **eaten**
4. VERB PHRASE: **should have thought** MAIN VERB: **thought**
5. VERB PHRASE: **will be going** MAIN VERB: **going**
6. VERB: **is** MAIN VERB: **is**
7. VERB PHRASE: **has been working** MAIN VERB: **working**
8. VERB PHRASE: **will watch** MAIN VERB: **watch**
9. VERB: **moved** MAIN VERB: **moved**
10. VERB PHRASE: **could have asked** MAIN VERB: **asked**

EXERCISE 6: *page 37.*

1. **three, her, new** *Three* describes how many companies. *Her* describes whose job. Remember, when a noun or pronoun is possessive, it works like an adjective. *New* describes what type of job.
2. **My, small, monthly** *My* describes whose paycheck. *Small* describes what type of paycheck. *Monthly* describes what type of bills.
3. **kind, our, poor** *Kind* describes what type of friends. *Our* and *poor* describe *family.*
4. **old, brick, violent** *Old* and *brick* describe what type of building. *Violent* describes what type of earthquake.
5. **hard** *Hard* describes what type of language.
6. **best, final** *Best* describes which team. *Final* describes which round.
7. **his, right, hard** *His* describes whose elbow. *Right* describes which elbow. *Hard* describes what type of ground.
8. **good, child, expensive** *Good*, *child*, and *expensive* describe what type of care. Normally *child* is a noun. However, if it works like an adjective, it is an adjective.
9. **Many, more, their** *Many* describes how many parents. *More* describes how much time. *Their* describes whose children.
10. **high-paying, good** *High-paying* describes which jobs. *Good* describes what kind of education.

EXERCISE 7: *page 38.*

1. **brave** Susan is the only person mentioned.
2. **best** A football team has more than three people.

3. **more** The new phone is compared to the old one.
4. **most** A staff most likely has three or more people.
5. **easier** Spanish is compared to one other language, French.
6. **more** Wayne is compared to one other person, his partner.
7. **best** Most likely the company has three or more people.
8. **shortest** The sophomore class probably has three or more people.
9. **worst** *I* probably has seen at least three movies.
10. **better** *You* is compared to one other person, *Ken*.

EXERCISE 8: *page 39.*

1. **very, hard** *Hard* explains how the crew worked. *Very* tells to what extent for the adverb *hard*.
2. **often, late** *Often* tells when the bills are paid. *Late* tells how the bills are paid.
3. **today, beautifully** *Today* tells when the chorus sang. *Beautifully* tells how the chorus sang.
4. **never** *Never* tells when we told. (We told at no time.)
5. **quite** *Quite* tells to what extent for the adjective *talented*.
6. **quickly** *Quickly* tells how the dog ate his food. *Friendly* is an adjective that describes the dog.
7. **really, soon** *Really* tells to what extent Jay wants a raise. *Soon* tells when he wants a raise.
8. **truly** *Truly* tells to what extent the plumber fixed the problem.
9. **away, yesterday** *Away* tells where the cat ran. *Yesterday* tells when the cat ran.
10. **promptly, straight, home** *Promptly* and *straight* tell how she walked. (In this sentence, *straight* means directly.) *Home* tells where she walked.

EXERCISE 9: *pages 39–40.*

1. **faster** The hiker entered the cave twice.
2. **harder** The team played twice, yesterday and today.

3. **most** People spoke six times.
4. **best** There are at least three dressed women in Hollywood.
5. **more** Eve ran twice, today and Friday.
6. **most** The store probably has at least three colorful shirts.
7. **louder** Ted yelled at two people, his secretary and me.
8. **worse** Two speakers, Guy and you, ramble.
9. **more** Two buildings were destroyed, this one and that one.
10. **less** Two types of annoying calls are compared.

EXERCISE 10: *page 42.*

1. **with the red hat** *With the red hat* describes *the student.*
   to her class *To her class* tells where the student is running.
2. **after the storm** *After the storm* tells when the rainbow appeared.
   across the sky *Across the sky* tells where the rainbow stretched.
3. **In spite of her broken arm** *In spite of her broken arm* tells how she rode.
   into town *Into town* tells where she rode.
4. **During spring break** *During spring break* tells when she went.
   to Florida *To Florida* tells where she went.
   with her friends *With her friends* tells how she went.
5. **Before noon** *Before noon* shows when the president will tell.
   about his new staff *About his new staff* describes *something.*
6. **up the steps** *Up the steps* tells where Jong climbed.
   behind me *Behind me* shows where Jong sat.
7. **Because of the cramp** *Because of the cramp* tells how she will run.
   in her leg *In her leg* shows where the cramp is.
   as far as that tree *As far as that tree* tells where she will run.
8. **on many issues** *On many issues* describes how the parties differ.
   besides crime *Besides crime* describes which issues.

9. **below the shelf** *Below the shelf* tells where you will find the box.
   in the basement *In the basement* describes which shelf.
10. **Because of her hard work** *Because of her hard work* tells how Rose earned more vacation.
    with pay *With pay* describes what type of *days*.

CHAPTER REVIEW

EXERCISE 1: *pages 42–44.*

1. **Preposition** *The hall* is the object of the preposition. The prepositional phrase *down the hall* works as an adverb. It shows where the student ran.
2. **Adverb** *Down* tells where the opponent was knocked.
3. **Adjective** *Down* describes the pillows. It tells what type of pillows they are.
4. **Verb** *Would like* is a verb phrase. *Would* is the helping verb, and *like* is the main verb.
5. **Preposition** *A child* is the object of the preposition. The prepositional phrase *like a child* describes how *she acts.* Thus the phrase works as an adverb.
6. **Adverb** *Carefully* tells how he guided the wire. Like many adverbs, it ends in *-ly*.
7. **Adjective** *Careful* follows the linking verb *is* and describes *Karen*.
8. **Verb** *Was concerned* is a verb phrase. *Was* is the helping verb, and *concerned* is the main verb.
9. **Adjective** *Concerned* describes the citizens. It tells what type of citizens went to the meeting.
10. **Noun** *Concerns* follows the linking verb *are* and refers to the subject of the sentence.
11. **Noun** *Success* is an idea. It is also the object of the preposition *about.*
12. **Preposition** The prepositional phrase *over the bridge* works like an adverb and tells where the horse trotted. Note that *into the pasture* is also a prepositional phrase.
13. **Adverb** *Over* shows where the coffee spilled.
14. **Preposition** *Behind the door* is a prepositional phrase that works like an adverb. The phrase shows where the basket was hidden.
15. **Adverb** In this sentence, *behind* shows where John was running.
16. **Adverb** *Behind* tells where she fell.
17. **Adjective** *Mary's* tells who owns the stained glass windows.
18. **Adverb** *By* shows where the car raced.
19. **Preposition** *By the store* is a prepositional phrase that works like an adverb and shows where he must stop.
20. **Adjective** *Running* describes the type of water. Remember, the function of a word determines its part of speech.
21. **Adjective** *Past* describes which days. Note that *for the past five days* is a prepositional phrase that works like an adverb. It explains when the weather was terrible.
22. **Noun** In this sentence, *the past* is a thing. Whenever you see an article, a noun soon follows.
23. **Preposition** *Past noon* is a prepositional phrase that works like an adverb. The phrase tells when Bruce will have to work.
24. **Adjective** *Was* is a linking verb. *Exhausted* describes Bob.
25. **Noun** The article *the* is a clue. In addition, *from the car* is a prepositional phrase that works like an adjective and describes the exhaust.

EXERCISE 2: *page 44.*

1. ARTICLE: **The** ADJECTIVE: **dedicated** NOUN: **athlete** ADVERB: **eventually** VERB: **became** ARTICLE: **a** ADJECTIVE: **professional** ADJECTIVE: **tennis** NOUN: **player**. *Tennis* is an adjective that describes the type of player.
2. PREPOSITION: **With** ADJECTIVE: **steady** NOUN: **hands** NOUN: **Megan** ADVERB: **expertly** VERB: **completed** ARTICLE: **the** ADJECTIVE: **delicate** NOUN: **surgery**.

3. NOUN: **He** VERB: **studied** ARTICLE: **the** ADJECTIVE: **weather** NOUN: **reports** ADVERB: **very** ADVERB: **carefully**.
   Weather is an adjective describing the type of reports.

4. NOUN: **Cricket** VERB: **is** ARTICLE: **a** ADVERB: **very** ADJECTIVE: **popular** NOUN: **sport** PREPOSITION: **in** NOUN: **England**.

5. ADJECTIVE: **Christine's** ADJECTIVE: **new** NOUN: **suitcase** VERB: **was** VERB: **destroyed** PREPOSITION: **during** ADJECTIVE: **her** NOUN: **flight** PREPOSITION: **to** NOUN: **Chicago**.
   Was is a helping verb. *Destroyed* is the main verb.

6. NOUN: **Jason** ADVERB: **constantly** VERB: **searched** PREPOSITION: **for** ARTICLE: **a** ADJECTIVE: **new** NOUN: **job** PREPOSITION: **with** ADJECTIVE: **better** NOUN: **hours**.

7. ARTICLE: **The** ADJECTIVE: **retired** NOUN: **pilot** ADVERB: **still** VERB: **flies** ADJECTIVE: **his** ADJECTIVE: **small** NOUN: **plane** ADVERB: **regularly**.

8. PREPOSITION: **Without** NOUN: **help** NOUN: **she** VERB: **carried** ARTICLE: **the** NOUN: **furniture** PREPOSITION: **into** ARTICLE: **the** NOUN: **house**.

9. ARTICLE: **The** NOUN: **basket** PREPOSITION: **of** NOUN: **flowers** VERB: **filled** ARTICLE: **the** NOUN: **room** PREPOSITION: **with** ARTICLE: **a** ADJECTIVE: **wonderful** NOUN: **scent**.

10. PREPOSITION: **Before** NOUN: **dark** VERB: **collect** ADJECTIVE: **your** NOUN: **toys** PREPOSITION: **in** ARTICLE: **the** NOUN: **yard**.
    In this sentence, *dark* is a noun because it means "nightfall."

CHAPTER 2: PARTS OF A SENTENCE

EXERCISE 1: *page 46.*

There is more than one correct revision for each fragment.

1. **F** The women with the pink shirt missed the train.
2. **C** The subject is *the tall man in the red hat*, and the predicate is *asked me for directions*.
3. **C** This is a command. The subject, *you*, is implied.
4. **F** This is a command. The subject, *you*, is implied.
5. **F** The group of words does not have a verb. *You did a great job!* is a complete sentence.
6. **C** *I* is the subject. *Need to find a good baby-sitter* is the predicate.
7. **F** This group of words does not have a subject or a predicate. *By midnight, I was tired.*
8. **C** This is a command. The subject, *you*, is implied.
9. **C** What about *the man in charge of payroll. The man in charge of payroll has many friends on Fridays.*
10. **C** This is a command. The subject, *you*, is implied.

EXERCISE 2: *page 47.*

1. This past winter was terrible. **C** 2. The snow! **F** 3. Schools were closed for several days, and many people could not get to work. **C** 4. Water pipes froze. **C** 5. Some roofs collapsed. **C** 6. Bridges, too. **F** 7. Luckily, no one was seriously injured. **C** 8. Next winter may be even worse. **C** 9. Watch out! **C** Sentences 2 and 6 are fragments because they do not have verbs, and they do not express complete thoughts. Sentence 9 is a command; the subject is implied.

EXERCISE 3: *page 47.*

1. **her baby** Jasmine bathed whom? Her baby. *Her* is an adjective that describes *baby*.
2. **X** *Across the sky* is a prepositional phrase that shows where *the thunder rolled*.
3. **his math test** Abdul passed what? His math test. *His* and *math* are adjectives that describe *test*.
4. **X** *Hard* is an adverb that tells how she tried.
5. **the sunrise** I saw what? The sunrise.

EXERCISE 4: *page 48.*

1. **free tickets, me** Doyle offered what? Free tickets. Doyle offered free tickets to whom? Me.
2. **The check.** We mailed what? The check. *Yesterday* is an adverb that tells when the check was mailed.
3. **the mail, us** The post office sent what? The mail. The post office sent the mail to whom? Us.
4. **award, Mansi** The coach gave what? An award. The coach gave an award to whom? Mansi.
5. **the cookies** Kim baked what? The cookies. *Friday* tells when the cookies were baked.

EXERCISE 5: *page 49.*

1. **lilacs, noun** Those flowers ↔ lilacs.
2. **costly, adjective** The cars ↔ costly.
3. **deep, adjective** The water ↔ deep.
4. **a lawyer, noun** He ↔ a lawyer.
5. **thrilled, adjective** Megan ↔ thrilled.
6. **sad, adjective** Courtney ↔ sad.
7. **gifts, noun** The books ↔ gifts.
8. **sour, adjective** The milk ↔ sour.
9. **late, adjective** My ride ↔ late. *For work* is a prepositional phrase that describes *ride*.
10. **friends, noun** My guests ↔ friends.

EXERCISE 6: *page 51.*

1. **Mike nor Joe** subject
2. **a check and a nice plaque** object of the verb
3. **my mom and dad** subject
   my brothers and me object of the verb
4. **Hard work and discipline** subject
   not only in school, but also in life object of the preposition
5. **Rita and I** subject
6. **Either Bob or Colleen** subject
   you and your friend object of the verb
7. **jobs and wages** object of the verb
8. **not only gifts, but also great memories** object of the verb
9. **run, bike, and skate** verb
10. **Ruth and me** object of the verb

EXERCISE 7: *page 55.*

1. **subject** Keep in mind, *who* is a pronoun. Who or what is going? Who is going.
2. **object of the verb** Ginny bought concert tickets for whom? Blake.
3. **subject complement** Sometimes *felt* is a linking verb. *Cold* is an adjective that describes Skeeter and Lynne. Skeeter and Lynne ↔ cold at the football game. If you substitute *are* for *felt*, the sentence still makes sense.
4. **subject** Ask yourself, who or what are? Seats are. *There* cannot be the subject of a sentence. In this sentence, it is an adverb describing where the seats are.
5. **object of the verb** Who called what? The police.
6. **verb** *Drive* shows the action in the sentence.
7. **object of the verb** Our boss will pay more money to whom? Us.
8. **object of the verb** The strike slowed what? Shipments.

9. **subject complement** We ↔
    drenched. *Drenched* follows the
    linking verb *were* and describes *we*.
10. **subject** Who wants help? The man.

CHAPTER REVIEW

EXERCISE 1: *pages 56, 57.*

1. SENTENCE: Laura, Jen, and Kathy
    skated ~~on the pond behind their home in Connecticut~~.
    VERB: **skated** (action) *Skated* shows
    that action in the sentence.
    SUBJECT: **Laura, Jen, and Kathy**
    Who skated? Laura, Jen, and Kathy
    SUBJECT COMPLEMENT: **X**
    OBJECT(S): **X**
2. SENTENCE : They drove the car
    ~~with the sunroof to the beach on the Fourth of July~~.
    VERB: **drove** (action) *Drove* shows
    the action in the sentence.
    SUBJECT: **They** Who drove? They.
    SUBJECT COMPLEMENT: **X**
    OBJECT(S): **the car** They drove
    what? The car.
3. SENTENCE: Anne gave Khoa and
    Marie surprise parties ~~for their birthdays~~.
    VERB: **gave** (action) *Gave* shows the
    action in the sentence.
    SUBJECT: **Anne** Who gave? Anne.
    SUBJECT COMPLEMENT: **X**
    OBJECT(S): **surprise parties** Anne
    gave what? Surprise parties.
    Khoa and Marie Anne gave surprise
    parties to whom? Khoa and Marie.
4. SENTENCE: Khan is a caring person
    and a great doctor.
    VERB: **is** (linking) *Is* is a form of *be*.
    It is on the list of linking verbs.
    SUBJECT: **Khan** Who is? Khan.
    SUBJECT COMPLEMENT: **caring
    person and a great doctor** Khan ↔
    caring person and a great doctor
    OBJECT(S): **X**

5. SENTENCE: The pie ~~in the oven~~
    smells delicious.
    VERB: **smells** (linking) *Smells* is a
    linking verb in some situations. The
    pie ↔ delicious.
    SUBJECT: **The pie** What smells?
    The pie.
    SUBJECT COMPLEMENT: **delicious**
    The pie ↔ delicious. *Delicious* is an
    adjective.
    OBJECT(S): **X**
6. SENTENCE: Here are the drapes ~~for the windows~~.
    VERB: **are** (linking) *Are* is a form of
    be. It is on the list of linking verbs.
    SUBJECT: **the drapes** What are?
    The drapes. *Here* is an adverb that
    describes where the drapes are.
    SUBJECT COMPLEMENT: **X**
    OBJECT(S): **X**
7. SENTENCE: Anh bought food, made
    dinner, and cleaned the house.
    VERB: **bought, made, and cleaned**
    (action) *Bought*, *made*, and *cleaned*
    show the action in the sentence.
    SUBJECT: **Anh** Who bought, made,
    and cleaned? Anh.
    SUBJECT COMPLEMENT: **X**
    OBJECT(S): **food, dinner, the
    house** Anh bought what? Food. Anh
    made what? Dinner. Anh cleaned
    what? The house.
8. SENTENCE: My dog ran ~~across the yard~~, swam ~~in the pond~~, and rolled ~~in the mud~~.
    VERB: **ran, swam, and rolled**
    (action) *Ran*, *swam*, and *rolled* show
    the action.
    SUBJECT: **My dog** What ran, swam,
    and rolled? My dog.
    SUBJECT COMPLEMENT: **X**
    DIRECT OBJECT(S): **X**

EXERCISE 2: *pages 57, 58.*

1. SENTENCE: ~~After work~~, Joe gave his wife and his daughter a hug and a kiss.
   SUBJECT: **Joe** Who gave? Joe.
   VERB: **gave** (action) *Gave* shows the action in the sentence.
   SUBJECT COMPLEMENT: **X**
   OBJECT(S): **hug and a kiss** Joe gave what? A hug and a kiss.
   his wife and his daughter Joe gave a hug and a kiss to whom? His wife and his daughter.

2. SENTENCE: The horse stalls and the doghouse smelled awful.
   SUBJECT: **The horse stalls and the doghouse** What smelled? The horse stalls and the doghouse.
   VERB: **smelled** (linking) The horse stalls and the doghouse ↔ awful. *Smells* is a linking verb in this sentence.
   SUBJECT COMPLEMENT: **awful** (adjective) The horse stalls and the doghouse ↔ awful.
   OBJECT(S): **X**

3. SENTENCE: There are three people ~~on the court without racquets~~.
   SUBJECT: **Three people** Who are? Three people. *There* cannot be a subject. It is an adverb describing where.
   VERB: **are** (linking) *Are* is a form of be. It is on the list of linking verbs.
   SUBJECT COMPLEMENT: **X**
   OBJECT(S): **X**

4. SENTENCE: The hard, driving rain fell ~~throughout the night and into the day~~.
   SUBJECT: **The hard, driving rain** What fell? The hard, driving rain. *Hard* and *driving* are adjectives that describe *rain*.
   VERB: **fell** (action) *Fell* shows action in the sentence.
   SUBJECT COMPLEMENT: **X**
   OBJECT(S): **X**

5. SENTENCE: Some ~~of my friends~~ went ~~to the magic show at the old movie house on 5ᵗʰ street~~.
   SUBJECT: **Some** Who went? *Some* is a pronoun and the subject of the sentence.
   VERB: **went** (action) *Went* shows the action.
   SUBJECT COMPLEMENT: **X**
   OBJECT(S): **X**

6. SENTENCE: ~~After training hard for many years~~, Sean became an excellent athlete.
   SUBJECT: **Sean** Who became? Sean.
   VERB: **became** (linking) *Became* is a linking verb. Sean ↔ excellent athlete.
   SUBJECT COMPLEMENT: **an excellent athlete** Sean ↔ excellent athlete. *Athlete* is a noun. *Excellent* is an adjective that tells what kind of athlete.
   OBJECT(S): **X**

7. SENTENCE: ~~On our trip to Europe~~, we bought gifts ~~for our friends and family~~.
   SUBJECT: **we** Who bought? We.
   VERB: **bought** (action) *Bought* shows the action.
   SUBJECT COMPLEMENT: **X**
   OBJECT(S): **gifts** We bought what? Gifts. *Our friends and family* is not an object of the verb. It is an object of the preposition *for*. The whole prepositional phrase should have been crossed out in the first step.

8. SENTENCE: Who ran ~~to the phone~~ and called the police?
   SUBJECT: **Who** Who ran? *Who* is a pronoun and the subject of the sentence.
   VERB: **ran and called** (action) *Ran* and *called* show the action in the sentence.
   SUBJECT COMPLEMENT: **X**
   OBJECT(S): **the police** Called whom? The police.

9. SENTENCE: Here are the photos ~~from our trip to Greece~~.
   SUBJECT: **The photos** What are? The photos. *Here* cannot be the subject of a sentence. It is an adverb that tells where the photos are.
   VERB: **are** (linking) *Are* is a form of *be*. It is on the list of linking verbs.
   SUBJECT COMPLEMENT: **X**
   OBJECT(S): **X**

10. SENTENCE: Watch your step ~~on the stairs~~!
    SUBJECT: **(You)** Who watch? This sentence is a command. The implied subject is *you*.
    VERB: **watch** (action) *Watch* shows the action.
    SUBJECT COMPLEMENT: **X**
    OBJECT(S): **your step** (You) watch what? Your step.

CHAPTER 3: VERB USAGE

EXERCISE 1: *pages 62, 63.*

1. **bakes** Every Monday shows that the action happens repeatedly.
2. **helped, played** *Last week* shows that the action happened in the past.
4. **will start** *Next fall* shows that the action will happen in the future.
5. **ripped** *Yesterday* shows that the action happened in the past.
6. **will show** *Tomorrow night* shows the action will happen in the future.
7. **bloom or will bloom** This action happens repeatedly. However, *in the spring* does suggest that the action will happen in the future.
8. **exploded** *Noticed* is in the past tense. *He exploded* when *he noticed*. Both actions happened in the past.
9. **rows** *Often* shows that the action happens repeatedly.
10. **raved** *Last night* shows that action happened in the past.

EXERCISE 2: *page 64.*

1. **had considered** *Last year* and *before running for office* show that the action was completed before another action in the past. The past perfect tense is used.
2. **will have** *By tomorrow* shows that the action will be completed by a specific time in the future. The future perfect tense is used.
3. **has jogged** *Since last week* and *every day* show that the action began in the past and continues into the present. The present perfect tense is used.
4. **has studied** *Already* shows that the action was just completed. The present perfect tense is used.
5. **will have finished** *By next spring* shows that the action will be completed by a specific time in the future. The future perfect tense is used.
6. **have painted** *Already* shows that the action was just completed. The present perfect tense is used.
7. **had dreamed** *Before July 4, 1776* shows that the action was completed before a specific time in the past. The past perfect tense is used.
8. **will have traveled** *By 2050* shows that the action will be completed by a specific time in the future. The future perfect tense is used.
9. **had destroyed** *Before. . . last year,* shows that the action was completed before a specific time in the past. The past perfect tense is used.
10. **will have applied** *By next fall* shows that the action will be completed by a specific time in the future. The future perfect tense is used.

EXERCISE 3: *page 66.*

1. **am working** *Right now* shows that the verb should be in the present continuing tense.

2. **were watching** *Yesterday* shows that the verb should be in the past continuing tense.
3. **will be living** *Next year* shows that the verbs should be in the future continuing tense.
4. **were shoveling** *Last Friday* shows that the verb should be in the past continuing tense.
5. **will be playing** *Next fall* shows that the verb should be in the future continuing tense.
6. **were barking** *This morning* shows that the verb should be in the past continuing tense.
7. **will be studying** *Next spring* shows that the verbs should be in the future continuing tense. 8. **was trying** *All morning yesterday* shows that the verb should be in the past continuing tense.
9. **will be struggling** *In the spring next year* shows that the verb should be in the future continuing tense.
10. **are putting** *At present* shows that the verb should be in the present continuing tense.

EXERCISE 4: *page 67.*

1. *be* Last week I **was**. This week I have **been**.
2. *be* Last week they **were**. This week they have **been**.
3. *bring* Last week I **brought**. This week I have **brought**.
4. *buy* Last week I **bought**. This week I have **bought**.
5. *come* Last week I **came**. This week I have **come**.
6. *do* Last week I **did**. This week I have **done**.
7. *go* Last week I **went**. This week I have **gone**.
8. *have* Last week I **had**. This week I have **had**.
9. *run* Last week I **ran**. This week I have **run**.
10. *see* Last week I **saw**. This week I have **seen**.

EXERCISE 5: *pages 67, 68.*

1. **seen** *Have* signals the perfect tenses. The past participle *seen* must be used.
2. **went** *Yesterday*, shows that the action happened in the past.
3. **run** *Have* signals the perfect tenses. The past participle *run* must be used.
4. **come** *Have* signals the perfect tenses. The past participle *come* must be used.
5. **done** *Has* signals the perfect tenses. The past participle *done* must be used.
6. **bought** *Have* signals the perfect tenses. The past participle *bought* must be used.
7. **had** *Have* signals the perfect tenses. The past participle *had* must be used.
8. **brought** *Last Friday* signals the past tense.
9. **been** *For the past two weeks* and *has* signal the present perfect tense. The past participle *been* must be used.
10. **came** *Last night* signals the past tense.

EXERCISE 6: *page 68.*

1. *begin* Last week I **began**. This week I have **begun**.
2. *dig* Last week I **dug**. This week I have **dug**.
3. *drink* Last week I **drank**. This week I have **drunk**.
4. *ring* Last week I **rang**. This week I have **rung**.
5. *shrink* Last week I **shrank**. This week I have **shrunk**.
6. *sing* Last week I **sang**. This week I have **sung**.
7. *sinks* Last week I **sank**. This week I have **sunk**.
8. *swim* Last week I **swam**. This week I have **swum**.
9. *win* Last week I **won**. This week I have **won**.

EXERCISE 7: *page 68.*

1. **dug** *Brought* is in the past tense. This suggests that the action happened in the past.
2. **begun** *By nine o'clock tomorrow* and *will have* signal that the action will be completed by a specific time in the future. The future perfect tense needs the past participle *begun.*
3. **won** *Have* signals the present perfect tenses. The past participle *won* must be used.
4. **rang** *Last night* signals that the action happened in the past.
5. **shrunk** *In the past year* and *have* signal an action that began in the past and continues in the present. The past participle *shrunk* must be used for the present perfect tense.
6. **drunk** *Had* and *before the race* signal that this action was completed before another action in the past. The past participle *drunk* must be used for the past perfect tense.
7. **sung** *Have* signals the perfect tenses. The past participle *sung* must be used.
8. **sang** *Last night* signals the past.
9. **began** *Yesterday* signals the past.
10. **won** *Has* signals the present perfect tense. The past participle *won* must be used.

EXERCISE 8: *page 69.*

1. *break* Last week I **broke**. This week I have **broken**.
2. *choose* Last week I **chose**. This week I have **chosen**.
3. *eat* Last week I **ate**. This week I have **eaten**.
4. *fall* Last week I **fell**. This week I have **fallen**.
5. *freeze* Last week I **froze**. This week I have **frozen**.
6. *get* Last week I **got**. This week I have **gotten**.
7. *give* Last week I **gave**. This week I have **given**.

8. *grow* Last week I **grew**. This week I have **grown**.
9. *know* Last week I **knew**. This week I have **known**.
10. *ride* Last week I **rode**. This week I have **ridden**.
11. *speak* Last week I **spoke**. This week I have **spoken**.
12. *take* Last week I **took**. This week I have **taken**.
13. *tear* Last week I **tore**. This week I have **torn**.
14. *wear* Last week I **wore**. This week I have **worn**.
15. *write* Last week I **wrote**. This week I have **written**.

EXERCISE 9: *pages 69, 70.*

1. **broken** *Had* signals the past perfect tense, which needs the past participle.
2. **chosen** *By nine o'clock last night* and *had* signal the past perfect tense. The past participle is needed.
3. **ate** *Last year* signals the past tense.
4. **fell** *Yesterday* signals the past tense.
5. **given** *Have* signals the present perfect tense.
6. **spoken** *Has* signals the present perfect tense. The past participle is needed.
7. **took** *This morning* signals the past tense.
8. **written** *Have* and *just* signal the present perfect tense. The past participle is needed.
9. **knew** *Yesterday* signals the past tense.
10. **ridden** *Has* signals the present perfect tense. The past participle is needed.

EXERCISE 10: *page 70.*

1. *arise* Last week I **arose**. This week I have **arisen**.
2. *bid* Last week I **bid**. This week I have **bid**.
3. *bite* Last week I **bit**. This week I have **bitten**.

4. *blow* Last week I **blew**. This week I have **blown**.
5. *build* Last week I **built**. This week I have **built**.
6. *burst* Last week I **burst**. This week I have **burst**.
7. *catch* Last week I **caught**. This week I have **caught**.
8. *cost* Last week I **cost**. This week I have **cost**.
9. *cut* Last week I **cut**. This week I have **cut**.
10. *draw* Last week I **drew**. This week I have **drawn**.

EXERCISE 11: *page 71.*

1. *dream* Last week I **dreamed**. This week I have **dreamed**.
OR
Last week I **dreamt**. This week I have **dreamt**.
2. *feed* Last week I **fed**. This week I have **fed**.
3. *feel* Last week I **felt**. This week I have **felt**.
4. *fight* Last week I **fought**. This week I have **fought**.
5. *find* Last week I **found**. This week I have **found**.
6. *flee* Last week I **fled**. This week I have **fled**.
7. *fly* Last week I **flew**. This week I have **flown**.
8. *hang* (an object) Last week I **hung**. This week I have **hung**.
9. *hang* (a person) Last week I **hanged**. This week I have **hanged**.
10. *hear* Last week I **heard**. This week I have **heard**.

EXERCISE 12: *page 72.*

1. *hide* Last week I **hid**. This week I have **hidden**.
2. *hold* Last week I **held**. This week I have **held**.
3. *hurt* Last week I **hurt**. This week I have **hurt**.
4. *keep* Last week I **kept**. This week I have **kept**.

5. *lay* Last week I **laid**. This week I have **laid**.
6. *lead* Last week I **led**. This week I have **led**.
7. *leave* Last week I **left**. This week I have **left**.
8. *let* Last week I **let**. This week I have **let**.
9. *lie* Last week I **lay**. This week I have **lain**.
10. *lose* Last week I **lost**. This week I have **lost**.

EXERCISE 13: *pages 72, 73.*

1. *make* Last week I **made**. This week I have **made**.
2. *meet* Last week I **met**. This week I have **met**.
3. *pay* Last week I **paid**. This week I have **paid**.
4. *prove* Last week I **proved**. This week I have **proved, proven**.
5. *put* Last week I **put**. This week I have **put**.
6. *read* Last week I **read**. This week I have **read**.
7. *rise* Last week I **rose**. This week I have **risen**.
8. *say* Last week I **said**. This week I have **said**.
9. *set* Last week I **set**. This week I have **set**.
10. *shoot* Last week I **shot**. This week I have **shot**.

EXERCISE 14: *page 73.*

1. *sit* Last week I **sat**. This week I have **sat**.
2. *slide* Last week I **slid**. This week I have **slid**.
3. *spend* Last week I **spent**. This week I have **spent**.
4. *stand* Last week I **stood**. This week I have **stood**.
5. *strike* Last week I **struck**. This week I have **struck**.
6. *teach* Last week I **taught**. This week I have **taught**.

7. *tell* Last week I **told**. This week I have **told**.
8. *think* Last week I **thought**. This week I have **thought**.
9. *understand* Last week I **understood**. This week I have **understood**.

EXERCISE 15: *page 74.*

1. **flew** *Last week* signals the past tense.
2. **hung** Keep in mind, pictures were hung, people were hanged.
3. **blew** *Last week* signals the past tense.
4. **heard** *Has* signals the present perfect tense. The past participle is needed.
5. **fought** *Last year* signals the past tense.
6. **drew** *Yesterday* signals the past tense.
7. **built** *Had* and *by dinner time* signal the past perfect tense. The past participle is needed.
8. **hidden** *Had* signals the past perfect tense. The past participle is needed.
9. **understood** *Have* signals the present perfect tense. The past participle is needed.
10. **struck** *Fell* is in the past tense.

EXERCISE 16: *page 75.*

1. *lie* Last week I **lay**. This week I have **lain**.
2. *sit* Last week I **sat**. This week I have **sat**.
3. *rise* Last week I **rose**. This week I have **risen**.

EXERCISE 17: *page 75.*

1. *lay* Last week I **laid** a book. This week I have **laid** a book.
2. *set* Last week I **set** a book. This week I have **set** a book.
3. *raise* Last week I **raised** a book. This week I have **raised** a book.

EXERCISE 18: *pages 75, 76*

1. **rises** The subject, *Jong*, moves. *Every morning* shows that the action is repeated, and the present tense should be used.
2. **sat** *My car keys* is the object of the verb. The subject handles *car keys*.
3. **laid** *Her notes* is the direct object.
4. **sat** The subject, *we*, moves. *In the same seats* is **not** an object of the verb. Remember, you should cross out prepositional phrases when you look for parts of the sentence.
5. **lain** The subject, *I*, is moving equalize — or in this case, not moving. *Have* signals the present perfect tense. The past participle must be used.
6. **raised** *Flowers* is the object of the verb. The subject handles *flowers*.
7. **lay** The subject, *I*, is moving. *Yesterday* shows that the verb is in the past tense. The past tense of lie is lay.
8. **rose** The subject, *José*, is moving.
9. **set** *All* is the object of the verb. *Jill* handles *all*. Keep in mind, *all* is a pronoun in this sentence.
10. **laid** *The new roof* is the object of the verb. *The workers* handle *the new roof*.

CHAPTER REVIEW

EXERCISE 1: *page 76.*

Yesterday I **decided** to change my study habits. I **want** to be more successful in school. I *always* work hard, but my hard work does not pay off. I **will study** differently *from now on*. *Tomorrow*, I will go to my teacher, and I **will ask** her for suggestions. *Then* I **will list** all of the changes that I will make. I *will put* that list on my desk, and I **will look** at it at night when I study. The list **will frustrate** me sometimes, but I know it *will help* me *in the long run*. If I **improve** my skills *now*, I **will study** better *in the future*.

EXERCISE 2: PAGE 76.

Brie has **gone** through a major change. *Last year*, she **was** in terrible shape. She could not run a mile, and she **had** bad eating habits. *Recently* Brie has **been** training for a triathlon. *For the past six months*, she has **gone** to the gym *every day*. In February, she **saw** a great bike in a store window, and she **bought** it. *Now* she *rides* her bike and **runs** as often as she can. I **saw** her last week, and I **did** not even know her. She **is** so different *now*. She **came** up to me and *introduced* herself. This new lifestyle has **been** good for her.

EXERCISE 3: *page 77.*

1. **working** The helping verb *is* and the adverb *now* signal the present continuing tense.
2. **known** *Had* signals the past perfect tense. The past participle is needed.
3. **speaking** *Will . . . be* signal the future continuing tense.
4. **slid** *Yesterday* signals the past tense.
5. **winning** *Are* signals the present continuing tense. Sometimes it helps to rewrite questions as statements. *We are _____ the race.*
6. **fled** *Robbed* is in the past tense.
7. **thinking** *Were* signals the present continuing tense.
8. **flew** *Last winter* signals the past tense.
9. **hid** *Yesterday* signals the past tense.
10. **lost** *Over the past two weeks* and *have* signal the present perfect tense. The past participle is needed.
11. **hanged** *Last Monday* signals the past tense. People were hanged. Pictures were hung.
12. **writing** *Will be* signals the future continuing tense. The *-ing* form is needed.
13. **rides** *Often* signals a repeated action. The present tense is needed.

14. **given** *Had* signals the past perfect tense. The past participle is needed.
15. **gone** *Have* signals the present perfect tense. The past participle is needed.
16. **stumbled** *Scared* is in the past tense.
17. **taken** *By next week* and *will have* signal the future perfect tense. The past participle is needed.
18. **sang** *Last Friday* signals the past tense.
19. **drunk** *Had* signals the past perfect tense. The past participle is needed.
20. **swum** *Will … have* and *this afternoon* signal the future perfect tense. The past participle is needed.
21. **talking** *Were* signals the past continuing tense. The *-ing* form is needed.
22. **rang** *Last year* signals the past tense. *Often* may have confused you. In this case, *often* is an adverb telling to what extent the doorbell rang last year. If *last year* were omitted, then *rings* would be correct because the sentence would be about a repeated action.
23. **arose** *This morning* signals the past tense.
24. **chose** *Last week* signals the past tense.
25. **tore** *Yesterday* signals the past tense.

CHAPTER 4: SUBJECT-VERB AGREEMENT

EXERCISE 1: *page 79.*

1. **itches** *Skin* is singular.
2. **read** When *you* is the subject, the verb does not have an *-s*.
3. **look** When *I* is the subject, the verb does not have an *-s*.
4. **practice** *Players* is plural.
5. **think** *They* is a plural pronoun.

6. **wants** *Ted* is one person.
7. **open** *Children* is plural.
8. **fall** *Peaches* is plural.
9. **wears** *Kay* is one person.
10. **dress** *The girls* is plural.

EXERCISE 2: *page 80.*

1. **were** *We* is plural.
2. **has** *Megan* is one person.
3. **have** *Children* is plural.
4. **are** *They* is plural.
5. **is** *He* is singular.
6. **Are** When *you* is the subject, the verb does not end in *-s*. If in doubt, reword the question as a statement. *You are sure that the movie starts at 7 o'clock.*
7. **were** *The boys* is plural.
8. **have** When *I* is the subject, the verb does not end in *-s*.
9. **is** *Steve* is one person.
10. **Is** If in doubt, reword the question as a statement. *The last flight to New York is about to leave. Last flight* is singular.

EXERCISE 3: *page 81.*

1. **is** Beware of words that are set off by commas, *which*, or *that*. The horse ~~that jumped over four fences~~ is in the lead.
2. **sits** Cross out prepositional phrases. The crate ~~of bananas~~ sits next to the pears.
3. **works** Beware of words that make the subject appear plural or are set off by commas. Juan, ~~together with his brothers~~, works at the paper mill.
4. **needs** Cross out prepositional phrases. The fence ~~in the backyard by the barn~~ needs a repair.
5. **was** Cross out prepositional phrases. Rose, ~~along with her children~~, was at the mall today.
6. **is** Beware of words that are set off by commas, *which*, or *that*. The desk ~~that has two chairs~~ is mine.
7. **have** Cross out prepositional phrases. The plants ~~on the shelf over by the window~~ have died.

8. **like** Cross out prepositional phrases. The workers ~~with long trips home~~ like to leave early on Fridays.
9. **increases** Beware of words that make the subject sound plural or are set off by commas. Nga's salary, ~~as well as her benefits~~, increases every fall.
10. **scares** Beware of words that are set off by commas, *which*, or *that*. The haunted house, ~~full of rats and bats~~, scares many people at night.

EXERCISE 4: *page 82.*

1. **are** My <u>shoes</u> are where?
2. **are** Reword the sentence, and cross out the prepositional phrase. Two reasons ~~for your success~~ are there.
3. **want** <u>You</u> do want more sugar for your coffee.
4. **goes** <u>Khan</u> goes there.
5. **is** <u>Joe</u> is going where on his trip?
6. **are** <u>You</u> are doing what with my new coat?
7. **is** The <u>horse</u> ~~from the stable across the road~~ is here.
8. **Does** Your <u>mother</u> does still drive to the store every day.
9. **do** <u>You</u> do win every time you play chess.
10. **Does** <u>Chad</u> does believe in ghosts.

EXERCISE 5: *pages 82, 83.*

1. **wants** *No<u>body</u>* is always singular.
2. **Does** *Any<u>one</u>* is always singular.
3. **likes** *Neither (one)* is always singular.
4. **Has** *Every<u>body</u>* is always singular.
5. **knits** *Each (one)* is always singular.
6. **cares** *No <u>one</u>* is always singular.
7. **is** *Either (one)* is always singular.
8. **cuts** *Some<u>body</u>* is always singular. *Everyday* signals that the verb should be in the present tense because the action happens repeatedly.
9. **Does** *Any<u>body</u>* is always singular.
10. **needs** *Some<u>thing</u>* is always singular.

EXERCISE 6: *pages 83, 84.*

1. **are** The verb must be plural. <u>Some</u> of my <u>friends</u>
2. **want** The verb must be plural. <u>Several</u> of my <u>peers</u>
3. **falls** The verb must be singular. <u>All</u> of my <u>change</u>
4. **Do** Reword questions. <u>Any</u> of your <u>brothers</u> do need a new coat. The verb must be plural.
5. **is** The verb must be singular. <u>Most</u> of my <u>time</u>
6. **are** The verb must be plural. <u>None</u> of my <u>siblings</u>
7. **Do** Reword questions. A <u>few</u> of your <u>shirts</u> do need to be washed. The verb must be plural.
8. **Are** Reword questions. <u>Most</u> of your <u>gifts</u> are wrapped. The verb must be plural.
9. **have** The verb must be plural. <u>Many</u> of my <u>socks</u>
10. **think** The verb must be plural. <u>Both</u> of the <u>coaches</u>

EXERCISE 7: *pages 84, 85.*

1. **growls** The tiger or <u>the bear</u> <u>growls</u>. When *or* is the conjunction, the verb agrees with the closest subject.
2. **work** The chef <u>and</u> the waiters work. When *and* is the conjunction, the verb is plural.
3. **know** Neither the coach nor <u>his players know</u>. When *nor* is the conjunction, the verb agrees with the closest subject.
4. **are** Red, blue, <u>and</u> yellow are. When *and* is the conjunction, the verb is plural.
5. **think** The doctor <u>and</u> the nurses think. When *and* is the conjunction, the verb is plural.
6. **join** Carl or <u>his sisters</u> <u>join</u>. When *or* is the conjunction, the verb agrees with the closest subject.
7. **knocks** The cats or <u>the dog</u> <u>knocks</u>. When *or* is the conjunction, the verb agrees with the closest subject.

8. **make** The cold air, snow, <u>and</u> high winds make. When *and* is the conjunction, the verb is plural.
9. **flourishes** The flowers nor <u>the tree</u> flourishes. When *nor* is the conjunction, the verb agrees with the closest subject.
10. **erase** The teacher or the students <u>erase</u>. When *or* is the conjunction, the verb agrees with the closest subject.

EXERCISE 8: *page 85.*

1. **is** The subject is *athlete*.
2. **were** The subject is *cars*.
3. **is** The subject is *interest*, which is singular.
4. **is** The subject is *sight*, which is singular. Don't forget to cross out prepositional phrases. A lovely sight ~~in the fall~~ is . . .
5. **are** The subject is *trees*.
6. **is** The subject is *his main concern*.
7. **idea** The subject is *idea*.
8. **were** The compound subject is *a bigger backstop and more bleachers*. When the conjunction *and* is used for a compound subject, the verb must be plural.
9. **were** The compound subject is *a nicer sign or more ads*. When the conjunction *or* is used for a compound subject, the verb must agree with the closest subject, *more ads*.
10. **were** The compound subject is *More voter turnout and better polls*. When the conjunction *and* is used for a compound subject, the verb must be plural.

CHAPTER REVIEW

EXERCISE 1: *page 86.*

1. **was** The bag ~~of balls~~ was. . . Cross out prepositional phrases.
2. **forgets** *Someone* is always singular.
3. **are** For *all*, you must look at the prepositional phrase *of my peers*. *Peers* is plural.

4. **are** For *none*, you need to look at the prepositional phrase *of the cookies. Cookies* is plural.

5. **wants** *Everyone* is always singular.

6. **think** The conjunction *and* makes the subject and the verb plural.

7. **need** When *or* is used, focus on the subject closest to the verb. *The children need.*

8. **is** For *most*, you must look at the prepositional phrase *of my money. Money* is singular.

9. **is** When a linking verb is used, focus on the subject. *Her idea* is singular.

10. **was** When *or* is used, focus on the subject closest to the verb. *The flute was.*

11. **has** When *or* is used, focus on the subject closest to the verb. *The new shop around the corner has.*

12. **have** When *or* is used, focus on the subject closest to the verb. *I have.*

13. **is** Beware of words set off by commas, *that*, or *which*. The subject is *the coat.*

14. **is** Cross out prepositional phrases. The fire hydrant ~~down the street by Beth's trees~~ is leaking.

15. **have** Beware of words set off by commas, *that*, or *which*. The subject is *my shoes.*

16. **plays** Cross out prepositional phrases. Grandma, ~~along with her friends~~, plays bridge each week.

17. **were** Reword sentences that begin with *there*. Five tickets for the show are there on the table.

18. **Do** Rewrite questions as statements. *You do know the name of the new girl.*

19. **are** *Both* is always plural.

20. **is** For *none* you need to look at the prepositional phrase *of the change. Change* is singular.

EXERCISE 2: *page 86.*

Health care is a tough issue for many people these days. Everybody **wants**[1] to have the best care at the lowest cost. Yet, poor people and ill people lack the health care that they need. The problem **is**[2] high costs and scanty coverage. Neither medicine nor doctors are affordable for many people. Every year politicians, looking for votes and full of hot air, **promise**[3] to improve health care, but nothing seems to change.

Even the thought of choosing a health plan is hard for some. In our office alone, there **are**[4] five different health plans. My boss, along with some others, **belongs**[5] to an HMO. Many of the other employees see private doctors. Yet, no one is happy. The forms that we all complete **seem**[6] endless. Few of the doctors **are**[7] available when we need them, and the cost keeps rising. Better health plans **are**[8] a great idea, but who knows how to improve them? Somebody is going to find a solution to this problem, but it will not be soon enough.

1. *Everybody* is always singular.
2. *Problem* is the subject, and it is singular.
3. *Politicians* is the subject, and it is plural. *Looking for votes and full of hot air* is set off with commas. It should be ignored.
4. *Health plans* is the subject, and it is plural. *In our office alone* is a prepositional phrase that works like an adverb, and *there* is an adverb. Try rewording the sentence: *Five different health plans are there in our office alone.*
5. *My boss* is the subject, and it is singular. Cross out the prepositional phrase *along with some others.*
6. *Forms* is the subject, and it is plural. Ignore *that we all complete.*

7. *Few* is the subject, and it is always plural.
8. *Better health plans* is the subject, and it is plural.

CHAPTER 5: PRONOUNS

EXERCISE 1: *page 88.*

1. **She** Subject
2. **They** Subject
3. **I** Subject
4. **He** Subject
5. **he** Subject Complement
6. **He, she** Subject
7. **she** Subject Complement
8. **She** Subject
9. **they** Subject Complement
10. **she** Subject Complement

EXERCISE 2: *page 89.*

1. **she**
2. **they**
3. **she, he**
4. **he**
5. **she**
6. **she, he**
7. **she**
8. **he, I**
9. **she**
10. **She**

EXERCISE 3: *page 90.*

1. **me** *Me* is an object of the verb. The little girl sprayed whom?
2. **him, me** *Him and me* form an object of the verb. The manager promised a good job to whom?
3. **him** *Him* is an object of the verb. Congress sent a bill to whom?
4. **us** *Us* is the object of the preposition *for.* If you need to review the prepositions, see Chapter 1.
5. **him, her** *Him and her* form an object of the verb. Did you give enough paint to whom?

6. **me** *You and me* form the object of the preposition *between.* Many people incorrectly choose *I* because they think it "sounds" right. Practice saying *between you and me.*
7. **him, her** *Him and her* form an object of the verb. Why did Nga tell that story to whom?
8. **me** *Dade and me* form the object of the preposition *behind.* If you need to review prepositions, see Chapter 1.
9. **him** *Di and him* form an object of the verb.
10. **her** *Him and her* form the object of the preposition *about.*

EXERCISE 4: *page 91.*

1. **her** The singer brought two people. The singer brought Anne and her.
2. **me** The team chose the player of the year. The team chose me.
3. **me** Yu Lin bought her best friends nice gifts. Yu Lin bought you and me nice gifts.
4. **me** The program gave two troubled kids a chance. The program gave Carlos and me a chance.
5. **me** Ingrid sent her sisters flowers. Ingrid sent you and me flowers.
6. **me** Taxes are a burden for me. Taxes are a burden for a hard worker.
7. **me** Dr. Koo gave her nurses a lot of grief. Dr. Koo gave Jane and me a lot of grief.
8. **him** Ty tipped the waiters too much. Ty tipped Fred and him too much.
9. **me** The mentors helped two students learn more. The mentors helped Ian and me learn more.
10. **me** Leaving home was hard for one person. Leaving home was hard for me.

EXERCISE 5: *page 92.*

1. **hers** Possessive pronouns do not have apostrophes.

2. **My** *My* shows ownership.
3. **his, her** *His* and *her* show ownership.
4. **His** *Chewing* is an *-ing* verb that acts like a noun. Use a possessive pronoun.
5. **his** Possessive pronouns do not have apostrophes.
6. **They** This pronoun should not be possessive.
7. **his** *Putting* is an *-ing* verb that acts like a noun. Use a possessive pronoun.
8. **its** Possessive pronouns do not have apostrophes.
9. **theirs** Possessive pronouns do not have apostrophes.
10. **his** *Speaking* is an *-ing* verb that acts like a noun. Use a possessive pronoun.

EXERCISE 6: *page 93.*

1. **Who** *Who* is the subject. Who or what asked?
2. **whom** *Whom* is the object of the preposition. Lee gave money to whom or what?
3. **Who** *Who* is the subject. Who or what was elected president?
4. **Whom** We should send whom to the training program?
5. **whom** *Whom* is an object of the verb. Cal gave the game ball to whom or what?
6. **Whom** Brazil did defeat whom to win the World Cup in 1994?
7. **Who** Be careful. You might reword this sentence and make *the new law* the subject. *The new law will hurt whom.* However, *by the new law* is a prepositional phrase; *the new law* cannot be the subject. The subject of the sentence is *who.* Who or what will be hurt?
8. **whoever** *Whoever* is the subject. Who or what thought?

9. **whomever** *Whomever* is an object of the verb. The volunteers help whom or what?
10. **Whom** Jack did pay whom?

EXERCISE 7: *page 94.*

1. **whoever** *Whoever* is the subject of the clause *whoever had the greatest need.*
2. **who** *Who* is the subject of the clause *who granted the money.*
3. **whom** *Whom* is the object of the verb in the clause *whom we just met.* Rewrite the clause *we just met whom.*
4. **who** *Who* is the subject of the clause *who took the new sign.*
5. **Whoever** *Whoever* is the subject of the clause *whoever committed the war crimes.*
6. **who** *Who* is the subject of the clause *who are injured.*
7. **whomever** *Whoever* is the object of the verb in the clause. Try rewording the clause. *She chooses whomever.*
8. **Whoever** *Whoever* is the subject of the clause *whoever wins the war.*
9. **whom** *Whom* is the object of the verb in clause. Try rewording the clause. *She saved whom.*
10. **who** *Who* is the subject of the clause *who come to America.*

EXERCISE 8: *page 95.*

1. **correct** Mom planned the whole trip without any help.
2. **It** *Itself* does not refer to another noun or pronoun in the sentence.
3. **correct** *We* performed the action on *ourselves.*
4. **correct** You need to get the job done alone.
5. **me** *Myself* does not refer to another noun or pronoun in the sentence.
6. **correct** *They* performed the action on *themselves.*

7. **yourself** *You* performed the action on *yourself.*
8. **He** *Himself* does not refer to another noun or pronoun in the sentence.
9. **correct** She paid for night school without any help.
10. **correct** Rachel performed the action on *herself.*

EXERCISE 9: *page 96.*

1. **I** Mr. Pyo is as careful with the car as <u>I am.</u>
2. **she** Sasha bikes more often than <u>she bikes.</u>
3. **he** Shane skates as well as <u>he skates.</u>
4. **they** If we work hard, we can play as well as <u>they play.</u>
5. **we** Beth and Phil are good athletes, but they are not better than <u>we are.</u>
6. **he** Kyle runs less often than <u>he runs.</u>
7. **we** When they finish their dance lessons, they will be as good as <u>we are.</u>
8. **I** The drummer in the band isn't any better than <u>I am.</u>
9. **she** As an artist, Pam is much more creative than <u>she is.</u>
10. **he** The umpire had a better view of the play than <u>he had.</u>

EXERCISE 10: *page 96.*

1. **We** We ~~children~~ look forward to the holidays.
2. **us** The owner gave a higher wage to us ~~waiters~~.
3. **we** How will we ~~reporters~~ know when you will take action?
4. **We** We ~~parents~~ must make sure that our children stay away from drugs.
5. **us** Art and music classes are important for us ~~students~~.
6. **we** Are we ~~workers~~ in danger of losing our jobs?
7. **We** We ~~voters~~ must choose the best leaders for our country.

8. **us** This memo is about us ~~managers~~.
9. **us** The road crew helped us ~~commuters~~ get to work in the snow.
10. **us** When will he give us ~~drivers~~ a break?

EXERCISE 11: *page 97.*

1. **his** *His* agrees with *Juan or Carlos.*
2. **one** *One* agrees with *if <u>one</u> eats well.*
3. **their** *Their* agrees with *few people,* which is plural.
4. **their** *Their* agrees with *Kerry and Katherine,* which is plural.
5. **their** *Their* agrees with *many people,* which is plural.
6. **their** *Their* agrees with *none of the pilots,* which is plural because *pilots* is plural.
7. **his** *His* agrees with *everyone,* which is singular.
8. **his** *His* agrees with *each,* which is singular.
9. **his** *His* agrees with *nobody,* which is singular.
10. **their** *Their* agrees with *several birds,* which is plural.

CHAPTER REVIEW

EXERCISE 1: *pages 98, 99.*

1. **no error**
2. **We** We ~~coal miners~~ need to earn higher wages.
3. **he** *Be* is a linking verb, and *he* is a subject complement.
4. **no error** Remember, *whoever* is the subject of the clause *whoever needs it.*
5. **she** Two people welcomed us into their homes. Kim welcomed us. She welcomed us.
6. **no error** Remember, *running* is a verb that acts like a noun. *His* is an adjective that describes *running.*

7. **she** This judge is more strict than *she is.*
8. **no error** We did meet *whom?*
9. **hers** Possessive pronouns do not have apostrophes.
10. **no error** Drug use is rising among us ~~teenagers~~.
11. **she** He does not want to work as hard as *she works.*
12. **no error** *Whoever* is the subject of the clause *whoever was hurt.*
13. **his** *Singing* is a verb that acts like a noun. *His* is an adjective that describes *singing.*
14. **no error** We ~~women~~ give our hearts to whomever we choose. *Whomever* is the object of the verb in the clause *whomever we choose.* Try rewording the clause as *we choose whomever.*
15. **me** *You and me* is the object of the preposition *between.*
16. **no error**
17. **his** The pronoun must be singular because *everyone* is singular.
18. **no error** *Who ran his car into the wall* is a clause that describes the driver. *Who* is the subject of the clause.
19. **me** Dr. Lee loves to give advice to you and me. *You and me* is the object of the preposition *to.*
20. **no error** *Their* is used because *workers* is plural.
21. **no error** *One* is used because the sentence is about anyone.
22. **no error** *You and me* is the object of the preposition *about.*
23. **him** *Him and me* is the object of the verb. Coach Ngyun benched him. Coach Ngyun benched me.
24. **he** He gave a raise to the wait staff. A reflexive pronoun (ends with *-self*) must refer to another noun or pronoun in the sentence.
25. **whoever** *Whoever* is the subject of the clause *whoever gives them money.*

EXERCISE 2: *page 99.*

Everybody who comes to America brings **his**[1] hopes for a better life. For example, Juan and Rose always believed in the American dream. When they arrived, Juan and Rose promised to work hard for **whoever**[2] gave them a job. Juan's brothers gave Rose and **him**[3] money to get started, but it was not enough. Juan often thought that no person ever worked as hard as **he** [4]. In time, life slowly improved for Rose and him. **Their**[5] working for the future paid off. Before too long, they earned fair wages and provided a good home for their children. Juan told **whomever**[6] he met about his new life. He was proud of his success. **We**[7] native-born Americans can learn a lot from these new arrivals.

1. *Everybody* is singular.
2. *Whoever* is the subject of the clause *whoever gave them a job.*
3. *Rose and him* form an object of the verb. Juan's brothers gave Rose money. Juan's brothers gave him money.
4. ...no one person ever worked as hard as he worked.
5. *Working* is a verb that works like a noun, and it is the subject of the sentence. *Their* is an adjective that describes working.
6. *Whomever* is the subject of the clause *whomever he met.* Try to reword the clause as *he met whomever.*
7. We ~~native-born Americans~~ can learn...

CHAPTER 6: PHRASES

EXERCISE 1: *page 104.*

1. **Sitting on the wall** What is dangerous? *Sitting on the wall* is the subject of the sentence.
2. **eating finger foods** *Eating finger foods* is the object of the preposition *on.*

3. **singing on the stage** Rose recalls what? *Singing on stage* is the object of the verb.

4. **to trick us** *To trick us* is a subject complement.

5. **To read often** What is important? *To read often* is the subject of the sentence.

6. **to hire good workers** Jan asked what? *To hire good workers* is an object of the verb.

7. **Painting a huge sign** What is a great idea? *Painting a huge sign* is the subject of the sentence.

8. **biking in Maine** *Biking in Maine* is the object of the preposition *about*.

9. **running in the rain** Russ enjoys what? *Running in the rain* is the object of the verb.

10. **Sailing into the wind** What is hard? *Sailing into the wind* is the subject of the sentence.

EXERCISE 2: *pages 104, 105.*

1. **Angered by the vote** *Angered by the vote* describes *he*, the first noun after the comma.

2. **thrilled with the news** *Thrilled with the news* describes *Jack.*

3. **Sailing into the storm** *Sailing into the storm* describes *boat*, the first noun after the comma. *Small* is an adjective that also describes *boat.*

4. **driving into town** *Driving into town* describes *Russ.*

5. **affected by his remarks** *Affected by his remarks* is a subject complement that follows the linking verb *seems.* The phrase describes *judge.*

6. **Hunting in the woods** *Hunting in the woods* describes *Pete*, the first noun after the comma.

7. **biking fast** *Biking fast* describes *Joe.*

8. **Excited about Santa** *Excited about Santa* describes *Katherine*, the first noun after the comma.

9. **drifting in the sky** *Drifting in the sky* describes *clouds.*

10. **decorated with lights** *Decorated with lights* describes *tree.*

EXERCISE 3: *page 105.*

1. **to finish the project** *To finish the project* tells how we are anxious.

2. **to answer that question** *To answer that question* tells how it is unwise.

3. **to be home alone at night** *To be home alone at night* tells why Zach is scared.

4. **to balance work and family** *To balance work and family* tells how it is hard.

5. **to maintain their bodies** *To maintain their bodies* tells why athletes train daily.

CHAPTER REVIEW

EXERCISE 1: *page 106.*

1. **Running errands** *Running errands*, a **noun**, is the subject.

2. **to write thank-you notes for the gifts** *To write thank-you notes for the gifts* works as a **noun**. Nga needs what?

3. **him (to) leave the house before six o'clock** *Him (to) leave the house before six o'clock* works as a **noun**. I wanted what?

4. **Hurried by my friend** *Hurried by my friend* works as an **adjective** that describes *I.*

5. **playing ball with his friends** *Playing ball with his friends* works as a **noun**. Sean enjoys what?

6. **her to work more hours** *Her to work more hours* works as a **noun**. Juan does not want *her;* Juan wants *her to work more hours.*

7. **Waiting on tables** *Waiting on tables* works as a **noun** and is the subject. What is hard work?

8. **to see his mom** To see his mom works as an **adverb**. Keep in mind, *to the door* is a prepositional phrase (*to* + noun).

9. **her to wash her hands before dinner** *Her to wash her hands before dinner* works as a **noun**. I wanted what?

10. **Injured from the crash** *Injured from the crash* works as an **adjective** that describes *Carlos*.

11. **standing by the side of the road** *Standing by the side of the road* works as an **adjective** that describes *deer*.

12. **to run on solar power** *To run on solar power* works as an **adverb** that shows how the car was designed.

13. **running a red light** *Running a red light* works as an **adjective** that describes *him*.

14. **me to think about my faults** *Me to think about my faults* works as a **noun**. The book forced what?

15. **Running after the bus** *Running after the bus* works as an **adjective** that describes *he*.

16. **Skating on the pond** *Skating on the pond* works as a **noun** and is the subject of the sentence.

17. **To travel abroad** *To travel abroad* works as a **noun** and the subject of the sentence.

18. **Educated by the warnings** *Educated by the warnings* works as an **adjective** that describes *Jill*.

19. **gathering flowers on the side of the road** *Gathering flowers on the side of the road* works as an **adjective** that describes *Grandma*.

20. **Leaving our homeland** *Leaving our homeland* works as a **noun**. It is the subject of the sentence.

21. **helping me** *Helping me* works as a **noun**. It is the object of the preposition *for*.

22. **armed with a gun** *Armed with a gun* works as an **adjective** that describes *thief*.

23. **Trained in CPR** *Trained in CPR* works as an **adjective** that describes *Fred*.

24. **the sitter to watch the baby carefully** *The sitter to watch the baby carefully* works as a **noun**. We want what?

25. **her to keep costs down** *Her to keep costs down* works as a **noun**. The boss wants what?

CHAPTER 7: CLAUSES

EXERCISE 1: *pages 107, 108.*

1. **independent** *I cleaned up the mess* could be a sentence.

2. **dependent** *As long as I pay my bills on time* is not a complete thought. The reader needs to know what happens when the bills are paid on time.

3. **independent** *Drunk driving arrests increased* could be a sentence.

4. **dependent** *That our leaders use* is not a complete thought. The reader needs more information.

5. **independent** *No one cares* could be a sentence.

6. **independent** *He makes sure that it will last a long time* could be a sentence.

7. **dependent** *Until she pays off all of the loans* is not a complete thought. What happens until she pays the loans?

8. **independent** *Rich cleaned the house* could be a sentence.

9. **dependent** *Who scored the last goal* could be a question, but as a statement it does not express a complete thought. The reader needs more information.

10. **dependent** *Which parents want all-day kindergarten* does not express a complete thought.

EXERCISE 2: *page 109.*

1. **what happened in the store** *What happened in the store* is the object of the verb. We discussed whom or what?
2. **who will win the race today** *Is* is a linking verb. Nga ↔ who will win the race today.
3. **whoever walks through the door** *Whoever walks through the door* is the object of the preposition *to*. They will give the prize to whom or what?
4. **which person is guilty** *Which person is guilty* is the object of the verb. We must decide whom or what?
5. **whose story was true** *Whose story was true* is the object of the verb. The judge did not know whom or what?
6. **What the customer wanted** Who or what was not on the menu?
7. **whomever his boss wants** *Whomever his boss wants* is the object of the preposition *to*. Carlos will give the job to whom or what?
8. **that the house needed some repairs** *That the house needed some repairs* is the object of the verb. Jim knew whom or what?
9. **whoever feels lonely** *Whoever feels lonely* is an object of the verb. I will send a card to whom or what?
10. **Whoever needs food or shelter** Who or what can get help from the church?

EXERCISE 3: *pages 110, 111.*

1. **whose face is etched in my mind** *Whose face is etched in my mind* describes *victim.*
2. **that will hold more fans** *That will hold more fans* describes *stadium.*
3. **who finds a cure for AIDS** *Who finds a cure for AIDS* describes *person.*
4. **that I saw in the pet store** *That I saw in the pet store* describes *dog.*
5. **whose record is spotless** *Whose record is spotless* describes *person.*
6. **whom he met on the plane** *Whom he met on the plane* describes *man.*
7. **who work overtime** *Who work overtime* describes *drivers.*
8. **which will care for all three children** *Which will care for all three children* describes *center. Day-care* also modifies *center.* Both the adjective clause and the adjective tell what type of center.
9. **whose hand went through the glass** *Whose hand went through the glass* describes *person.*
10. **which will have meat for dinner** *Which will have meat for dinner* describes *store.*

EXERCISE 4: *page 112.*

1. **After I paid off all my debts** *After I paid off all my debts* tells *when* I felt a sense of relief.
2. **before the cold weather comes** *Before the cold weather comes* tells *when* we need to call the landlord.
3. **provided that the students earn good grades** *Provided that the students earn good grades* tells *how* schools offer aid.
4. **As long as Rose works two jobs** *As long as Rose works two jobs* tells *how often* Juan will have to do more housework.
5. **wherever the soil and sunlight are good** *Wherever the soil and sunlight are good* tells *where* Salma will plant.
6. **as soon as he completes high school** *As soon as he completes high school* tells *when* Nasser will go to work.
7. **before you cross the street** *Before you cross the street* tells *when* you should look both ways.

8. **Even though Kate is smart** *Even though Kate is smart* tells *how* she still needs to work.

9. **If I don't pass this test** *If I don't pass this test* tells *why* I will not get my driver's license. Keep in mind, *not* is an adverb that tells *when* something will happen. *Don't* combines *do* and *not*.

10. **unless more people come** *Unless more people come* tells *how much* we have.

EXERCISE 5: *page 113.*

1. **who** Use *who* for people.
2. **that** Use *that* for things or animals.
3. **which** *Which needs repair* is not important; we already know that the barn is Doug's. In addition, *which needs repair* is set off by commas. *Which* is used with commas.
4. **who** *Who* is used with people.
5. **that** Khan does not want just any job. He wants a job *that will pay him more money*. The clause limits the noun and does not have commas. *That* must be used.
6. **whom** *Whom* is used with people.
7. **which** *Which kills many people* is not important. We already know that lung cancer kills. In addition, *which* is used with clauses that are set off by commas.
8. **that** There are many jokes, but I told a joke *that he had not heard before*. The clause limits the noun and does not have commas. *That* must be used.
9. **who** *Who* is used for people.
10. **that** Joe will not buy just any dog. He wants a dog *that will be good with children*. The clause limits the noun and does not have commas. *That* must be used.

EXERCISE 6: *pages 113, 114.*

1. **(that) we knew we could afford** *(That) we knew we could afford* describes *house.*

2. **so (that) she can lose a few extra pounds** *So (that) she can lose a few extra pounds* tells why Ramla runs.
3. **(that) her staff is working hard** Our boss thinks whom or what? *(That) her staff is working hard* is the object of the verb.
4. **so (that) no one will get hurt** *So (that) no one will get hurt* tells why Jihye put a fence around the pool.
5. **(that) we stay for lunch, noun clause** *(That) we stay for lunch* is the object of the verb. Kim insists whom or what?
6. **(that) we knew would hurt the poor** *(That) we knew would hurt the poor* describes *bill.*
7. **(that) he will go to college** Ty thinks what? *(That) he will go to college* is the object of the verb.
8. **(that) he could eat quickly** *(That) he could eat quickly* describes *snack.*
9. **(that) we don't know how to cure** *(That) we don't know how to cure* describes *disease.*
10. **so (that) he can keep the deer out of the garden** *So (that) he can keep the deer out of the garden* tells why he bought the repellent.

CHAPTER REVIEW

EXERCISE 1: *pages 114, 115.*

1. **adjective** *Working in the yard* is a phrase that describes *Nate.*
2. **noun** *That we should eat five fruits and vegetables a day* is the object of the verb. Food experts say what?
3. **noun** *Whatever is on the menu* is the object of the verb. Blair will eat what?
4. **noun** *To bring ethics to the White House* is a phrase and the object of the verb. The president needs what?
5. **adverb** *Before you start exercising* tells when you should see your doctor.
6. **noun** *To enter a marathon* is a phrase and the subject of the sentence. What takes courage?

7. **noun** *To stay after school for extra help* is a phrase and the object of the verb. Thän wanted what?

8. **adverb** *Provided that you buy me coffee and a paper* tells when and why I will drive you.

9. **noun** *Flying a kite* is a phrase and the subject of the sentence.

10. **adverb** *If Ben does not learn to control his temper* tells why he will get himself in trouble.

11. **noun** *His driving in the snow* is a phrase and the subject. What upsets Jan?

12. **noun** *Anne to get a job in retail* is a phrase and the object of the verb. The social worker wanted what?

13. **noun** *That you want to learn about cars* is the object of the verb. I understand what?

14. **adjective** *Running away from the scene* describes *thief.*

15. **noun** *What José needs* is the subject. What is?

16. **adverb** *After his parents divorced* tells when Sal spent weekends with his dad.

17. **adjective** *Racing to catch the train* is a phrase that describes *Paula,* the first noun after the comma.

18. **adjective** *Whom she helped* describes *women.*

19. **adverb** *As soon as there is a cure for the common cold* tells when we will stop sneezing.

20. **adjective** *Troubled by the flu* is a phrase that describes *Fran,* the first noun after the comma.

21. **noun** *To work harder* is a phrase and the object of the verb in the sentence.

22. **adjective** *Who spilled wine on my dress* describes *waiter.*

23. **adjective** *That is on Elm Street* describes *store.*

24. **noun** *Driving to New York* is a phrase and the object of the verb in the sentence.

25. **adverb** *Whenever you are in town* tells when you should come see us.

26. **adverb** *While we were at the bus stop* tells when a car jumped the curb.

27. **noun** *Whoever wants to earn more money* is the subject of the sentence.

28. **adjective** *Burning my skin* is a phrase that describes *sun.*

29. **noun** *To be the best student in his class* is the object of the verb. Manuel wants what?

30. **adjective** *Tired from the trip* is a phrase that describes *Al.*

CHAPTER 8:
END MARKS AND COMMAS

EXERCISE 1: *page 120.*

1. ... **miles.** This is a polite command.
2. ... **book?** This is a direct question.
3. ... **alone!** This is an emotional command.
4. ... **leaking.** This is an indirect question. These are not the plumber's exact words.
5. **Hey!** This is an emotional interjection.
6. ... **gone.** This is an indirect question.
7. ... **name.** This is a polite command.
8. ... **you!** This is an emotional command.
9. ... **party?** This is a direct question.
10. ... **night.** This is a statement.

EXERCISE 2: *pages 121, 122.*

1. Kim wants to travel with her **family, but** they cannot afford to take a trip this year. The comma and conjunction *but* join independent clauses.
2. Meg bought **clothes, toys, and food** for the children at the shelter. The commas separate items in a series.

3. The sitter cares for four children during the day and goes to school at night. Do not add commas. This sentence has a compound verb.
4. She **sang, danced, and acted** like the star of the show. The commas separate verbs in a series.
5. The house was **big, well kept, and costly**. The commas separate adjectives in a series.
6. I will work longer **hours, and** Fred will help more at home. The comma and conjunction *and* join two independent clauses.
7. Jong missed his **train, yet** he did not call for a ride. The comma and the conjunction *yet* join two independent clauses.
8. The **gloves, hats, and scarves** make a mess in the hall closet. The commas separate nouns in a series.
9. They played all day and laughed all night. Do not add commas. *Played* and *laughed* form a compound verb.
10. The trial will be **delayed, so** both sides will have more time to gather evidence. The comma and the conjunction *so* join two independent clauses.

EXERCISE 3: *page 122.*

1. The **clear, blue** sky did not have a cloud. *Clear* and *blue* describe *sky*, and they are equally important.
2. Three soup bowls need to be cleaned. Do not add commas. Numbers should not be separated from other adjectives.
3. **Thick, black** smoke from the fire filled the room. *Thick* and *black* describe *smoke*, and they are equally important.
4. Dr. Lee's **shiny, new** dental chair scares many patients. *Shiny* and *new* both describe dental chair. *Dental* is an adjective, but it is more important than *shiny* and *new*.

5. They searched the woods for five straight days. Do not add commas. Numbers should not be separated from other adjectives.
6. The new brick building will be our town hall. *New* and *brick* are both adjectives that describe *building*, but they are not equally important.
7. **Fresh, white** paint will help the shabby old shelves. *Fresh* and *white* both describe *paint*, and they are equally important.
8. The old bathroom sink is cracked. *Old* and *bathroom* both describe *sink*, but they are not equally important.
9. It is hard to find **good, low-cost** health care. *Good* and *low-cost* describe *health care*, and they are equally important.
10. We filled six large bags with sand. Do not add commas. Numbers should not be separated from other adjectives.

EXERCISE 4: *page 123.*

1. **Ty, weary** from the long **trip, drank** coffee to wake himself. Without the phrase, the reader still knows who drank coffee.
2. The waiter who spilled soup down my back still got a tip. Do not add commas. *Who spilled soup down my back* is a restrictive clause. It tells which waiter.
3. The **hiker, cold** and **alone, tried** to find help. Without the phrase *cold and alone*, the sentence still makes sense.
4. **Nate, a lawyer, has** won some hard cases. Without the appositive, the reader still knows who won some hard cases.
5. The artist Renoir painted many works. Do not add commas. Without *Renoir*, the reader does not know which artist painted many works.
6. Judge **Car, who** is on my **case, is** strict. Without the phrase *who is on my case*, the reader still knows which judge is strict.

7. The judge who is on my case is strict. This time *who is on my case* is important. It tells the reader which judge is strict.
8. The ratings that are used for TV shows are vague. The clause *that are used for TV shows* tells which ratings are vague. *That* is only used with restrictive clauses.
9. **Jake, tired** of reading the same **books, went** to the library to find something new. Without *tired of reading the same books*, the reader still knows who went to the library.
10. *Cheers,* **a** great **show, aired** for many years. Without *a great show*, the reader still knows which program aired for many years.

EXERCISE 5: *page 124.*

1. After the rain **came, the** streams overflowed and the streets flooded. Place a comma after introductory clauses.
2. **Yes, I** will work a few extra hours. *Yes* is an introductory word. It is an unemotional interjection.
3. Once the food **arrives, we** can serve the children. Place a comma after introductory clauses.
4. **Bob, leave** the flashlight in the car. Place a comma after a direct address.
5. Scared of the wind and **noise, Rick** hid under the bed during the storm. Place a comma after an introductory phrase.
6. As soon as we get to the **beach, I** will jump in the water. Place a comma after an introductory clause.
7. Between the seat and the door of the **car, Rita** found some loose change. Place a comma after an introductory phrase.
8. I checked the lights and turned down the heat before we left. Do not add commas. *Checked* and *turned* form a compound verb.

9. **Juan, did** you learn to swim when you were a child? Place a comma after a direct address.
10. For **example, some** movies have good soundtracks. Place a comma after opening words.

EXERCISE 6: *pages 124, 125.*

1. He **sang, "We** shall be free." Place a comma after the "talking" word *sang* to set apart the speaker.
2. "It's just a **job," Tom said, "I** need the money." Place commas inside the quotation marks and after the "talking" word *said* to set apart the speaker.
3. "Watch your language!" my mom scolded. Do not add commas. Exclamation marks work alone.
4. "Once we finish this **project," he said, "I** will take a few days off." Place commas inside the quotation marks and after the "talking" word *said* to set off the speaker.
5. "When can we go home?" Jane asked. Do not add commas. Question marks work alone.
6. Ned **shouted, "We** need to win this game!" Place a comma after the "talking" word *shouted*.
7. "When I was a **boy," he declared, "I** had to walk to school in the snow." Place commas inside the quotation marks and after the "talking" word *declared*.
8. "The ballot is stronger than the **bullet," Abraham** Lincoln said. Place a comma inside the quotation marks.
9. "Why will they fire so many workers?" Rose asked. Do not add commas. Question marks work alone.
10. "Stay out of the water!" the lifeguard yelled. Do not add commas. Exclamation marks work alone.

EXERCISE 7: *page 125.*

1. The best **sales, I think, are** at the malls. *I think* is an interruption that connects ideas.
2. Are you **sure, Jeff, that** this car is safe? *Jeff* is a direct address.
3. **Meat, on** the other **hand, should** be refrigerated right away. *On the other hand* is an interruption that connects ideas.
4. Singers who top the charts can make a lot of money. Do not add commas. *Who top the charts* is a restrictive clause. Without it, the reader would not know which singers make a lot of money.
5. **Sue, in fact, works** hard to save money. *In fact* is an interruption that connects ideas.
6. **You, along** with your **doctor, need** to take care of your health. *Along with your doctor* is an interruption that provides explanation.
7. Her wrist that had the cast is pale. Do not add commas. *That had the cast* is a restrictive clause that tells which wrist.
8. I **hope, Kay, that** we can hire more waiters. *Kay* is a direct address.
9. The judge **ruled, of course, that** Dale should stand trial. *Of course* is an interruption that connects ideas.
10. **Surgeons, besides** making a lot of **money, earn** respect. *Besides making money* is an interruption that provides explanation.

EXERCISE 8: *page 126.*

1. On December **7, 1941, the** Japanese bombed Pearl Harbor. Don't forget to place a comma after the year.
2. We sent all of the cards to 10 King **Street, Wilton, Maine** 12543. Place a comma between each part of the address, except for the state and zip code.
3. Many babies were born in September 1996, nine months after the big snow storm. Do not add commas.
4. Carl spent over **$40,000** for that car. Add a comma after every three numbers counting from the right.
5. We may have some bad luck on **Friday, May** 13. Place a comma after the day.
6. Please send our mail to Box **12, Rush, New** York **54693, after** June **4, 1997.** Place a comma between parts of the address, except the state and zip code. Place a comma after the entire address when it is in a sentence. Place a comma between the date and the year.
7. The moon is about **240,000** miles from the earth. Place a comma after every three numbers counting from the right.
8. I arrived in Glens **Falls, New York, at** three o'clock. Place a comma between a city and state and after the state.
9. Sayre will have the book done by June 1997. Do not add commas.
10. On **Friday, March 15, Ruth** will have her birthday party. Place a comma after the day and after the entire date.

EXERCISE 9: *page 127.*

1. To **Jen, Laura** was a great friend. The reader needs to pause after *Jen* to separate it from *Laura*.
2. In **baseball, fans** are a key part of the game. The reader needs to pause after *baseball* to separate it from *fans*.
3. For **some, dogs** help cure loneliness. The reader needs to pause after *some* to separate it from *dogs*.
4. Before **nine, guests** had to leave. The reader needs to pause after *nine* to separate it from *guests*.

5. Though **sad, Meg** put a smile on her face for all to see. The reader needs to pause after *sad* to separate it from *Meg*.

CHAPTER REVIEW

EXERCISE 1: *page 127.*

Looking for a job is hard,[1] but there are ways to get help.[2] Most people will change jobs many times during their life,[3] so it is important to learn job-search skills.[4] Where can you get these skills?[5] The public library has helpful books, articles, [6]and computer programs. High schools and colleges have career counselors who aid students in the job market.[7] For a fee,[8] employment services will help workers find jobs in a particular field.[9] There even is information on-line.[10] So if resumes, applications,[11] and interviews are in your future,[12] get the help you need.[13] Make this job search your last one![14]

1. Place a comma before the conjunction *but.*
2. Place period at the end of a statement.
3. Place a comma before the conjunction *so.*
4. Place a period at the end of a statement.
5. Place a question mark after a direct question.
6. Place a comma between items in a series.
7. Place a period at the end of a statement.
8. Place a comma after an introductory phrase.
9. Place a period at the end of a statement.
10. Place a period at the end of a statement,
11. Use commas for items in a series.
12. Place a comma after an introductory clause.

13. Place a period at the end of a statement.
14. This is a command. It should have a period or an exclamation point.

EXERCISE 2: *page 128.*

Every year children are injured by accidents that could have been prevented.[1] Even before a baby is brought home from the hospital,[2] parents should do a safety check.[3] What should parents inspect?[4] Cribs, playpens, and highchairs[5] must meet federal safety guidelines.[6] Car seats, which are crucial,[7] should fit securely in the back seat of the car.[8] Small objects, medicines, knives, cleaning products,[9] and cords must be kept out of reach.[10] Bathtubs, toilets, and buckets[11] should be off-limits; children, in fact,[12] can drown in only a few inches of water.[13] If parents inspect their homes carefully,[14] they can prevent many accidents.[15] Safe homes save lives.[16]

1. Place a period at the end of a statement.
2. Place a comma after an introductory clause.
3. Place a comma at the end of a statement.
4. Place a question mark after a direct question.
5. Use commas for items in a series.
6. Place a comma at the end of a statement.
7. Use commas to set off nonrestrictive clauses.
8. Place a comma at the end of a statement.
9. Use commas for items in a series.
10. Place a period at the end of a statement.
11. Use commas for items in a series.
12. Use commas to set off interrupters.
13. Place a period at the end of a statement.

14. Place a comma after an introductory clause.
15. Place a period at the end of a statement.

EXERCISE 3: *page 128.*

I went to a concert with some friends last night,[1]and we had a great time.[2] As we walked through the gate,[3] a man shouted,[4] "I have front row seats!" [5]to my friend Sean.[6] We bought the tickets, ordered some food, [7] and made ourselves comfortable.[8] After the first song,[9]Jack yelled, [10] "This band is awesome!" [11]The lead singer looked down at us and mouthed,[12]"What did you say?[13]" Jack was too embarrassed to repeat what he yelled,[14]so I did. Do you believe that they invited me up on stage?[15] "Just my luck,[16]" Jack said,[17] "I get their attention,[18] and you go up on stage.[19]" "Remember,[20] I got these seats,[21]" Sean remarked.[22] By the end of the concert, [23] there were no hard feelings.[24] We had too much fun to hold grudges.[25]

1. Place a comma before the conjunction and.
2. Place a period at the end of a statement.
3. Place a comma after an introductory clause.
4. Place a comma after the talking word to separate the speaker from the quotation.
5. Exclamation marks work alone. Do not use commas with exclamation points.
6. Place a period at the end of a sentence.
7. Use commas to separate items in a series.
8. Place a comma at the end of a statement.
9. Place a comma after an introductory phrase.
10. Place a comma after the talking word to separate a speaker from the quotation.

11. Exclamation marks work alone. Do not use commas with exclamation points.
12. Place a comma after the talking word to separate the speaker from the quotation.
13. Question marks work alone. Do not add commas or periods.
14. Place a comma before the conjunction so.
15. Place a question mark after a direct question.
16. Use commas to separate speakers from quotations.
17. Place a comma after the talking word to separate the speaker from the quotation.
18. Place a comma before the conjunction and.
19. Place a period at the end of a statement.
20. Place a comma after an introductory word.
21. Use commas to separate a speaker from the quotation.
22. Place a period at the end of a statement.
23. Place a comma after an introductory phrase.
24. Place a period at the end of a statement.
25. Place a period at the end of a statement.

CHAPTER 9: MORE PUNCTUATION

EXERCISE 1: *page 130.*

1. Many people went home when the team started to **lose; the** true fans stayed until the end. The semicolon joins two independent clauses.
2. Fakih saved enough money to buy a nice **house; now, he** can afford to live in a great town. The semicolon joins two independent clauses. The comma follows *now*, a conjunctive adverb.

3. Ann took the children to the playground and pushed them on the swings. Do not add commas or a semicolon. *Took* and *pushed* form a compound verb.

4. Many women who have small children work full **time; others** stay home. The semicolon joins two independent full-clauses. Do not add commas. *Who have small children* is a restrictive clause that tells which women.

5. When she was young, Heidi ran in road races to stay in **shape, but** she preferred biking. The comma and *but* join two independent clauses. A semicolon could be used, but the comma after *young* does not confuse the reader.

6. Iron pills can poison **children; therefore, adults** must store the pills safely. The semicolon joins two independent clauses. A comma follows *therefore*, a conjunctive adverb.

7. The detective searched the crime scene, traced phone calls, and questioned **suspects; but** no arrests have been made. A semicolon joins the two independent clauses because the first clause has commas.

8. When the news called for snow, we were ready for a bad rush **hour; however, the** snow never came. A semicolon joins the two independent clauses that have a conjunctive adverb, however. A comma follows *however*.

9. Garth sang for **hours, and** the crowd cheered. The comma and *and* join two independent clauses.

10. When we went on the boat, we wore **lifejackets; the** water was rough, and we are not good swimmers. The semicolon joins two independent clauses. In this sentence, the commas could be confusing.

EXERCISE 2: *page 131.*

1. During the strike, the union negotiated the **contract; organized** the picket lines, which no one **crossed; began** a **boycott; and** helped strikers with financial problems.
The semicolons separate the items and make the sentence easier to read.

2. On our trip to Washington, D.C., I saw the White House, which I had seen **before; the** Capitol, where they never seem to do any **work; and** the Supreme Court. The semicolons separate the items, which have commas.

3. Parents today can choose to stop work and stay home with their **children; to** work from **home; to** work part time, which some people **prefer; or** to work full time. The semicolons separate the items, which have commas.

4. People who want freedom, refugees, and entrepreneurs come to the United States to improve their lives. Do not add punctuation. The commas separate items in a series.

5. Before Jane got to work, she walked the **dog; gave** medicine to her son, who has a bad **cold; and** went to school to drop off her daughter, who forgot to do her homework. The semicolons separate items, which are long and have commas.

EXERCISE 3: *page 132.*

1. Please check the following **things: gas**, oil, tires, and wiper fluid. The colon is placed before a list.

2. The weather was **great: sunny**, cool, and pleasant. *Sunny, cool, and pleasant* summarize the weather.

3. The best sports for children are T-ball, soccer, and basketball. Do not add a colon. This list follows a linking verb, and colons are not placed after linking verbs.

4. Ray was **thrilled: he** earned a huge bonus and got a raise. *He earned a huge bonus and got a raise* explains why Ray was thrilled.
5. The store will be closed on the following **days: May** 7, 8, and 9. The colon is placed before a list.
6. Franklin D. Roosevelt's words have been quoted **often: "Let** me assert my firm belief that the only thing we have to fear is fear itself." The colon is placed before a long quotation.
7. Dear Dr. **Kim:** The colon is placed after a greeting in a business letter. (If the letter were personal, one would not use *Dr. Kim.*)
8. We need to take care of some problems in the house, such as dirt, leaks, and mice. Do not add a colon after *such as.*
9. The rule is **simple: don't** talk when I am talking. The colon is placed before an explanation.
10. In small towns across the United States, strong values still **matter: hard** work, honesty, and family. *Hard work, honesty,* and *family* summarize strong values.

EXERCISE 4: *pages 133, 134.*

1. **Lori's** Add *'s* after a singular noun.
2. **anyone's** Add *'s* after an indefinite pronoun.
3. **lawyers'** Add *'* after a plural noun that ends in *-s.*
4. **his** Possessive pronouns do not have apostrophes.
5. **voters'** Add *'* after a plural noun that ends in *-s.*
6. **hers** Possessive pronouns do not have apostrophes.
7. **James's** Add *'s* after a singular noun. Some writers will add only an apostrophe to a name that ends in -s. In some situations, omitting the *-s* is acceptable. However, adding *'s* after a singular noun is always correct, so include the *-s.*
8. **children's** Add *'s* to a plural noun that does not end in *-s.*

9. **ours** Possessive pronouns do not have apostrophes.
10. **baby's** Add *'s* to a singular noun.
11. **Everybody's** Add *'s* to an indefinite pronoun.
12. **theirs** Possessive pronouns do not have apostrophes.
13. **year's** Add *'s* to a singular noun.
14. **people's** Add *'s* to a plural noun that does not end in *-s.*
15. **Stephens's** Add *'s* after a singular noun. Some writers will add only an apostrophe to a name that ends in -s. In some situations, omitting the *-s* is acceptable. However, adding *'s* after a singular noun is always correct, so you might as well include the *-s.*

EXERCISE 5: *page 134.*

1. **Gale and Myleen's** Gale and Myleen shared one trip. Note that *trip* is singular.
2. **step-sister's** Add *'s* to the last word in the compound.
3. **Kristin and Pat's** Kristin and Pat share a son. Note that *son* is singular.
4. **Kay's and Phil's** Kay and Phil each have their own writing skills.
5. **brother-in-law's** Add *'s* to the last word in the compound.
6. **Brian, Rachel, Deena, and David's** They all share the same day-care center. Note that *center* is singular.
7. **mother-in-law's** Add *'s* to the last word in the compound.
8. **Greg's and Rye's** Greg and Rye each have their own bad habits. Note that *habits* is plural.
9. **Erin's and Doris's** Erin and Doris each have their own reasons. Note that *reasons* is plural.
10. **Rose and Juan's** Rose and Juan share a car. Note that *car* is singular.

EXERCISE 6: *page 135.*

1. **your** *You* owns the hair.
2. **Whose** *Who* owns the car. Possessive pronouns do not have apostrophes.

3. **It's** It is a bad habit.
4. **Their** They own the check.
5. **Who's** Who is the lead actor?
6. **you're** I want to be sure that you are ready.
7. **they're** Jim just heard that they are moving.
8. **its** It owns the back wheel.
9. **Whose** *Who* owns the toys. Possessive pronouns do not have apostrophes.
10. **It's** It is a great day.

EXERCISE 7: *page 136.*

1. **"Golf** is good walk **spoiled,"** said Mark Twain. These are his exact words.
2. Our boss announced that we will have fewer hours this year. This is an indirect quotation. Note *that.* Do not add quotation marks.
3. **"I** don't want **much,"** he said, **"I** just want to spend more time with my **family."** These are his exact words.
4. **"I** remain just one thing, and one thing only — and that is a **clown,"** said Charlie Chaplin. These are his exact words.
5. John said that he wants to take a trip to Greece. This is an indirect quotation. Note *that.* Do not add quotation marks.
6. **"The** day has just **begun,"** she sang. These are her exact words.
7. He argued that we spent too much time on this project. This is an indirect quotation. Note *that.* Do not add quotation marks.
8. During the speech Barb whispered, **"If** we all put our heads down, maybe he will stop talking, and we will go **home."** These are her exact words.
9. Will Rogers said that he didn't know jokes, he just watched the government and reported the facts. This is an indirect quotation. Note *that.* Do not add quotation marks.

10. **"I** need a **break!"** he yelled. These are his exact words.

EXERCISE 8: *page 137.*

1. The article **"New** Toys for **Fishermen"** appeared in the last issue of *Field and Stream. New Toys for Fisherman* is the title of an article in a magazine.
2. Billy Joel's song **"Goodnight** My **Angel"** will put her to sleep. A song is part of a larger work, an album.
3. Chapter 7, which is titled **"What** We Live **By,"** made me think about many things in my life. A chapter is part of a larger work, a book.
4. **"The** Stone in the **Road"** is a story that you will like. Short stories need quotation marks.
5. In my view, **"discipline"** means setting limits. *Discipline* is defined.
6. Have you read the poem titled **"The Busy Man?"** Poems need quotation marks.

EXERCISE 9: *pages 137, 138.*

1. They say, **"there** are at least one thousand chips in every bag of **cookies"; but** how do they know? Semicolons are place outside quotation marks.
2. When he shouted," Ump, you are **crazy!" he** was thrown out of the game. Only the quotation needs the exclamation mark.
3. Have you heard the song called **"The Dance"** on the radio? The name of the song has quotation marks.
4. When he asked, "Why do teens join **gangs?"** I did not know what to say. The question mark is only for the quotation.
5. The sign says, "You must be as tall as my hand to go on this **ride."** Periods go inside quotation marks.
6. He shouted, "You're out**!"** Only the quotation needs the exclamation point.

7. Are you sure he said, "we need to hire four more **drivers**"? The question mark is for the whole sentence.
8. I now know the real meaning of **"taxes":** watching someone else spend your money. Colons are placed outside of quotation marks.
9. She said, "We need to talk." Periods are placed inside quotation marks.
10. Jim screamed, "I want to go **home!"** as his mother pushed the cart through the food store. Only the quotation needs an exclamation mark.

CHAPTER REVIEW

EXERCISE 1: *page 138.*

We have moved many times,[1] but moving does not get much easier with experience. When we search for a new home, we look for the following features:[2] an affordable house, a nice neighborhood, excellent schools,[3] and a good commute to work. Generally we've[4] moved into homes that we've[5] enjoyed,[6] but finding a nice home in a new town is hard. One needs to learn about the town, which can vary from one neighborhood to another; the schools, which are different for every child;[7] and the surrounding area. The meetings with realtors seem endless; however,[8] a good realtor can help make the move a little easier. Every move is hard;[9] it's[10] important to take the time to do it right.

1. Use a comma with the conjunction *but* to join two independent clauses.
2. Use a colon to introduce a list. *The following* signals a list.
3. Use commas to separate items in a series. This series includes *house, neighborhood,* and *schools.*
4. Use an apostrophe for contractions. *We've* is a contraction of *we have.*
5. Use an apostrophe for contractions. *We've* is a contraction of *we have.*
6. Use a comma with the conjunction *but* to join two independent clauses.

7. Use semicolons to separate items in the series that also use commas. *Which can vary from one neighborhood to another* and *which are different for every child* are clauses that should be set off with commas because they are not important.
8. *However* is a conjunctive adverb. It should have a semicolon before and a comma after it. Inserting a period after *endless* and capitalizing *however* also would be correct.
9. Use a semicolon to join two independent clauses without a conjunction.
10. Use an apostrophe for contractions. *It's* is a contraction of *it is.*

EXERCISE 2: *pages 138, 139.*

We promised to help celebrate Kathy's[1] birthday. Nonetheless, when we walked into the house,[2] I knew we were in trouble. As we strolled through the front door,[3] Ruth said,[4] "There must be thirty children here."[5] "Yeah,"[6] Russ added,[7] "and they're climbing the walls."[8] We couldn't[9] believe our eyes:[10] two adults were trying to entertain thirty six-year-olds without driving themselves crazy. It seemed impossible. Suddenly Joe yelled,[11] "Toss me some eggs,"[12] and he started to juggle. Ruth's[13] magic tricks also got their attention. Before long the children were spellbound, and the adults regained their sanity:[14] mission accomplished.

1. Use an apostrophe to show possession. Whose birthday? Kathy's.
2. Use a comma to separate the dependent clause *when we walked into the house.*
3. Use a comma to separate the introductory clause *as we strolled through the front door.*
4. Use a comma to separate the speaker from the quotation. Insert the comma after the "talking" word *said.*
5. Use quotation marks for direct quotations. Note that the period is inside the quotation marks.

6. Use quotation marks for direct quotations. Note that the comma is inside the quotation marks.

7. Use commas to separate the speaker from the quotation.

8. Use quotation marks for direct quotations. Note that the period is inside the quotation marks.

9. Use an apostrophe for contractions. *Couldn't* is a contraction of *could not.*

10. Use a colon to show that an explanation will follow. *Two adults...crazy* explains why *we couldn't believe our eyes.* A semicolon also would be appropriate.

11. Use a comma to separate the speaker from the quotation. Place the comma after the "talking" word.

12. Use quotation marks for direct quotations, and a comma to join two independent clauses with the conjunction *and.* Note that the comma is placed inside the quotation marks.

13. Use an apostrophe to show possession. Whose magic tricks? Ruth's

14. Use a colon to show that a summary will follow. *Mission accomplished* summarizes what happened.

EXERCISE 3: *page 139.*

By now everyone knows that eating right and exercising are important; however,[1] life is not that easy. Every time I see the doctor, she asks,[2] "How often do you exercise?"[3] "Not often enough,"[4] I respond. People who travel struggle to find decent meals and a place to work out. Parents'[5] schedules are hectic:[6] work, trips to the doctor, soccer games, PTA meetings. Students even have trouble fitting good food and exercise into their lives. We all need to step back and look at our priorities. If we don't[7] take care of ourselves,[8] who will? Even though it's[9] hard,[10] we need to take the frustrations out of our lives and put the healthy habits back in.

1. *However* is a conjunctive adverb. Use a semicolon before and a comma after *however.*

2. Use a comma to separate the speaker from the quotation. Place the comma after the "talking" word *asks.*

3. Use quotation marks for direct quotations. Note that the question mark is inside the quotation because only the quotation is a question.

4. Use quotation marks for direct quotations and commas to separate the quotation from the speaker. Note that the comma is inside the quotation mark.

5. Use an apostrophe to show possession. Whose schedules are hectic? Parents'. Note that *parents* is plural and it ends in *-s.* Add just an apostrophe.

6. Use a colon to signal that a summary or explanation will follow. *Work, trips to the doctor, soccer games,* and *PTA meetings* explain why parents' schedules are hectic.

7. Use an apostrophe for contractions. *Don't* is a contraction of *do not.*

8. Use a comma after an introductory clause.

9. Use an apostrophe for contractions. *It's* is a contraction of *it is.*

10. Use a comma after an introductory clause.

CHAPTER 10: CAPITALIZATION

EXERCISE 1: *pages 140, 141.*

1. **My** boss said, "**We** need a longer lunch break. **A** half hour is not enough time." *My, We* and *A* all begin sentences.

2. I wrote a letter about health care to **Senator** Robb, and **I** sent a copy to Vi Rus, my doctor. *Senator* is a title, and the pronoun *I* is always capitalized. *Doctor* is not capitalized because it appears after the name.

3. **no changes** *A professor* is a title that follows a name. It should not be capitalized.

4. **In** her book, Jan wrote, "**Meeting** friends is hard for some people." *In* is the first word of the sentence. *Meeting* is the first word of a sentence that is a quotation.

5. **Dr**. Seuss's book, ***The Cat** in the **Hat***, is a big hit with children. *Dr.* is a title and the first word of a sentence. *The, cat,* and *hat* should be capitalized because they are major words in a title.

6. Susan said, "**We** get more conservative as we age." *We* is the first word of a sentence that is a quotation.

7. **no changes** The title *mayor* comes after the name.

8. The song "**Let's Give Them Something To Talk About**" reminds me of you. Each word in the title is a major word. *To* is not a preposition; it is part of the infinitive *to talk. About* is a preposition, but it is the last word in the title, so it is a major word.

9. Some people want **Governor** Weld and **Vice President** Gore to run in the next election. Both *Governor* and *Vice President* are titles that appear before names.

10. Ellen's music box plays "**Ring** around the **Rosie**." *Ring* and *Rosie* are major words. *Around* is a preposition, and *the* is an article.

EXERCISE 2: *page 142.*

1. On **Monday, Hope Church** will open a new soup kitchen at **Park Street** and **King Street**. *Monday* is a day of the week. *Hope Church* is an institution. *Park, King,* and *Street* are common nouns that are part of a name.

2. Blair **High School** held classes on **Veterans' Day**, but the students were off for **Labor Day**. *Blair High School* is an institution. *Veterans' Day* and *Labor Day* are holidays.

3. Christians read the **Bible**, and **Jews** read the **Talmud**. *Christians* and *Jews* are worshippers. The *Bible* and *Talmud* are holy books.

4. **My** mom came all the way from **France** to see me. *My* is the first word of the sentence. *France* is a geographical name. Do not capitalize *mom*, which is a common noun in this sentence.

5. **The Purple Heart** and the **Bronze Star** are meaningful awards. *The Purple Heart* and *Bronze Star* are names of specific awards.

6. The **Renaissance** was a time of great art and music. The Renaissance is a historic period.

7. Aunt Sue and **Uncle** Peter are from the **South**, but they enjoyed traveling to **Vermont** and **New York**. *Uncle* is a common noun that is used as part of a name. *South* refers to the place, not the direction. *Vermont* and *New York* are states.

8. Dad studied **Russian** and **Spanish** when he worked for the **FBI**. *Russian* and *Spanish* are languages. *FBI* is an abbreviation of a proper noun (Federal Bureau of Investigation).

9. Many lakes, such as **Lake Champlain** and **Squam Lake**, attract tourists in the summer. When *lake* is part of a name, it is capitalized.

10. Did you know that **Grandma** liked **Nike's** commercials that aired during the **Super Bowl**? *Grandma* names a person. *Nike* is a company name. The *Super Bowl* is an event.

CHAPTER REVIEW

EXERCISE 1: *page 142.*

Reading is part of life. We[1] read road signs, recipes, directions, and newspapers daily. Your mom[2] may be able to prepare dinner without a recipe, but the rest of us depend on *Dinner in No Time*[3] or some other cookbook for help. Likewise, when we program the VCR, we read the directions. We check the paper for TV shows, such as *Wings,*[4] or special movies like *Twister*. At the health club, some people read the *New York Times* while they ride the bike. We even read our junk[5] mail. Reading doesn't just get us through the day; it opens up a whole new world.

1. Capitalize the first word in a sentence.
2. Do not capitalize common nouns. In this case, *mom* is not used as a name.
3. Capitalize major words in titles.
4. Capitalize major words in titles.
5. *Junk* is simply an adjective. Do not capitalize it.

EXERCISE 2: *page 143.*

Art, music, and literature touch our lives. A French[1] playwright said, "A[2] work of art is above all an adventure of the mind." Some people travel the world to see great works, such as *David* or the *Mona Lisa.*[3] Other people simply go to the library or turn on the radio to find great works. Books, such as the *Road Less Traveled,* make us think about our lives. Songs, such as "My Hometown," describe our feelings. We all can't travel to see art from the Renaissance[4] or hear great music, but we can enjoy the simple works that reach us every day.

1. Capitalize people and languages.
2. Capitalize the first word in a direct quotation.
3. Capitalize major words in titles.
4. Capitalize historic periods.

EXERCISE 3: *page 143.*

No one likes going to the dentist, but my dentist is good. Dr.[1] Aldrege, whose office is on Park Street,[2] has new issues of Time in her waiting room, and she is rarely late for an appointment. Her dental chair looks like the space shuttle Columbia, but she is great with my teeth. Dr.[3] Aldrege uses methods that the ADA[4] (American Dental Association) supports. When I leave her office, my teeth look and feel much better. I tell everyone, even my dad,[5] to go to Dr.[6] Aldrege. After all, going to the dentist does not have to be a bad experience.

1. Capitalize titles that appear before names.
2. Capitalize proper nouns.
3. Capitalize the first word in a sentence and proper nouns.

4. Capitalize abbreviations for proper nouns. *ADA* is an abbreviation for the American Dental Association.
5. Do not capitalize common nouns. In this sentence, *dad* is a common noun, not a name.
6. Capitalize titles that appear before names.

CHAPTER 11: SPELLING

EXERCISE 1: *page 145.*

1. separate
2. tear
3. raise
4. would
5. answer
6. busy
7. beginning
8. courses
9. February
10. forty
11. grammar
12. every
13. built
14. been
15. friends
16. hour
17. chose
18. wear
19. business
20. minute

EXERCISE 2: *page 146.*

1. balloon
2. athlete
3. awful
4. address
5. balance
6. argument
7. amount
8. accept
9. available
10. apply
11. attendance
12. approval
13. article
14. angles
15. no error

EXERCISE 3: *page 147.*

1. career
2. cigarette
3. no error
4. Beautiful
5. bicycle
6. citizen
7. ceiling
8. color
9. careful
10. breathe
11. committee
12. column
13. common
14. no error
15. company

EXERCISE 4: *page 148.*

1. decide
2. education
3. daughter
4. congratulate
5. dollar
6. death
7. doubt
8. corner
9. confident
10. eighth
11. early
12. dropped
13. dozen
14. dying
15. compliment

EXERCISE 5: *pages 148, 149.*

1. knife
2. island
3. immigrant
4. healthy
5. government
6. kindergarten
7. no error
8. holiday
9. foreign
10. finally
11. interesting
12. no error
13. fourth
14. jewelry
15. knock

EXERCISE 6: *pages 149, 150.*

1. misspelled
2. library
3. prejudice
4. medicine
5. niece
6. perform
7. no error
8. pencil
9. muscle
10. neighbor
11. maintenance
12. movable
13. no error
14. parallel
15. noticeable

EXERCISE 7: *page 150.*

1. recommend
2. no error
3. refugee
4. promptly
5. no error
6. probably
7. recognize
8. responsibility
9. realize
10. prescription
11. no error
12. afford
13. realistic
14. repetition
15. no error

EXERCISE 8: *page 151.*

1. stomach
2. soldiers
3. useful
4. temperatures
5. no error
6. sophomore
7. stopped
8. surprise
9. shoulder
10. source
11. succeed
12. no error
13. surrounded
14. reason
15. toward

EXERCISE 9: *page 151.*

1. Vegetables
2. weather
3. welfare
4. weird
5. view
6. valuable

EXERCISE 10: *pages 152, 153.*

1. believe
2. taxes
3. receive
4. caffeine
5. no error
6. seats
7. no error
8. protein
9. weight
10. boats

EXERCISE 11: *page 154.*

1. movement
2. meaningful
3. dazing
4. lovable
5. confused
6. arguing
7. advantageous
8. married
9. swimming
10. noticeable
11. stayed
12. misstate
13. tipped
14. likeness
15. unnatural
16. bountiful
17. consumable
18. disservice
19. beautifying
20. caring

CHAPTER REVIEW

EXERCISE 1: *page 155.*

1. different
2. Athletes
3. muscles
4. kitchen
5. shoppers
6. comfortable

7. really
8. Everybody
9. healthy
10. successful

EXERCISE 2: *page 155.*

1. stayed
2. factory
3. restaurants
4. secretaries
5. forty
6. doctors
7. fields
8. valuable
9. typically
10. controlled

CHAPTER 12: WORD CHOICE

EXERCISE 1: *page 158.*

1. accept
2. already
3. affect
4. between
5. number
6. as
7. bored
8. lend
9. take
10. buy
11. capital
12. dessert
13. emigrate
14. less
15. hear
16. desert
17. immigrate
18. fewer
19. like
20. except

EXERCISE 2: *pages 160, 161.*

1. whole
2. imply
3. know
4. teach
5. let
6. meat
7. plain
8. principle

9. quiet
10. stationary
11. sweat
12. there
13. too
14. whether
15. two
16. they're
17. teach
18. infer
19. quit
20. stationery

CHAPTER REVIEW

EXERCISE 1: *page 161.*

Exercise is important, but ~~less~~[1] young Americans are staying fit. While some young adults and children have become quite active, ~~to~~[2] many have ignored their bodies. ~~Stationery~~[3] lifestyles cause health problems. However, a good diet with few ~~sweats~~[4] and a decent exercise program can favorably affect our health. Most people already know what they need to do to improve their fitness; ~~their~~[5] just not doing it. We Americans need to quit making excuses and start breaking a sweat. We can't all look like the top athletes, but we can have healthy lifestyles.

1. Use *fewer* because one can count the number of young Americans.
2. In this case, *too* means "extremely."
3. Use *stationary* because the lifestyles don't have movement.
4. Sweets are sugary foods.
5. *They're* is a contraction for *they are.*

EXERCISE 2: *page 161.*

Buying a car takes time and effort. First, the buyer must ~~teach~~[1] about the different cars that are on the market and decide what type of car she wants. She may need to ~~lend~~[2] money and get insurance, ~~two~~.[3] After the preparations, the buyer and salesperson ~~meat~~[4] to agree upon a price. If the buyer already knows a lot about the car, she may get a better deal. After the sale, even more paperwork needs to be done. Many people are glad when the ~~hole~~[5] process is finally over.

1. Use *learn* because the buyer is gaining information about the cars.
2. Use *borrow* because she will receive money that she must return.
3. *Too* means "also."
4. Use *meet* to show that the buyer and salesperson get together.
5. *Whole* means "complete."

EXERCISE 3: *page 162.*

The number of people ~~emigrating~~[1] to America has increased in recent years, but the challenges they face are still the same. When people leave ~~there~~[2] native land, they have to ~~let~~[3] family and friends behind. When they arrive here, their lives change forever. ~~Weather~~[4] or not they are skilled, many immigrants have to accept jobs with low wages. Most immigrants also have to learn a whole new language and culture. In spite of these hardships, many immigrants are ~~quiet~~[5] successful in America.

1. Use *immigrate.* An immigrant goes into a country.
2. Use *their* to show possession.
3. Use *leave* to show that they go away.
4. Use *whether* when there is an option. In this case, the option is between having skills and not having skills.
5. Use *quite* to show that something happens to a degree. In this sentence, *quite* shows to what degree immigrants are successful.

PRACTICE FOR UNITS 1 THROUGH 4

1. **3** *For the past few decades* signals that the action began in the past and continues today. *Have neglected* is in the present perfect tense, which shows actions that started in the past and continue into the present. *Had neglected* is in the past perfect tense, which shows actions that were completed before a specific time or event in the past.

2. **5** The conjunction *but* joins two independent clauses. A comma is needed before the conjunction. The clauses could be joined with a semicolon because the first clause is long. However, *but* should not be capitalized as it is in option (2).

3. **4** Use the possessive form to show whose lives.

4. **2** Words are too full for two *L*'s on the end.

5. **5** The sentence is correct.

6. **4** When these sentences are joined, *which* introduces a clause that describes *fund*. The clause is nonrestrictive, so *which* should be used instead of *that*. *First, they must create an emergency fund, which holds enough money to cover expenses for three to six months.*

7. **3** *Which* introduces a nonrestrictive clause. The sentence makes sense without the clause. Nonrestrictive clauses are set off with commas.

8. **1** *Instead of saving for the future* is an introductory phrase. It should be set off with a comma.

9. **5** The sentence is correct.

10. **4** *Home, college, and retirement* form a series. Commas separate items in a series.

11. **1** *Learn* means "to gain understanding or information." *Teach* means "to give understanding or information." The planners give understanding.

12. **4** *Child car, work, and lifestyle changes* form a series. Commas separate items in a series.

13. **3** The new sentence joins two independent clauses. The first clause has commas, so the clauses must be combined using a semicolon.

14. **5** The semicolon shows that the two independent clauses are related. The two statements are not equal, and they do not give an option. Therefore, neither *and* nor *but* can be used.

15. **2** *Two* is the number 2. *Too* means "also or excessive."

16. **3** *The cost of child care, commuting, and services may outweigh the benefit of a second income in some families.*

17. **5** This sentence is correct.

18. **1** The new sentence combines two independent clauses that share the same subject. The new sentence has a compound verb. *Parents need to evaluate their concerns carefully and make choices that will have a lasting influence on themselves and their children.*

19. **3** *Every day* signals that the action happens repeatedly. In addition, the rest of the paragraph is in the present tense. Thus, the verb *emerge* should be in the present tense.

20. **4** In this sentence, *too* means also.

21. **1** This sentence has two independent clauses that are joined by *and*. A comma must be placed after the first independent clause.

22. **4** The paragraph is in the present tense.

23. **2** This sentence has a series that uses commas. Semicolons should separate the three items—income taxes, sales taxes, and property taxes.

24. **3** This word is often misspelled. Try the following: A license means you can start driving.

25. **2** *Their* is used to show possession. *They're* is the contraction of *they are*.

26. **1** Insert a comma between items in a series. A comma should not be placed after *police* because *police* and *fire* are adjectives that describe what type of protection.

27. **4** *Nobody* is singular. It should have the singular verb *wants*.

28. **4** *Departments* is a common noun. It should not be capitalized.

29. **3** *In the past* is an introductory phrase. Insert a comma after an introductory phrase.

30. **1** *Now* shows that this sentence is in the present tense.

31. **4** This is a common spelling mistake. Try the following: I want your <u>attention</u> <u>at</u> <u>ten</u>.

32. **2** *When all laws are upheld* is an introductory clause. Insert a comma after an introductory clause.

33. **5** This sentence is correct.

34. **2** *But* is a conjunction that joins two independent clauses.

35. **1** *That works to protect people's rights* is a nonrestrictive clause that is set off by commas. Without the clause, the reader still knows which group has noted the complaints against the police. Use *which*, instead of *that*, for nonrestrictive clauses.

36. **3** This is a common spelling mistake. Try the following: The <u>baby</u> <u>probably</u> cried.

37. **3** This is a common spelling mistake. Try the following: Was the <u>interview</u> <u>interesting</u>?

38. **5** In the first sentence *the market* is the subject, and *was dominated* is the verb. *By business programs and computer games* is a prepositional phrase that tells how the market was dominated. The new sentence reads, "Business programs and computer games dominated the market for years." In the new sentence, *business programs and computer games* is the subject. *Dominated* is the verb, and *the market* is the object of the verb. Both sentences have the same meaning.

39. **1** *Now* signals the present tense.

40. **2** *However* is a conjunctive adverb, which joins two independent clauses. Place a semicolon before conjunctive adverbs and a comma after them.

41. **3** *Software can't solve every problem; nonetheless, computer programs do help children with their homework and adults with their taxes. Nonetheless* is a conjunctive adverb. It forms a relationship between the two independent clauses. *Nonetheless* shows that even though software can't solve every problem, it still is helpful. The other options—*and, so, or,* and *therefore*—do not show the correct relationship between the two sentences.

42. **4** *Trace* and *track* are in the present tense. *Create* is part of the compound verb, and it should be in the same tense as the other verbs.

43. **1** The list ~~of programs~~ keeps growing. The verb must agree with the subject, *list*.

44. **5** *By making computers more accessible, manufacturers have increased the number of computer users.* In both sentences, *by making computers more accessible* is a phrase that describes how manufacturers have increased the number of computer users. In the new sentence, the phrase is simply moved to the front.

45. **4** This word is often misspelled. Try the following: <u>Differ</u> to be <u>different</u>

46. **3** *However* is a conjunctive adverb. It shows the relationship between the two independent clauses. Place semicolons before conjunctive adverbs and commas after them.

47. **2** *When parents regularly participate in school activities* is an introductory clause. It must be followed by a comma.

48. **1** *Education matters* summarizes the message that parents must send. The other options do not show the relationship between the two sentences.

49. **4** *Confident* and *eager* describe *children*. Because the adjectives are equally important, they must be separated by a comma.
50. **2** *Their* is used to show possession. In this sentence, *their* refers to *schools*.
51. **3** *Who* is used for people, and *which* is used for animals or things.
52. **2** The word is often misspelled. Try the following: Let them be ath<u>le</u>tic.
53. **5** This sentence is correct.
54. **1** Assist whom or what? *Whoever needs help. Whoever* is the subject of the clause.
55. **4** Whose schools? *America*'s. The apostrophe is needed to show possession.

CHAPTER 13: WRITING CLEAR SENTENCES

EXERCISE 1: *page 180.*

1. **and** *And* adds two equal statements.
2. **so** *So* shows why something happened. Why did Lou save his money?
3. **yet, but** *Yet* means however. *But* shows that something is unexpected. The reader may not expect that some people will love snakes.
4. **or** *Or* shows an option, ordering pizza or preparing food.
5. **yet, but** *Yet* means however. *But* shows that something is unexpected.
6. **so** *So* shows why something happens. Why did Kyle work hard?
7. **and** *And* adds two equal statements.
8. **so** *So* shows why something happens. Why did Nu work hard?
9. **or** *Or* shows an option, go to college or go to work.
10. **and** *And* adds two equal statements.

EXERCISE 2: *pages 181, 182.*

1. **to charm his girlfriend, to impress his friends, and to please his parents** In the original sentence, *to charm* and *to impress* are in the infinitive form. All of the verbs in a series should be in the same form.
2. **Free food, great music, and good weather** *That was free*, *great*, and *good* all work like adjectives. They should be in the same form.
3. **carefully, regularly, and knowledgeably** *Carefully*, *regularly*, and *with knowledge* all work like adverbs. They should be in the same form.
4. **quiet, bright, relaxing place to study** *Quiet*, *bright*, and *that is relaxing* are all adjectives that describe *place*. They should be in the same form.
5. **through town, over the bridge, and past the town pool** *Through town*, *over the bridge*, and *past the town pool* are prepositional phrases that work as adverbs. They tell where to drive, and they should be in the same form.
6. **ignored scientific research, testified before Congress, and fought lawsuits against them** *Ignored*, *testified*, and *fought* are verbs that should be in the same form.
7. **happily, repeatedly, and kindly** *Happily*, *repeatedly*, and *with kindness* describe how people volunteer. They should be in the same form.
8. **a good reputation, athletic programs, and a reasonable tuition** *Good*, *athletic*, and *that is reasonable* work like adjectives. They should be in the same form.

9. **various books, on-line computers, and children's materials** *Various, on-line, and that are for children* work like adjectives. They should be in the same form.
10. **large, open, well-designed gym** *Large*, *open*, and *that is well designed* work like adjectives and describe *gym*. They should be in the same form.

EXERCISE 3: *pages 183, 184.*

Each question has more than one correct answer.

1. **The new player is tall and athletic.** *Tall* and *athletic* are adjectives that describe *player*. They should be in the same form.
2. **Running daily and eating well are important for me.** *Running daily* and *eating well* are phrases that work like nouns. They form the compound subject.
   OR
   To run daily and to eat well are important to me. *To run daily* and *to eat well* are phrases that work like nouns. They form the compound subject.
3. **Nate shops for food each week and does the laundry.** *Nate* performs both actions. This sentence has a compound verb *shops* and *does*.
   OR
   Nate shops for food each week, and he does the laundry. *Nate* performs both actions. This compound sentence has a pronoun.
4. **The coach thinks that playing well is more important than winning every game.** This sentence compares *playing* and *winning*. Both words should be in the same form.
   OR
   The coach thinks that to play well is more important than to win every game. This sentence compares *to play* with *to win*.

5. **Matt works late and prepares dinner when he gets home.** *Matt* performs both actions. *Works* and *prepares* form a compound verb.
6. **Many doctors think that finding a cure for cancer is as important as researching heart disease.** This sentence compares *finding a cure* to *research on heart disease.* Both phrases should be in the same form.
7. **In the city, many people argue that improving the schools is as important as lowering crime rates.** In this sentence, *improving the schools* is compared to *to lower crime rates.* Both phrases should be in the same form.
8. **Tourists enjoy hearing the Cleveland Orchestra and visiting the Cleveland Museum of Art.** *Hearing* and *to visit* should be in the same form. They are both things that tourists enjoy.
9. **Ray fixed the car and stained the deck.** Ray performed both actions. *Fixed* and *stained* form a compound verb.
10. **Writing poetry and composing music have some similarities.** *Writing* and *to compose* work as subjects in this sentence. They should be in the same form.

EXERCISE 4: *page 184.*

1. **watches** *Every Friday* shows that the action happens repeatedly. Therefore, both verbs, *orders* and *watches*, should be in the present tense.
2. **will cut** *Next week* signals that the action will happen in the future. Both verbs, *will clean* and *will cut*, should be in the future tense.
3. **moved** *Last month* signals that the action happened in the past. Both verbs, *bought* and *moved*, should be in the past tense.
4. **will pass** *Next year* signals that the action will happen in the future. Both verbs, *will pass* and *will sign*, should be in the future tense.

5. **acted** *On Monday* does not give enough information. The actions could have happened last Monday, or they may occur next Monday. However, *walked* is in the past tense, so *acted* should be in the past tense.

6. **ended** *Last week* signals the past tense. Both verbs, *signed* and *ended*, should be in the past tense.

7. **will invest** *In the next few years* signals the future tense. Both verbs, *will invest* and *will bring*, should be in the future tense.

8. **attracts** *Every year* signals that the actions occur regularly. Both verbs, *lures* and *attracts*, should be in the present tense.

9. **established** In this sentence, the only signal word is the verb *overturned*, which is in the past tense. Both verbs, *overturned* and *established*, should be in the past tense because they occur at the same time.

10. **taught** *Last year* signals the past tense. Both verbs, *took* and *taught*, should be in the past tense.

EXERCISE 5: *pages 185, 186.*

1. **had won** <u>After</u> Shantae won, he waved. Both actions occurred in the past, but one action was completed before the other action began. Use the past perfect tense (had + verb) for the first action.

2. **rush** <u>When</u> the weather reports predict, people rush. Both actions happen repeatedly at the same time. Both verbs should be in the present tense.

3. **will find** If he does not return, I will find. *Return* is in the present tense. Any action that happens next is in the future, so *will find* is in the future tense.

4. **will be** Because it will rain, the traffic will be. Both actions occur at the same time in the future. *Will rain* and *will be* should be in the future tense.

5. **talked or was talking** I washed <u>while</u> I talked. Both actions occur at the same time in the past. *Was talking* shows that the subject talked on the phone for some time.

6. **will win** Anne will win, if she gives. *Gives* is in the present tense. Any action that happens next is in the future, so *will win* is in the future tense.

7. **had cleaned** Before my friends arrived, I had cleaned. Both actions occurred in the past, but one action was finished before the other began. Use the past perfect tense (had + verb) for the first action.

8. **had studied** After we had studied, we relaxed and watched. All three actions occurred in the past, but one action was completed before the other actions began. Use the past perfect tense (had + verb) for the first action.

9. **will have cooked** John will have cooked before next Sunday. The action will be completed before a specific time in the future. Use the future perfect tense (will have + verb).

10. **will put** As soon as the check arrives, Han will put. *Arrives* is in the present tense. Any action that happens next is in the future, so *will put* is in the future tense.

EXERCISE 6: *pages 186, 187.*

1. **Used properly, air bags and seat belts can save lives.** *Used properly* describes *air bags*, the first noun after the comma.

2. **After school, children often watch TV until their parents come home.** *After school* describes when children watch TV.

3. **Homes with flood damage are being moved to higher ground.** *With flood damage* describes *homes*. Who would move <u>to</u> ground with flood damage?

4. **The working poor, struggling to pay the bills, often cannot afford good health care.** *Struggling to pay the bills* describes *working poor.* In the original sentence, *struggling to pay the bills* describes *health care.*

5. **Tired from the flu, I called in sick to work.** *Tired from the flu* describes *I*, which is the first noun after the comma. In the original sentence, *tired from the flu* describes *work.*

6. **Lim unintentionally found a good plumber to fix his sink.** *Unintentionally* is an adverb that shows how Lim found the plumber. The original sentence does not make sense; *unintentionally* describes how the plumber fixes the sink.

7. **Dr. Tim tells people with weight problems to eat a low-fat diet and exercise.** *With weight problems* describes *people.* In the original sentence, *with weight problems* describes *exercise.*

8. **Some people who want to choose their own doctors are frustrated with HMOs.** *Who want to choose their own doctors* describes *people.* In the original sentence, *who want to choose their own doctors* describes *HMOs.*

9. **Concerned about the risk of inflation, the Chair of the Federal Reserve will raise interest rates.** *Concerned about the risk of inflation* describes *Chair.* In the original sentence, the phrase describes *rates.*

10. **Some people use dogs that are trained to help the visually impaired.** *Trained to help the visually impaired* describes *dogs.* In the original sentence, the phrase describes *people*, which does not make sense.

EXERCISE 7: *pages 188, 189.*

There is more than one possible answer to each question.

1. **While I was climbing up the mountain face, my foot slipped.** In the original sentence, my foot climbed up the mountain face alone.

2. **While the police were searching for clues to the crime, the police car was stolen.** In the original sentence, the police car was searching for clues to the crime.

3. **When we were tired and hungry, our museum tour ended.** In the original sentence, the museum tour was tired and hungry.

4. **While I was checking my watch, the sun came out from behind the clouds.** In the original sentence, the sun was checking my watch.

5. **When the voters became frustrated with campaign funding, reform bills quickly passed through Congress.** In the original sentence, the reform bills were frustrated.

6. **After Kim checked all the numbers, she mailed her tax return to the IRS.** In the original sentence, the tax return checked the numbers.

7. **Ty searched the want ads for a job with steady hours and good pay.** In the original sentence, Ty had steady hours and good pay.

8. **When I was running to catch the bus, my briefcase spilled all over the sidewalk.** In the original sentence, the briefcase was running to catch the bus.

9. **When we became angered by the slow response, the ambulance finally arrived at the scene.** In the original sentence, the ambulance was angered.

10. **The salesperson showed us the new cars, which were fresh off the delivery truck.** In the original sentence, the salesperson was fresh off the delivery truck.

EXERCISE 8: *page 189.*

1. **they** *They* refers to *doctors.*
2. **she** *She* refers to *Ms. Tran.*
3. **it** *It* refers to the drug test, which is singular.
4. **It** *It* refers to our food store, which is singular. (To agree with *it, open* should be changed to *opens. Close* should be changed to *closes,* and *carry* should be changed to *carries.*)
5. **they** *They* refers to the school board members. The board members were on TV, not the budget cut. (To agree with *they, was* should be changed to *were.*)
6. **it** *It* refers to CPR. *During her first aid classes* is a prepositional phrase that shows when Jill learned CPR. Therefore, the pronoun should refer to *CPR,* not *classes.*
7. **she** The pronoun should refer to *Kathy,* not *classes.*
8. **one** Use *one* for a general statement. (To agree with *one, need* should be changed to *needs.*)
9. **it** The pronoun refers to Japan. Glen was not the only person hit by the earthquake.
10. **it** The pronoun refers to the Smithsonian Institution, not James Smithson. He has been dead for years.

EXERCISE 9: *pages 190, 191.*

1. Because ivory tusks are valuable, hunters slaughter elephants.
2. Although wildlife groups work hard to save species, some animals may not survive.
3. TV violence affects children.
4. Gas, maintenance, and insurance are expensive, so car owners must be prepared to spend a lot of money. OR Gas, maintenance, and insurance are expensive; therefore, car owners must be prepared to spend a lot of money.
5. Whenever one lifts something heavy, back support is important.
6. Rabid animals sometimes infect persons.
7. Because they do not pay their bills on time, some persons earn bad credit ratings.
8. People with bad debts are helped by financial planners.
9. The liver and other organs can be destroyed by alcoholism over time.
10. Because their child would go to college, Jim and Pat saved money each year.

EXERCISE 10: *pages 192–194.*

Each question has more than one correct answer.

1. **a.** Kay was struggling to pay her **bills, so** she took an extra job on weekends.
   b. Kay was struggling to pay her **bills; therefore, she** took an extra job on weekends.
   Kay was struggling to pay her bills shows why *she took an extra job on weekends.*
2. **a.** Han wants to let her daughter play **outside, but** there is too much violence in their neighborhood.
   b. Han wants to let her daughter play **outside; however, there** is too much violence in their neighborhood.
   There is a difference between what Han wants to do and what she can do.

3. **a.** Tim drops Greg off at day-care in the **morning, and** Shavone picks Greg up after work.

   b. Tim drops Greg off at day-care in the **morning; likewise, Shavone** picks Greg up after work

   And and *likewise* show that two equal statements are added together.

4. **a.** Ray wants to star in the school **play, but** he has not learned his lines.

   b. Ray wants to star in the school **play; still, he** has not learned his lines.

   But and *still* show that there is a difference between what Ray wants and what may happen.

5. **a.** Eve wants to learn a new software program by **Friday, yet** she needs to prepare for her presentation, which is tomorrow.

   b. Eve wants to learn a new software program by **Friday; instead, she** needs to prepare for her presentation, which is tomorrow.

   Yet and *instead* show that there is a difference between what Eve wants to do and what she needs to do.

6. **a.** Credit card debt can destroy a family's **finances, so** it is better to buy only what one can afford to pay in cash.

   b. Credit card debt can destroy a family's **finances; thus, it** is better to buy only what one can afford to pay in cash.

   So and *thus* show that the first statement explains why the second statement is true.

7. **a.** Most people know the dangers of **smoking, yet** teenage tobacco use continues to increase.

   b. Most people know the dangers of **smoking, nonetheless, teenage** tobacco use continues to increase.

   Yet and *nonetheless* shows that there is a difference between what people know about smoking and what they do about it.

8. **a.** Politicians keep talking about cutting government **spending, but** few people want to give up the government services that they use.

   b. Politicians keep talking about cutting government **spending; however, few** people want to give up the government services that they use.

   But and *however* show that there is a difference between what politicians talk about and what actually happens.

9. **a.** The tax code in America is **complex, so** many Americans must pay a professional to do their taxes.

   b. The tax code in America is **complex; consequently, many** Americans must pay a professional to do their taxes.

   So and *consequently* show that the first statement explains why the second statement is true.

10. **a.** Ray needs more training for his **job, so** he is taking a computer class on weekends.

    b. Ray needs more training for his **job; therefore, he** is taking a computer class on weekends.

    So and *therefore* show that the first statement explains why the second statement is true.

EXERCISE 11: *pages 195, 196.*

These are suggestions. There is more than one possible answer to each question.

1. **When Matt's mom came home from work, he was excited to see her.** The original sentences are related by time.

2. **We were sitting at the stoplight, and we could hear music blaring from another car, which was across the street.** In the original sentences, the second sentence gives additional information about the car in the first sentence.

3. **Because Salma had a bad cold, Salma's mother could not leave her at day-care.** The original sentences are related by cause and effect. The first sentence shows the cause, and the second sentence tells the effect.

4. **Although Anh finished his test in less than thirty minutes, he did not have many correct answers.** The original sentences show a contrast. One might expect that Anh would do well on the test because he finished so quickly.

5. **Whenever the lights on a school bus flash, cars must stop so that students can exit the bus safely.** The original sentences are related by time.

6. **Nathan paints landscapes as well as Kayla does.** The original sentences show a comparison between Nathan and Kayla.

7. **While the tornado whipped through the town, people huddled in their basements hoping they would be safe.** The original sentences are related by time.

8. **Very few people voted in the primary elections, which will determine the Republican candidates.** The original sentences are related by information. The second sentence provides additional information about the elections.

9. **Although Wolf wanted to swim to cool off from the hot weather, the water in the pool was too cold.** The original sentences show a contrast. There is a difference between what Wolf wanted to do and what he did.

10. **Many people in the Midwest desperately need flood relief, which politicians promised to give a month ago.** The original sentences are related by information. The second sentence gives additional information about flood relief.

CHAPTER REVIEW

EXERCISE 1: *pages 196–198.*

1. **3 areas and creating** *Discovering* and *creating* form a compound verb. Both verbs should be in the same form.

2. **4 now** *Townhouses and strip malls now dominate the land where farms and orchards once stood.*

3. **1 but** *Although* and *but* show a contrast. There is a difference between how some people feel about the developments and how others feel. *These new developments delight some people, but they frustrate others.*

4. **5 burdens local services** *Changes, crowds,* and *are burdened* form a compound verb. All of the verbs should be in the same form.

5. **5 no correction necessary** Option (1) is wrong because a comma after *housing* is unnecessary. Option (2) is wrong because *are working* shows that the action is in the present tense. Option (3) is wrong because a comma after *leaders* is unnecessary. Option (4) is wrong because *with the need* does not modify *setting.*

6. **3 which protects** The second sentence gives additional information about the project. *Which protects over 93,000 acres of land from development* is an adjective clause that modifies *project. In Montgomery County, Maryland, county leaders established a preservation project, which protects over 93,000 acres of land from development.*

7. **5 want** *Although* and *but* both show a contrast. There are different views of the project. *Although many people want the preservation project to continue, others want it to end.*

8. **1 move *that is preserved* after land** *That is preserved* is an adjective clause. In the original sentence, the clause modifies *money*. The clause should modify *land*. *Farmers, who own much of the land that is preserved, are losing money.*

9. **3 change *stores for retail* to *retail stores*** New housing, *office space, and stores for retail* form a series. Each item in the series should be in the same form (adjective + noun).

10. **5 no correction necessary** Option (1) is wrong because a comma after *jobs* is unnecessary. Option (2) is wrong because *they* is used for people, and *it* is used for things. Option (3) is wrong because the subject and verb should be plural. Option (4) is wrong because *to the county* works as an adverb clause that answers the question where.

11. **2 move *between developers and preservationists* after *debate*** *Between developers and preservationists* is a prepositional phrase that describes *debate*. In the original sentence, the phrase describes *years*.

EXERCISE 2: *pages 198, 199.*

1. **3 parties that are used** The second sentence gives additional information about *parties*. The adjective phrase *that are used to sell products* describes *parties*. *Home parties that are used to sell products are making a comeback.*

2. **2 move *with friends and neighbors* after *socializing*** *With friends and neighbors* is a prepositional phrase that describes *socializing*. In the original sentence, the phrase describes *goods*. The goods do not have friends and neighbors.

3. **4 , now many** *Although* and *but* show a contrast. There is a difference between home parties in the past and home parties today. *Although Tupperware has sold its products through home*

parties *for years, now many different companies use home parties to market their goods.*

4. **5 no correction necessary** Option (1) is wrong because the comma sets off an introductory phrase. Option (2) is wrong because *parties* is the plural of party. It is not possessive. Option (3) is wrong because a comma after *baskets* is unnecessary. Option (4) is wrong because *today* signals that the sentence is in the present tense.

5. **1 trend, which started** The second sentence provides additional information. *Which started in the early nineties* is an adjective clause that describes *trend*. *This sales trend, which started in the early nineties, has developed for a number of reasons.*

6. **5 have become** *Have become* is in the present perfect tense so that it will agree with the rest of the paragraph.

7. **3 have been encouraged** In the original sentence, *busy lifestyles* is the subject. In the new sentence, *some people* is the subject, and *by busy lifestyles* is part of a prepositional phrase that tells how some people have been encouraged. *Some people have been encouraged by busy lifestyles to shop in these social settings.*

8. **4 replace *have* with *has*** *Inventory*, the subject, is singular. (Do not be fooled by *of goods*, a prepositional phrase that should be ignored.) The verb should also be singular.

9. **5 no correction necessary** Option (1) is wrong because *whatever the reason* is an introductory phrase that should be set off by a comma. Option (2) is wrong because *this* is singular; therefore, the verb should be singular. Option (3) is wrong because *that will continue* is a restrictive clause; it tells which trend. Restrictive clauses use *that* and do not have commas. Option (4) is wrong because the sentence is about the future.

CHAPTER 14: WRITING PARAGRAPHS

EXERCISE 1: *pages 201–203.*

These topic sentences are suggestions. There is more than one correct answer for each question.

1. **Dan is not doing well in school.** The first four sentences give examples of Dan's poor performance. The fifth sentence shows what Dan needs to do about his poor performance.
2. **Even though this was the worst flood in years, our town will survive.** The first three sentences in the paragraph show how destructive the flood was. The last two sentences show why the town will survive.
3. **Although activities are important for children, they can become overwhelming.** The first two sentences show why children are involved in activities. The last three sentences tell what can happen if children have too many activities.
4. **Aggressive drivers have become a concern recently.** The first two sentences show how aggressive driving has changed recently. The last two sentences show why aggressive driving is a concern.
5. **The labor laws in France hurt the nation's economy.** The first sentence explains what the labor laws do. The other sentences show why the labor laws are bad for the economy of France.
6. **The snow storm on April Fool's Day was frustrating.** Each sentence in the paragraph tells why the storm was frustrating.
7. **The symptoms of appendicitis are important to recognize**. The first three sentences describe the symptoms, and the last sentence tells what one should do about the symptoms.
8. **Walkers are dangerous.** The first sentence explains how walkers have been used. The second sentence tells how doctors' views on walkers have changed because of the danger. The last four sentences explain why walkers are dangerous.
9. **Red meat is not as popular as it was years ago.** The first and second sentences show that red meat was popular in the past. The last three sentences explain why red meat is not as popular as it used to be.
10. **Construction equipment thrills young children.** The first and second sentences tell why children like construction equipment. The last sentence shows one effect of children's interest in construction equipment.

EXERCISE 2: *pages 203, 204.*

1. TOPIC SENTENCE: Searching for a new job requires a lot of hard work and patience.
   d. **Congress recently increased the minimum wage.** This sentence is related to work, but it has nothing to do with searching for new job.
2. TOPIC SENTENCE: Soccer has become a popular sport in America.
   c. **Leg injuries are common in many sports.** Leg injuries have nothing to do with soccer becoming a popular sport.
   e. **Lacrosse is also very popular in some areas.** The popularity of lacrosse is not related to soccer.
3. TOPIC SENTENCE: Americans need to take food poisoning seriously.
   a. **Many Americans each too much.** Although this is true, it has nothing to do with food poisoning.
   e. **In England, mad cow disease poisoned the beef and sickened several people.** This sentence may be deleted or left in the paragraph. Even though it focuses on food poisoning in England, it does show that food poisoning is a serious issue.

4. TOPIC SENTENCE: More Americans are investing in mutual funds than ever before.

   d. It is important to save money for the future. Although this is true, it is not related to the fact that more people are investing in mutual funds.

5. TOPIC SENTENCE: A good baby-sitter is hard to find.

   c. Some local hospitals offer baby-sitting classes that teach teenagers to care for young children. This sentence may be deleted or left in the paragraph. It does not clearly support the idea that a baby-sitter is hard to find. However, it does show what is being done about the shortage of baby-sitters.

   d. Parents are having fewer children these days. Although this is true, it does not show that a good baby-sitter is hard to find.

EXERCISE 3: *pages 205, 206.*

These answers are suggestions. Each question has more than one correct answer.

1. EXAMPLE: On Friday and Saturday nights, many people watch rented movies with family or friends.
   FACT: Most major towns have at least one movie rental store, such as Blockbuster or Hollywood Video.
   OPINION: Watching a movie at home is more relaxing than going to a movie theater.

2. EXAMPLE: Children and adults enjoy roller coasters, flumes, and haunted houses.
   FACT: King's Dominion, Great Adventure, and Disney World attract families throughout the spring, summer, and fall.
   OPINION: Disney World is the best family amusement park because it really has something for everyone.

3. EXAMPLE: My neighbor, who has twins, did not sleep well for months after the babies were born.
   FACT: Many adults enroll in parenting classes that help people deal with their children more effectively.
   OPINION: Before becoming parents, adults must make sure that they are ready not only for the joy, but also for the hard times.

4. EXAMPLE: Running, in-line skating, and biking are all great forms of exercise.
   FACT: Many studies show that Americans neither eat properly nor exercise enough.
   OPINION: As a nation, we need to make healthy lifestyles a priority.

5. EXAMPLE: Few of my friends have saved any money for emergencies or retirement.
   FACT: In other countries, such as Japan, individuals save much more money than Americans.
   OPINION: Saving money is an important habit that many Americans need to develop.

EXERCISE 4: *pages 207, 208.*

These answers are suggestions. Each question has more than one possible answer.

1. **It would take ten minutes to transmit one page, which would be hard for the recipient to read. Now, some fax machines are the size of a large book, and they can send multiple pages in minutes.** *Which would be hard for the recipient to read* is an adjective clause that describes *page*. The second sentence combines two equally important ideas. Both independent clauses in the second sentence focus on how fax machines will improve.

2. **They often focus on improving their athletic ability and neglect their education. Very few athletes turn pro, and those who do often have short careers.** *Focus and neglect* form a compound verb. The second sentence combines two ideas that are equally important.

3. **Meanwhile, more schools are introducing science topics to elementary students. Second and third graders now learn about basic biology and physics.** *Basic biology and physics* is a compound object of the preposition.

4. **Often, many features that make computers helpful and easy to use expose private information. When people use computers for banking and investments, hackers enter their files and learn personal information**. The new sentences present the same information in a different way.

5. **Check the car carefully or hire a good mechanic to inspect the car for you. Get insurance, and, if necessary, arrange for a loan.** The original paragraph gives the reader advice. However, it repeats *you* far too often. The new sentences are commands, so the subject, *you*, is implied.

EXERCISE 5: *pages 208, 209.*

These answers are suggestions. Each question has more than one possible answer.
1. **whispered, shouted, announced**
2. **productive, relaxing, fun-filled**
3. **tremendous, huge, overweight**
4. **minor, insignificant, tiny**
5. **rainy, exhausting, boring**
6. **spicy, inexpensive, healthy**
7. **bumped, crushed, sideswiped**
8. **crashed, lingered, broke**
9. **daily, weekly, biweekly**
10. **noisy, never ending, not moving**

CHAPTER REVIEW

EXERCISE 1: *pages 209, 210.*

These are suggestions. Each question has more than one possible answer.
1. **Researchers are studying how day-care affects children.** Each sentence is related to the topic sentence. The first supporting detail describes a particular study. The second and third supporting details focus on the positive and negative effects of day care. The fourth supporting detail states that research will continue because day care is popular.

2. **Roads and bridges in America need to be maintained more carefully.** Each sentence is related to the topic sentence. The first supporting detail shows that routes in America have not been well maintained. The second supporting detail explains that even though maintenance is costly, it must be done. The third and fourth supporting details show how poor maintenance affects us, and the fifth supporting detail emphasizes that road maintenance is a safety issue.

3. **Homeowners' associations are powerful in some neighborhoods.** Each sentence is related to the topic sentence. The first, second, and third supporting details show what types of power the associations have. The fourth supporting detail shows that some people like the power and others do not.

4. **Spring is a great time of year**. Each sentence is related to the topic sentence. The first, second, third, and fourth supporting details show why spring is great.

5. **People save money in many different ways**. Each sentence is related to the topic sentence. The first, second, and third supporting detail show how people save their money. The fourth supporting detail explains that one can use any technique to create a savings account.

6. **We need to teach our children to pursue their dreams**. The first and second supporting details show that children have many dreams when they are young. The third supporting detail notes that children often lose their dreams as they age, and the fourth supporting detail explains why it is important for children to follow their dreams.

7. **Babies are expensive**. Each sentence is related to the topic sentence. The first, second, third, and fourth supporting details show why babies are expensive. The fifth supporting detail emphasizes that parents need to prepare themselves for these costs.

8. **Today, many people depend on gadgets in their homes.** The first and second supporting details show what types of gadgets people have. The third and fourth sentences tell people's different reactions to these devices.

9. **School busses are not used effectively**. The first supporting detail explains why buses are needed. The second and third supporting details show why buses are underused. The fourth supporting detail tells that under-used school buses are costly. The fifth supporting detail suggests that there must be a solution to the problem.

10. **Music is everywhere.** The first supporting detail tells where music is often found. The second, third, fourth, and fifth supporting details show where there is music in our daily lives. The sixth supporting detail suggests choosing one form of music over another.

EXERCISE 2: *page 211.*

These are suggestions. Each question has more than one possible answer.

1. a. **During the summer, the lawn needs to be mowed once a week.**
   b. **Every few years, the house needs to be painted.**
   Supporting details for this paragraph should include examples of work that needs to be done around the home.

2. a. **One can bike alone or with a friend.**
   b. **In just a half hour, one can get a great workout.**
   Supporting details for this paragraph should include reasons why biking is a good form of exercise.

3. a. **For a person who lives alone, a pet may be the only family member.**
   b. **Many families travel with their pets.**
   Supporting details for this paragraph should include ways that pets are members of the family.

4. a. **Love letters and greeting cards travel by mail.**
   b. **Likewise, newsletters and magazines are delivered to some people's mailboxes.**
   Supporting details for this paragraph should focus on items that travel through the mail.

5. a. **Many children like the ladders and hoses that firefighters use.**
   b. **Other children are fascinated by all of the equipment that firefighters wear.**
   Supporting details for this paragraph should include reasons why children like fire engines.

6. a. **Some people can work from home because of computers.**
   b. **In schools, computers help students learn at their own pace.**
   Supporting details for this paragraph should include specific ways that computers have changed our lives.

7. a. **More restaurants offer delivery services.**
   b. **Many companies have in-house day care centers so parents can be near their children.**
   Supporting details for this paragraph should include new services that help people who are busy.
8. a. **Parents can volunteer in their child's classroom or coach an after-school sport.**
   b. **In some schools, parents can eat lunch with their children in the school cafeteria.**
   Supporting details for this paragraph should include ways that parents can be active in their children's education.
9. a. **Free trial offers encourage us to test a new product.**
   b. **Sports figures, musicians, and other famous people help products become popular.**
   Supporting details for this paragraph should include specific ways advertisers get people to buy a product.
10. a. **Walking or biking places, instead of driving, can help save gas.**
   b. **Likewise, buying only what one needs and searching for sales can cut costs.**
   Supporting details for this paragraph should include specific actions that can help save money.

CHAPTER 15: PLANNING THE ESSAY

EXERCISE 1: *page 217.*

1. **Your thoughts on whether both parents should work or one should stay home with the children** *State your opinion* are the signal words.
2. **Reasons why teenagers should be allowed to drink alcohol or more efforts should be made to stop teenage drinking** *Tell how* are the signal words.

3. **The effects that television has had** *Effects* is the signal word.
4. **Steps that should be taken to help homeless persons** *Describe how* are the signal words.
5. **Steps to take to teach new drivers** *Describe how* are the signal words.

EXERCISE 2: *pages 218, 219.*

These answers are suggestions. Each question has more than one correct answer.
1. **Parents should do what is best for their children.** *State your opinion* are the signal words.
2. **As a nation, we must work harder to stop teenage drinking.** *Tell how* are the signal words.
3. **Televisions have helped Americans learn more about themselves and the world.** *Effects* is the signal word.
4. **There are many ways to help homeless people.** *Describe how* are the signal words.
5. **Drivers need to experience many different driving situations before they earn a license.** *Explain how* are the signal words.

EXERCISES 3 AND 4: *pages 220, 221.*

These answers are suggestions. Each question has more than one correct answer.
1. good day care is hard to find, both parents may want to work, both parents may have to work to support their children, many jobs can't be done from home, children need excellent care, working and caring for children is exhausting, parents can return to work when their children go to school, children need a lot of attention, day care is expensive, leaving the workforce makes it harder to advance
2. the legal age doesn't really affect teenage drinking; teenagers need more education about alcohol; ad campaigns could teach teens about the dangers of alcohol; parents need to be more involved in their teenagers' lives; teens need more

programs for sports, music, and art to keep them busy and away from alcohol; teens should learn how to drink responsibly; teens drink alcohol, in part, because it is forbidden; some advertisers target teens; teens need stiffer penalties for underage drinking; teens should learn the difference between alcohol use and alcohol abuse before they go off to college or live on their own

3. some good education programs, connects people to the outside world, people watch too much TV, a lot of sex and violence on TV, inexpensive entertainment, easy to learn about the news, creates a common culture because people all over America see the same shows, influences the way people dress and behave, children are exposed to too much at young ages, families can watch shows together, some immigrants use TV to learn English

4. more drug and alcohol counseling services; shelters should be temporary; homeless children should be in school; more job training programs; people should give panhandlers food, not money that can be used to buy drugs; more mental health services; panhandlers should not be allowed to harass people; people convicted of petty crimes should do community service in shelters; hold a "Thanksgiving in March" food drive; collect clothes for homeless

5. a minimum of 40 hours behind the wheel; require driving school; start with a daytime only license; drivers must practice on highways, curvy roads, etc.; start with drivers license for only school or work; practice driving in rain and snow on a practice track; learn to drive an automatic and standard car; use machines that simulate different driving conditions like flight simulators; videos on driving safety; driving tests on different types of driving conditions

EXERCISE 5: *page 222.*

There is more than one possible answer.
THESIS STATEMENT ➡ High schools should require community service because it helps students become more thoughtful, responsible citizens.

A. students can learn about careers that might interest them; community service improves many students' self-esteem; students learn to work with other adults; students can learn important job skills

B. students can volunteer in programs that interest them; students help in nursing homes and day-care centers; teens work as tutors and hospital aides; students clean roadways and improve playgrounds

C. teenagers become more interested in community issues; students learn how important it is to volunteer; when people volunteer as teens, they are more likely to volunteer as adults; high school community service programs have made students more active in college volunteer programs

A. **Students learn from their experiences.**

B. **Students become involved in many different types of service.**

C. **Community service helps students become more confident, active adults.**

EXERCISE 6: *page 224.*

This is a suggestion. There is more than one possible answer.

I. Teaches Students

A. Students can learn about careers that might interest them

B. Students learn to work with other adults

C. Students can learn important job skills

D. Students learn how important it is to volunteer

II. Different Types of Service
A. Students can volunteer in programs that interest them
B. Students help in nursing homes and day-care centers
C. Teens work as tutors and hospital aides
D. Students clean roadways and improve playgrounds
III. More Confident, Active Adults
A. Community service improves many students' self-esteem

B. When people volunteer as teens, they are more likely to volunteer as adults
C. High school community service programs have made students more active in college volunteer programs
D. Teenagers become more interested in community issues

EXERCISE 7: *pages 225, 226.*

This is a suggestion. There is more than one possible answer.

Main Ideas	Details
Teaches Students	➡ Students learn to work with other adults ➡ Students can learn important job skills ➡ Students can learn about careers that might interest them ➡ Students learn the importance of volunteering
Different Types of Service	➡ Students can volunteer in programs that interest them ➡ Students help in nursing homes and day-care centers ➡ Teens work as tutors and hospital aides ➡ Students clean roadways and improve playgrounds
More Confident, Active Adults	➡ Community service improves many student's self-esteem ➡ When people volunteer as teens, they are more likely to volunteer as adults ➡ High school community service programs have made students more active in college volunteer programs ➡ Teenagers become more interested in community issues

EXERCISE 8: *pages 227, 228.*

This is a suggestion. There is more than one possible answer.

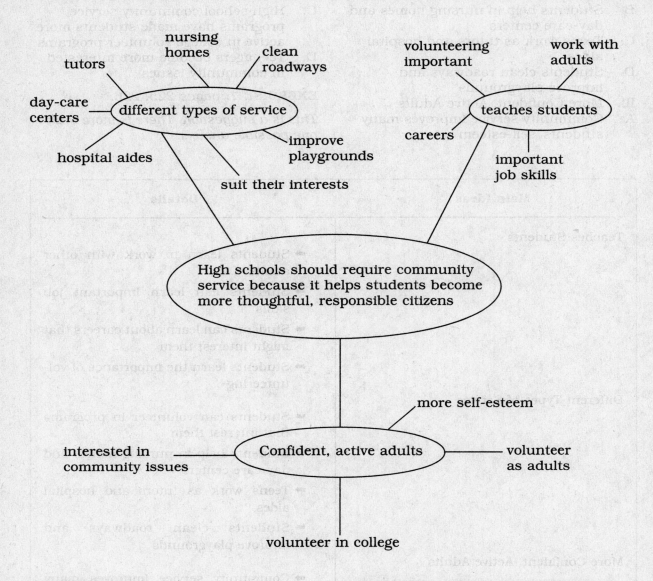

CHAPTER REVIEW

EXERCISE 1: *pages 228, 229.*

These are suggestions. There is more than one possible answer.

Part A:

SIGNAL WORDS: positive and negative effects The signal words show that the essay should be about the effects of cellular phones.

THESIS STATEMENT: Cellular phones have had positive and negative effects on modern life. The thesis statement points the writer's thoughts in the right direction. First, the writer will focus on the positive effects, then he or she will write about the negative affects.

Part B:

POSITIVE EFFECTS

children can always get in touch with

their parents
it's easy to make a call in an emergency
employees and employers can keep in touch
when stuck in traffic, can talk to people
can call home or work to say you will be late
don't need to find a pay phone to make a call
can report traffic accidents and bad

driving to police right away
NEGATIVE EFFECTS
cell phone use may cause traffic accidents
cell phones don't always work
other people can easily listen to your cell phone calls
cell phones can be expensive
don't always want people to contact you

Part C:

Main Ideas	Details
Can stay in touch with family, friends, work	➡ Children can talk to parents ➡ Call home or work to say you will be late ➡ When stuck in traffic, can talk to people

Cell phones are convenient	➡ It is easy to make a call in an emergency
	➡ Do not need to find a pay phone to make a call
	➡ Can report to police
	    traffic accidents
	    bad driving

Cell phones have drawbacks	➡ Cell phone use may cause traffic accidents ➡ Cell phones can be expensive ➡ Do not always want people to contact you ➡ Other people can easily listen to your cell phone calls
Cell phones don't always work	

EXERCISE 2: *pages 229, 230.*

Part A:
SIGNAL WORDS: Tell how The essay should be about the steps that should be taken to improve public education in America.
THESIS STATEMENT: Educators, parents, and community members need to work together to improve public education.
Part B:

EDUCATORS:
set higher expectations
all students must pass tests in major subjects to graduate
students prepare for college, job training, or both
all students should take at least three years of English, math, science, social studies, and physical education
more programs to help elementary children with problems in school
demand discipline and keep schools safe

PARENTS:
parents should promise to volunteer in schools for a certain number of hours each year
parents must attend parent-teacher conferences
parents should read to young children
parents should check homework
parents need to further their own education to show learning is important

parents should have high expectations for academics and discipline
COMMUNITY MEMBERS:
donate equipment to the schools
local businesses should work with job-training programs
mentors for students
more after-school activities for students
keep school buildings well maintained

Part C:

Main Ideas	Details
Educators raise standards and provide extra help	➡ At least three years of English, math, science, social studies, and physical education ➡ Pass tests in major subjects to graduate ➡ Prepare for college, job training, or both ➡ More programs to help elementary children 　　Extra help for struggling students ➡ Demand discipline and keep schools safe
Parents get involved and show education is important	➡ Volunteer in schools for a certain number of hours each year ➡ Attend parent-teacher conferences ➡ Read to young children ➡ Check homework ➡ Further their own education 　　Show learning is important ➡ High expectations 　　Academics 　　Discipline
Community support	➡ Donate equipment ➡ Local businesses work with job-training programs ➡ Mentors for students ➡ After-school activities for students ➡ Keep buildings well maintained

CHAPTER 16: WRITING THE ESSAY

EXERCISE 1: *pages 232–234.*

These are suggestions. Each question has more than one correct answer.

1. For generations fathers and mothers had clearly defined roles. Fathers went off to work while mothers stayed home with the children. Now, parents have more options not only for work, but also for child care. Unfortunately, some adults use these options to benefit themselves and not their families. Parents should do what is best for their children.

2. Alcohol abuse is a national problem not only for adults, but also for teenagers. Even though the drinking age is twenty-one, minors regularly drink alcohol. Teenage alcohol abuse leads to deadly car accidents, violence, and numerous health problems. As a nation, we must work harder to stop teenage drinking.

3. Throughout history different inventions have changed people's lives. However, few inventions have had as much influence as the television. The television has had some negative effects, but overall it has been a great invention. Televisions have helped Americans learn more about themselves and the world.

4. Men, women, and children become homeless for many different reasons. When they are on the streets, homeless people depend on shelters, soup kitchens, and free counseling. Unfortunately, these programs often are overwhelmed. Homelessness is an old problem that needs new solutions. There are many ways to help homeless people.

5. Many Americans depend on their cars. As a result, getting a driver's license is very important for some people. Unfortunately, inexperienced drivers cause many accidents. Tougher standards for new drivers could save lives. Drivers should experience many different driving situations before they earn a license.

EXERCISE 2: *pages 235, 236.*

These paragraphs are suggestions. There is more than one correct answer.

Television can help people learn. Some immigrants use TV programs to learn English. Shows, such as *Barney*, *Sesame Street*, and *The Magic School Bus,* help children discover new things. News programs help people quickly learn about local, national, and international events. In addition, some shows focus on history, different cultures, or even animals in the wild. Television is a good form of entertainment. A plain television set is fairly inexpensive, and it can offer many different channels. Television programs are created for children, teenagers, and adults. Families and friends can watch TV shows together, or they can enjoy a show by themselves. Many people like to see their favorite stars on TV every week.

On the other hand, television has some negative effects. Some children watch over four hours of television a day. Parents often do not even know what their children are watching. Many television programs that children watch have a lot of sexual situations, bad language, and violence. Unfortunately, children often imitate what they see on television. As a result, they do things that are inappropriate.

EXERCISE 3: *page 237.*

1. **however** *However* shows that there is a difference between the two statements. The first sentence focuses on positive features, and the second sentence notes a negative feature.
2. **For example** *For example* shows that the snail darter and the spotted owl are examples of protected species.
3. **Likewise** *Likewise* connects similar ideas. Both sentences focus on difficult transitions in school.
4. **First**, **Then** *First* and *then* show in what order the different actions take place.
5. **As a result** *As a result* shows a cause and effect relationship. Because many people cannot afford college, many students do not get the education that they need.
6. **Instead** *Instead* shows that there is a difference between where *we* wanted to go and where *we* actually went.
7. **Now** *Now* shows a change in time. The first sentence is about what happened in the past, and the second sentence is about what is happening in the present.
8. **for instance** *For instance* shows that the second sentence gives a specific example. The second sentence tells how immigrants work hard.
9. **Instead** *Instead* shows that there is a difference between what *we* thought *we* were buying and what *we* actually bought.
10. **However** *However* shows that there is a difference between what children need and what they are getting.

EXERCISE 4: *page 238.*

1. **For example** *For example* shows that the paragraph will focus on specific examples of positive effects.
2. **As a result** *As a result* shows a cause and effect relationship. People can telecommute because they can use computers to communicate.
3. **Likewise** *Likewise* shows that this sentence has a similar idea. Companies can hold meetings without getting people together because they can use computers to communicate.
4. **also** *Also* shows that this paragraph will explain more benefits.
5. **In addition** *In addition* shows that this sentence has a similar idea. It gives another way that computers help people learn more easily.
6. **On the other hand** *On the other hand* connects ideas that are different. The second paragraph focused on positive effects. This paragraph emphasizes negative effects.
7. **Likewise** *Likewise* shows that this sentence has a similar idea. This sentence also focuses on how computers isolate people.
8. **Nonetheless** *Nonetheless* shows a contrast. Even though computers have had positive and negative effects, they will continue to be an important invention.

EXERCISE 5: *page 239–241.*

These are suggestions. Each question has more than one correct answer.

1. Parents should choose work and child-care arrangements that are good for their children. It is important that children have the financial and emotional support that they need. After reviewing different options, parents may decide to work, stay home with their children, or work from home. Whatever the decision, it is important to build strong families, which are good for children and society as a whole.

2. Clearly, teenage drinking must be stopped. We need not only to teach teenagers about the dangers of alcohol, but also to create positive activities for minors. Likewise, teenagers must be held responsible for their actions. As a nation, we must make sure that teenagers develop into healthy, responsible adults. Today's teenagers are tomorrow's leaders.

3. Televisions help Americans learn. Television programs focus on many different subjects, and they create a common culture. In addition, televisions connect people to the outside world. If you want to learn something new, turn on the TV.

4. Clearly, homeless people should be helped in many ways. Groups that help the homeless should coordinate their efforts, create more counseling programs, and focus on homeless children. Homeless people do not need to suffer. This is one problem that has some solutions.

5. People need a lot of driving experience before they earn a license. More practice driving, restricted licenses, and tougher driving tests could improve driver safety. If the states do not force new drivers to gain more experience, drivers should set higher standards for themselves. A license gives people a lot of freedom, but it also requires a lot of responsibility.

CHAPTER REVIEW

EXERCISE 1: *pages 241, 242.*

This essay is a suggestion. Each essay has more than one correct answer.

New inventions are created every day. Often they make our lives easier, but sometimes they can be frustrating. The cellular phone, which is a recent invention, has changed the way people communicate. Not all of the changes have been helpful. Cellular phones have had positive and negative effects on modern life.

For example, cellular phones help people stay in touch with family, friends, and employers. If a child has a problem, he or she can always call a parent. Some children regularly call their parents after school. Likewise, adults can call home or work when they are going to be late. When people get stuck in traffic, they can make phone calls and still get some work done.

Cellular phones also are convenient. It is easy to make a phone call in an emergency. Many people keep the phones in their cars, but others take them jogging, biking, or walking to make themselves feel safer. Cell phones also are more convenient than pay phones. Sometimes it is hard to find a pay phone that works. Likewise, drivers can use cellular phones to report traffic accidents or bad driving to the police.

Nonetheless, cellular phones do have drawbacks. Some studies show that cell phone use while driving actually causes accidents. Even basic cellular phone rates can be expensive, and other people can listen into your conversations. In addition, cell phones may make it too easy for people to contact you; there are times when you do not want phone calls.

Clearly, cellular phones have affected our lives in positive and negative ways. Even though cell phones are helpful and convenient, they do cause some problems. Like many inventions, cell phones can make our lives easier. We simply need to use them wisely.

EXERCISE 2: *page 242.*

This essay is a suggestion. Each essay has more than one correct answer.

Public education is an important part of American society. Through public education, every child in the United States has the opportunity to achieve his or her dreams. Unfortunately, many public schools in America do not educate children well. As a result, we have many students who do not have the skills that they need. Educators, parents, and community members need to work together to improve public education in America.

First, parents and educators need to set higher expectations for students. They must demand discipline and set high academic standards. Children learn more when they are challenged. High school students should take at least three years of English, math, science, social studies, and physical education. Students also should be required to pass tests in all major subjects in order to graduate from high school. In addition, courses for high school students should prepare them for college, job training, or both.

Likewise, parents need to get more involved in the schools and show their children that education matters. Parents must do more than check homework. Parents also should attend parent-teacher conferences and volunteer in the schools. In addition, parents must improve their own education to show their children that learning does not stop at the school door.

The community also needs to support the local schools. Community leaders can donate equipment to the schools and arrange more after-school activities for students. Local businesses can work with job-training programs. Adults in the community can serve as mentors for students. In addition, the community as a whole can work together to make sure that school buildings are well maintained.

Clearly, educators, parents, and community members can improve public education in America. Higher standards, greater parental involvement, and more local support can make the public schools more successful. If we work together, public schools can help students develop their skills and achieve their dreams.

CHAPTER 17: REVISING THE ESSAY

EXERCISE 1: *pages 244, 245.*

Public education is an important part of American society. Many public schools in America do not educate children well. As a result, too many students do not have the skills that they need. **Parents, teachers, and community leaders must work together to improve our public schools.**

First, parents and educators need to set higher expectations for students. Children learn more when they are challenged. High school students should take at least three years of English, math, science, social studies, and physical education. **Students also should pass standardized tests to prove that they have learned the material. In addition,** courses for high school students should prepare them for college, job training, or both.

Likewise, parents need to get more involved in the schools and show their children that education matters. Parents should attend parent-teacher conferences and volunteer in the schools. **They should get involved in after-school activities that their children enjoy.** Parents **also** must improve their own education to show their children that learning does not stop at the school door.

The community also needs to support the local schools. Community leaders can donate equipment to the schools and arrange more after-school activities for students. ~~Often teachers live in the community~~. Adults in the community can serve as mentors for students. **In addition,** the community as a whole can work together to make sure that school buildings are well maintained.

Parents, teachers, and community members can improve public education in America. Higher standards, greater parental involvement, and more local support can make the public schools more successful. If we work together, public schools can help students develop their skills and achieve their dreams.

Add a thesis statement to the first paragraph to give the essay direction. Insert at least one more supporting detail to both the second and third paragraphs. In the fourth paragraph, cross out the sentence that is not related to the topic. For each body paragraph, add transitional words to make the information flow more smoothly. At the start of the concluding paragraph, insert a sentence that rewords the thesis statement.

EXERCISE 2: *page 246.*

Throughout history, new inventions have changed **people's** lives. Inventions often make our lives easier or our work more productive. Sometimes, however, they seem to make life more difficult. The telephone is one invention that has had mixed results. The telephone is helpful in many **ways, but** it also has drawbacks.

Telephones help people communicate with family, friends, and the world. With telephones, people can keep in touch with family members who may be across town or across the country. **Phones** help friends communicate, and they help people check on older relatives or neighbors who may need assistance. Telephones **create** a connection to the outside world.

Telephones are practical. Making a phone call is easier than writing a letter. In much less time, you can pick up the phone and talk with a **friend**. While talking on the phone, you can do other things, such as dishes or laundry. In an emergency, a telephone can get you help quickly.

Although telephones are helpful in many ways, phone calls can be expensive and annoying. Monthly **bills, which** are based on the calls you **make, can** be costly. In addition, telephones help people contact you—even when you do not want them to call. For example, an employer can call you at home. Likewise, people call during dinner or in the middle of the night.

Clearly, the telephone can be both beneficial and frustrating. Telephones help people **communicate, and** they have many practical uses. However, they also are expensive and annoying. Like many inventions, the telephone is a great tool when it is used wisely.

In the introductory paragraph, insert an apostrophe to show possession in *peoples.* Add a comma to the thesis statement before the conjunction *but.* In the second paragraph, capitalize *phones* and add a verb to complete the last sentence. Spell *friend* correctly in the third paragraph. In the fourth paragraph, insert commas to set apart the nonrestrictive clause. Likewise, add a comma in the concluding paragraph before the conjunction *and.*

EXERCISE 3: *pages 246, 247.*

Many people are active in volunteer activities. These projects not only get people involved in **their** communities, but also help people in need. Some people want to make community service a high school graduation requirement; others think that schools should not force students to "volunteer." High schools should require community service because it helps students become more thoughtful, responsible adults.

Students learn from community service. Students discover different careers that might **interest** them, such as medicine or teaching. Students also learn to work with adults. **In addition,** teens develop important job skills that will help them in the future. They learn to be on time, to follow directions, and to complete projects.

Students also get involved in many different types of community service. Teenagers can choose volunteer programs that interest them. **Students help in nursing homes and day-care centers. They work as tutors and hospital aids. Students also clean roadways and improve playgrounds.**

Likewise, when students are involved in community service, they develop into more **active, confident** adults. Community service improves **students'** self-esteem. People who volunteer as teens **are** more likely to volunteer as adults. High school community service programs have made students more active in college volunteer programs. In addition, teenagers who are involved in community programs are more interested in local issues.

Clearly, community service can be an important part of one's high school education. Community service programs positively **affect** students not only when they are teens, but also when they become adults. **Community service should not just be a graduation requirement; it should be a way of life.**

In the first paragraph, use *their* to show possession. Add a topic sentence to the second paragraph and spell *interest* correctly. In addition, add transitional words. In the third paragraph, add at least three supporting details. For the fourth paragraph, add a comma between *active* and *confident*, two adjectives that describe *adults*. Likewise, add a verb to the third sentence, which is incomplete. In the fifth paragraph, change *effect* to *affect*, which means "to influence." In addition, add a general, insightful statement to the end of the paragraph.

POSTTEST

1. **4 home schooling** (See Chapter 13—Writing Clear Sentences: Rewriting Sentences) *Home schooling* is the subject of the sentence. *In the last decade* is a prepositional phrase that works as an adverb; it answers the question *when*. When you move *in the last decade* to the start of the sentence, the rest of the sentence remains the same. *In the last decade, home schooling has become a popular trend throughout the United States.*

2. **1 change *dominate* to *dominated*** (See Chapter 3—Verb Usage: Verb Tense) *In the past* signals that the verb should be in the past tense. Option (2) is wrong because *religious* is spelled correctly. Option (3) is wrong because *conservatives* is a common noun, which should not be capitalized. Option (4) is wrong because there is no reason to insert a comma after *home*.

3. **3 replace resons with reasons** (See Chapter 11—Spelling) *Reason* is often misspelled. Try this: you need <u>a</u> good reason. Option (1) is wrong because *now* is an introductory word, which needs a comma. Option (2) is wrong because *their* shows possession. Option (4) is wrong because *teach* means "to give understanding or information."

4. **1 replace *will be* with *are*** (See Chapter 13—Writing Clear Sentences: Consistent Verb Tense) Both verbs in the sentence should be in the present tense, *are concerned* and *do (not) teach*. Option (2) is wrong because there is no reason to insert a comma after *concerned*. Option (3) is wrong because *parents* is not possessive in this sentence. Option (4) is wrong because the sentence is in the present tense.

5. **2 drug use, teen pregnancy, and violence** (See Chapter 8—End Marks and Commas: Independent Clauses and Items in a Series) Use commas to separate items in a series. Do <u>not</u> place a comma after the last item in the series. Option (1) is wrong because commas are not used to separate the items. Option (3) is wrong because it has a comma after the last item in the series. Option (4) is wrong because it does not have a comma separating the first two items. Option (5) is wrong because it uses a semicolon instead of a comma.

6. **4 replace *childrens* with *children's*** (See Chapter 9—More Punctuation: Apostrophes) Use an apostrophe to show possession. Whose education? Their children's. Option (1) is wrong because *their* should be used to show possession. Option (2) is wrong because *families* is the plural form of family. It is not possessive in this sentence. Option (3) is wrong because *as a result* is an introductory phrase, which should be set apart with a comma.

7. **2 in kindergarten through** (See Chapter 13—Writing Clear Sentences: Misplaced Modifiers and Rewriting Sentences) *In kindergarten through twelfth grade* is a prepositional phrase that modifies *children*. In the new sentence, it should immediately follow *children*. Otherwise, the phrase would be a misplaced modifier. *Nationally since 1990, the number of home-schooled children in kindergarten through twelfth grade has almost doubled to 500,000 students.*

8. **3 special support groups, teaching materials, and athletic organizations** (See Chapter 13—Writing Clear Sentences: Parallel Structure) Items in a series should be in the same form. *Special* describes *support groups*, and *athletic* describes *organizations*. Likewise, *teaching* describes *materials*. Options (1), (4), and (5) are wrong because they are not parallel. Option (2) is wrong because it uses semicolons instead of commas.

9. **1 replace *Colleges and Universities* with *colleges* and *universities*** (See Chapter 10—Capitalization) *Colleges* and *universities* are common nouns. These words should be capitalized only when they are part of a name for a specific institution. Option (2) is wrong because *at the same time* is an introductory phrase, which needs a comma to set it apart. Option (3) is wrong because the sentence is in the present perfect tense, not the future tense. Option (4) is wrong because there is no reason to insert a comma. A series consists of at least three items.

10. **3 for many families; however, it** (See Chapter 13—Writing Clear Sentences: Rewriting Sentences) *Although* and *however* signal a contrast between the first statement and the second one. The other options do not show the same relationship between the statements.

11. **3 insert a comma after *declined*** (See Chapter 8—End Marks and Commas: Opening Words, Phrases, and Clauses) *At the same time that adult smoking has declined* is an introductory clause. It should be set apart with a comma. Options (1) and (2) are wrong because the verbs in the sentence should be consistent. Option (4) is wrong because *increased* is spelled correctly.

12. **5 no correction necessary** Option (1) is wrong because *teenagers* is not possessive. Option (2) is wrong because the comma is needed before the *but* to show contrast. Option (3) is wrong because *cigarettes* is spelled correctly. Option (4) is wrong because the sentence should be in the present tense.

13. **2 pressure, others insist** (See Chapter 9—More Punctuation: Semicolons) The semicolon joins two independent clauses that are related. The other options do not punctuate the sentence correctly.

14. **3 replace *are* with *is*** (See Chapter 4—Subject-Verb Agreement: Special Situations) The verb, *is*, must agree with *nicotine*, which is the subject of the sentence. *Of cigarettes* is a prepositional phrase that describes *nicotine*. Option (1) is wrong because *unfortunately* is an introductory word, which should be set apart with a comma. Option (2) is wrong because *for many people* should be placed near *addictive*, the word that is modified. Option (4) is wrong because *cigarettes* is a common noun, which should not be capitalized.

15. **4 replace *which* with *who*** (See Chapter 7—Clauses: Who, Which, and That) *Who* is used for people. *Which* is used for animal and things. Option (1) is wrong because *their* is used to show possession. Option (2) is wrong because *thus* is an introductory word, which needs a comma to set it apart. Option (3) is wrong because *are* must agree with the subject, *teens*.

16. **1 replace *is* with *are*** (See Chapter 4—Subject-Verb Agreement: General Guidelines and Special Situations) The verb, *are*, must agree with the subject of the sentence, which is *efforts*. *To stop teenage smoking* is a phrase that describes *efforts*. Option (2) is wrong because *across the nation* is an introductory phrase, which should be set apart with a comma. Option (3) is wrong because there is no reason to place a comma after *smoking*. Option (4) is wrong because *efforts* is spelled correctly.

17. **2 that** (See Chapter 7—Clauses: Who, Which, and That and Chapter 14—Writing Clear Sentences: Combining Sentences) When the sentences are joined, *that* introduces a clause that describes *identification*. People who want to buy tobacco products may soon have to show photo identification that proves they are at least 18 years old.

18. **4 replace *them* with *underage smokers*** (See Chapter 13—Writing Clear Sentences: Consistent Pronouns) In the original sentence, *them* is too vague. Does it refer to *persons* or *underage smokers*? Pronouns with vague references should be replaced with nouns that clarify the sentence. Option (1) is wrong because the sentence is in the present tense. Option (2) is wrong because there is no reason to place a comma after *persons*. Option (3) is wrong because the past tense does not agree with the rest of the sentence.

19. **5 no correction necessary** Option (1) is wrong because *likewise* is an introductory word, which should be set apart by a comma. Option (2) is wrong because *smokers* should not be possessive. Option (3) is wrong because the paragraph focuses on possible changes in the future. Option (4) is wrong because *vending machines* is a common noun, which should not be capitalized.

20. **3 smoking, but they** (See Chapter 8—End Marks and Commas: Independent Clauses and Items in a Series) *But* is a conjunction that joins two independent clauses. Commas should be placed before coordinating conjunctions. Options (1), (2), (4), and (5) are wrong because they do not punctuate the independent clauses properly.

21. **1 change *Doctors* to *doctors*** (See Chapter 10—Capitalization) *Doctors* is a common noun. It should only be capitalized when it is used as a title and placed before a doctor's name. Option (2) is wrong because *in the past decade* is an introductory phrase, which should be set apart with a comma. Option (3) is wrong because *have emphasized* shows that the action began in the past and continues into the present. Option (4) is wrong because *good* and *prenatal* are not equal adjectives. There should not be a comma between them.

22. **4 replace *she* with *they*** (See Chapter 5—Pronouns: Pronoun Agreement) The pronoun refers to *women*, which is plural. Therefore, the pronoun must be plural. Option (1) is wrong because *even before women become pregnant* is an introductory clause, which should be set apart with a comma. Option (2) is wrong because both verbs in the sentence, *become* and *consider*, should agree. Option (3) is wrong because there is no reason to place a comma after *prenatal*.

23. **2 replace *that* with *who*** (See Chapter 7—Clauses: Who, Which, and That) *Who* is used for people, and *that* is used for animals or things. Option (1) is wrong because *prescribe* is spelled correctly. Option (3) is wrong because the clause is restrictive. It tells which women. Option (4) is wrong because *doctors* should not be possessive.

24. **3 monitor the** (See Chapter 13—Writing Clear Sentences: Rewriting Sentences) In the original sentence, *the baby's health and the mother's condition* form a compound subject, and *are* is the verb. In the new sentence, *doctors* is the subject and *monitors* is the verb. *During checkups throughout the pregnancy, doctors monitor the developing baby's health and the mother's condition.*

25. **4 replace *it's* with *its*** (See Chapter 5—Pronouns: Possessive Case) Possessive pronouns do not have apostrophes. Option (1) is wrong because *baby's* is possessive. Doctors listen to whose heartbeat? Option (2) is wrong because the paragraph is in the present tense. Option (3) is wrong because there is no reason to place a comma after *heartbeat*.

26. **5 mother's nutrition, exercise, and emotional well-being** (See Chapter 8—End Marks and Commas: Independent Clauses and Items in a Series) Items in a series should be separated by commas. Options (1), (2), (3) and (4) are wrong because they do not have commas separating the items. Option (2) also changed *mother's* to *mothers*, which is not possessive.

27. **1 change *taught* to *teach*** (See Chapter 13—Writing Clear Sentences: Consistent Verb Tense) The verb, *teach*, should be in the present tense because the rest of the paragraph is in the present tense. Option (2) is wrong because *they* must agree with *doctors*, which is plural and gender neutral. Option (3) is wrong because there is no reason to place a comma after *childbirth*. Option (4) is wrong because *parents* should not be possessive.

28. **1 move *who have good prenatal care* after *women*** (See Chapter 7—Clauses: Adjective Clauses) In the original sentence, *who have good prenatal care* is a misplaced modifier. It describes *women*. Therefore, it should be placed next to *women*. Option (2) is wrong because *babies* should be plural, not possessive. Option (3) is wrong because *healthier* is spelled correctly. Option (4) is wrong because *deliver* should agree with *women*, the subject of the sentence.

29. **3 insert a comma after *result*** (See Chapter 8—End Marks and Commas: Opening Words, Phrases, and Clauses) *As a result* forms an introductory phrase, which should be set apart with a comma. Option (1) is wrong because a singular noun is made possessive by adding *'s*. Option (2) is wrong because *every* is spelled correctly. Option (4) is wrong because *should be* is in the present tense, and it is consistent with the paragraph.

30. **2 replace *that* with *which*** (See Chapter 7—Clauses: Restrictive and Nonrestrictive Clauses) *Was created by George C. Marshall* is part of a nonrestrictive clause. The clause should begin with *which*, and it should be set apart with commas. Option (1) is wrong because *World War II* names a specific event. Option (3) is wrong because the action occurred in the past. Option (4) is wrong because commas are used to set apart nonrestrictive clauses.

31. **4 replace *gives* with *gave*** (See Chapter 3—Verb Usage: Verb Tense) *From 1948 to 1951* shows that the action occurred in the past. Therefore, *gave*, the past tense of *give*, should be used. Option (1) is wrong because *from 1948 to 1951* is an introductory phrase, which should be set apart with a comma. Option (2) is wrong because *Western Europe* is a specific region in Europe that should be capitalized. Option (3) is wrong because *worth $13 billion* should be near the noun it modifies, *services*.

32. **4 replace *todays* with *today's*** (See Chapter 9—More Punctuation: Apostrophes) *Today's* describes dollars and shows *whose* dollars. The possessive form should be used. Option (1) is wrong because *in today's dollars* is an introductory phrase, which should be set apart with a comma. Option (2) is wrong because *dollars* is spelled correctly. Option (3) is wrong because *billion* is a common noun.

33. **4 change *prevent* to *prevented*** (See Chapter 13—Writing Clear Sentence: Balanced Structure) Both verbs should be in the same tense. *Stimulated* and *prevented* should be used because the action occurred in the past. Option (1) is wrong because the *Marshall Plan* names a specific program. Option (2) is wrong because there is no reason to place a comma after *Europe*. Option (3) is wrong because *in Europe* modifies *economy*. Modifiers should be placed next to the nouns that they describe.

34. **3 provide food, reconstruct factories, and recreate businesses** (See Chapter 13—Writing Clear Sentences: Parallel Structure) Items in a series should be in the same form. In the original sentence, *businesses were recreated* is not in the same form

as the other two items. Options (1), (4), and (5) are wrong because they do not have parallel structure. Option (2) is wrong because it uses semicolons, instead of commas, to separate the items.

35. **1 insert a comma after *Plan*** (See Chapter 8—End Marks and Commas: Opening Words, Phrases, and Clauses) *As a result of the Marshall Plan* is an introductory phrase, which should be set apart with a comma. Option (2) is wrong because *Western Europe* is a specific region that should be capitalized. Option (3) is wrong because there is no reason to place a comma after *economy*. Option (4) is wrong because the sentence should be in the past tense.

36. **2 move *for their children* after *safely*** (See Chapter 13—Writing Clear Sentences: Misplaced Modifiers) *For their children* describes *safely*. Modifiers should be placed next to the words that they describe. Option (1) is wrong because there is no reason to place a comma after *seats*. Option (3) is wrong because *parents* is not possessive in this sentence. Instead, *parents* is the subject of the sentence. Option (4) is wrong because *their* is the possessive form. It answers the question whose children.

37. **1 remove the comma after *correctly*** (See Chapter 8—End Marks and Commas: Adjectives) *Correctly* is an adverb that describes *installed*. A comma should be used to separate two adjectives that are equally important, not an adverb and an adjective. Option (2) is wrong because *accident* is spelled correctly. Option (3) is wrong because *percent* is a common noun, which should not be capitalized. Option (4) is wrong because there is no reason to place a comma after *accident*.

38. **3 change *carefull* to *careful*** (See Chapter 11—Spelling: Spelling Rules) Words are too full to have two *l*'s on the end. Option (1) is wrong because *they* is the subject of the independent clause. Option (2) is wrong because *follow* must agree with *they*, the subject of the clause. Option (4) is wrong because *parents* should not be possessive. *Parents* is the subject of the sentence.

39. **4 replace *is* with *are*** (See Chapter 4—Subject-Verb Agreement: General Guidelines and Difficult Subjects) The verb must agree with *car seats*, the subject of the sentence. *There* never is the subject of a sentence. It is an adverb that tells *where*. *For each stage of development* is a phrase. Option (1) is wrong because *different* is spelled correctly. Option (2) is wrong because *there* is an adverb that answers the question where. Option (3) is wrong because *for each stage of development* is an introductory phrase, which should be set apart with a comma.

40. **5 no correction necessary** Option (1) is wrong because *newborns* is the subject of the sentence. It should not be possessive. Option (2) is wrong because *pounds* is a common noun, which should not be capitalized. Option (3) is wrong because there is no reason to place a comma after *car seat*. Option (4) is wrong because *are* must agree with *they*, the subject of the dependent clause.

41. **2 replace *which* with *that*** (See Chapter 7—Clauses: Restrictive and Nonrestrictive Clauses) Use *that* for restrictive clauses. *Is designed for children between 20 and 40 pounds* is a restrictive clause. It shows which car seat. Option (1) is wrong because *After that stage* is an introductory phrase, which should be set apart with a comma. Option (3) is wrong because *between* is used when two things are compared. In this case,

20 pounds and *40 pounds* are compared. Option (4) is wrong because there is no reason to place a comma after *forward-facing*.

42. **1 a booster, which works** (See Chapter 7—Clause: Who, Which, and That) The original is best. Use *which* and commas for nonrestrictive clauses. Options (2), (3), (4), and (5) use either the wrong signal word or the wrong form of punctuation.

43. **3 replace *they* with *car seats*** (See Chapter 13—Writing Clear Sentences: Consistent Pronouns) *They* is too vague. Should car seats or parents be positioned properly? Pronouns with unclear references should be replaced with specific nouns. Option (1) is wrong because *sure* modifies *to make*. Option (2) is wrong because *check* must agree with *parents*, the subject of the sentence. Option (4) is wrong because *to make* is an infinitive, which should not be divided.

44. **5 no correction necessary** Option (1) is wrong because *of the car* modifies *seat*. Option (2) is wrong because the sentence should be in the present tense, not the past tense. Option (3) is wrong because there is no reason to place a comma after *seat*. Option (4) is wrong because *car seats* is the subject, and it is not possessive.

45. **3 to the car; the seat should** (See Chapter 9—More Punctuation: Semicolons) This sentence has two independent clauses that are related. The second clause explains how tightly car seats should be secured. Option (3) shows the correct relationship between the two clauses.

46. **1 replace *whomever* with *whoever*** (See Chapter 5—Pronouns: Who and Whom) *Whoever needs help with car-seat installation* is a clause. Use *whoever* because it is the subject of the clause. Option (2) is wrong because *police* and *departments* are common nouns. Option (3) is wrong because there is no reason to place a comma

after *help*. Option (4) is wrong because the verb should be in the present tense.

47. **1 change *american cancer society* to *American Cancer Society*** (See Chapter 10—Capitalization) Capitalize proper nouns. The American Cancer Society is an organization. Option (2) is wrong because *has* agrees with *American Cancer Society*, the subject of the sentence. Option (3) is wrong because *years* should not be possessive. Option (4) is wrong because there is no reason to place a comma after *people*.

48. **4 insert a comma after *disease*** (See Chapter 8—End Marks and Commas: Nonrestrictive Words, Phrases, and Clauses) *A deadly disease* is an appositive that renames *skin cancer*. Nonrestrictive appositives should be set apart with commas. Option (1) is wrong because the comma after *cancer* is necessary to set apart the appositive *a deadly disease*. Option (2) is wrong because *Americans* is a proper noun, which should be capitalized. Option (3) is wrong because *every* is spelled correctly.

49. **3 apply sunscreen, wear hats, use sunglasses, and limit sun exposure** (See Chapter 13—Writing Clear Sentences: Parallel Structure) Items in a series should be in the same form, and they should be set apart with commas. Each of the first three items has a verb and a noun. The fourth item should have a verb and a noun, also. Options (1), (2), and (5) are wrong because the items are not in the same form. Option (4) is wrong because the items are separated with semicolons instead of commas.

50. **2 people, unfortunately, do** (See Chapter 8—End Marks and Commas: Interruptions) *Unfortunately* is an interrupter, which should be set apart with commas. Options (1), (3), and (4) are wrong because *unfortunately* is not

set apart with commas.

51. **1 replace *them* with *it*** (See Chapter 5—Pronouns: Pronoun Agreement) The pronoun refers to *sunscreen*, which is singular. Therefore, the pronoun also should be singular. Option (2) is wrong because *although most children wear sunscreen at the beach* is an introductory clause, which should be set apart with a comma. Option (3) is wrong because there is no reason to place a comma after *outside*. Option (4) is wrong because *wear* is spelled correctly.

52. **4 change *themselves'* to *themselves*** (See Chapter 5—Pronouns: Special Situations) *Themselves* is a reflexive pronoun. It shows that the subject performs and receives the action. It should not be possessive because it does not own anything. Option (1) is wrong because *likewise* is an introductory word, which should be set apart with a comma. Option (2) is wrong because *half* is spelled correctly. Option (3) is wrong because there is no reason to place a comma after *sunscreen*.

53. **3 move *prematurely* after *age*** (See Chapter 1—Parts of Speech: Verbs) *To age* is an infinitive. Never split an infinitive; keep *to* and the verb together. *Prematurely* is an adverb that tells when. Option (1) is wrong because *besides skin cancer* is an introductory phrase, which should be set apart with a comma. Option (2) is wrong because *causes* agrees with *sun exposure*, which is singular. Option (4) is wrong because *causes* is spelled correctly.

54. **5 no correction necessary** Option (1) is wrong because *which are well documented and highly publicized* is a nonrestrictive clause. It should be set apart with a comma. Option (2) is wrong because *which* is used for nonrestrictive clauses. Option (3) is wrong because there is no reason to place a comma after *documented*. Option (4) is wrong because *are* agrees with *risks*, which is plural.

55. **2 replace *there* with *their*** (See Chapter 12—Word Choice) *Their* is used to show possession. Option (1) is wrong because *Americans* is not possessive in this sentence. It is the subject of the clause. Option (3) is wrong because *if Americans changed their habits* is an introductory clause, which should be set apart with a comma. Option (4) is wrong because *could* is spelled correctly.

Glossary

ABBREVIATION a shortened form of a word or phrase EXAMPLES: Dr. and FBI (Federal Bureau of Investigation)

ACTION VERBS show the subject either performing an action or receiving an action EXAMPLES: She <u>swam</u> to shore. He <u>was hit</u> by the ball.

ADJECTIVE a word that tells the size, shape, number, owner, or appearance of a noun or pronoun EXAMPLES: large, round, jagged

ADVERB a word that gives information about verbs, adjectives or other adverbs EXAMPLES: carefully, soon, quickly

ANTECEDENT a particular word, phrase, or clause to which a pronoun refers EXAMPLE: The <u>dancers</u> shined <u>their</u> shoes before the show.

APPOSITIVE a word or phrase that renames or explains a noun or pronoun EXAMPLE: Megan, <u>a lawyer</u>, works long hours.

ARTICLE a word that is used to signal a noun EXAMPLES: a, an, the

CAPITALIZATION the use of capital letters EXAMPLES: <u>W</u>e donated to the <u>R</u>ed <u>C</u>ross.

CASE a form of a pronoun that is based on its role in the sentence—pronouns with related jobs are part of the same case. EXAMPLES: <u>He</u> drove. I drove <u>him</u>. Dave drove <u>his</u> car.

CLAUSE a group of words with a subject and a predicate—the group works together to send a message (see independent clause and dependent clause)

COMMA (,) a punctuation mark that is used to separate ideas, parts of a sentence, or items in a series EXAMPLE: Kay bought flowers, fertilizer, and a watering can.

COMMAND a sentence that tells someone to do something EXAMPLE: Drive slowly.

COMMON NOUN a noun that names a general group of people, places, or things EXAMPLES: brother, street, house

COMPOUND PART one part of a sentence (subject, verb, etc.) that has two or more components EXAMPLES: Joe and Brie walked for miles (compound subject). Sean relaxed and read until noon (compound verb).

CONJUNCTION a word that connects words, phrases, or clauses (and, but, yet, so, for, nor, or) EXAMPLE: Ruth and Russ looked at houses, <u>but</u> they did not see one that they liked.

CONJUNCTIVE ADVERB a word that connects two independent clauses and shows the relationship between them EXAMPLE: They wanted to swim; <u>however</u>, the water was too cold.

CONSONANT a letter of the alphabet that is not *a, e, i, o, u,* or sometimes *y*

CONTRACTION a word that combines two words and leaves out one or more letters EXAMPLES: can't (can not), it's (it is)

DANGLING MODIFIER a descriptive word or phrase that has nothing to describe—a sentence with a dangling modifier must be rewritten EXAMPLE: *Wrong* <u>Swimming in the cold water</u>, the towel looked cozy. *Right* When I was swimming in the cold water, the towel looked cozy.

DEPENDENT CLAUSE a group of words with a subject and predicate that does not express a complete thought EXAMPLE: <u>When Ty was a boy</u>, his mother taught him to play soccer.

DIRECT OBJECT a noun or pronoun that receives the action in a sentence (see object of the verb) EXAMPLE: Rhea asked <u>him</u> to the dance.

DIRECT QUOTATION someone's exact words EXAMPLE: Mark Twain said, "<u>Wrinkles should merely indicate where smiles have been</u>."

END MARK a punctuation mark that appears at the end of a sentence EXAMPLES: Where have you been<u>?</u> That was the best joke I have ever heard<u>.</u> Watch out<u>!</u>

EXCLAMATION POINT (!) an end mark that shows emotion EXAMPLE: Ouch<u>!</u>

FRAGMENT an incomplete sentence—a fragment may lack a subject or a verb, or it may be a dependent clause that needs other words to have meaning EXAMPLES: Whenever we need help. Before noon.

FUTURE PERFECT TENSE a verb form that shows an action will be completed before a specific time in the future EXAMPLE: Before the curtain falls, we <u>will have sung</u> for hours.

FUTURE TENSE a verb form that shows that an action will take place in the future EXAMPLE: Vera <u>will take</u> the test tomorrow.

GERUND a verb that ends in *-ing* and acts like a noun EXAMPLE: <u>Running</u> is a great form of exercise.

INDEFINITE PRONOUN a word that does not refer to a specific person, place or thing EXAMPLE: <u>Everybody</u> needs to write well.

INDEPENDENT CLAUSE a group of words that expresses a complete thought and has a subject and a verb EXAMPLES: Vahid needs a date for the dance. After Kate changed her clothes, <u>she went to the store</u>.

INDIRECT OBJECT shows to or for whom or what an action was performed (see object of the verb) EXAMPLE: We bought <u>her</u> a birthday gift.

INDIRECT QUOTATION tells what someone said, but does not use that person's exact words EXAMPLE: Salma said that she will run for reelection.

INFINITIVE a verb form that usually begins with *to* EXAMPLE: He wanted <u>to see</u> the results.

INTERJECTION a word that bursts with emotion EXAMPLES: Wow! Ouch!

INTERRUPTER a word or group of words that breaks the flow of a sentence EXAMPLE: The car, <u>however</u>, would not start.

IRREGULAR VERB a verb that does not follow the usual pattern to form the past or past participle EXAMPLE: swim (present), swam (past), swum (past participle)

LINKING VERB a verb that connects the subject to words that rename or describe the subject EXAMPLES: was, are, were, look, become, appear

MISPLACED MODIFIER a descriptive word or phrase that blurs the meaning of a sentence because it is misplaced EXAMPLE: Nadine with the cloudy water swam in the pool.

MODIFIER a word or group of words that describes another word or phrase EXAMPLE: The child <u>who lost his truck</u> cried <u>endlessly</u>.

NONRESTRICTIVE CLAUSE a clause that is not critical to the meaning of the sentence EXAMPLE: Joe's truck, which has over 100,000 miles, is in good shape.

NOUN a word that names a person, place, thing, or idea EXAMPLES: George Jones, Maine, bus, fear

OBJECTIVE CASE a group of pronouns (me, you, him, her, it, us, them, whom, whomever)—a pronoun in the objective case can work as an object of a verb or an object of a preposition EXAMPLES: Kim tripped <u>her</u>. Phil gave <u>her</u> a ticket. Tim knew about <u>her</u>.

OBJECT OF THE PREPOSITION a noun or pronoun that is connected to a preposition EXAMPLE: Nate ran into <u>the wall</u>.

OBJECT OF THE VERB a noun or pronoun that receives the action in a sentence, either directly or indirectly EXAMPLES: Megan mailed <u>the letters</u>. Megan mailed <u>Sean</u> the letters.

PARTICIPLE a form of a verb that works as an adjective or creates certain tenses with a helping verb EXAMPLES: The <u>running</u> water is cold. I have <u>seen</u> that movie.

PAST PARTICIPLE a form of a verb that works as an adjective or forms the perfect tenses—most past participles end in *-ed*. EXAMPLE: The <u>exhausted</u> workers have <u>labored</u> for days.

PAST PERFECT TENSE a verb form that shows that an action was finished before a specific time in the past EXAMPLE: Bill <u>had wanted</u> to be a doctor before he went to college.

PAST TENSE a verb form that shows an action took place in the past EXAMPLES: Yu Lin <u>worked</u> last weekend. Fran <u>was</u> at the game.

PERIOD (.) a punctuation mark that is used at the end of a statement—it is also used for abbreviations EXAMPLE: <u>Dr.</u> Hawk said that all of the guests arrived<u>.</u>

PHRASE a group of words that work together to perform one job EXAMPLE: <u>Wearing a seat belt</u> can save your life.

PLURAL more than one EXAMPLES: we, they, cats

POSSESSIVE a noun or pronoun that shows ownership EXAMPLES: <u>Tony's</u> basketball, <u>her</u> room

POSSESSIVE CASE a group of pronouns (my, your, his, her, its, our, their, whose)—pronouns in the possessive case can be placed before a noun to show ownership or before an "ing" verb that is used as a noun—possessive pronouns also can substitute for nouns EXAMPLES: That is <u>his</u> book. <u>His</u> driving is awful. The bike is <u>his</u>.

PREDICATE part of a sentence that describes the subject or shows the subject in action EXAMPLES: Jihye <u>is a great lawyer</u>. He <u>ran across the field</u>.

PREDICATE ADJECTIVE an adjective that follows a linking verb and describes the subject of the sentence (see subject complement) EXAMPLES: This movie is <u>boring</u>. The milk smelled <u>sour</u>.

PREDICATE NOUN a noun that follows a linking verb and renames the subject of the sentence (see subject complement) EXAMPLE: Jeff is a <u>pilot</u>.

PREFIX letters that are placed in front of a word to change its meaning EXAMPLE: Gail <u>pre</u>viewed the show.

PREPOSITION a word that links words or groups of words EXAMPLES: after, between, under, near

PREPOSITIONAL PHRASE a group of words that includes a preposition, its object, and any modifiers EXAMPLE: Dave ran <u>after the wild horse</u>.

PRESENT PARTICIPLE a form of a verb that works as an adjective or forms the continuing tenses—most present participles end in *-ing* EXAMPLE: The <u>running</u> water is <u>filling</u> the pool.

PRESENT PERFECT TENSE a verb form that shows an action that began in the past and continues to the present—it also shows actions that have just finished EXAMPLE: We <u>have been working</u> on this project for months.

PRESENT TENSE a verb form that shows that an action is taking place now EXAMPLES: People <u>ignore</u> the stop sign on Main Street. Joel <u>is</u> a lawyer.

PRONOUN a word that substitutes for a noun and works like a noun EXAMPLES: I, you, she, they, everybody

PROPER NOUN a noun that names a specific person, place, or thing EXAMPLES: Jesse Owens, Florida, Pepsi

QUESTION MARK (?) a punctuation mark that ends a question EXAMPLE: What movie will you see?

QUOTATION MARKS ("") punctuation marks that are used in pairs to set apart someone's exact words, the title of something that is part of a larger work, or words that are being defined EXAMPLES: Kim yelled, "Put on your coat!" "Expensive" is anything that I can not afford.

REFLEXIVE PRONOUN a pronoun that ends in *-self* or *selves*—these pronouns show that someone did something to himself EXAMPLE: Fay hit herself with the car door.

REGULAR VERB a verb that follows a common pattern to change form—add *-d* or *-ed* to the present tense to form the past tense or the past participle EXAMPLE: talk (present tense), talked (past tense), talked (past participle)

RESTRICTIVE CLAUSE a clause that helps identify a noun in the sentence—without the clause, the sentence would not have the same meaning EXAMPLE: The doctor who put in my stitches was very careful.

SEMICOLON (;) a punctuation mark that joins independent clauses and separates items in a series—use a semicolon for a series when the items already have commas EXAMPLE: We were frustrated; the mayor would not give us a straight answer.

SENTENCE a group of words with a subject and a predicate that expresses a complete thought EXAMPLE: Lee quit his job on Friday.

SINGULAR one EXAMPLES: I, you, horse

SPLIT INFINITIVE an infinitive that has been divided into two parts EXAMPLE: *Wrong* They wanted to really work hard. *Right* They really wanted to work hard.

SUBJECT someone or something that a sentence is about EXAMPLE: He trained for the Olympics.

SUBJECT-VERB AGREEMENT the subject and verb in a sentence send the same message—they refer to the same number and gender

SUBJECTIVE CASE a group of pronouns (I, you, he, she, we, they, who)—pronouns in the subjective case can work as a subject or a subject complement EXAMPLES: Vera and I went to the mall. The top lawyers are Jake and she.

SUFFIX letters that are placed at the end of a word to change its meaning EXAMPLE: She was knowledgeable.

VERB a word that connects related words or shows action EXAMPLES: run, show, are, were

VERB TENSE the form of a verb that tells when an action took place (past, present, future) EXAMPLE: Yesterday, Shantae planted the garden.

VOWEL the letters *a, e, i, o, u,* and sometimes *y*—all other letters are called consonants.

Index

NOTES

NOTES